D. Timoney   083   333   9283

GW01395846

DIPLOMA IN FINANCIAL MANAGEMENT

MODULE B

Subject Area 3

FINANCIAL STRATEGY

DipFM

Study Text

BPP)))
LEARNING MEDIA

First edition 2001
Seventh edition July 2007

ISBN 9780 7517 4279 4 (Previous edition 0 7517 2696 6)

British Library Cataloguing-in-Publication Data
A catalogue record for this book
is available from the British Library

Published by

BPP Learning Media Ltd
BPP House, Aldine Place
London W12 8AA

www.bpp.com/learningmedia

Printed in Great Britain by
WM Print
45-47 Frederick Street
Walsall
West Midlands
WS2 9NE

We are grateful to the Association of Chartered
Certified Accountants for permission to reproduce past
examination questions. The suggested solutions in the
exam answer bank have been prepared by BPP
Learning Media Ltd.

Your learning materials, published by BPP Learning
Media Ltd, are printed on paper sourced from
sustainable, managed forests.

BPP
LEARNING MEDIA

Contents

How to use this interactive text

This is the seventh edition of the BPP Learning Media textbook for the Diploma in Financial Management Module B, subject area 3 *Financial Strategy*. It has been specifically written to cover the Syllabus and Study Guide, and has been fully reviewed by the examiner.

To pass the examination you need a thorough understanding in all areas covered by the syllabus and study guide.

Recommended approach

(a) To pass you need to be able to answer questions on **everything** specified by the syllabus and study guide. Read the text very carefully and do not skip any of it.

(b) Learning is an **active** process. Do **all** the activities as you work through the text so you can be sure you really understand what you have read.

(c) After you have covered the material in the Interactive Text, work through the questions in the Practice and Revision Kit for Module B.

(d) Before you take the exam, check that you still remember the material using the following quick revision plan.

(i) Read through the chapter learning objectives. Are there any gaps in your knowledge? If so, study the section again.

(ii) Read and learn the key terms.

(iii) Read and learn the key learning points, which are a summary of each chapter.

(iv) Do the quick quizzes again. If you know what you're doing, they shouldn't take long.

This approach is only a suggestion. You or your college may well adapt it to suit your needs.

Remember this is a **practical** course.

(a) Try to relate the material to your experience in the workplace or any other work experience you may have had.

(b) Try to make as many links as you can to subject area 2 of Module A, and also to Module B.

Further question practice

Practice and Revision Kit

A substantial further bank of questions including past exam questions is available in the BPP Learning Media Practice and Revision Kit for this module.

i-Pass CD Rom

BPP Learning Media's i-Pass product is an invaluable aid to revision. We produce one each for Module A and Module B. These interactive CD Roms provide numerous multiple choice and data response questions for each of the two subject areas in the module. Ideal for question practice and revision, they are designed to test knowledge and perfect exam technique.

You can order both these products by telephoning 0845 0751 100 (+44(0)20 8740 2211 for overseas customers) or on line at www.bpp.com/learningmedia.

Revision

Revision is made easier with BPP Learning Media's Passcards. These are pocket sized revision cards, corresponding to each chapter of the study text and covering the essential key points of the topics. The perfect solution for revision on the move.

BPP
LEARNING MEDIA

Help yourself study for your DipFM exams

Exams for professional bodies such as ACCA are very different from those you have taken at college or university. You will be under **greater time pressure before** the exam – as you may be combining your study with work. There are many different ways of learning and so the BPP Learning Media Study Text offers you a number of different tools to help you through. Here are some hints and tips: they are not plucked out of the air, but **based on research and experience**. (You don't need to know that long-term memory is in the same part of the brain as emotions and feelings - but it's a fact anyway.)

The right approach

1   **The right attitude**

Believe in yourself	Yes, there is a lot to learn. Yes, it is a challenge. But thousands have succeeded before and you can too.
Remember why you're doing it	Studying might seem a grind at times, but you are doing it for a reason: to advance your career.

2   **The right focus**

Read through the Syllabus and Study guide	These tell you what you are expected to know and are supplemented by Exam focus points in the Text.
Study the Exam Paper section	Past papers are likely to be good guides to what you should expect in the exam.

3   **The right method**

The whole picture	You need to grasp the detail - but keeping in mind how everything fits into the whole picture will help you understand better. • The **Introduction** of each chapter puts the material in context. • The **Syllabus content, Study guide** and **Exam focus points** show you what you need to **grasp**.
In your own words	To absorb the information (and to practise your written communication skills), it helps to **put it into your own words**. • **Take notes.** • Answer the **questions** in each chapter. You will practise your written communication skills, which become increasingly important as you progress through your DipFM exams. • Try **'teaching' a subject** to a colleague or friend.
Give yourself cues to jog your memory	The BPP Study Text uses **bold** to **highlight key points**. • Try **colour coding** with a highlighter pen. • Write **key points** on cards.

4   **The right review**

Review, review, review	It is a **fact** that regularly reviewing a topic in summary form can **fix it in your memory**. Because **review** is so important, the BPP Study Text helps you to do so in many ways.
	• **Chapter roundups** summarise the 'Fast forward' key points in each chapter. Use them to recap each study session.
	• The **Quick quiz** is another review technique you can use to ensure that you have grasped the essentials.
	• Go through the **Examples** in each chapter a second or third time.

Developing your personal Study Plan

BPP's **Learning to Learn Accountancy** book emphasises the need to prepare (and use) a study plan. Planning and sticking to the plan are key elements of learning success.

There are four steps you should work through.

Step 1   **How do you learn?**

First you need to be aware of your style of learning. The BPP **Learning to Learn Accountancy** book commits a chapter to this **self-discovery**. What types of intelligence do you display when learning? You might be advised to brush up on certain study skills before launching into this Study Text.

BPP's **Learning to Learn Accountancy** book helps you to identify what intelligences you show more strongly and then details how you can tailor your study process to your preferences. It also includes handy hints on how to develop intelligences you exhibit less strongly, but which might be needed as you study accountancy.

Are you a **theorist** or are you more **practical**? If you would rather get to grips with a theory before trying to apply it in practice, you should follow the study sequence on page (vii). If the reverse is true (you like to know why you are learning theory before you do so), you might be advised to flick through Study Text chapters and look at examples, case studies and questions (Steps 8, 9 and 10 in the **suggested study sequence**) before reading through the detailed theory.

Step 2   **How much time do you have?**

Work out the time you have available per week, given the following.

- The standard you have set yourself
- The time you need to set aside later for work on the Practice & Revision Kit and Passcards
- The other exam(s) you are sitting
- Very importantly, practical matters such as work, travel, exercise, sleep and social life

Hours

Note your time available in box A.   A [   ]

BPP LEARNING MEDIA

Step 3   Allocate your time

- Take the time you have available per week for this Study Text shown in box A, multiply it by the number of weeks available and insert the result in box B.

  B [   ]

- Divide the figure in box B by the number of chapters in this text and insert the result in box C.

  C [   ]

Remember that this is only a rough guide. Some of the chapters in this book are longer and more complicated than others, and you will find some subjects easier to understand than others.

Step 4   Implement

Set about studying each chapter in the time shown in box C, following the key study steps in the order suggested by your particular learning style.

This is your personal **Study Plan**. You should try and combine it with the study sequence outlined below. You may want to modify the sequence a little (as has been suggested above) to adapt it to your **personal style**.

BPP's **Learning to Learn Accountancy** gives further guidance on developing a study plan, and deciding where and when to study.

Suggested study sequence

It is likely that the best way to approach this Study Text is to tackle the chapters in the order in which you find them. Taking into account your individual learning style, you could follow this sequence for each chapter.

Key study steps	Activity
Step 1 **Topic list**	Note the topics covered in the chapter. Each numbered topic is a numbered section in the chapter.
Step 2 **Introduction**	This gives you the big picture in terms of the context of the chapter. The content is referenced to the Study Guide, and Exam Guidance shows how the topic is likely to be examined. In other words, it sets your objectives for study.
Step 3 **Knowledge brought forward boxes**	In these we highlight information and techniques that it is assumed you have 'brought forward' with you from your earlier studies. If there are topics which have changed recently due to legislation for example, these topics are explained in more detail.
Step 4 **Fast forward**	Fast forward boxes give you a quick summary of the content of each of the main chapter sections. They are listed together in the roundup at the end of each chapter to provide you with an overview of the contents of the whole chapter.
Step 5 **Explanations**	Proceed methodically through the chapter, reading each section thoroughly and making sure you understand.
Step 6 **Key terms and Exam focus points**	• Key terms can often earn you *easy marks* if you state them clearly and correctly in an appropriate exam answer (and they are highlighted in the index at the back of the Text). • Exam focus points state how we think the examiner intends to examine certain topics.
Step 7 **Note taking**	Take brief notes, if you wish. Avoid the temptation to copy out too much. Remember that being able to put something into your own words is a sign of being able to understand it. If you find you cannot explain something you have read, read it again before you make the notes.

Key study steps	Activity
Step 8 **Examples**	Follow each through to its solution very carefully.
Step 9 **Case studies**	Study each one, and try to add flesh to them from your own experience. They are designed to show how the topics you are studying come alive (and often come unstuck) in the real world.
Step 10 **Questions**	Make a very good attempt at each one.
Step 11 **Answers**	Check yours against ours, and make sure you understand any discrepancies.
Step 12 **Chapter roundup**	Work through it carefully, to make sure you have grasped the significance of all the fast forward points.
Step 13 **Quick quiz**	When you are happy that you have covered the chapter, use the Quick quiz to check how much you have remembered of the topics covered and to practise questions in a variety of formats.
Step 14 **Question practice**	Either at this point, or later when you are thinking about revising, make a full attempt at the suggested Question(s). If you have bought i-Pass, use this too.

Short of time: Skim study technique?

You may find you simply do not have the time available to follow all the key study steps for each chapter, however you adapt them for your particular learning style. If this is the case, follow the **skim study** technique below.

- Study the chapters in the order you find them in the Study Text.
- For each chapter:
  - Follow the key study steps 1-3
  - Skim-read through step 5, looking out for the points highlighted in the fast forward boxes (step 4)
  - Jump to step 12
  - Go back to step 6
  - Follow through steps 8 and 9
  - Prepare outline answers to questions (steps 10/11)
  - Try the Quick quiz (step 13), following up any items you can't answer
  - Do a plan for the Question (step 14), comparing it against our answers
  - You should probably still follow step 7 (note-taking), although you may decide simply to rely on the BPP Learning Media Passcards for this.

Moving on...

However you study, when you are ready to embark on the practice and revision phase of the BPP Effective Study Package, you should still refer back to this Study Text, both as a source of **reference** (you should find the index particularly helpful for this) and as a way to **review** (the Fast forwards, Exam focus points, Chapter roundups and Quick quizzes help you here).

And remember to keep careful hold of this Study Text – you will find it invaluable in your work.

> More advice on Study Skills can be found in BPP's **Learning to Learn Accountancy** book.

Syllabus

Aim

To develop an understanding of the role of financial strategy in the investing, financing and resource allocation decisions within an organisation.

Objectives

On completion of this paper candidates should be able to:

- Explain the role and nature of financial strategy and its relationship to shareholder value
- Identify the main elements of investment appraisal
- Evaluate long-term decision opportunities through the use of appropriate techniques
- Identify and evaluate the major sources of finance available to an organisation
- Explain the role of capital markets in raising finance
- Discuss the main methods of managing working capital and analyse working capital policies
- Evaluate the motives for, and financial implications of, mergers and acquisitions
- Discuss the impact of taxation and inflation on financial strategy decisions

Position of the paper in the syllabus

This subject area is directly related to the management decision-making theme of the Diploma in Financial Management and links closely with the other three subject areas within the scheme. Some overlap between these subject areas is inevitable. For example, financial statements and ratios that are considered in subject area 1, fixed and variable costs and relevant and irrelevant costs that are considered in subject area 2, and gearing that is considered in subject area 4, may also be considered in this paper.

Syllabus content

Chapter where covered in Text

1 **The nature and scope of financial strategy**

(a)	Financial strategy and organisational objectives	1
(b)	Financial strategy and the role of the finance function	1

2 **Investment appraisal**

(a) Evaluation of long-term investment opportunities through the use of:

(i)	net present value	3, 5
(ii)	internal rate of return	3
(iii)	accounting rate of return	2
(iv)	payback period (including discounted payback period)	2, 3
(v)	profitability index	4

(b)	Advantages and disadvantages of each appraisal technique	2–4
(c)	Asset replacement decisions	3
(d)	Simple single-constraint capital rationing decisions	4
(e)	Sensitivity analysis	4
(f)	Methods available to approve, monitor and control investment projects	2
(g)	Non-financial issues in investment appraisal	2

BPP
LEARNING MEDIA

Excluded topics

The following topics are specifically excluded from the syllabus:

- Calculations to derive discount factors. Candidates will always be supplied with discount tables
- The mathematical derivation of any formulae
- The use of statistical probabilities for measuring the risk of a particular investment or policy

Key areas of the syllabus

The key topic areas are as follows:

- Investment decision making
- Raising finance
- Capital markets
- Working capital management
- Business combinations
- Share valuation

Study Guide

Financial Strategy

1   The nature and scope of Financial Strategy

Syllabus reference 1a, b

- Broadly describe the relationship between financial strategy, management accounting and financial accounting

- Identify the possible aims and objectives of organisations, both profit seeking and non-profit seeking

- Identify the key stakeholders of a company including shareholders, lenders, directors, employees, customers, suppliers and the government and the importance of each group to the company

- Identify the role of the finance function in management decision making

2/3   Investment appraisal – I

Syllabus reference 2a, b, f

- Explain the key features of long-term investment decisions

- Describe methods available to approve, monitor and control investment projects

- Explain the Accounting Rate of Return and evaluate its usefulness as a measure of investment worth

- Explain the Payback method and evaluate its usefulness as a measure of investment worth

- Calculate the Accounting Rate of Return and Payback Period for an investment project from given data

4   Investment appraisal – II

Syllabus reference 2a, b

- Explain the importance of the time value of money in appraising investments

- Identify relevant cash flows relating to potential investments

- Explain the Discounted Payback Period method and evaluate its usefulness as a measure of investment worth

- Explain the Net Present Value and Internal Rate of Return methods of investment appraisal and evaluate their usefulness as measures of investment worth

- Calculate the Discounted Payback Period, Net Present Value and Internal Rate of Return for an investment project from given data

- Compare the Net Present Value and Internal Rate of Return methods

- Explain the advantages of DCF methods (Net Present Value and Internal Rate of Return) over Payback and Accounting Rate of Return

5   Investment appraisal – III

Syllabus reference 2c, e

- Apply DCF methods to asset replacement decisions

- Identify and discuss the sources of risk affecting the viability of a project

- Analyse and evaluate the sensitivity of Net Present Value outcomes to changes in key variables
- Evaluate sensitivity analysis as a tool of investment appraisal

6 Investment appraisal – IV

Syllabus reference 2a, d, g

- Distinguish between hard and soft capital rationing
- Apply the profitability index technique to single-period, divisible projects
- Explain how non-financial factors can influence the investment decision
- Explain how inflation and taxation should be taken into account when making investment decisions

7 Raising finance - I

Syllabus reference 3a

- Explain financing in terms of the risk/return trade off
- Discuss the main features of ordinary shares and preference shares
- Describe the main features of
    - straight long-term loan capital and mortgages
    - convertible loans, subordinated loans and warrants
    - deep discount bonds and junk (high yield) bonds
- Discuss the reasons for issuing each particular form of loan capital
- Distinguish between fixed and floating rates of interest
- Explain the factors to be taken into account when considering a financing choice between ordinary shares, preference shares and loan capital

8/9 Raising finance – II

Syllabus reference 3a

- Explain the main advantages and disadvantages of leasing rather than purchasing assets
- Distinguish between finance leases and other leases
- Describe the main features of a sale-and-lease-back agreement and explain the advantages and disadvantages of raising finance in this way
- Explain the advantages and disadvantages of hire-purchase agreements
- Describe the main features of securitisation
- Explain the role and nature of PFI and PPP in raising finance
- Explain the importance of internally-generated sources of long-term finance to a business

10 Raising finance – III

Syllabus reference 3a, g

- Describe the main features of:
    - invoice discounting and debt factoring
    - bills of exchange and acceptance credits
    - bank overdrafts

- Discuss the advantages and disadvantages of the various forms of external short-term finance available to a business

- Identify and evaluate the main internal sources of short-term finance

- Describe the problems faced by small businesses seeking external finance (such as inadequate information, inadequate security, funding gap etc)

11/12 Financing options

Syllabus reference 3b, c, d, e

- Prepare forecast financial statements in order to examine financing options or to identify funding needs

- Analyse past, current and expected future performance of a business through the use of ratios and other techniques to examine the implications of different financing options

- Evaluate the effect of financing options on the risks and returns to investors

- Evaluate the suitability of different forms of financing for given situations

- Explain the problem of overtrading (undercapitalisation) and describe the symptoms and remedies

13 Cost of capital

Syllabus reference 3f

- Explain the term 'cost of capital' and its importance in investment decision making

- Calculate

    - cost of equity (including a basic understanding of CAPM)
    - cost of preference shares
    - cost of loan capital
    - weighted average cost of capital

- Discuss the assumptions underlying the use of weighted average cost of capital in investment decision making

14/16 Capital markets

Syllabus reference 3a, 4a, b, e, f, g

Stock markets

- Outline the nature and purpose of a Stock Exchange

- Describe how stock markets operate

- Calculate, analyse and evaluate appropriate financial ratios (eg EPS, P/E, dividend yield and dividend cover)

- Explain the advantages and disadvantages of a company seeking a stock market listing

- Describe the main international capital markets for bonds and equities

Share issues and redemptions

- Explain the main forms of issuing shares and the advantages and disadvantages of each method

- Describe the advantages and disadvantages of rights issues

- Calculate the price of rights

- Explain the purpose, and effect on shareholder wealth, of bonus issues, scrip dividends and share splits

- Discuss reasons for the repurchase or redemption of shares

Venture capital

- Identify and discuss the main types of investment that are suitable for venture capital funds

- Explain the investment process for venture capitalists and the main factors that are taken into account by venture capitalists when assessing investment potential

- Analyse and evaluate an investment proposal from the perspective of a venture capitalist

17 Market efficiency

Syllabus reference 4c, d

- Explain the term 'market efficiency'

- Describe the main forms of market efficiency

- Examine the implications of market efficiency for managers and investors

- Discuss in broad terms the applicability of the Efficient Market Hypothesis to stock markets

18 Working capital management – I

Syllabus reference 5a, b, e

- Explain the nature and scope of working capital management

- Explain the need for effective working capital management

- Distinguish the working capital needs of different types of business

- Analyse and evaluate the financial implications of different working capital policies

Management of inventory

- Calculate and interpret inventory ratios

- Explain the role of inventory in the working capital cycle

- Describe and evaluate the tools and techniques of inventory management

- Apply the basic EOQ model

19 Working capital management – II

Syllabus reference 5b, c

Management of receivables

- Explain the role of receivables in the working capital cycle

- Describe the factors to be taken into account when assessing the creditworthiness of customers

- Describe the main sources of information to assess the creditworthiness of customers

- Identify and discuss the main factors involved in deciding on terms of sale

- Explain the role of settlement discounts

- Describe policies for the effective and efficient collection of debts

- Analyse and evaluate the financial implications of different credit policies

- Calculate and interpret receivables ratios

20   Working capital management – III

Syllabus reference 5b, d

Management of cash

- Explain the role of cash in the working capital cycle

- Describe and apply the tools and techniques of cash management

- Identify and discuss the main factors to be taken into account when deciding upon the level of cash to be held

- Calculate and interpret cash ratios

- Describe methods of managing a bank overdraft

21   Working capital management – IV

Syllabus reference 5d, f

Management of payables

- Explain the role of payables in the working capital cycle

- Describe the advantages of trade credit

- Identify the risks of taking increased credit and the role of guarantee

- Describe policies for effective management of payables

- Calculate and interpret payables ratios

Working capital management and the small business

Explain the problems confronted by small businesses in managing working capital (eg market power, poor financial management skills, inadequate information systems)

22   Business combinations

Syllabus reference 6a, b, c, d

- Explain the motives for business combinations

- Analyse and evaluate the impact of a proposed acquisition on financial performance and shareholder wealth

- Evaluate the various forms of bid consideration

- Identify and discuss the main areas for investigation when considering a proposed takeover

- Describe the methods available to resist a takeover bid

23/24 Share valuation

Syllabus reference 6e

- Explain the basic principles of valuation

- Discuss the relevance of accounting information to share valuation

- Apply share valuation methods based on:
  - net assets
  - income flows and cash flows
  - dividends
  - price earnings ratio

- Discuss the theoretical and practical limitations of the valuation methods

- Describe the practical influences on share price including reasons why share prices may differ from their theoretical values

- Explain the role of share valuation models in negotiations regarding business combinations

25/26 Company restructuring

Syllabus reference 6f

Divestments

- Describe the nature of, and reasons for, divestments

- Discuss sell-offs, spin-offs and liquidation as forms of divestment

- Analyse and evaluate the financial effects of proposals for divestment

Management buy-outs and buy-ins

- Discuss the advantages and disadvantages of buy-outs and describe the issues that a management team should address when preparing a buy-out proposal

- Assess the financial benefits of a buy-out from both the buy-out team and the financial backer

- Identify the advantages and disadvantages of management buy-ins

Going private

Explain the reasons for a public company changing to private company status

27/28 Revision

Reading list

This reading list has been compiled by the examiner. It includes some books which you may find useful for wider reading around topics, and in the course of research into the Module B Project.

- P F Atrill
  Financial Management for Non-specialists (2nd edition)
  Financial Times Prentice Hall
  ISBN 0-13-022775-7

- R A Brealey, S C Myers, A J Marcus
  Fundamentals of Corporate Finance (2nd edition)
  Irwin Mc Graw Hill
  ISBN 0-07-11545-0

- EJ McLaney
  Business Finance Theory and Practice (5th edition)
  Financial Times Prentice Hall
  ISBN 0-273-64636-2

Wider reading is also desirable, particularly relevant articles in *Finance Matters*.

The exam paper

The examination for each module will cover the two subject areas in that module. The examination for Module B will cover both 'Financial Strategy' (subject area 3) and 'Risk Management' (subject area 4) topics.

The structure of the examination for Module B will be as follows.

Section A

20 multiple choice questions (10 covering subject area 3 and 10 covering subject area 4) of 2 marks each.

Section B

3 written questions of 20 marks each - covering subject area 3.

Section C

3 written questions of 20 marks each - covering subject area 4.

Candidates will be required to attempt all questions in Section A, one question from Section B, one question from Section C and one final question from either Section B or C.

The time allowed will be 3 hours.

The structure of the Module A examination follows the same format, but will cover Interpretation of Financial Statements and Performance Management.

The pass mark for each examination is 50%.

Analysis of past papers

We analyse here the topics which have been examined in Section B of the pilot paper and the examinations set to date.

	Marks
June 2007	
Relevant costs and DCF project appraisal	20
Financial forecasts and capital structure	20
Preparation and commentary on a monthly forecast cash flow statement	20
December 2006	
Investment appraisal using NPV, including sensitivity analysis	20
Debt factoring	20
Share valuation and rights issues/debt issues	20
June 2006	
Investment appraisal using NPV and discounted payback	20
Takeover pricing, synergies and post acquisition share price	20
Credit policy and customer credit management	20
December 2005	
Investment appraisal by calculating NPVs	20
'Spinning off' a successful subsidiary	20
Efficiency of stock markets	20

Marks

June 2005

Divestment and share valuation	20
Working capital management, receivables	20
Nature and purpose of a Stock Exchange, advantages and disadvantages of obtaining a listing	20

December 2004

IRR calculation and discussion	20
Operating cash cycle calculation and discussion	20
Venture capital	20

June 2004

Project appraisal, NPV and sensitivity analysis	20
Theoretical ex-rights price, value of rights, shareholders' options, and comment	20
Debt factoring and invoice discounting	20

December 2003

Investment appraisal, incremental cash flows and NPV	20
Takeover, EPS and shareholders' wealth post-acquisition	20
Costs of inventory, just-in-time and order size	20

June 2003

Investment appraisal with sensitivity analysis	20
Forecasting and financing options	20
Shareholder wealth maximisation and takeovers	20

December 2002

Receivables' discount policy – effects on profit and investment	20
Share valuation for takeover	20
Small business finance – problems and sources	20

June 2002

Operating cash cycle: explanations and calculations	20
Share valuation and rights issues	20
Efficient market hypothesis	20

Pilot Paper

Valuation of an acquisition	20
Receivables' collection period and terms given to customers	20
Choosing between financing methods; gearing policies	20

Projects

General

Candidates are required, as part of their assessment, to submit a project for each module of the Diploma in Financial Management qualification.

The Module B project is a 5,000 word project which covers both Financial Strategy (subject area 3) and Risk Management (subject area 4).

The nature of the projects is such that they will not require extensive research and can be completed without reference to sensitive work situations. The projects will relate to the subject matter of the individual papers, and candidates who have studied the syllabus of each paper should be able to have a good attempt at the projects. Each project should be approximately 5,000 words in length, including appendices, but excluding the bibliography. The assignments will involve a mixture of calculation and narrative. The project will be an integrated assignment covering the two subject areas together; there will not be separate assignments.

The BPP Learning Media Project textbook will help you prepare for the Project element of Module B. You can order by calling 0845 751 100 (within the UK) +44 (0)20 8740 2211 (from overseas) or by visiting www.bpp.com/learningmedia.

Part A
The nature and scope of financial strategy

The nature and scope of financial strategy

Topic list	Syllabus reference
1 Financial management and financial strategy	1a
2 Financial objectives of private sector companies	1a
3 Stakeholders in a company	1a
4 Non-financial objectives	1a
5 Objectives of not-for-profit organisations	1a
6 Role of the finance function in financial strategy	1b

Introduction

This opening chapter sets the scene for the whole Study Text, by exploring the meaning of financial strategy. A strategy is a course of action designed to achieve a specific objective, so you will see that financial strategy is concerned with strategic decisions of a financial nature. Since strategy is tied in with achieving objectives, we consider in this chapter what the objectives of an organisation should be.

1 Financial management and financial strategy

Financial strategy is a key element in **corporate strategy and decision-making.**

Financial management is concerned with setting and achieving **corporate financial targets,** and so with decisions about investment and disinvestment by a company, obtaining and using finance, dividend decisions and the control of cash flows and assets and liabilities, including working capital.

Key term

Financial management can be defined as the management of the finances of an organisation in order to achieve the financial objectives of the organisation.

The usual assumption in financial management for the private sector is that the objective of the company is to **maximise shareholders' wealth**. Broadly, there are two aspects of financial management: **financial planning** and **financial control.**

1.1 Financial management decisions

The financial manager gives advice or makes decisions relating to **investment**, **financing**, **dividends** and the **management of operating cash flows and working capital**.

Examples of different types of **investment decision** are as follows.

- (a) Decisions internal to the business enterprise

  - (i) Whether to undertake new capital expenditure projects
  - (ii) Whether to invest in new plant and machinery
  - (iii) Research and development decisions
  - (iv) Investment in a marketing or advertising campaign

- (b) Decisions involving external parties

  - (i) Whether to carry out a takeover involving another business
  - (ii) Whether to engage in a joint venture with another enterprise

- (c) Disinvestment decisions

  - (i) Whether to sell off unprofitable segments of the business
  - (ii) Whether to sell old or surplus plant and machinery
  - (iii) The sale of subsidiary companies

Investments in assets must be **financed** somehow. Financial management is also concerned with how funds can be raised over the long term, for example by the following methods.

- (a) Retention of profits for reinvestment in the business
- (b) The issue of new shares to raise capital
- (c) Borrowing, from banks or other lenders
- (d) Leasing of assets, as an alternative to outright purchase

Retention of profits was mentioned above as a financing decision. The other side of this decision is that if profits are retained, there is less to pay out to shareholders as dividends, which might deter investors. An appropriate balance needs to be struck in addressing the **dividend decision**: how much of its profits should the company pay out as dividends and how much should it retain for investment to provide for future growth and new investment opportunities?

Financial management is also concerned with the **management of cash flows**. The operations of a business tie up 'working capital', because money has to be invested in purchasing inventories, and giving credit to customers, before money comes back into the business from sales. The **management of working**

capital (inventories, receivables and payables) is largely concerned with optimising cash flows and the investment in working capital.

1.2 Financial management, financial accounting and management accounting

Financial management calls for financial skills or awareness, and is closely related to both financial accounting and management accounting.

Financial accounting is concerned with:

Maintaining records of business transactions, including records of purchases, invoices to customers, payments and receipts. The accounts department is responsible for collecting money from customers and making payments to creditors. One aspect of financial management is the control of operating cash flows and working capital.

Providing financial statements that report the financial performance and financial position of a company. This information is made available to the public, and is used by investors to assess the value of the company and its investment potential. It is also used by management to monitor the success of their financial strategy, when the objective of a company is to achieve increases in reported earnings and earnings per share.

Management accounting is concerned with providing financial information for:

(a)   Decision-making. The principles of relevant costing, used by management accountants to assess the financial merits of taking a particular course of action, are also used in decisions on capital expenditure.

(b)   Performance measurement and management. Management accounting is concerned with the implementation of financial strategy decisions, setting targets for achievement and monitoring actual results.

1.3 Financial strategy

Every organisation should have **objectives** for achievement, and should define those objectives. For example, the main objective of a company might be to increase the wealth of its shareholders. It will probably have other objectives too, not all of them financial in nature.

Key term

> **Strategy** may be defined as a course of action, including the specification of resources required, to achieve a specific objective.

The above definition indicates that since strategy depends on objectives or targets, the obvious starting point for a study of corporate strategy and financial strategy is the **identification and formulation of objectives**.

Johnson and Scholes (*Exploring Corporate Strategy*) summarise the characteristics of strategic decisions for an organisation as follows.

(a)   Strategic decisions are concerned with the **scope** of the organisation's activities.

(b)   Strategy involves the matching of an organisation's activities to the **environment** in which it operates.

(c)   Strategy also involves the matching of an organisation's activities to its **resource capability**.

(d)   Strategic decisions therefore involve major decisions about the **allocation** or **re-allocation of resources**.

(e)   Strategic decisions **affect operational decisions**, because they set off a chain of 'lesser' decisions and operational activities, involving the use of resources.

(f)   Strategic decisions are affected not just by environmental considerations and the availability of resources, but also by the **values and expectations of the people in power** within the organisation.

(g)   Strategic decisions are likely to affect the **long-term direction** that the organisation takes.

(h)   Strategic decisions have implications for change throughout the organisation, and so are likely to be **complex in nature**.

Financial strategy is concerned with strategic decisions of a financial nature, and is an area of strategy falling within the scope of financial management.

Three levels of strategy can be identified.

(a)   **Corporate strategy** is concerned with broader issues, such as that of 'what business are we in?' Financial aspects of this level of strategic decision-making include the choice of method in entering a market or business. Whether entry should be accomplished through an acquisition or through organic growth, for example, is a question with financial implications.

(b)   **Business strategy** or **competitive strategy** covers the question of how the company competes in its markets, and the resources that should be invested into each area of operations. The financial aspects of business strategy include making decisions about capital investments, and raising finance for capital expenditure.

(c)   **Operational strategy** is concerned with how different functions within the business - including the finance function - contribute to corporate and business strategies. For example, a strategy to implement a new credit policy to stimulate sales might be developed and implemented by the finance function.

Question 1.1   Corporate strategy

For any company you are familiar with, through your own work experience or from news reports, try to state what its overall corporate strategy might be.

(For the answer to this question, see the Answer section at the end of this book.)

---

2 Financial objectives of private sector companies

FAST FORWARD

The main objective of a for-profit company is usually financial, e.g. **maximising the wealth of shareholders** as a long-term objective, with shorter-term financial targets for growth in profits and earnings per share, etc.

Financial strategy involves making decisions about investing and obtaining finance to fund those investments. Investment should have a purpose. Why should a company make new investments? What is it trying to achieve by investing? Does it matter how new investments are funded, and if so, why? A starting point for a study of financial strategy should be an understanding of financial objectives, and the rationale on which financial management decisions, particularly investment decisions, are made.

A company is owned by its ordinary shareholders (the 'equity' shareholders) but governed by its board of directors. The board of directors is responsible for the way in which the company is managed and for the investments that the company makes, and the directors are accountable to the shareholders for the company's performance. Decisions taken by the directors and their management team should be focused towards obtaining benefits for the shareholders.

The assumption underpinning financial management decisions is that **the main objective of a company should aim to maximise the wealth of its owners, the equity shareholders**. Financial strategy should therefore be directed towards making investments that maximise **shareholder wealth**.

Other individuals and groups have an interest or stake in a company. The executive directors, managers and employees make their living out of working for their company, and might expect secure employment, career development and a good salary and other rewards. However, although managers and employees might have expectations of what their company should do for them, the objective of a company cannot be expressed satisfactorily in terms of increasing employee benefits. In truth, there are many such stakeholders in a business, and a genuine conflict exists between the interests of the stakeholders and those of other stakeholders that we examine later.

Despite such conflicts, the overriding objective of a company should be to maximise shareholder wealth, decision-makers need to know whether investment decisions will increase shareholder wealth or not. An investment decision should be taken if it is likely to increase shareholder wealth, but should not be taken if it will reduce shareholder wealth. But how can it be decided in advance whether shareholders are likely to benefit or not from a particular investment decision?

2.1 Expected returns for shareholders

Shareholders invest in a company in the expectation of obtaining a return on their investment. Return is obtained in the form of both dividends and increases in the value of the shares. The size of return that shareholders expect depends on a number of different factors, such as:

(a) **Opportunity cost:** the size of returns available on other investments. If investment A is identical in virtually every respect to investment B, and investment A is yielding a return of 10% per annum, investors will expect a 10% yield from investment B.

(b) **Inflation.** Investors expect a 'real' return on their investment, after allowing for the effect of inflation. Broadly speaking, if the rate of inflation rises from 2.5% per annum to 3% per annum, investors are likely to expect an increase In the return on their investment of 0.5%, to allow for the higher inflation rate.

(c) The **risk** in the investment. Some investments are more risky than others. Investment risk is assessed in terms of how much higher or lower the actual returns might be, compared with the expected returns. For example, the **expected** returns on both investment X and investment Y might be 10%. However, the **actual** returns on investment X could be anywhere in the range 0% to 20%, whereas the range of possible returns for investment Y is 8% - 12%. Although the expected returns are the same for both investments, investment X is more risky, because of the greater variation or volatility in the potential return. Investors generally expect a higher return on investment to compensate them for higher investment risk.

The return shareholders expect to receive varies from one company to another, and one of the issues described in this text is how to establish the expected return on the shares of a particular company, and the expected returns that a company should make on its investments.

2.2 Investments by a company and shareholder wealth

When a company makes an investment, the investment might be financed partly by debt capital and partly by shareholders' capital. The investment returns will be used to pay interest on the debt and repay the debt principal, and any additional returns after debt payments are profits attributable to shareholders. The returns are either paid out as dividends, or reinvested in the business, to provide even higher returns in the future (i.e. invested for growth). Maximising shareholder wealth depends on the returns a company makes on its investments.

(a) If the investment returns available for the shareholders are higher than the returns expected by the shareholders, the value of the shareholders' investment (i.e. the share price) should rise.

(b) On the other hand, if the returns available to shareholders from a company's investments are less than the shareholders expect, the share price will fall.

Key term

> **Increases in shareholder wealth** can be measured by increases in the market value of the shares (net of any equity capital contributed for, say, new investment).

The market value of a public company's shares depends on the price investors in the stock market put on it. Share prices are driven by investors' expectations of how well the company will perform, and what the future prospects are for dividends and profit growth. Share prices fluctuate continually, due to short-term supply and demand factors in the stock market, but over a slightly longer period, the following presumptions about share prices can be made.

(a) **The value or price of a share will depend on the money returns that shareholders expect to receive in the future from the share (i.e. dividends), and the yield or return that investors require.**

For example, if a share is expected to pay a dividend of 50 cents per annum into the foreseeable future, and investors in the share expect a yield of 15%, the value of the share will be determined by the expected future dividends and the required investment return.

(b) **Expectations about future returns change from time to time.**

A company might announce better-than-expected dividends and make more optimistic forecasts for the future. If investors decide that future returns will be higher than previously expected, the share price will rise. Similarly, if a company disappoints investors with its performance and prospects for the future, the share price will fall.

(c) **Investors might change their view about the size of return they want to receive.**

For example, a company might alter its investment strategy, and start investing in high-risk projects. If it does this, future returns will be more at risk, and the return that shareholders expect from their investment might be increased as a result. This will have an effect on the share price.

The fundamental issues in financial strategy can be summarised as follows.

(a) The objective of a company should be to maximise shareholder wealth.

(b) Shareholder wealth is measured by the market value of their shares.

(c) Share prices are determined by the future returns that investors expect on the shares, in terms of future dividends, and the investment yield they require.

(d) Future returns and dividends will depend on the returns that a company makes from its own investments.

(e) A company, when making new investments, should therefore consider the effect on future returns for shareholders and should only undertake new investments if they are expected to increase shareholder wealth.

These issues underpin most of the topics covered by this Study Text.

3 Stakeholders in a company

There are various **'stakeholder groups'** in a company, each with its own interests and objectives.

Key term

There is a variety of different groups or individuals whose interests are directly affected by the activities of a firm. These groups or individuals are referred to as **stakeholders** in the firm.

Sharplin (*Strategic Management*) has listed the various stakeholder groups in a firm as follows.

Stakeholder groups	
• Common shareholders	• Competitors
• Preferred shareholders	• Neighbours
• Trade creditors	• The immediate community
• Holders of unsecured debt securities	• The national society
• Holders of secured debt securities	• The world society
• Intermediate (business) customers	• Corporate management
• Final (consumer) customers	• Organisational strategists
• Suppliers	• The chief executive
• Employees	• The board of directors
• Past employees	• Government
• Retirees	• Special interest groups

It is probably convenient to categorise the main stakeholder groups as:

    (a)   The shareholders
    (b)   Lenders
    (c)   Employees
    (d)   Senior management (the directors)
    (e)   Customers
    (f)   Suppliers
    (g)   The Government

Stakeholder groups can exert influence on strategy, and strategic decisions can be affected by concerns for stakeholder groups other than the shareholders. The greater the power of the stakeholder group, the greater its influence will be.

3.1 Objectives of stakeholder groups

The various groups of stakeholders in a firm have different goals and interests.

    (a)   **Ordinary (equity) shareholders** are the providers of the risk capital of a company and their goal might be to maximise the wealth they obtain from their investment in the company.

    (b)   **Long-term creditors or lenders** have the objective of receiving payments of interest and capital on the loan by the due date for the repayments. Where the loan is secured on assets of the company, the creditor will be able to appoint a receiver to dispose of the company's assets if the company defaults on the repayments. To avoid the possibility that this may result in a loss to the lender if the assets are not sufficient to cover the loan, the lender will wish to minimise the risk of default and will not wish to lend more than is prudent.

(c)   **Employees** might want to maximise their rewards paid to them in salaries and benefits, according to their particular skills and the rewards available in alternative employment. Most employees will also want security and continuity of employment.

(d)   **Directors**, like other employees, have the objective of maximising their own rewards. Their personal interests might conflict with the interests of shareholders. They are accountable to the shareholders, but are the decision-makers within a company. They formulate policy and set targets, both financial and non-financial. They might also seek to persuade shareholders of the need to consider the interests of other stakeholders in the company.

(e)   **Customers** buy goods or services from the company, and expect to receive good value for the money they pay. They might also consider that they have a right to expect certain standards of quality, and certain minimum standards of service. In some industries, such as the provision of utility services like water and electricity, the general public might even believe they have a *right* to receive the service.

(f)   **Trade creditors (suppliers)** provide goods or services to the firm on credit, and have the objective of being paid the full amount due by the date agreed. They usually wish to maintain their trading relationship with the firm and may sometimes be prepared to accept later payment to avoid jeopardising that relationship.

(g)   **Government** objectives can be formulated in political terms, and terms relating to the national economy. Government affects the activities of businesses in numerous ways, for example through taxation of profits, the provision of grants, health and safety legislation, training initiatives and so on. Government policies will often be related to economic objectives such as sustained economic growth and high levels of employment.

Key term

> The **stakeholder view** of company objectives is that many groups of people have a stake in what the company does. Shareholders own the business, but there are also suppliers, managers, workers and customers. Each of these groups has its own objectives so that a compromise or balance is required. Management must balance the profit objectives with the pressures from the non-shareholder groups in deciding the strategic targets of the business.

3.2 Financial objectives – shareholder v stakeholder

We noted earlier that the overriding financial objective of a company should be to maximise shareholder wealth, and reasons commonly put forward for this are

- Shareholders can force change if they do not receive what they consider to be adequate returns or are not happy with how the company is being run.

- Shareholders will sell their shares if they are not satisfied by their returns, driving down the share price.

- The company will be taken over by outsiders if it fails to satisfy current shareholders, with these new shareholders imposing their own policies.

As such, a company must adapt to the desires of its shareholders. This shareholder view sees the company as an efficiency-seeking, shareholder value-maximising, economic entity. Within this view, financial discipline is enforced by competitive markets for products, technologies, capital, managerial talent and corporate control.

In contrast, stakeholders see the company as a collective that comes together to achieve a common purpose. Stakeholders emphasise the duty of managers to all stakeholders and relationships based on trust, and that the role of law and government is primarily to ensure fairness. Their view is that the interests of key stakeholders must be integrated into the goals of the company, that the shareholder view is narrow and simplistic, and that the goal of managers must be to address the interests of all groups and individuals who can affect, or be affected by, corporate activities

Clearly there is a conflict between these views that needs to be examined. Should a business be managed for the shareholders or for all stakeholders? In this respect, the following points should be noted.

- **Clarity of purpose** – Irrespective of the opinion that the shareholder view is rather simplistic, it does have the advantage of offering managers clarity of purpose. In contrast, though the stakeholder view may be put forward as more principled and high-minded, it is impractically wide in scope – you can't please all the people all the time. Stakeholders are not a homogeneous group, their goals are often in conflict. As a result, the stakeholder approach creates a recipe for confusion in decision-making, and reduces opportunities for creating value, to the benefit of no one other than competitors.

- **Residual claimants** – Maximising shareholder value is the only approach that can increase the returns for everyone. Ordinary shareholders are the residual claimants of the business, i.e. they are paid only after all other claimants. It is only when we manage for residual claimants that we have the incentive to increase the size of the returns as much as possible. By contrast, claimants such as creditors, suppliers and employees, have no incentive to increase value beyond the point at which their claims are assured. As such, shareholder-value maximisation works to the benefit of all stakeholders.

- **Risk tolerance and innovation** – Managing for stakeholders may lead managers to assume lower levels of entrepreneurial risk. Fixed claimants worry about total risk, that is all of the risks associated with a company's cash flows, and will, therefore, be too risk-averse in the choices they want managers to make. Shareholders, however, care only about systematic risk, the portion of the overall risk related to the market, as a result of their diversification. They tend to be less risk-averse and, as a result, are more likely to induce managers to invest in new growth opportunities, markets and products, and in innovative, cutting edge technologies. Such risk taking is essential if a business is to maintain and enhance its position in a highly competitive and increasingly internationalised market.

- **Stakeholder involvement** – Non-shareholding stakeholders can easily become shareholders, but the reverse is not possible. Given that, stakeholder-based governance will necessarily leave out a key constituency while shareholder-based governance will not.

- **Legal protection** – The legal system provides safeguards for non-shareholding stakeholders, but often does not do so for shareholders. The relationship of employees, suppliers, creditors, consumers and society at large with the company is mostly covered by contract law, tort law or regulation. For example, employees have contractual provisions covering discrimination, health and safety, pensions, etc. In contrast the law provides little protection for shareholders.

The above points clearly support the shareholder view, however, as with any debate, there are counterarguments such as lack of corporate citizenship, contract failure, imposition of third party externalities and exposure to corporate malfeasance.

- **Corporate citizenship** – Corporate citizenship is a term used to describe the contribution a company makes to society through its core business activities, its social investment and philanthropy programmes, and its engagement in public policy. That contribution is determined by how well a company manages its economic, social and environmental impacts, as well as its relationships with stakeholders.

- **Contract failure** – Stakeholders emphasise the duty of managers to all stakeholders and relationships based on trust, with law and the government ensuring fairness. Such an approach, stakeholder proponents argue, should minimise the likelihood and effect of any business contract failures. However, all contracts are prone to failure because of factors such as inadvertence, unforeseen contingencies, disputes concerning interpretation and pre-contract intentions.

- **Third party externalities** – Third party externalities arise when corporate decisions have an influence, good or bad, on any third parties. Examples would include pollution or planning blight. Arguably a stakeholder view would have more regard to such consequences.

- **Corporate malfeasance** – There have been may examples of corporate malfeasance perpetrated by the managers of companies, allegations of fraud, bribery and corruption. The stakeholder view is that if a business is managed for all interested parties there would be no incentive for this type on activity. It should be noted, however, that such actions have rarely gained the prior approval of the shareholders who are usually the biggest losers in the event of a corporate scandal, and are frequently undertaken for the benefit of managers (one of the stakeholder groups).

Shareholders would argue that all of these critiques could equally apply to stakeholder-managed companies with their heterogeneous aims and expectations. The issues they raise do not arise just because the system focuses on shareholder-value maximisation, rather they are issues that arise as a result of the nature of the business.

Clearly, there are no right or wrong answers to this debate, however the balance, if only as a result of the legal ownership position, is in favour of the shareholder approach. Irrespective of whether a shareholder or stakeholder approach is adopted, problems to be considered include the following.

- **Short-run v the long-run** – Businesses should concern themselves with the long-run, however managers may be tempted to concentrate on the short-run for their own benefit.

- **Excessive risk-taking** – When management incentives for entrepreneurial risk taking mutate into those for excessive risk taking, e.g. through the use of executive stock options. Many option grants are tied to short-term performance and have become one-sided bets for managers. Since option values increase with risk, they can tip the balance towards excessive risk taking.

- **CEO compensation** – The suggestion that the remuneration of many CEOs has become unrelated to overall business performance.

In conclusion, 'There can be no debate about whether corporations should acknowledge and respond to the interest of every stakeholder to the extent that the interests are embodied in law or enforced by market forces .... The debate is ongoing, however, about whether the plural stakeholders should be served as legitimate claimants in their own right rather than simply as a way of serving the primary corporate constituency, the common shareholder' (Sharplin).

In addition, many managers acknowledge that the interests of some stakeholder groups – e.g. themselves and employees - should be recognised and provided for, even if this means that the interests of shareholders might be adversely affected. However, from a practical perspective, not all stakeholder group interests can be given specific attention in the decisions of management. Those stakeholders for whom management recognises and accepts a responsibility are referred to as **constituents** of the firm giving rise to certain non-financial objectives discussed below.

3.3 Shareholders and the directors

Although ordinary shareholders (equity shareholders) are the owners of the company to whom the board of directors are accountable, the actual powers of shareholders tend to be restricted, except in companies where the shareholders are also the directors. The **day-to-day** running of a company is the responsibility of the **management**, and although the company's results are submitted for shareholders' approval at the annual general meeting (AGM), there is often apathy and acquiescence in directors' recommendations. AGMs are often very poorly attended.

Key term

> The relationship between management and shareholders is sometimes referred to as an **agency relationship**, in which managers act as agents for the shareholders.

Shareholders are often ignorant about their company's current situation and future prospects. They generally have no right to inspect the books of account, and their forecasts of future prospects are gleaned from the annual report and accounts, stockbrokers, investment journals and daily newspapers.

A reason why directors might do their best to improve the financial performance of their company and identify with shareholder interests is that their remuneration is often related to the profitability of the company. Managers in very large companies, or in very profitable companies, will normally expect to earn higher salaries than managers in smaller or less successful companies. There is also an argument for giving managers some profit-related pay, or providing other incentives (such as share options) that are related to profits or the share price.

4 Non-financial objectives

FAST FORWARD

> A company might also have **non-financial objectives**, which it also seeks to achieve, even though this might not be consistent with profit maximisation.

A company may have important **non-financial objectives**, which will limit the achievement of its financial objectives. Examples of non-financial objectives are as follows.

(a) **The welfare of employees.** A company might try to provide good wages and salaries, comfortable and safe working conditions, good training and career development, and good pensions. If redundancies are necessary, many companies will provide generous redundancy payments, or spend money trying to find alternative employment for redundant staff.

(b) **The welfare of management.** Managers will often take decisions to improve their own circumstances, even though their decisions will incur expenditure and so reduce profits. High salaries, company cars and other perks are all examples of managers promoting their own interests.

(c) **The welfare of society as a whole.** The management of some companies are aware of the role that their company has to play in exercising **corporate social responsibility** and providing for the well-being of society. As an example, many oil companies are aware of their role as providers of energy for society, faced with the problems of **protecting the environment** and preserving the Earth's dwindling energy resources. Companies may be aware of their responsibility to minimise pollution. In delivering 'green' environmental policies, a company may improve its corporate image as well as reducing harmful externality effects.

(d) **The provision of a service.** The major objectives of some companies will include fulfilment of a responsibility to provide a service to the public. Examples are the privatised British Telecom and British Gas.

(e) **The fulfilment of responsibilities towards customers and suppliers.** Responsibilities towards **customers** include providing a product or service of a quality that customers expect, and dealing honestly and fairly with customers. Responsibilities towards **suppliers** are expressed mainly in terms of trading relationships. A company's size could give it considerable power as a buyer. The company should not use its power unscrupulously. Suppliers might rely on getting prompt payment, in accordance with the agreed terms of trade.

Other non-financial objectives are **growth**, **diversification** and **leadership in research and development**.

4.1 Financial and non-financial objectives

A problem for many companies is the **divorce of management from ownership.** The management of a company might pursue interests and objectives that are not necessarily in the shareholders' best interests.

Non-financial objectives do not negate financial objectives, but they do suggest that the simple theory of company finance, that the objective of a firm is to maximise the wealth of ordinary shareholders, is too simplistic. Financial objectives may have to be compromised in order to satisfy non-financial objectives.

On the other hand, a counter-argument is that a company might fail to maximise shareholder wealth unless it considers other stakeholders and non-financial objectives.

(a) Unless managers and employees are rewarded sufficiently, and given incentives to work towards achieving better returns for the company, they might lack the motivation. Companies need to align the interests of the directors, managers and employees with the interests of the shareholders.

(b) Non-financial issues such as customer satisfaction and ethical investment could also affect the share price. Unless a company can satisfy its customers more than its competitors are able to, it will lose market share and profitability, and might fail to survive in a competitive market. If a company makes non-ethical investments, some investment institutions might refuse to buy the shares and some consumers might refuse to buy the company's products.

However, although non-financial objectives can be important, the main focus of attention in this text will be on financial returns and shareholder wealth maximisation.

5 Objectives of not-for-profit organisations

Not-for-profit organisations should have a non-financial primary objective, but with supporting financial objectives. The main financial objective might be to achieve value for money (economy, efficiency and effectiveness).

Not-for-profit organisations include national and local government bodies, organisations providing public services such as the police, fire services, hospital authorities, schools and armed forces, and charity organisations. The main objective of a not-for-profit organisation is not financial, and depends on the nature of its activities.

However, there are financial constraints limiting what any such organisation can do. They must operate within the limits of the money available to them.

(a) A not-for-profit organisation needs money to pay for its operations, and the major financial constraint is the amount of funds that it can obtain.

(b) Having obtained funds, a not-for-profit organisation should seek to get **value for money** from use of the funds:

(i)   **Economically**: not spending $2 when the same thing can be bought for $1
(ii) **Efficiently**: getting the best use out of what money is spent on
(iii) **Effectively**: spending funds so as to achieve the organisation's objectives

The nature of financial objectives in a not-for-profit organisation can be explained in more detail, using **government departments** in the UK as an illustration.

5.1 Government departments

Financial management in government departments is different from financial management in an industrial or commercial company for some fairly obvious reasons.

(a) Government departments do not operate to make a profit and are not subject to competitive reasons for controlling costs, being efficient or, when services are charged for (such as medical prescriptions), keeping prices down.

(b) Government decisions are driven by political imperatives rather than commercial ones.

(c) The government gets its money for spending from taxes, other sources of income and borrowing (such as issuing government bonds), whether financial markets regard as totally secure.

(d) In the UK, additional finance for capital expenditure projects, such as building hospitals and schools and modernising public transport has been sought from the private sector. Raising finance from businesses to pay for public projects is referred to as the **Private Finance Initiative (PFI)** or **Public-Private Partnership (PPP).** The involvement of companies in public projects emphasises the growing significance of financial strategy for the public sector.

Since managing government is different from managing a company, a different financial framework is needed for planning and control. This is achieved by setting objectives for each department, by careful planning of public expenditure proposals, and by emphasis on getting value for money.

A good deal of government work is carried out by **executive agencies** (vehicle licensing, Companies House, the Royal Mint and so on). Executive agencies are answerable to the government for providing a certain level of service, but are independently managed on business principles.

Question 1.2   PFI

Critics of the Private Finance Initiative, whereby private sector finance is used to pay for the building of public facilities such as hospitals and schools, claim that the government is mortgaging state services for future generations to pay. What do you suppose is meant by this?

(For the answer to this question, see the Answer section at the end of this book.)

---

6 Role of the finance function in financial strategy

In a company, major strategic decisions are made or approved by the board of directors. The role of the finance director or financial manager is to:

(a) Give advice to the board to assist with decision-making, such as capital expenditure decisions, company restructuring decisions or decisions about the method of financing an acquisition

(b) Monitor capital expenditure projects, and carry out post-completion audits

(c) Prepare long-term financial projections or plans (a business plan), setting out the company's targets in money terms

(d) Provide financial information to the Board, so that the directors can assess actual performance against the plan

(e)   Implement strategy in areas where the finance function has direct management responsibility. These areas might include raising new finance from external sources, as well as the management of receivables and cash

(f)   Make proposals for new strategic initiatives in areas where the finance function has direct management responsibility, for example proposing a new credit policy

The remainder of this text explains these various aspects of financial strategy.

Chapter roundup

- Financial strategy is a key element in **corporate strategy and decision-making.**

- Financial management is concerned with setting and achieving **corporate financial targets,** and so with decisions about investment and disinvestment by a company, obtaining and using finance, dividend decisions and the control of cash flows and assets and liabilities, including working capital.

- The main objective of a for-profit company is usually financial, e.g. **maximising the wealth of shareholders** as a long-term objective, with shorter-term financial targets for growth in profits and earnings per share, etc.

- A company might also have **non-financial objectives**, which it also seeks to achieve, even though this might not be consistent with profit maximisation.

- A problem for many companies is the **divorce of management from ownership.** The management of a company might pursue interests and objectives that are not necessarily in the shareholders' best interests.

- There are various **'stakeholder groups'** in a company, each with its own interests and objectives.

- **Not-for-profit organisations** should have a non-financial primary objective, but with supporting financial objectives. The main financial objective might be to achieve value for money (economy, efficiency and effectiveness).

Quick quiz

1   How is shareholder wealth measured?

2   Why might a company pursue a demerger strategy?

3   What is the difference between financial accounting and management accounting?

4   What is the problem of the divorce of ownership from management?

5   What are the main stakeholder groups in a public company?

Answers to quick quiz

1   By the value of the company's shares, and increases in the share price, together with any cash payments by the company to shareholders (dividends), net of any equity contributions (e.g. rights issue).

2   To maximise shareholder wealth. A demerger involves splitting a company into two (or more) separate companies. The aim would be to increase shareholder wealth, in the expectation that the total value of the two demerged companies will exceed the value of the company as a single entity.

3   Financial accounting is concerned with external financial reporting, to shareholders and the general public. Management accounting is concerned with providing internal financial information for use by management to help managers reach well-informed decisions.

4   Management who do not own their company might pursue strategies that are in their own interests rather than in the best interests of shareholders (e.g. resisting a hostile takeover bid, or pursuing growth of sales revenue rather than earnings per share growth).

5   Shareholders, senior management, other employees, trade creditors (suppliers), providers of debt finance, customers, the government.

Part B
Investment appraisal

2

Capital investment

Topic list	Syllabus reference
1 Investment	2a
2 Investment decisions	2a
3 Steps in project appraisal	2a
4 Methods of project appraisal	2a
5 Non-financial factors in a capital investment decision	2a, g
6 The accounting rate of return (ARR) method	2a
7 The payback method	2a
8 The payback and ARR methods in practice	2a, b

Introduction

Companies will be faced with possible investment opportunities, ie the possibility of paying out cash now, in the anticipation of receiving cash inflows in the future. Managers at companies need a basis on which to decide whether to accept or reject each possible opportunity. This chapter considers two methods of appraising investments, the ARR method and the payback period method.

1 Investment

Investment is any expenditure made with the expectation of future benefits or 'returns'. Expenditure can be divided into two categories: **capital expenditure** and **revenue expenditure**.

1.1 Capital expenditure and revenue expenditure

Capital expenditure is spending on non-current assets. **Investment** is spending with a view to obtaining future benefits, and might be long-term or short-term. **Capital projects** involve capital expenditure with a view to obtaining long-term benefits, and there may also be some investment in working capital.

Capital expenditure is expenditure resulting in the acquisition of non-current assets or an *improvement* in their earning capacity.

Revenue expenditure is expenditure incurred for either of the following reasons.

(a) For the purpose of the trade of the business - this includes expenditure classified as cost of sales, selling and distribution expenses, administration expenses and finance charges

(b) To maintain the existing earning capacity of non-current assets

Case Study

Suppose that a business purchases a building for $300,000. It then adds an extension to the building at a cost of $100,000. The building needs to have a few broken windows mended, its floors polished and some missing roof tiles replaced. These cleaning and maintenance jobs cost $9,000. The original purchase ($300,000) and the cost of the extension ($100,000) are capital expenditure because they are incurred to acquire and then improve a non-current asset. The other costs of $9,000 are revenue expenditure because they merely maintain the building and thus the earning capacity of the building.

Capital expenditures differ from day to day revenue expenditures in two ways. Firstly, they often involve a bigger outlay of money. Secondly, the benefits will accrue over a long period of time, usually well over one year and often much longer, so that the benefits cannot all be set against costs in the current year's income statement.

1.2 Non-current asset investment and working capital investment

A capital investment in non-current assets will lose value over the life of the project, and the asset might have no value at all at the end of the project. Working capital investment, on the other hand, will be recovered at the end of the project.

Investment can be made in **non-current assets** or **working capital**.

(a) An investment in non-current assets typically involves a cash outlay when the asset is acquired, and the benefits of the investment are obtained from the returns (extra net revenue or reduced costs) over the life of the asset.

(b) Investment in working capital is represented in the balance sheet of the organisation as inventories plus receivables minus trade payables. An investment in working capital arises because an organisation has to buy resources, such as raw materials, before the investment can be recovered from sales of the finished product or service. In addition, the finished product or service may be sold on credit, in which case the organisation has to wait until some time after the sale until it gets its return in cash.

It may help to think of an investment in working capital as the difference between the operating profits reported by an organisation (ignoring depreciation costs of non-current assets) and the cash returns the organisation receives.

1.3 Example

A company makes an investment in a non-current asset costing $50,000. The asset has a life of three years, and the net operating profit from the asset, ignoring depreciation costs, will be $20,000 in Year 1, $30,000 in Year 2 and $25,000 in Year 3. The project will require an investment of $15,000 in working capital.

What are the cash flows of this project?

Solution

The investment in working capital means that cash flows in Year 1 will reduce cash flows from operations by $15,000 below the operating profit figure. However, at the end of the project, the working capital investment will come to an end, and will be converted into cash (eg as outstanding debtors pay what they owe). The cash flows are therefore as follows.

Year	Capital expenditure $	Working capital investment $	Net operating profit $	Net cash flow pa $	Cumulative net cash flow $
0	(50,000)	(15,000)		(65,000)	(65,000)
1			20,000	20,000	(45,000)
2			30,000	30,000	(15,000)
3		15,000	25,000	40,000	25,000

Notes

1   By convention in capital investment appraisal, it is normally assumed that cash flows during each time period (year) all take place at the end of the period. If a cash flow or investment takes place at or near the beginning of a period, it is normally assumed that it occurs at the end of the previous time period.

2   A capital investment that takes place 'now', at the start of Year 1, is therefore assumed to have taken place at the end of the period that has just ended, which is Year 0.

3   The recovery of the working capital investment at the end of the project will take place early in Year 4, which is therefore regarded, by convention, as taking place at the end of Year 3.

2 Investment decisions

FAST FORWARD

Commercial investment decisions are largely determined by financial considerations. (Are the returns sufficient? Is it the cheapest option available?)

Key term

An **investment decision** is a decision:

(a)   whether or not to undertake an investment

(b)   when there are alternative choices for an investment, selecting which of the mutually exclusive investments to undertake

(c)   when capital for spending is in short supply, deciding which investments to undertake with the money that is available.

2.1 Investment by the commercial sector and by not-for profit organisations

For investments by **commercial organisations**, a major consideration is finance. An investment should be justified in financial terms, and should not be undertaken if it is not expected to meet the minimum financial requirements. However, non-financial considerations could influence an investment decision.

Investment by not-for-profit organisations differs from investment by commercial organisations.

(a) Relatively few capital investments by not-for-profit organisations are made with the intention of earning a financial return. For example, government spending on roads, hospitals, schools, the defence forces and the police service, nuclear waste dumps and so on are not made with an eye to profit and return. Similarly, investments by charities would not be made with profit in mind.

(b) Rather than considering financial cost and financial benefits (if any) alone, not-for-profit organisations will often have regard to the **social costs** and **social benefits** of investments when making capital expenditure decisions. The social costs of building a new motorway into a city might include the loss of people's homes, more pollution and health hazards whereas the social benefits might include faster travel, the ability of the road to carry a larger volume of traffic and the environmental benefits for the people in the city from reduced traffic congestion.

The investment appraisal techniques described in this chapter and the chapters that follow are based on the assumption that the investment decision is a commercial one, and that financial considerations will therefore predominate.

3 Steps in project appraisal

FAST FORWARD

There is a need for **management control** over capital spending. Projects, once identified as potential investments, should be properly **evaluated** and a formal proposal to invest submitted to the managers responsible for authorising the spending. The spending should be **authorised**. Once authorised, the spending on the project and benefits from the project should be **monitored**. After the project has been completed, there should be a **post-completion audit**.

Capital expenditure proposals should go through a formal decision making and control cycle with the following key stages.

- Identification
- Appraisal
- Proposal
- Approval and authorisation
- Implementation
- Monitoring and control
- Performance review and post completion audit

The benefits of a formal system of authorisation and monitoring are as follows.

3.1 Identification

Projects originate from the identification of a problem or the opportunity to do something new. If the issue identified matches the long-term strategic objectives of the business then an initial proposal may be made which, if approved, will result in a formal project.

At this point management must ensure that the project is established with clear terms of reference, an appropriate management structure and a carefully selected project team. The project team will have to study, discuss and analyse the problem, from a number of different aspects (e.g. technical, financial etc.) so must have the appropriate skills and authority to carry out the task.

It is important at this stage to establish general project goals which can be developed into specific objectives Clear goals and objectives give team members quantifiable targets to aim for. This should improve motivation and performance, as attempting to achieve a challenging goal is more inspiring than simply being told 'do your best'.

3.2 Appraisal

Appraisal has a number of elements

- Feasibility study financial appraisal
- Risk assessment
- Finance source selection

3.2.1 Feasibility study and financial appraisal

FAST FORWARD

A feasibility study undertaken by a carefully selected team covering all aspects of a project's feasibility is a vital stage in assessing whether an investment is worthwhile. Feasibility studies are particularly important for investments and projects that are likely to be long and complicated and for very large projects where it will be essential to be able to develop a clear business case.

A more realistic judgement as to the overall feasibility of the project can now be made. Some large projects may involve a pre-project feasibility study, which establishes whether it is feasible to undertake the project at all. For complex projects, a detailed feasibility study may be required to establish if the project can be achieved within acceptable cost and time constraints.

A feasibility study team might be appointed to carry out the study (although individuals might be given the task in the case of smaller projects).

- Members of the team should be drawn from the departments affected by the investment.

- At least one person must have relevant detailed technical knowledge, and one other person must be able to assess the organisational implications of the new system.

- It is possible to hire consultants to carry out the feasibility study, but their lack of knowledge about the organisation may adversely affect the usefulness of their proposals.

- Before selecting the members of the study group, the steering committee must ensure that they possess suitable personal qualities, e.g. the ability to be objectively critical.

There are five key areas in which a project must be feasible if it is to be selected.

- **Operational feasibility** – Operational feasibility is a key concern. If an investment makes technical sense but conflicts with the way the organisation does business, the solution is not feasible. Thus an organisation might reject a solution because it forces a change in management responsibilities, status and chains of command, or does not suit regional reporting structures, or because the costs of redundancies, retraining and reorganisation are considered too high.

- **Technical feasibility** – The requirements, as defined in the feasibility study, must be technically achievable. For a computer system for example, any proposed solution must be capable of being implemented using available hardware, software and other technology. Technical feasibility considerations could include the following.

- Volume of transactions that can be processed within a given time
- Capacity to hold files or records of a certain size
- Response times (how quickly the computer does what you ask it to)
- Number of users that can be supported without deterioration in the other criteria

- **Social feasibility** – An assessment of social feasibility will address a number of areas, including the following.

    - Personnel policies
    - Redrawing of job specifications
    - Threats to industrial relations
    - Expected skills requirements
    - Motivation

- **Ecological feasibility** – Ecological feasibility relates to environmental considerations. A particular course of action may be rejected on the basis that it would cause too much damage to the environment. In some markets customers may prefer to purchase ecologically sound products. Ecological feasibility issues could include the following.

    - What waste products are produced?
    - How is waste disposed of?
    - Is use of the product likely to damage the environment?
    - Could the production process be 'cleaner'?
    - How much energy does the process consume?

- **Economic feasibility** – Any project will have economic costs and economic benefits. Economic feasibility has three strands.

    - The benefits must justify the costs.

    - The project must be the 'best' option from those under consideration for its particular purpose.

    - The project must compete with projects in other areas of the business for funds. Even if it is projected to produce a positive return and satisfies all relevant criteria, it may not be chosen because other business needs are perceived as more important.

The methods available for financially appraising a proposed project are discussed below.

3.2.2 Risk assessment

At this initial stage, risks that could affect project implementation need to be carefully identified. Once this has happened, risks need to be ranked according to their seriousness and likelihood, and measures taken to transfer, minimise, accept or eliminate project risks. What happens to the risk will depend on the severity of the risk and the cost of management action.

The risk situation also needs to be reviewed every time key project decisions are taken.

From the point of view of any financial risks it may be necessary to consider sensitivity or scenario analysis (covered later).

3.2.3 Finance source selection

The alternative sources of finance available to businesses and the methods of selecting the most appropriate one are covered later in Part C of this manual.

3.3 Proposal

Once the feasibility study has been completed, the project team should prepare a formal proposal to put to the business executives with a recommended course of action. The contents of the proposal will largely follow on directly from the feasibility study, the proposal being a formalised document setting out the business case for the proposal and how it should be financed.

It is likely that the results of various studies undertaken for the feasibility study will be included as appendices in this report, though the information may well be in a more summarised form.

The proposal must stand alone. It must provide all of the information that the executives may need in order to come to a conclusion. It would typically start with an executive summary, followed by the detail of the report, the conclusion and recommendations, and any appendices.

3.4 Approval and authorisation

The specific authorisation requirements will depend on the financial and strategic significance of the proposal. Senior managers may have the authority to decide on small projects in their area. Directors are liable to be able to authorise larger projects on their own, but for the most significant projects approval will be required from the full board of directors.

Those making the decision must be satisfied that an appropriately-detailed evaluation has been carried out, that the proposal meets the necessary criteria to contribute to profitability, and that it is consistent with the overall strategy of the enterprise.

The benefits of a formal system of authorisation and monitoring are as follows.

(a) Capital expenditure projects often involve **large amounts of spending and resource utilisation**. In view of their importance for a business, they should be planned, approved and controlled with as much care as revenue spending is controlled (eg through budgeting and budgetary control).

(b) A capital investment decision may be **difficult to reverse**. When a spending decision is reversed, considerable costs might already have been incurred for little or no benefit.

(c) Investment decisions need to be considered in the light of **strategic and tactical plans** of the company. Investment decisions should be consistent with the company's long-term objective, which will usually be the maximisation of the wealth of shareholders. A formal process of project appraisal and approval is a way of checking consistency with strategic objectives.

(d) Capital projects might have an expected life of many years, and **estimates of future returns will inevitably be uncertain**. Consequently, there may be a high degree of risk and uncertainty in investment decisions. A formal appraisal procedure provides an opportunity for assessing the risk.

3.5 Implementation

Once the decision has been made that the project will be undertaken, responsibility for the project should be assigned to a **project manager** or other responsible person. The required resources will need to be made available to this manager, who should be given specific targets to achieve.

The project manager is concerned with co-ordinating people and other resources to carry out the project plan and has two phases.

- Design and development
- Distribution

3.5.1 Design and development

The design and development stage is where the actual product, service or process that will be the end result of the project is worked on. The activities carried out in this stage will vary greatly depending on the type of project. For example, in a software implementation, this is when the programming of the software would take place; in a construction project, the building design would be finalised.

The main aim is to produce a design that will meet user requirements; for this to happen, the design has to be tested against what users want. Subsequent phases may have to be altered if the product design changes as a result of the testing process.

3.5.2 Distribution

After the process, service or product has been developed it will be made available or installed so it is available to be used.

Products can be launched globally, or on a country-by-country basis, depending on the markets involved. Launch plans may have to be modified if competitors change their response.

If the project involves a new system or process, a period of parallel running alongside the existing system or process may be carried out. This enables results to be checked, and any last-minute problems to be ironed out before the organisation is fully reliant on the new system or process. However implementation is not the time for adding new features or enhancements in response to user comments. Pressure for new features should have been dealt with earlier; if demand arises at this stage, there may need to be a follow-on project.

At this stage communication with internal users and customers is essential to ensure that they are happy and will start using what has been developed. Communication needs to be two-way, with those affected by the project being able to discuss their initial needs and requirements for ongoing support.

3.6 Monitoring and control

Monitoring and control is concerned with ensuring project objectives are met by monitoring and measuring progress and taking corrective action when necessary.

At the start of each project, an overall project plan needs to be produced to enable the business to monitor project delays. This should be supplemented by detailed project plans and budgets describing the tasks, resources and links. At the initial stage, the plan needs to highlight resource and time constraints, and also project date constraints.

Quality standards also need to be established before the project commences and ongoing quality control procedures defined.

Managers and project monitoring committees should be kept informed of progress, with achievements measured against the project's critical success factors being regularly reported. Cost control systems also need to be established that will monitor actual against planned expenditure.

Actual performance should be reviewed against the objectives identified in the project plan. If performance is not as expected, control action will be necessary.

3.7 Performance review and post implementation audit

3.7.1 Performance review

The nature of an investment or project will determine how its success is measured. Performance reviews will vary in content from organisation to organisation, and from investment to investment. Organisations will need to consider carefully the following factors.

- What is evaluated
- Who decides what constitutes performance and whether it is good or bad
- Does the investment have a single clear purpose, or a number of different purposes which will complicate the targets that are set for it
- How important will quantitative measures be and how important will qualitative measures be

Financial measures are an important measure of many investments' success. Organisations will assess whether the investment is generating the expected positive cash flows and whether it is fulfilling other targets, for example a payback period of less than a certain number of years, or a target return on investment.

With many investments, the key success indicators factors are likely to be direct improvements in production. Likely important measures here include:

- Number of customer complaints and warranty claims
- Rework
- Delivery time
- Non-productive hours
- Machine down time
- Stock-outs

Some investments will be undertaken to improve internal procedures, and will be assessed on the basis of whether they have fulfilled the needs that prompted the investment. The performance of a computer system for example will be evaluated on the basis of whether it meets the basic needs to provide information of the required quality (timely, accurate, relevant to business needs, clear etc), or improves turnaround time for information.

3.7.2 Post implementation audit

FAST FORWARD

A post-completion audit is designed to identify improvements not only over the remaining life of a specific project, but in the business's budgeting and management procedures.

A post audit or a post-completion audit is a review of the cash inflows to and outflows from a project after it has reached the end of its life, or at least some years after it began. As far as possible, the actual cash flows should be measured and compared with the estimates contained in the original capital expenditure appraisal. The manager responsible for the project should be asked to explain any significant variances.

A post-completion audit is an objective, independent assessment of the success of a capital project in relation to plan. It covers the whole life of the project and provides feedback to managers to aid the implementation and control of future projects.

Benefits of post-completion audits

Post completion audit checking cannot reverse the decision to make the capital expenditure because the expenditure will already have taken place, however it does have a certain control value.

- If a manager asks for and gets approval for a capital project, and knows that in due course the project will be subject to a post-completion audit, then the manager will be more likely to pay attention to the benefits and the costs than if no post audit were threatened.

- If the post audit takes place before the project life ends, and if it finds that the benefits have been less than expected because of management inefficiency, steps can be taken to improve efficiency and earn greater benefits over the remaining life of the project. Alternatively, the post-completion audit may highlight those projects which should be discontinued.

- A post-completion audit can help to identify managers who have been good performers and those who have been poor performers.

- A post-completion audit might identify weaknesses in the forecasting and estimating techniques used to evaluate projects, and so should help to improve the quality of forecasting for future investment decisions.

- A post-completion audit might reveal areas where improvements can be made in methods so as to achieve better results from capital investments in general.

- The original estimates may be more realistic if managers are aware that they will be monitored, but post-completion audits should not be unfairly critical.

It may be too expensive to post-completion audit all capital expenditure projects; therefore managers may need to select a sample for a post-completion audit. A reasonable guideline might be to audit all projects above a certain size, and a random sample of smaller projects.

Problems with post-completion audits

- There are many uncontrollable factors in long-term investments such as environmental changes. Since such factors are outside management control there may be little to gain by identifying the resulting variances.

- This means that it may not be possible to identify separately the costs and benefits of any particular project or, due to uncertainty, to identify the costs and benefits at all.

- Post-completion audit can be a costly and time-consuming exercise. Labour, which may be a scarce resource, is required to undertake the task.

- Applied punitively, post-completion audit exercises may lead to managers becoming over cautious and unnecessarily risk averse.

- The strategic effects of a capital investment project may take years to materialise and it may never be possible to identify or quantify them effectively.

4 Methods of project appraisal

There are several methods for the financial appraisal of a project, and evaluating whether the project would be of value to the organisation.

(a) **The accounting rate of return method** (or **return on investment**). This method calculates the profits that will be earned by a project and expresses these as a percentage return on the capital invested in the project. The higher the rate of return, the higher a project is ranked. A project might be undertaken if its expected accounting rate of return exceeds a minimum target amount. This method of project appraisal is based on **accounting results** rather than cash flows.

(b) **The payback period.** This method of investment appraisal calculates the length of time a project will take to recoup the initial investment, in other words how long a project will take to pay for itself. A capital project might not be undertaken unless it achieves payback within a given period of time. This method of project appraisal is based on the anticipated **cash flows**.

(c) A **discounted cash flow (DCF)** appraisal. There are three methods of project appraisal using DCF.

(i) The **net present value (NPV) method**. This takes into consideration all the relevant cash flows associated with a project over the whole of its life, and also when the cash flows will occur. Cash flows occurring in future years are then adjusted to a **'present value'**. The process of re-valuing all project cash flows to a 'present value' is known as discounting. The present value of benefits (revenues or savings) are then compared with the present value of expenditures. The difference is the net present value. If the present value of benefits exceeds the present value of costs, the project is financially justified. If the present value of benefits is less than the present value of costs, the project is not justified financially. The NPV method is the recommended method of project appraisal, since it is consistent with the objective of maximising shareholder wealth.

(ii) The **internal rate of return (IRR) method**. This method uses discounting arithmetic to calculate the return expected from the project calculated on a discounted cash flow basis. This 'internal rate of return' for the project is then compared with the target rate of return. The project is justified financially if the IRR of the project exceeds the target rate of return.

(iii) The **discounted payback method**. This method converts all the expected cash flows from a project to a present value, and calculates how long it will take for the project to payback the capital outlay on a discounted cash flow basis. It is similar to the non-discounted payback method, except that it uses discounted cash flows.

Each of these methods will be described in either this chapter or the next chapter.

4.1 Reliability of forecasts

Before looking at each of these appraisal methods in turn, it is worth emphasising one problem common to all of them. Capital projects often have an expected commercial life of many years, and project appraisal calls for an estimate of future returns over the project's life. **Forecasting** is never easy, but in capital budgeting the problems are particularly acute. Forecasts must always be treated with some suspicion, and a large margin for error might have to be allowed.

Exam focus point

The Financial Strategy Examiner has highlighted investment appraisal as one of the key areas of the syllabus – and it in fact, 'could appear in every examination paper, or nearly every examination paper, in one form or another.' It is therefore essential that you have a good grasp of this area. The June 2003 exam contained a good example of the type of question that might be asked. The topic featured again in December 2003, June 2004 and December 2005 bearing out the examiner's comment on the importance of this area.

5 Non-financial factors in a capital investment decision

FAST FORWARD

Although capital investment decisions by commercial organisations are largely finance-driven, **non-financial factors** can affect a decision. Non-financial factors include legal issues, ethical issues, political and regulatory issues, quality issues and employee issues.

Relevant to Q's on Invet Apprasal

A decision maker should always bear in mind **non-financial factors** that affect a decision, and you may be asked to identify these from a case described in your examination. Such 'non-financial' factors may have indirect financial implications, at some time in the future.

Possible non-financial factors that could influence an investment decision include:

(a) **Legal issues**. There may be a risk of legal action against the company as a result of its investment.

(b) **Ethical issues**. Unethical investments or actions by a company could be damaging to its public reputation.

(c) **Government regulation**. Investment decisions might be affected by the risk of government regulation.

(d) **Political issues**. A future change of government in the country concerned could affect the future returns from an investment. Political uncertainty often has a deterrent effect on investment decisions, persuading companies to defer their spending decisions until the future is more certain.

(e) **Quality implications**. Although financial objectives are important for commercial investments, other strategic objectives may also be relevant. In particular, the perceived quality of output produced by the company could be important for its relations with customers. A profitable investment might therefore be turned down if there are quality implications.

(f) **Personnel issues**. Employees might be affected significantly by a capital investment decision, and the impact on employee relations, motivation and working culture might need to be considered.

6 The Accounting rate of return (ARR) method

FAST FORWARD

ARR = the accounting profits from the project, expressed as a percentage of the amount invested. Typically, profit is the average annual profit and the amount invested is measured as the average investment over the life of the project. A project would be undertaken if its expected ARR exceeds the company's minimum required ARR. If there are two mutually exclusive investments, the investment with the higher ARR would be chosen.

A capital investment project may be assessed using the accounting rate of return method of appraisal. The expected accounting **return on investment (ROI)** or **accounting rate of return (ARR)** for the project is calculated, and compared with a pre-determined minimum target accounting rate of return. The project is justified financially if its expected ARR exceeds the minimum target.

Key term

> The **accounting rate of return (ARR)** measures the profitability of an investment by expressing the expected accounting profits as a percentage of the book value of the investment. There are several different possible formulae for its calculation.

The organisation must define ARR, and specify how it should be calculated, since various methods are possible. A formula for calculating ARR that is common in practice is:

$$ARR = \frac{Estimated\ average\ profits}{Estimated\ average\ investment} \times 100\%$$

The **average** investment is the average of the investment at the start of the project and the investment at the end of the project, allowing for depreciation of the non-current asset or assets. For example, suppose that a capital investment will call for spending of $100,000 on a non-current asset that will have a four-year life and zero value at the end of this time, and for a working capital investment of $20,000. The average investment would be $70,000 (half of $100,000 plus the working capital investment of $20,000).

Another method of calculating ARR is for the figure below the line to be the total initial investment, rather than the average investment over the life of the project.

$$ARR = \frac{Estimated\ average\ profits}{Estimated\ total\ investment} \times 100\%$$

A third method of calculating ARR is to have total expected profits above the line.

$$ARR = \frac{Estimated\ total\ profits}{Estimated\ total\ investment} \times 100\%$$

Profits are accounting profits, and are calculated after deducting a charge for depreciation of the non-current asset(s).

6.1 Example: the accounting rate of return

A company has a target accounting rate of return of 20%. ARR is calculated as estimated average annual profits over estimated average investment. The company is now considering the following project.

Capital cost of asset	$80,000
Estimated life	4 years
Estimated profit before depreciation	
Year 1	$20,000
Year 2	$25,000
Year 3	$35,000
Year 4	$25,000

The capital asset would be depreciated by 25% of its cost each year, and will have no residual value. You are required to assess whether the project should be undertaken.

Solution

The annual profits after depreciation, and the mid-year net book value of the asset, would be as follows.

Year	Profit after depreciation $	Average investment $	ARR
1	0		
2	5,000		
3	15,000		
4	5,000		
	25,000		
Average	6,250	40,000	15.625%

The project would not be undertaken because it would fail to yield the target return of 20%.

6.2 The ARR method and the comparison of mutually exclusive projects

The ARR method of capital investment appraisal can also be used to compare two or more projects which are mutually exclusive. The project with the highest ARR would be selected, provided that the expected ARR is higher than the company's target ARR.

Question 2.1   ARR method

Bee Limited is contemplating the purchase of a new machine and has two alternatives.

	Machine X	Machine Y
Cost	$10,000	$10,000
Estimated scrap value	$2,000	$3,000
Estimated life	4 years	4 years
Estimated future cash flows		
Year 1	$5,000	$2,000
2	$5,000	$3,000
3	$3,000	$5,000
4	$1,000	$5,000

The only difference between annual cash flows and annual profits is depreciation.

ARR is calculated as average annual profit over average investment, and the company has a target minimum ARR of 22%.

Based on the ARR method, which (if any) of the two machines would be purchased?

(For the answer to this question, see the Answer section at the end of this book.)

Note how, in the question above as much weight was attached to cash inflows at Year 4 as to those at Year 1, whereas the management of Bee would favour high cash inflows in the early years. Early cash flows are less risky and they improve liquidity. For this reason, they might choose machine X despite its lower ARR. One of the disadvantages of the ARR method is that it does not take account of the timing of cash inflows and outflows.

6.3 The drawbacks to the ARR method of capital investment appraisal

The ARR method of capital investment appraisal has several major weaknesses.

It does not take account of the *timing* of the profits from an investment. For example, suppose that investment A and investment B would both cost $1,000. Investment A would make a profit of $100 in Years 1- 4 and a profit of $2,000 in Year 5. Investment B would make a profit of $2,000 in Year 1, and $100 in each of Years 2 - 5. If the two investments are compared by their ARR, both would have exactly the same ARR.

It might be apparent, however, that investment B would be preferable because it provides most of its expected returns earlier. Whenever capital is invested in a project, money is tied up until the project begins to earn profits which pay back the investment. Money tied up in one project cannot be invested anywhere else until the profits come in. Management should be aware of the benefits of early repayments from an investment, which will provide the money for other investments.

A second major weakness of investment decisions based on ARR is the lack of a clear decision rule for deciding whether or not a project should be undertaken, based on its expected ARR. For example, suppose an investment is expected to achieve an average accounting rate of return of, say, 15% over the next five years. Does this suggest that the investment should be undertaken or not? The company might set a target ARR that investments must achieve, so that if the target is, say, 14%, a project expected to yield 15% would be undertaken. However, the choice of the ARR target return would be subjective, lacking a rational basis. In contrast, decision methods based on discounted cash flows (DCF), described in the next chapter, do have a rational basis for the target rate of return. With DCF, the target return is based on the expected returns of investors in the company, and investments are required to provide a return that is at least enough to meet investor requirements. Accounting returns, however, are not the same as investment returns, and a target investment return would be inappropriate for applying an ARR decision rule.

There are a number of other disadvantages with the ARR decision method.

(a) It is based on **accounting profits** and **not cash flows**. Accounting profits are subject to a number of different possible accounting treatments.

(b) It is a relative measure rather than an absolute measure and hence takes no account of the size of the investment.

(c) It takes no account of the length of the project.

(d) It ignores the **time value of money**. With the ARR method, $1 receivable in five years' time has exactly the same value as $1 spent now. Money 'now' is actually worth more than the same amount of money at a future date, because the money 'now' can be invested to earn a return, whereas future money can't be invested until it is received.

There are, however, advantages to the ARR method. It is a quick and simple calculation, it involves a familiar concept of a percentage return and it looks at the entire project life.

7 The payback method

Payback = the time required for the cash inflows from a project to recoup the cash outlays. A project would be undertaken if its expected payback is sooner than the maximum tolerated. If there are two mutually exclusive investments, the investment with the earlier payback would be chosen.

Key term

The **payback period** is the length of time required before the total of the cash inflows received from a project is equal to the cash outflows, and is usually expressed in years. In other words, it is the length of time the investment takes to pay itself back.

When deciding between two or more competing projects, the usual decision is to accept the one with the shortest payback. In the previous question (in Paragraph 6.2), machine X pays for itself after two years and machine Y after three years. Using the payback method of investment appraisal, machine X is preferable to machine Y.

Payback is often used as a 'first screening method'. By this, we mean that when a capital investment project is being considered, the first question to ask is: 'How long will it take to pay back its cost?' The organisation might have a target payback, and so it would reject any capital project unless its payback period were less than a certain number of years.

However, a project should not be evaluated on the basis of payback alone. Payback should be a *first* screening process, and if a project gets through the payback test, it ought then to be evaluated with a more sophisticated investment appraisal technique. You should note that when payback is calculated, we take profits *before* depreciation, because we are trying to estimate the *cash* returns from a project and profit before depreciation is likely to be a rough approximation of cash flows.

7.1 Example

A company is considering an investment in a project to acquire new equipment costing $80,000. The equipment would have a five-year life and no residual value at the end of that time. The straight-line method of depreciation is used. The expected profits after depreciation from investing in the equipment are as follows.

Year	Profit
	$
1	15,000
2	15,000
3	16,000
4	24,000
5	20,000

What is the payback period for the investment?

The payback period is calculated from the cumulative annual profits before depreciation. Annual depreciation is $16,000, and the profit before depreciation each year is found simply by adding $16,000 the annual profit estimate.

Year	Investment	Profit before depreciation	Cumulative profit before depreciation
	$	$	$
0	(80,000)		(80,000)
1		31,000	(49,000)
2		31,000	(18,000)
3		32,000	14,000
4		40,000	54,000
5		36,000	90,000

Payback occurs when the cumulative profits stop being negative and start to be positive. This will happen some time during year 3. If it is assumed that profits each year arise at an even rate throughout the course of the year, the payback period can be calculated in years and months.

$$\text{Payback} = \quad \text{Y years} \quad + \quad \left[\frac{B}{(B+E)} \times 12 \text{ months} \right]$$

Where

Y =   the number of complete years before payback. This is the year before the one in which payback occurs.

B =   the cumulative profits before depreciation at the beginning of the payback year, ignoring the negative value.

E =   the cumulative profits before depreciation at the end of the payback year.

In this example:

$$\text{Payback} = \quad \text{2 years} \quad + \quad \left[\frac{18,000}{(18,000 + 14,000)} \times 12 \text{ months} \right]$$

= 2 years 7 months (to the nearest month).

7.2 Disadvantages of the payback method

There are a number of serious drawbacks to the payback method.

(a)   The choice of a maximum payback period for an investment is arbitrary and subjective. For example, if a company establishes a rule that projects will not be undertaken unless they pay back within four years, where has the choice of a four year cut-off period come from?

(b)   It ignores all cash flows after the end of the payback period, and so is not concerned with the total expected returns from the investment. For example, suppose that the maximum payback period that a company selects for its investments is four years, and it is considering two mutually exclusive projects, X and Y, each costing $80,000. Project X would be expected to make total profits of $100,000 and pay back within two years. Project Y would be expected to make total profits of $500,000, but only pay back after five years. On the basis of payback alone, project X would be preferred, despite its lower total profitability.

(c)   If the objective of a company is to maximise the wealth of its shareholders, it would be wrong to ignore the future profits from an investment after an arbitrary cut-off date for payback. Using a payback cut-off limit is inconsistent with shareholder wealth maximisation.

(d)   The payback method ignores the timing of cash flows within the payback period and the time value of money (a concept incorporated into DCF appraisal methods). This means that it does not take account of the fact that $1 today is worth more than $1 in one year's time.

Other disadvantages of the payback method are that:

(a)   The method is unable to distinguish between projects with the same payback period.
(b)   It may lead to excessive investment in short-term projects.

7.3 Advantages of the payback method

In spite of its limitations, the payback method continues to be popular, and the following points can be made in its favour.

(a) It is simple to calculate and simple to understand, and this may be important when management resources are limited. It is similarly helpful in communicating information about minimum requirements to managers responsible for submitting projects.

(b) It can be used as a screening device as a first stage in eliminating obviously inappropriate projects prior to more detailed evaluation.

(c) The fact that it tends to bias in favour of short-term projects means that it tends to minimise uncertainty about both financial and business risk.

It can be used when there is a capital rationing situation to identify those projects which generate additional cash for investment quickly.

8 The payback and ARR methods in practice

The ARR method fails to give any consideration to the timing of cash flows over the life of a project, and is based on accounting profits, not cash flows. The payback method ignores the total amount of returns from a project over its life. Both methods therefore have serious weaknesses, and should not be used in isolation.

Despite the severe theoretical limitations of the payback method, it is widely used in practice. There are a number of reasons for this.

(a) It is a particularly useful approach for ranking projects where a firm faces liquidity constraints and requires a fast repayment of investments.

(b) It is appropriate in situations where risky investments are made in uncertain markets that are subject to fast design and product changes or where future cash flows are particularly difficult to predict.

(c) Most managers see risk as time-related: the longer the period, the greater the chance of failure. The payback method, by concentrating on the early cash flows, therefore uses data in which they have confidence. The justification for this is that cash flows tend to be correlated over time and hence if cash flows are below the expected level in early years, this pattern will often continue.

(d) The method is often used in conjunction with the NPV or IRR method and acts as a first screening device to identify projects which are worthy of further investigation.

(e) It is easily understood by all levels of management.

(f) It provides an important summary method: how quickly will the initial investment be recouped?

The ARR method is an unsatisfactory appraisal method, but remains popular despite its drawbacks mentioned above. Its popularity is probably due to the fact that, compared to DCF appraisal methods, it is more easily understood and calculated.

Although the ARR and payback methods are used in practice, they have no rational justification, and they provide only subjective rules for making investment decisions. Since the objective of a company should be to maximise shareholder wealth through investments, using a subjective basis for making investment decisions is inadequate. A rational approach to investment decision-making is provided by discounted cash flow methods of investment appraisal. These are described in the next chapter.

Question 2.2   ARR and payback methods

A company carries out capital project appraisal using a combination of the ARR and payback methods. It will not undertake any project unless the expected ARR is at least 15% and payback is within three years. ARR is measured as average annual profit as a percentage of the average investment over the life of the project.

A project is currently being considered. It would involve expenditure of $150,000 on an asset. The project's life would be five years and at the end of this time the asset would have no residual value. A working capital investment of $15,000 would be required.

The annual profits before depreciation from the project would be:

Year	$
1	10,000
2	40,000
3	80,000
4	70,000
5	50,000

Required

(a)   What is the ARR of the project?
(b)   What is the payback period for the project?
(c)   On the basis of the company's investment criteria, would this project be undertaken?

(For the answer to this question, see the Answer section at the end of this book.)

Chapter roundup

- **Capital expenditure** is spending on non-current assets. **Investment** is spending with a view to obtaining future benefits, and might be long-term or short-term. **Capital projects** involve capital expenditure with a view to obtaining long-term benefits, and there may also be some investment in working capital.

- A capital investment in non-current assets will lose value over the life of the project, and the asset might have no value at all at the end of the project. Working capital investment, on the other hand, will be recovered at the end of the project.

- Commercial investment decisions are largely determined by financial considerations. (Are the returns sufficient? Is it the cheapest option available?)

- There is a need for **management control** over capital spending. Projects, once identified as potential investments, should be properly **evaluated** and a formal proposal to invest submitted to the managers responsible for authorising the spending. The spending should be **authorised**. Once authorised, the spending on the project and benefits from the project should be **monitored**. After the project has been completed, there should be a **post-completion audit**.

- A problem with project evaluation is **uncertainty about future cash flows** over the life of a project.

- Although capital investment decisions by commercial organisations are largely finance-driven, **non-financial factors** can affect a decision. Non-financial factors include legal issues, ethical issues, political and regulatory issues, quality issues and employee issues.

- Methods of financial appraisal of capital projects include the ARR method, payback method and a number of DCF methods (NPV, IRR, discounted payback).

- **ARR** = the accounting profits from the project, expressed as a percentage of the amount invested. Typically, profit is the average annual profit and the amount invested is measured as the average investment over the life of the project. A project would be undertaken if its expected ARR exceeds the company's minimum required ARR. If there are two mutually exclusive investments, the investment with the higher ARR would be chosen.

- **Payback** = the time required for the cash inflows from a project to recoup the cash outlays. A project would be undertaken if its expected payback is sooner than the maximum tolerated. If there are two mutually exclusive investments, the investment with the earlier payback would be chosen.

- The ARR method fails to give any consideration to the timing of cash flows over the life of a project, and is based on accounting profits, not cash flows. The payback method ignores the total amount of returns from a project over its life. Both methods therefore have serious weaknesses, and should not be used in isolation.

1 Investment in a project would include a requirement for $20,000 of working capital at the start of Year 1, rising to $35,000 at the start of Year 2. The project would have a six-year life. In carrying out a financial appraisal of this project, what would be the investment 'cash flows' for working capital?

2 Non-financial factors in an investment decision might be legal issues, ethical issues, regulatory issues, political issues, quality issues, and employee issues. Can you think of another non-financial factor that might influence an investment decision?

3 How should project cash flows be monitored, for control purposes?

4 In calculating ARR, are the profit figures to be used before or after deducting depreciation charges?

5 A project would involve spending on a non-current asset of $50,000 and working capital investment of $10,000. The non-current asset is expected to have a residual value of $20,000, at the end of the project's three-year life. The average annual profit before depreciation would be $22,000. ARR is measured as average annual profit as a percentage of the average investment. What would be the average annual profit, the average investment and the ARR of this project?

6 Using the payback method, are the cash flows from the project before or after deducting depreciation?

Answers to quick quiz

1 Year 1 – $20,000. Year 2 – $15,000. Year 6 + $35,000. ('–' = cash outflow, '+' = cash inflow)

2 Environmental factors, or social responsibility factors.

3 By recording the capital spending, the revenues or savings from the project, and the revenue expenditure incurred. In practice, it might be difficult to identify all the cash flows directly attributable to a project. This can make monitoring very difficult.

4 ARR uses profits *after* deducting depreciation.

5 Annual depreciation = ($50,000 – $20,000)/3 years, = $10,000 per annum. Average annual profit is therefore $(22,000 – 10,000) = $12,000. The average non-current asset investment = ($50,000 + $20,000)/2 = $35,000. With the working capital investment of $10,000, the average investment is therefore $45,000. ARR = ($12,000/$45,000) × 100% = 26.7%

6 Depreciation is not a cash flow, and must be ignored in the calculation of payback. The cash flows are therefore *before* deducting depreciation.

3

DCF methods of investment appraisal

Topic list	Syllabus reference
1 Investment appraisal and cash flows	2a
2 The time value of money	2a
3 Discounted cash flow	2a
4 The net present value method of project appraisal	2a
5 Discounted payback	2a
6 The internal rate of return method of project appraisal	2a
7 NPV and IRR compared	2b
8 The NPV method and shareholder wealth creation	2b
9 Asset replacement decisions	2c
10 Multiple methods of investment appraisal	2b

Introduction

Discounted cash flow (DCF) methods of investment appraisal, such as the net present value (NPV) method and the internal rate of return (IRR) method, are superior to other methods since they take into account the time value of money. The NPV method is conceptually the best of all since it is directly consistent with the assumed objectives of maximisation of shareholder wealth. This chapter looks at the NPV method, the IRR method and the discounted payback method, and also considers the topic of asset replacement decisions.

We finish with the issue of multiple methods of investment appraisal, and the potential problems associated with it.

1 Investment appraisal and cash flows

With the exception of the ARR method, all methods of project appraisal focus on the expected **cash flows** of the project, not accounting profits. The cash flows to take into consideration are the **relevant cash flows** of the project. Relevant cash flows are future cash flows arising as a direct consequence of the investment. These may be extra revenues, extra costs, savings in costs or reductions in revenue.

The ARR method of project appraisal is based on accounting returns, with profits measured as profits after deducting depreciation. In contrast, the payback method of appraisal considers cash flows only.

An investment is the outlay of money with the expectation of getting more money back. When evaluating an investment, it is more appropriate to consider cash flows – money spent and received – rather than accounting profits. Accounting profits do not properly reflect investment returns, and this is a major weakness of the ARR method of project appraisal.

Cash flows represent the economic reality of investment and returns. An investment involves the outlay of money, in the expectation of getting more money back over the term of the investment. A company might pay out a sum of money to invest in a new business operation with an expected commercial life of several years. Over that period, it will expect to incur running costs to run the business, and to receive cash from sales. The returns on the investment will be the net cash inflows from the business operation.

In the same way, a shareholder's investment involves paying out cash to buy shares, and the returns are obtained in the form of dividends and the cash received from the eventual disposal of the shares.

Accounting profits are based on the accruals concept of accounting, and do not represent the reality of a company as a portfolio of many different investments. Instead of reporting the cash outlay on an investment, an income statement reports a depreciation charge on capital equipment over the economic life of the asset. Depreciation is a notional accounting charge, and does not represent a cash flow.

Thus cash flows and not accounting profits should be used for investment appraisal and decision-making.

1.1 Cash flows and profits compared

The cash flows involved in an investment should be measured as the relevant costs of the investment, as explained below. However, it is useful to remember the differences between operational cash flows and operating profit.

	$
Operating profit (accounting profit)	125,000
Add back depreciation	60,000
	185,000
Subtract the increase in working capital	(15,000)
Net cash flow from operations	170,000

In the example above, there are two reasons why cash flows differ from the accounting profit.

(a)   Depreciation is not a cash flow item, and to work out the actual cash flow depreciation has to be added back to the accounting profit.

(b)   Profit also differs from cash flow by the amount of the change in working capital in the period. Working capital means the investment in inventories and trade receivables, less any investment in trade payables. If there has been an increase in working capital due to larger inventories or more receivables, cash flow will be lower than profit. If working capital has been reduced in the period, eg by running down inventories, or extending credit taken from creditors, cash flow will exceed profit.

1.2 Example

A company invests $50,000 in a new item of equipment that has an expected life of five years and no residual value. Depreciation is charged by the straight-line method. The equipment is used to make a new product, and sales in Year 1 produce profits of $14,000. An additional investment in working capital of $3,000 is needed in Year 1.

The cash flows at the start of this project are as follows.

(a)   Immediate outlay at the start of the first year: $50,000 on equipment.

(b)   The cash profits for the first year, measured as operating profit plus depreciation added back, is $14,000 + $10,000 depreciation = $24,000.

(c)   Actual operational cash flows will not be $24,000 in Year 1, however, because of the increase in working capital. Some of the increase in profit is 'invested' in inventories and receivables. The actual cash flow is $3,000 lower.

(d)   However, it is generally assumed, in investment appraisal, that an investment in working capital occurs at the start of the year, and it is therefore treated as an initial investment rather than, in this example, as a cash flow in Year 1.

If the start of Year 1 is called Year 0 (i.e. the end of the current year), the cash flows in this example would be:

Year	Item	$
0	Purchase of equipment	(50,000)
0	Additional working capital	(3,000)
0	Total cash flow	(53,000)
1	Cash profits	24,000

1.3 Cash flows and relevant costs

Business decisions should be based on the expected cash flows arising as a consequence of the decision. The cash flows arising as a direct consequence of a decision are known as 'relevant costs'.

> The **relevant cash flows** for appraisal of a project are the *changes* in *future cash* flows that would arise from acceptance of the project.

(a)   **Relevant costs are future costs**. A decision is about the future; it cannot alter what has been done already. A cost that has been incurred in the past is totally irrelevant to any decision that is being made 'now'. Costs that have been incurred include not only costs that have already been paid, but also costs that are the subject of legally binding contracts, even if payments due under the contract have not yet been made. (These are known as **committed costs**.)

(b)   **Relevant costs are cash flows.**

(i)   The assumption used in relevant costing is that, in the end, profits earn cash. Accounting profits and cash flow are not the same in any period for various reasons, such as the timing differences caused by giving credit and the accounting treatment of depreciation. In the long run, however, a profit that is earned will eventually produce a net inflow of an equal amount of cash. Hence when decision making we look at **cash flow** as a means of measuring profits.

(ii)   Only cash flow information is required. This means that costs or charges which do not reflect additional cash spending should be ignored for the purpose of decision making. These include depreciation charges.

(c) **Relevant costs are incremental costs**. A relevant cost is one which arises as a direct consequence of a decision. Thus, only costs which will differ under some or all of the available opportunities should be considered; relevant costs are therefore sometimes referred to as incremental costs. For example, if an employee is expected to have no other work to do during the next week, but will be paid his basic wage (of, say, $200 per week) for attending work and doing nothing, his manager might decide to give him a job which earns only $140. The net gain is $140 and the $200 is irrelevant to the decision because although it is a future cash flow, it will be incurred anyway whether the employee is given work or not.

Relevant costs are therefore future, incremental cash flows.

Question 3.1   Annual cash flows

A company is considering an investment in a capital project to increase output and sales of one of its products, Product 123. As a result of the investment, sales of Product 123 would rise by 10,000 units each year. Product 123 sells for $20 each, and has variable costs of $8 per unit, and the current fixed cost per unit is $6. As a result of the project, fixed cost spending would rise from $600,000 each year to $680,000.

What would be the relevant annual cash flows, to take into account when evaluating this project?

(For the answer to this question, see the Answer section at the end of this book.)

Exam focus point

A 15 mark question was asked on relevant costs in the June 2007 exam.

1.4 Non-relevant costs

A number of terms are used to describe costs that are **irrelevant for decision making** because they are either not future cash flows or they are costs which will be incurred anyway, regardless of the decision that is taken.

Key term

A **sunk cost** is a cost which has already been incurred and hence should not be taken account of in decision making.

(a) A principle underlying decision making is that 'bygones are bygones'. In other words, what has happened in the past is done, and cannot be undone. Management decisions can only affect the future. In decision making, managers therefore require information about future costs and revenues which would be affected by the decision under review, and they must not be misled by events, costs and revenues in the past, about which they can do nothing.

Key term

A **committed cost** is a future cash outflow that will be incurred anyway, whatever decision is taken now about alternative opportunities.

(b) Committed costs may exist because of contracts already entered into by the organisation that it cannot get out of.

1.5 Working capital

You will be familiar with the concept of relevant costs already if you have studied the Performance Management syllabus. The same principles of relevant cash flows apply to long-term investment decisions as to short-term decision-making. However, there are some extra 'rules' to remember about the timing of cash flows for long-term investment projects.

(a)   A cash outlay incurred at the beginning of an investment project ('now') occurs in Year 0.

(b)   Cash flows that occur evenly **over the course of a year** are assumed to occur all at once at the end of the year. Receipts of $10,000 during Year 1 are therefore taken to occur at the end of Year 1.

(c)   A cash flow that occurs **at the beginning of a year** is taken to occur at the end of the previous year. Therefore a cash outlay of $5,000 at the beginning of Year 2 is taken to occur at the end of Year 1.

(d)   An **increase in working capital** during a year should normally be treated as occurring at the start of the year, and so is a cash outlay at the start of the year/end of the previous year.

(e)   A **decrease in working capital** during a year should also normally be treated as occurring at the start of the year. However, there is an **_important exception_** to this general rule. **_At the end of a project_**, any remaining investment in working capital is no longer required, and working capital will therefore be reduced to zero. This reduction in working capital to zero is treated as a cash inflow occurring at the end of the last year of the project.

1.6 Example

Bat has spent $2 million developing a new product and a further $800,000 on market research to find out whether a market launch would be worth undertaking. The findings of the market research were as follows.

(a)   To launch the product on the market, the company would have to spend a further $800,000 on equipment. This would be depreciated over three years by the straight-line method, and would have an estimated resale value of $200,000 at the end of this time.

(b)   The product would have a life of just three years, and profits after depreciation would be $500,000 in the first year, $600,000 in the second year and $300,000 in the third year.

(c)   There would be an initial investment of $120,000 in working capital in the first year and a further $140,000 of working capital would be needed in Year 2.

(d)   Instead of investing in the product launch, the company could sell the rights to the product to another company for $500,000.

What are the estimated cash flows from this project?

The annual depreciation charge would be $200,000. [($800,000 - $200,000)/3 years]. This should be added back to the annual profit after depreciation, to get the cash profit for each year. The resale value of the equipment is a cash inflow at the end of the project.

Costs already incurred are sunk costs and so irrelevant to the current investment decision. The sunk costs in this example are the development costs of $2 million and the market research cost of $800,000.

A decision to go ahead with the product launch will involve not just the cost of the equipment and the working capital investment. There would also be an opportunity cost by choosing not to sell the product rights.

Study the following cash flows carefully, and make sure that you understand how they have been derived.

	Year 0 $000	Year 1 $000	Year 2 $000	Year 3 $000
Equipment	(800)			200
Sale opportunity forgone	(500)			
Working capital	(120)	(140)		260
Cash profits		700	800	500
Total cash flow	(1,420)	560	800	960

2 The time value of money

DCF appraisal methods allow for the **time value of money**. $1 today is worth more than $1 at a future time, because money can be reinvested to earn more money over time.

Key term

> The **time value** of money describes the concept that the earlier cash is received, the greater value it has to the recipient. Conversely, the later a cash payment is made, the less the cost to the payer.

Investors put money into shares in the expectation of getting back, over time, an amount in excess of their original investment. The idea of investing cash to make more money should be a familiar concept to you. If you put money into a deposit account, you will expect to get your money back with interest. If the interest is not high enough, you will look somewhere else to invest.

In the same way, an investor buying shares expects a return in the form of dividends plus the eventual disposal price of the shares when he decides to sell them. If the expected returns are not high enough to justify the purchase price of the shares, he will not buy the shares, but put his money into another investment instead.

The same principle applies to investments by companies. The cash returns from long-term investments should be sufficient to provide an adequate return; otherwise, the investment should not be undertaken.

The required return on an investment consists of three elements, for any investor:

(a) An **opportunity cost**. This is the return that could be obtained by investing in something else. In financial management, the opportunity cost of an investment is usually expressed in terms of the return that could be obtained by putting money into a risk-free (and inflation-proof) investment.

(b) An amount to cover **inflation**. Inflation erodes the value of money over time, and an investor will expect the return on investment to cover the effect of inflation as well as to provide a 'real' return.

(c) An amount to reward the investor for the **risk** in the investment. Higher returns are expected from investments with a higher risk element.

An investment return is expressed as a percentage of the amount invested for each year of investment, in other words as a percentage amount each year. The longer the investment, the greater the required return. This too should be a familiar idea to you. If you put cash into a deposit account, you will expect to earn interest, and the longer you keep the money on deposit, the more interest you will expect to earn.

We must therefore recognise that if a capital investment is to be worthwhile, it must earn at least a minimum profit or return so that the size of the return will compensate the investor (the business) for the *length* of time which the investor must wait before the profits are made. For example, if a company could invest $60,000 now to earn revenue of $63,000 in one week's time, a profit of $3,000 in seven days would be a very good return. If it takes three years to earn the revenue, however, the return would be very low.

When capital expenditure projects are evaluated, it is therefore appropriate to decide whether the investment will make enough profits to allow for the 'time value' of capital tied up. The time value of money reflects people's **time preference** for $1 now over $1 at some time in the future. DCF is an evaluation technique which takes into account the time value of money.

3 Discounted cash flow

FAST FORWARD

In DCF, expected future cash flows (inflows and outflows) are converted into a **present value** equivalent amount. The present value of a future cash flow is the amount that would have to be invested now at the organisation's cost of capital to earn the future cash flow at the future time.

Key term

Discounted cash flow, or **DCF** for short, is an investment appraisal technique which takes into account both the timings of cash flows and also total profitability over a project's life.

Two important points about DCF are as follows.

(a) DCF looks at the **cash flows** of a project, not the accounting profits. Cash flows are considered because they show the costs and benefits of a project when they actually occur. For example, the capital cost of a project will be the original cash outlay, and not the notional cost of depreciation which is used to spread the capital cost over the asset's life in the financial accounts.

(b) The **timing** of cash flows is taken into account by discounting them. The effect of discounting is to give a bigger value per $1 for cash flows that occur earlier: $1 earned after one year will be worth more than $1 earned after two years, which in turn will be worth more than $1 earned after five years, and so on.

3.1 Compounding and discounting

Suppose that a company has $10,000 to invest, and wants to earn a return of 10% (compound interest) on its investments. This means that if the $10,000 could be invested at 10%, the value of the investment with interest would build up as follows.

(a) After 1 year $10,000 \times (1.10)$ = $11,000
(b) After 2 years $10,000 \times (1.10)^2$ = $12,100
(c) After 3 years $10,000 \times (1.10)^3$ = $13,310 and so on.

This is **compounding**. The formula for the future value of an investment plus accumulated interest after n time periods is:

$FV = PV (1 + r)^n$

where FV is the future value of the investment with interest

PV is the initial or 'present' value of the investment

r is the compound rate of return per time period, expressed as a proportion (so 10% = 0.10, 5% = 0.05 and so on)

n is the number of time periods.

Discounting starts with the future amount of a cash flow and converts it into a present value. A present value is the amount that would need to be invested now to earn the future cash flow, if the money is invested at the 'cost of capital'. For example, if a company expects to earn a (compound) rate of return of 10% on its investments, how much would it need to invest now to have the following investments?

(a) $11,000 after 1 year
(b) $12,100 after 2 years
(c) $13,310 after 3 years

The answer is $10,000 in each case, and we can calculate it by discounting. The discounting formula to calculate the present value of a future sum of money at the end of n time periods is:

$$PV = FV \frac{1}{(1+r)^n}$$

(a) After 1 year, $11,000 \times \frac{1}{1.10^1} = \$10,000$

(b) After 2 years, $12,100 \times \frac{1}{1.10^2} = \$10,000$

(c) After 3 years, $13,310 \times \frac{1}{1.10^3} = \$10,000$

Discounting can be applied to both money receivable and also to money payable at a future date. By discounting all payments and receipts from a capital investment to a present value, they can be compared on a common basis at a value which takes account of when the various cash flows will take place.

Key term

> **Present value** can be defined as the cash equivalent 'now' of a future sum of money receivable or payable at a future date, assuming that money 'now' can be invested at a given rate of return (known as the 'cost of capital'). A present value is calculated by **discounting** the future cash flow to its present value equivalent amount.

3.2 Discount factors

To make it easier to discount future cash flows to a present value, **discount factor** tables are available.

These tables give the value of $\frac{1}{(1+r)^n}$ for any cost of capital (value of r) and any future year (any value of n). In your examination, you will be given any discount factors that you might need to use to make a DCF appraisal. You will find the relevant tables at the back of this book.

Any cash flows that take place 'now', at the start of a project, take place in Year 0. The discount factor for Year 0 is 1.0. This means simply that cash flows occurring 'now' do not need to be discounted to convert them to a present value equivalent, because they are already at present value.

Question 3.2

Present value

Spender expects the cash inflow from an investment to be $40,000 after two years and another $30,000 after three years. Its target rate of return is 12%. Calculate the present value of these future returns, and explain what this present value signifies.

The following discount factors might be relevant.

Year	Discount factor at 12%
1	0.893
2	0.797
3	0.712
4	0.636

(For the answer to this question, see the Answer section at the end of this book.)

3.3 The cost of capital

The **cost of capital** used in DCF is the **cost of funds** that a company raises and uses, and the return that investors expect to be paid for putting funds into the company. It is therefore the **minimum return** that a company should make from its own investments, to earn the cash flows out of which investors can be paid their return. The cost of capital can therefore be measured by studying the returns required by investors, and used to derive a discount rate for DCF analysis and investment appraisal.

Calculating the cost of capital for a company is explained in a later chapter. For the time being, the 'cost of capital' is assumed to be a known figure.

4 The net present value method of project appraisal

With the **NPV method** of project appraisal, all expected cash inflows and all expected cash outflows from the project are discounted to a present value at the organisation's cost of capital. The net present value is the difference between the present value of total benefits and the present value of total costs. If the PV of benefits exceeds the PV of total costs, the NPV is positive, and the project is expected to earn a return in excess of the organisation's cost of capital. If the PV of benefits is less than the PV of total costs, the NPV is negative, and the project will earn a return that is lower than the organisation's cost of capital. Projects with a positive NPV are financially viable, but projects with a negative NPV are not.

Key term

Net present value or **NPV** is the value obtained by discounting all cash outflows and inflows of a capital investment project by a chosen target rate of return or cost of capital. The sum of the present value of all expected benefits from the project and the present value of all expected cash outlays is the 'net' present value amount.

The NPV method compares the present value of all the cash inflows from an investment with the present value of all the cash outflows from an investment. The NPV is thus calculated as the PV of cash inflows minus the PV of cash outflows.

(a)   **If the NPV is positive**, it means that the cash inflows from a capital investment will yield a return in excess of the cost of capital, and so the project should be undertaken if the cost of capital is the organisation's target rate of return.

(b)   **If the NPV is negative,** it means that the cash inflows from a capital investment will yield a return below the cost of capital, and so the project should not be undertaken if the cost of capital is the organisation's target rate of return.

(c)   **If the NPV is exactly zero**, the cash inflows from a capital investment will yield a return which is exactly the same as the cost of capital, and so if the cost of capital is the organisation's target rate of return, the organisation will be indifferent about whether it undertakes the project or not.

4.1 Example: NPV

Slogger is considering a capital investment, where the estimated cash flows are as follows.

Year	Cash flow
	$
0	(100,000)
1	60,000
2	80,000
3	40,000
4	30,000

The company's cost of capital is 15%. You are required to calculate the NPV of the project and to assess whether it should be undertaken.

The following discount factors might be relevant.

Year	Discount factor at 15%
1	0.870
2	0.756
3	0.658
4	0.572
5	0.497
6	0.432

Solution

Year	Cash flow $	Discount factor at 15%	Present value $
0	(100,000)	1.000	(100,000)
1	60,000	0.870	52,200
2	80,000	0.756	60,480
3	40,000	0.658	26,320
4	30,000	0.572	17,160
		Net present value	56,160

The PV of cash inflows exceeds the PV of cash outflows by $56,160, which means that the project will earn a DCF yield in excess of 15%. It should therefore be undertaken.

Question 3.3   To purchase or not to purchase?

LCH manufactures product X which it sells for $5 per unit. Variable costs of production are currently $3 per unit, and fixed costs 50c per unit. A new machine is available which would cost $90,000 but which could be used to make product X for a variable cost of only $2.50 per unit. Fixed costs, however, would increase by $7,500 per annum as a direct result of purchasing the machine. The machine would have an expected life of 4 years and a resale value after that time of $10,000. Sales of product X are estimated to be 75,000 units per annum. LCH expects to earn at least 12% per annum from its investments. Ignore taxation.

You are required to decide whether LCH should purchase the machine.

The following discount factors are relevant.

Year	Discount factor at 12%
1	0.893
2	0.797
3	0.712
4	0.636

(For the answer to this question, see the Answer section at the end of this book.)

4.2 Annuity discount factor tables

An annuity is a constant annual cash flow, for a number of years. An example of an annuity would be, say, cash receipts of $50,000 a year for six years, Years 1 – 6. To save time with calculating the present value of all the individual annual cash flows of an annuity, tables are available for the cumulative discount factors. Annuity tables give the total of all the discount factors for each year in Year 1 to Year n, for a given cost of capital r.

For example, the annuity factor for a cost of capital of 12% for Years 1 – 3 is 2.402. This is simply the sum of the discount factors for Year 1, 2 and 3.

Year	Discount factor at 12%	
1	0.893	
2	0.797	
3	0.712	
1 - 3	2.402	= Annuity factor at 12%, Years 1 - 3

If the amount of the annual cash flow for Years 1 – 3 is, say, $10,000 per annum, and the cost of capital is 12%, it is quicker to calculate the present value of these cash flows in one calculation ($10,000 × 2.402 = $24,020) instead of having to calculate the present value for the cash flow in each individual year and then add up the total.

These total discount factors could be described as 'same cash flow per annum' factors, or 'cumulative present value' factors, but the term 'annuity' factors is commonly used.

4.3 Example: NPV including use of annuity tables

IMC is considering the manufacture of a new product which would involve the use of both a new machine (costing $150,000) and an existing machine, which cost $80,000 two years ago but has no resale value. There is sufficient capacity on this machine, which has so far been under-utilised. Annual profits before deprecation would be $40,000.

The project would have a five-year life, after which the new machine would have a net residual value of $5,000.

Working capital requirements would be $10,000 in the first year, rising to $15,000 in the second year and remaining at this level until the end of the project, when it will all be recovered. The company's cost of capital is 10%.

You are required to assess whether the project is worthwhile.

Year	Discount factor at 10%
1	0.909
2	0.826
3	0.751
4	0.683
5	0.621
1 - 5	3.791

Solution

The project requires $10,000 of working capital at the end of Year 1 and a further $5,000 at the start of Year 2. Increases in working capital reduce the net cash flow for the period to which they relate. When the working capital tied up in the project is 'recovered' at the end of the project, it will provide an extra cash inflow (for example receivables will eventually be received in cash).

The historic cost of the current machine is not a relevant cost and must be ignored in the appraisal.

The NPV is calculated as follows.

Year	Equipment $	Working capital $	Contribution $	Net cash flow $	Discount factor 10%	PV of net cash flow $
0	(150,000)	(10,000)		(160,000)	1.000	(160,000)
1		(5,000)		(5,000)	0.909	(4,545)
1-5			40,000	40,000	3.791	151,640
5	5,000	15,000		20,000	0.621	12,420
					NPV =	(485)

The NPV is negative (although not by much) and the project is therefore not recommended for acceptance, because it fails to earn a return of 10%.

4.4 Strengths and weaknesses of the NPV method

The NPV method is the most valid of all the capital project appraisal methods.

(a) It recognises the time value of money, and evaluates cash flows, not accounting profits.

(b) When the cost of capital used in the appraisal is the organisation's cost of finance, a project with a positive **NPV should add to the overall value of the organisation**, and (in the case of a company) **increase shareholder wealth**.

The connection between NPV and creating shareholder wealth is very important, and is explained in more detail later.

Although it is the most appropriate method of project appraisal, the NPV method does have a drawback.

The net present value of a project is a money value. This is often difficult to understand. For example, it is easier to understand the comment: 'Project A will earn a return of 15% per annum' than it is to understand the comment 'Project A has an NPV of + $60,000 at a cost of capital of 10%'.

Exam focus point	NPV assessments can often appear as part of a question, as for example in June 2006 and December 2006.

5 Discounted payback

FAST FORWARD	The NPV method calculates a value for a capital project, taking into account all the expected cash flows over the entire life of the project. A company might want capital projects to earn a positive NPV, but also to pay back within a maximum time period. The **discounted payback method** is a way of combining DCF evaluation with a minimum payback period.

Key term	The **discounted payback** method of project appraisal is similar to the non-discounted payback method, except that payback is measured with the present value of cash flows.

A company might have an investment policy of undertaking projects only if:

(a) They have a positive NPV, and
(b) They pay back, in NPV terms, within a maximum time limit.

5.1 Example: discounted payback

TJ is considering two mutually-exclusive investments, Project A and Project B. It can undertake one of them, or neither, but it cannot undertake both.

Project A would involve expenditure on a non-current asset of $60,000 and a working capital investment of $5,000. The profits from the project, ignoring depreciation, would be:

Year	Cash profit
	$
1	15,000
2	20,000
3	20,000
4	25,000
5	20,000
6	15,000
7	10,000

BPP
LEARNING MEDIA

Project B would involve expenditure on a non-current asset of $50,000 and a working capital investment of $5,000. The profits from the project, ignoring depreciation, would be:

Year	Cash profit
	$
1	20,000
2	30,000
3	20,000
4	10,000
5	5,000
6	2,000

In both cases, the non-current asset would have nil residual value at the end of the project's life.

The company's cost of capital is 11%, and the discount factors are:

Year	Discount factor at 11%
1	0.901
2	0.812
3	0.731
4	0.659
5	0.593
6	0.535
7	0.482

It is company policy to require projects to pay back in discounted cash flow terms within four years.

Which project, if either, should be undertaken?

Solution

The NPV and discounted payback period for each project are calculated as follows.

Project A

Year		Cash flow $	Discount factor at 11%	Present value $	Cumulative present value $
0	(60,000 + 5,000)	(65,000)	1.000	(65,000)	(65,000)
1		15,000	0.901	13,515	(51,485)
2		20,000	0.812	16,240	(35,245)
3		20,000	0.731	14,620	(20,625)
4		25,000	0.659	16,475	(4,150)
5		20,000	0.593	11,860	7,710
6		15,000	0.535	8,025	15,735
7	(10,000 + 5,000)	15,000	0.482	7,230	22,965
NPV				+ 22,965	

$$\text{Discounted payback period} = 4 \text{ yrs} + \left(\frac{4{,}150}{4{,}150 + 7{,}710} \times 12 \text{ months} \right) = 4 \text{ yrs 4 months}$$

Project B

Year		Cash flow $	Discount factor at 11%	Present value $	Cumulative present value $
0	(50,000 + 5,000)	(55,000)	1.000	(55,000)	(55,000)
1		20,000	0.901	18,020	(36,980)
2		30,000	0.812	24,360	(12,620)
3		20,000	0.731	14,620	2,000
4		10,000	0.659	6,590	8,590
5		5,000	0.593	2,965	11,555
6	(2,000 + 5,000)	7,000	0.535	3,745	15,300
NPV				+ 15,300	

$$\text{Discounted payback period} = 2 \text{ yrs} + \left(\frac{12,620}{12,620 + 2,000} \times 12 \text{ months} \right) = 2 \text{ yrs } 10 \text{ months}$$

Project A has the higher NPV, but does not pay back until after 4 years 4 months, which is longer than the minimum acceptable payback period. Project B has a lower NPV but pays back within three years, which is less than the maximum acceptable. On the basis of the investment criteria used by this company, Project B would be undertaken.

5.2 Strengths and weaknesses of the discounted payback method

The discounted payback method of project evaluation is similar to the normal payback method, except that it allows for the time value of money.

    (a)   It establishes a requirement for projects to pay back within a maximum time period, although the maximum discounted payback is a subjective measure, for which there may be no rational justification.

    (b)   It gives recognition to the fact that for many companies liquidity is important, and projects need to provide returns fairly quickly.

    (c)   Unlike the non-discounted method of appraisal, it will not recommend any project for investment unless its NPV is expected to be positive.

The main disadvantage of the discounted payback method is that, as with the non-discounted payback method, it ignores all cash flows after payback has been reached. It does not take into consideration all the expected cash flows from the project. In the example above, for example, Project B is preferred even though the expected NPV from Project A is higher. By ignoring total returns from a project, its use is not consistent with the objective of maximising shareholder wealth.

Exam focus point

A 20 mark question involving the scheduling of cash flows, the determination of NPVs and the discounted payback period appeared in the June 2006 exam.

6 The internal rate of return method of project appraisal

FAST FORWARD

With the **IRR method** of project appraisal, the internal rate of return of the project is calculated. This is the cost of capital at which the NPV of the project would be zero, and so is the discount rate of return that the project is expected to earn. A project is financially viable if its IRR exceeds the company's target rate of return (its cost of capital).

Key term

> The **internal rate of return (IRR)** of a project is the discount rate at which the project NPV is zero. For a 'conventional' project – initial outflow followed by net inflows – this represents the maximum rate of return the project is able to cover before the NPV turns negative.

Using the **NPV method** of discounted cash flow, present values are calculated by discounting at a target rate of return, or cost of capital, and the difference between the PV of costs and the PV of benefits is the NPV. In contrast, the **internal rate of return (IRR)** method is to calculate the exact DCF rate of return which the project is expected to achieve, in other words the rate at which the NPV is zero.

The rule with the **internal rate of return (IRR)** method of project evaluation is that a project should be undertaken if it is expected to achieve a return in excess of the company's weighted average cost of capital. A project that has an IRR in excess of the cost of capital must have a positive NPV.

6.1 Estimating the IRR

Without a computer or calculator program, the calculation of the internal rate of return is made using a hit-and-miss technique known as the interpolation method. The **interpolation method** produces an estimate of the IRR, although it is not arithmetically exact.

The first step is to calculate two net present values, both as close as possible to zero, using rates for the cost of capital which are whole numbers. Ideally, one NPV should be positive and the other negative, although this is not essential.

Choosing rates for the cost of capital which will give an NPV close to zero (that is, rates which are close to the actual rate of return) is a hit-and-miss exercise, and several attempts may be needed to find satisfactory rates.

6.2 Example: the IRR method

A company is trying to decide whether to buy a machine for $80,000 which will save costs of $20,000 per annum for five years and which will have a resale value of $10,000 at the end of Year 5. If it is the company's policy to undertake projects only if they are expected to yield a DCF return of 10% or more, ascertain whether this project should be undertaken.

Use the following discount factors to estimate the IRR of the project.

Year	Discount factor at 9%	Discount factor at 12%
1 - 5	3.890	3.605
5	0.650	0.567

Solution

The IRR is the rate for the cost of capital at which the NPV = 0.

Try 9%:

Year	Cash flow	PV factor	PV of cash flow
	$	9%	$
0	(80,000)	1.000	(80,000)
1-5	20,000	3.890	77,800
5	10,000	0.650	6,500
		NPV	4,300

This is fairly close to zero. It is also positive, which means that the IRR is more than 9%. We can use 9% as one of our two NPVs close to zero, although for greater accuracy, we should try 10% or even 11% to find an NPV even closer to zero if we can. However, a discount rate of 12% will be used here, to see what the NPV is.

Try 12%:

Year	Cash flow	PV factor	PV of cash flow
	$	12%	$
0	(80,000)	1.000	(80,000)
1-5	20,000	3.605	72,100
5	10,000	0.567	5,670
		NPV	(2,230)

This is fairly close to zero and *negative*. The IRR is therefore greater than 9% (positive NPV of $4,300) but less than 12% (negative NPV of $2,230).

If we were to draw a graph of the NPV at different costs of capital of a 'typical' capital project, with a negative cash flow at the start of the project, and positive net cash flows afterwards up to the end of the project, it would look like Figure 1.

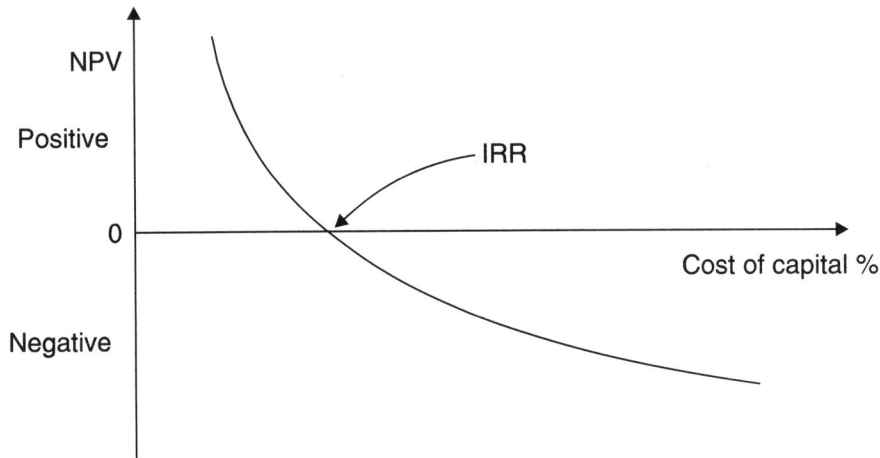

Figure 1

If we use a cost of capital where the NPV is slightly positive, and use another cost of capital where it is slightly negative, we can estimate the IRR - where the NPV is zero - by drawing a straight line between the two points on the graph that we have calculated.

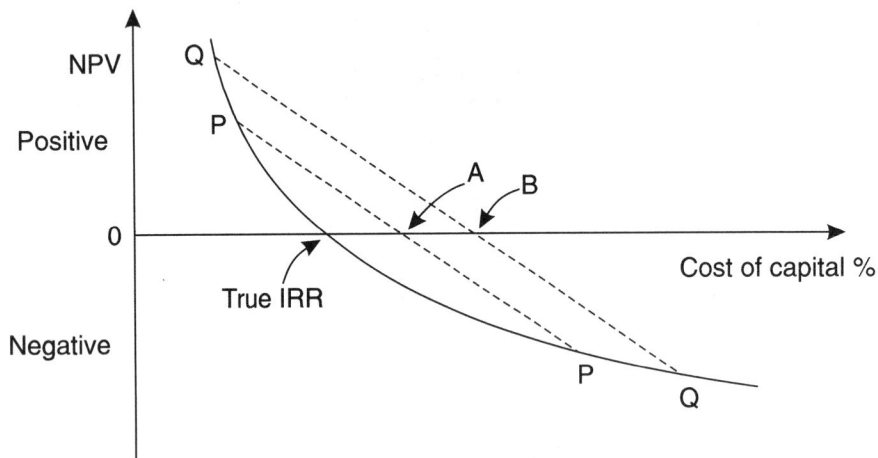

Figure 2

Study the diagram above carefully.

(a)   If we establish the NPVs at the two points P, we would estimate the IRR to be at point A.

(b)   If we establish the NPVs at the two points Q, we would estimate the IRR to be at point B.

The closer our NPVs are to zero, the closer our estimate will be to the true IRR.

We shall now use the two NPV values calculated earlier to estimate the IRR. The interpolation method assumes that the NPV rises in linear fashion between the two NPVs close to 0. The real rate of return is therefore assumed to be on a straight line between NPV = $4,300 at 9% and NPV = –$2,230 at 12%.

The formula to apply is as follows.

$$IRR = A + \left[\frac{N_A}{N_A - N_B} \times (B - A) \right]\%$$

where A is the lower rate of return
        B is the higher rate of return
        N_A is the NPV discounted at A
        N_B is the NPV discounted at B

Let us go back to our example.

$$IRR = 9 + \left[\frac{4,300}{4,300 - (-2,230)} \times (12 - 9) \right]\% = 10.98\%, \text{ say } 11\%$$

If it is company policy to undertake investments which are expected to yield 10% or more, this project would be undertaken.

Question 3.4   IRR

Find the IRR of the project given below and state whether the project should be accepted if the company requires a minimum return of 15%.

Time		$
0	Investment	(4,000)
1	Receipts	1,200
2	"	1,410
3	"	1,875
4	"	1,150

Use the following discount factors to estimate the IRR of the project.

Year	Discount factor at 14%	Discount factor at 16%
1	0.877	0.862
2	0.769	0.743
3	0.675	0.641
4	0.592	0.552

(For the answer to this question, see the Answer section at the end of this book.)

7 NPV and IRR compared

7.1 Advantages of IRR method

The main advantage of the IRR method is that the information it provides is more easily understood by managers, especially non-financial managers. For example, it is fairly easy to understand the meaning of the following statement.

'The project will be expected to have an initial capital outlay of $100,000, and to earn a yield of 25%. This is in excess of the target yield of 15% for investments.'

It is not so easy to understand the meaning of this statement.

'The project will cost $100,000 and have an NPV of $30,000 when discounted at the minimum required rate of 15%.'

7.2 Disadvantages of IRR method

A major weakness of the IRR method is its failure to take account of the total value of a capital project (the project's NPV). When there are mutually exclusive investments, the IRR method might favour a project with a higher IRR but a lower NPV. In this case NPV should be used.

It might be tempting to confuse IRR and accounting return on capital employed (ROCE). The accounting ROCE and the IRR are two completely different measures. If managers were given information about both ROCE (or ARR) and IRR, it might be easy to get their relative meaning and significance mixed up.

The IRR method ignores the relative size of investments. Both the following projects have an IRR of 18%.

	Project A	Project B
	$	$
Cost, year 0	350,000	35,000
Annual savings, years 1-6	100,000	10,000

Clearly, project A is bigger (ten times as big) and so more 'profitable' but if the only information on which the projects were judged were to be their IRR of 18%, project B would be made to seem just as beneficial as project A, which is not the case.

7.3 Mutually exclusive projects

Mutually exclusive projects are two or more projects from which only one can be chosen. Examples include the choice of a factory location or the choice of just one of a number of machines. The IRR and NPV methods can, however, give conflicting rankings as to which project should be given priority. Let us suppose that a company is considering two mutually exclusive options, option A and option B. The cash flows for each would be as follows.

Year		Option A	Option B
		$	$
0	Capital outlay	(10,200)	(35,250)
1	Net cash inflow	6,000	18,000
2	Net cash inflow	5,000	15,000
3	Net cash inflow	3,000	15,000

The company's cost of capital is 16%.

The NPV of each project is calculated below.

Year	Discount factor at 16%	Option A Cash flow $	Option A Present value $	Option B Cash flow $	Option B Present value $
0	1.000	(10,200)	(10,200)	(35,250)	(35,250)
1	0.862	6,000	5,172	18,000	15,516
2	0.743	5,000	3,715	15,000	11,145
3	0.641	3,000	1,923	15,000	9,615
		NPV =	+610	NPV =	+1,026

The DCF yield (IRR) of option A is 20% and the yield of option B is only 18% (workings not shown.) On a comparison of NPVs, option B would be preferred, but on a comparison of IRRs, option A would be preferred.

This situation can be illustrated diagrammatically:

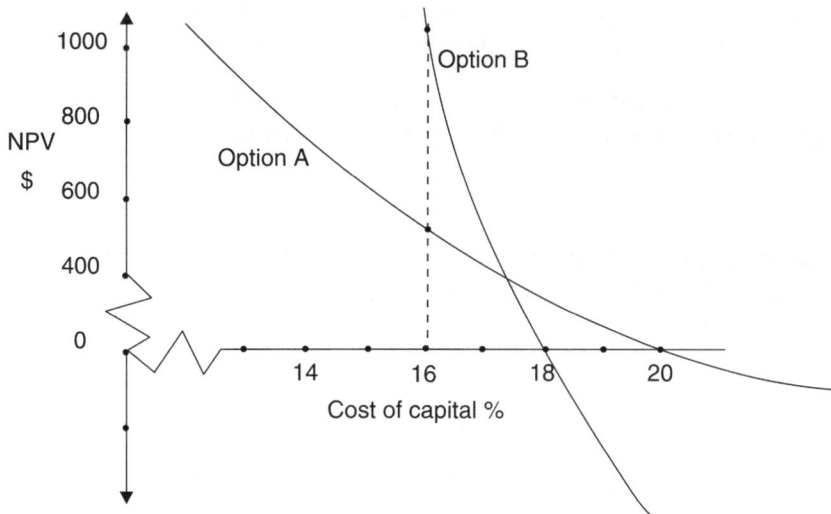

The fact that A has a higher IRR than B indicates that, if the company's cost of capital were to increase from 16%, A would yield a positive NPV for a larger range of costs than B. (It is 'less sensitive' to increases in the discount rate).

However, at the company's *actual* cost of capital, B gives a higher NPV, thereby increasing shareholder wealth by a greater amount than A.

Thus in the case of mutually exclusive projects where NPV and IRR rankings appear to conflict, the NPV approach should be used to decide between them.

Of course, if the projects were independent all this would be irrelevant since under the NPV rule both would be accepted and the organisation would be indifferent as to the order in which they were accepted.

7.4 Summary of NPV and IRR comparison

(a) Both methods gives the same accept or reject decision for individual projects.
(b) The IRR method is more easily understood.
(c) NPV is simpler to calculate than IRR.
(d) IRR and accounting ROCE can be confused.
(e) IRR ignores the relative sizes of investments.
(f) NPV is the preferred method for deciding between mutually exclusive projects.

Despite the advantages of the NPV method over the IRR method, the IRR method is widely used in practice. Even so, the NPV method is superior because it focuses on the measurement of shareholder wealth. This point is explained below.

Exam focus point

In the December 2004 exam candidates were required to assess the incremental cash flows of a new product using IRR and to discuss the strengths and weaknesses of the IRR.

8 The NPV method and shareholder wealth creation

FAST FORWARD

The NPV method of project appraisal is consistent with the financial objective of *maximising shareholder wealth*. Given certain assumptions, the value of a company should be expected to increase by the NPV of any projects that it undertakes.

The superiority of the NPV method of investment appraisal is that it provides a measurement of the expected increase in the value of a company, and so the increase in shareholder value, that might be expected from an investment. This is an important point, and is worth studying carefully.

Suppose that you invest $1,000 and want to earn a return of 10% per annum. If you are offered the chance to invest in a one-year project that will pay back $1,100 after one year, the investment will provide the 10% return you are looking for, and you will therefore think that it is worth the $1,000 that it will cost.

Suppose, however, that you are offered an investment with exactly the same risk characteristics that will pay back $1,200 after one year, on a $1,000 investment. This second investment will be more attractive, because it will provide a return higher than the 10% you are looking for. In NPV terms, the investment would have a positive net present value.

Year	Cash flow $	Discount factor at 10%	Present value $
0	(1,000)	1.000	(1,000)
1	1,200	0.909	1,091
NPV			91

If you acquire this investment for $1,000, another investor who also wants a return of 10% might immediately offer to buy it from you. He will offer more than $1,000. To obtain a return of at least 10% on his investment, this other investor will be prepared to offer you up to $1,091 ($1,200/1.10). If you sell at this price, you will have made $91 on your investment. In other words, you will have increased your wealth by $91. This increase in wealth is the NPV of the investment.

The same principle applies to investments by companies, for the same reason. If a project earns a return in excess of the returns expected by the providers of finance, the surplus belongs to the shareholders. The shareholders will expect this additional return to be paid to them as dividends, or reinvested by the company to provide even higher returns and dividends in the future. Either way, the perceived value of their investment will go up, and it should be expected to go up by the amount of the project NPV.

8.1 The fundamental theory of share values

The connection between a project NPV and changes in the total wealth of shareholders can be stated as a **fundamental theory of share values**, as follows.

Key term

> The **fundamental theory of share values** states that the market price of shares reflects investors' expectations of what the future returns from the shares will be. The share price represents the present value of all future returns, discounted at the investors' yield requirements (the cost of equity).

In theory, if a company undertakes a new capital investment and the net present value is positive when the cash flows are discounted at the company's cost of capital, the wealth of shareholders will be increased by the amount of the NPV.

(a)   The future cash flows from the project might be paid out to shareholders as dividends, so that future returns will be higher and the present value of future returns (i.e. the share price) will also be higher.

(b)   If the future cash flows from a project are not paid out as dividends, but are re-invested in another project with a positive net present value, the re-investment will achieve earnings and dividend growth and will add to shareholder wealth by the amount of the new project's NPV.

If this theory has validity, it is essential that investors:

(a)   Are aware of any new project undertaken by the company
(b)   Are aware of the future returns from the project, and
(c)   Share the same expectations as management about what the future returns will be.

Exam focus point

> For the purpose of your examination, you should assume that the fundamental theory of shareholder value is valid, unless the question indicates otherwise. Consequently, you should take as normal basic assumptions that:
>
> (a)   The objective of a firm is to maximise shareholder wealth
>
> (b)   Projects should be undertaken if they have a positive net present value when discounted at the company's cost of capital, and
>
> (c)   The increase in shareholder wealth should be the amount of the NPV
>
> These assumptions can be defended if it is also assumed that the capital markets display some form of *efficiency*. Market efficiency is explained in a later chapter.

9 Asset replacement decisions

FAST FORWARD

An **asset replacement decision** is a decision as to the optimal replacement cycle for a regularly-purchased asset. There are three techniques for using the NPV method to evaluate an asset replacement decision: the lowest common multiple method, the time horizon method and the equivalent annual cost method (which is probably the easiest of the three).

DCF techniques can be used for **asset replacement decisions**, to assess **when** and **how frequently** an asset should be replaced. When an asset is to be replaced by an 'identical' asset, the problem is to decide the optimum interval between replacements. As the asset gets older, it may cost more to maintain and operate, its residual value will decrease, and it may lose some productivity/operating capability. Consider the following example.

9.1 Example: replacement of an identical asset

James operates a machine which has the following costs and resale values over its three-year life.

Purchase cost: $25,000

	Year 1	Year 2	Year 3
	$	$	$
Running costs (cash expenses)	7,500	10,000	12,500
Resale value (end of year)	15,000	10,000	7,500

The organisation's cost of capital is 10%. You are required to assess how frequently the asset should be replaced.

Year	Discount factor at 10%
1	0.909
2	0.826
3	0.751
4	0.683
5	0.621
6	0.564
1 - 2	1.736
1 - 3	2.487

Solution

There are three possible methods of deciding the optimum replacement cycle: the **lowest common multiple method**, the **finite horizon method** and the **equivalent annual cost method**. Each method will usually give the same recommendation, as shown in the paragraphs below.

All three methods are concerned with the problem that a replacement asset will eventually be replaced itself by an asset which will also in its turn be replaced. Replacements are continuous, and are assumed to occur into the indefinite future. The replacement options in our example are assumed to be to replace the machine as frequently as shown below.

(a)   Every year
(b)   Every two years
(c)   Every three years (at the end of its useful life)

To compare these options, given that replacements will be continuous into the indefinite future, it is necessary to assess costs over a comparable period of time.

9.2 Lowest common multiple method

The lowest common multiple method works like this.

(a)   Estimate the cash flows over a period of time which is the lowest common multiple of all the replacement cycles under consideration. Thus for replacement cycles of one, two, or three years, the lowest common multiple of time is **six years**. In six years there would be the following numbers of replacement cycles.

(i)   Six complete replacement cycles of one year
(ii)   Three complete replacement cycles of two years
(iii)   Two complete replacement cycles of three years

(b)   Discount these cash flows over the lowest common multiple time period. The option with the lowest present value of cost will be the optimum replacement cycle.

In our example, we can calculate the annual cash flows as follows.

(a)   *Replacement every year*

Year		$	$
0	Purchase		(25,000)
1	Running cost	(7,500)	
	Resale value	15,000	
	New purchase	(25,000)	
			(17,500)
2-5	Same as year 1		(17,500)
6	Running cost	(7,500)	
	Resale value	15,000	
			7,500

The new purchase at the end of year 6 is ignored, because this starts a new six-year cycle for all three replacement options.

(b)   *Replacement every two years*

			$	$
Year				
0	Purchase			(25,000)
1	Running cost			(7,500)
2	Running cost		(10,000)	
	Resale value		10,000	
	New purchase		(25,000)	
				(25,000)
3,5	Same as year 1			(7,500)
4	Same as year 2			(25,000)
6	Running cost		(10,000)	
	Resale value		10,000	
				0

(c)   *Replacement every three years*

			$	$
Year				
0	Purchase			(25,000)
1	Running cost			(7,500)
2	Running cost			(10,000)
3	Running cost		(12,500)	
	Resale value		7,500	
	New purchase		(25,000)	
				(30,000)
4	Same as year 1			(7,500)
5	Same as year 2			(10,000)
6	Running cost		(12,500)	
	Resale value		7,500	
				(5,000)

We can now go on to calculate the PV cost for each replacement cycle, over a six-year period.

Year	Discount factor at 10%	Replacement every year Cash flow	Replacement every year PV of cash flow	Replacement every two years Cash flow	Replacement every two years PV of cash flow	Replacement every three years Cash flow	Replacement every three years PV of cash flow
		$	$	$	$	$	$
0	1.000	(25,000)	(25,000)	(25,000)	(25,000)	(25,000)	(25,000)
1	0.909	(17,500)	(15,908)	(7,500)	(6,818)	(7,500)	(6,818)
2	0.826	(17,500)	(14,455)	(25,000)	(20,650)	(10,000)	(8,260)
3	0.751	(17,500)	(13,143)	(7,500)	(5,633)	(30,000)	(22,530)
4	0.683	(17,500)	(11,953)	(25,000)	(17,075)	(7,500)	(5,123)
5	0.621	(17,500)	(10,868)	(7,500)	(4,658)	(10,000)	(6,210)
6	0.564	7,500	x4,230	0	0	(5,000)	(2,820)
			(87,097)		(79,834)		(76,761)

The cheapest replacement policy would be to replace the machine every three years, because this has the lowest total PV of cost.

9.3 The finite horizon method

As you will appreciate, the lowest common multiple method becomes a very long and tedious process when the maximum life of the asset is more than about three years. If the maximum life were, say, seven years, there would be seven different replacement options and the lowest common multiple would be 420 years. The **finite horizon method** is to calculate the present value of costs over a 'significant' time period (perhaps 15 or 20 years), because the present values of cash flows beyond this period are unlikely to affect the relative costs of the replacement options.

In our example, if the PV of costs had been calculated over a finite time period of five years, the three-year replacement option would still have been the cheapest. The finite time horizon method is therefore an approximation method which reduces the figure work needed, in the expectation that in spite of taking a short cut, the result is still the same.

9.4 The equivalent annual cost method

When there is no inflation, the **equivalent annual cost method** is the quickest method of deciding the optimum replacement cycle. To begin, it is necessary to calculate the present value of costs for each replacement cycle, but over one cycle only.

Year	Discount factor at 10%	Replacement every year		Replacement every two years		Replacement every three years	
		Cash flow	PV of cash flow	Cash flow	PV of cash flow	Cash flow	PV of cash flow
		£	£	£	£	£	£
0	1.000	(25,000)	(25,000)	(25,000)	(25,000)	(25,000)	(25,000)
1	0.909	7,500	6,818	(7,500)	(6,818)	(7,500)	(6,818)
2	0.826			0	0	(10,000)	(8,260)
3	0.751					(5,000)	(3,755)
			(18,182)		(31,818)		(43,833)

These costs are not comparable, because they relate to different time periods, whereas replacement is continuous. The equivalent annual cost method of comparing these cash flows is to calculate, for each length of replacement cycle, an annuity (equal annual cost) which has the same present value, discounted at the cost of capital, as the cost of repeated cycles of the various lengths under consideration.

In other words, we calculate the cash flows over one replacement cycle, and the PV of these cash flows, and then we turn this PV of cost into an equivalent annual cost.

The equivalent annual cost is calculated as follows.

$$\frac{\text{The PV of cost over one replacement cycle}}{\text{The cumulative present value factor for the number of years in the cycle}}$$

If there are three years in the cycle, the denominator will be the present value of an annuity for three years at 10% (2.487).

In our example, given a discount rate of 10%, the equivalent annual cost is calculated as follows.

(a)   Replacement every year:

Equivalent annual cost $= \dfrac{\$(18,182)}{0.909} = \$(20,002)$

(b)   Replacement every two years:

Equivalent annual cost $= \dfrac{\$(31,818)}{1.736} = \$(18,328)$

(c)   Replacement every three years:

Equivalent annual cost $= \dfrac{\$(43,833)}{2.487} = \$(17,625)$

Using the three year replacement as an example, this means that the uneven cash inflows and outflows of purchasing, running and selling the asset over the three year period are *equivalent* (i.e. in present value terms) to an *equal annual* cost of $17,625.

We can now compare the options on an 'equivalent cost per annum' basis. Thus the optimum replacement policy is the one with the lowest equivalent annual cost, which is every three years. This is the same conclusion reached by the earlier lowest common multiple method.

When a machine is to be **replaced by a machine of a different type**, there is a different replacement problem. The decision has to be made as to when the existing asset should be replaced rather than how frequently it should be replaced.

The optimum replacement cycle for the new machine may be calculated by one of the methods described previously. This does not resolve the further problem as to whether the old machine should be replaced now, or in one year's time, two years' time, and so on.

Question 3.5 — Equivalent annual cost method

Use the equivalent annual cost method to determine the optimum asset replacement cycle for Asset X, which has a maximum life of three years. The cost, annual running costs and sale value of Asset X are as follows.

Year	Cost $	Annual running cost $	Residual value at end of year $
0	30,000		
1		14,000	18,000
2		18,000	10,000
3		27,000	0

The company's cost of capital is 12% and the following discount factors apply.

Year	Discount factor at 12%
1	0.893
2	0.797
3	0.712
1 - 2	1.690
1 - 3	2.402

(For the answer to this question, see the Answer section at the end of this book.)

10 Multiple methods of investment appraisal

Throughout the last two sections we have been considering four different investment appraisal methods and each has its own advantages and disadvantages.

- **Accounting rate of return** – The return on investment has the advantages of being easy to calculate, easy to understand and clearly demonstrates profitability. However it takes no account of cash flow timings, differing project lives or the size of initial investment needed.

- **Payback period** – The payback period has the advantages of being easy to calculate and understand. It is also considers the earlier (more certain) cash flows and is useful if there are liquidity problems. However the measure ignores completely all cash flows outside the payback period and completely ignores the timing of cash flows within the period.

- **NPVs** – NPVs consider all cash flow returns from a project and their timings, cash being a much less subjective measure than profits. Unfortunately NPVs are harder to calculate and harder for the layman to understand. In addition, a number of uncertainties arise, e.g. exact cash flow timings or future interest rates, and it is often necessary to make some assumptions to complete any calculations.

- **IRRs** – The IRR or yield is an easier idea for the layman to interpret than the NPV and gives an indication of the sensitivity of the project to rate changes. It cannot, however, be used to decide between mutually exclusive projects as illustrated earlier.

Since they all have advantages and disadvantages, none of them can be considered to be the one-and-only ultimate method. Though the NPV approach is probably considered the primary technique, they all have their uses and limitations.

As a consequence, some businesses employ multiple methods of investment appraisal. They may use accounting returns to demonstrate profitability, payback to demonstrate liquidity, NPV to demonstrate commercial viability and IRR to demonstrate the risk inherent in the NPV assessment as a result of the potential for interest rate changes.

Where multiple methods are used, however, the question arises of how the results can be assessed to decide on a project or, more awkwardly, how to decide between projects. As we have already seen with mutually exclusive projects the highest IRR and the highest NPV do not necessarily coincide, and this fact can be extended to all of the techniques. The ideal project would have the highest return on investment, the shortest payback period, the highest NPV and highest IRR, but when assessing a range of alternatives this is unlikely to be the case.

If multiple methods are to be used then it will be important to have a pre-determined approach for prioritising the various results. Without such an approach, uncertainty will exist. Unfortunately there are no financial theories that support any such approach and consequently it will be somewhat subjective, being based on opinions and experience. But this fact alone reduces the appraisal process from an objective one to a subjective one.

The situation could be even worse if the business allows appraisal to be undertaken using just a selection of these methods. This would result in inconsistencies within assessments, and offer the possibility of manipulation of conclusions through the careful selection of appraisal techniques, rendering the process unreliable and casting doubt on the decision making process.

In conclusion, though at first glance there may appear to be advantages in utilising as many appraisal techniques as possible, in practice there are some significant problems to overcome.

Chapter roundup

- With the exception of the ARR method, all methods of project appraisal focus on the expected **cash flows** of the project, not accounting profits. The cash flows to take into consideration are the **relevant cash flows** of the project. Relevant cash flows are future cash flows arising as a direct consequence of the investment. These may be extra revenues, extra costs, savings in costs or reductions in revenue.

- DCF appraisal methods allow for the **time value of money**. $1 today is worth more than $1 at a future time, because money can be reinvested to earn more money over time.

- In DCF, expected future cash flows (inflows and outflows) are converted into a **present value** equivalent amount. The present value of a future cash flow is the amount that would have to be invested now at the organisation's cost of capital to earn the future cash flow at the future time.

- With the **NPV method** of project appraisal, all expected cash inflows and all expected cash outflows from the project are discounted to a present value at the organisation's cost of capital. The net present value is the difference between the present value of total benefits and the present value of total costs. If the PV of benefits exceeds the PV of total costs, the NPV is positive, and the project is expected to earn a return in excess of the organisation's cost of capital. If the PV of benefits is less than the PV of total costs, the NPV is negative, and the project will earn a return that is lower than the organisation's cost of capital. Projects with a positive NPV are financially viable, but projects with a negative NPV are not.

- The NPV method calculates a value for a capital project, taking into account all the expected cash flows over the entire life of the project. A company might want capital projects to earn a positive NPV, but also to pay back within a maximum time period. The **discounted payback method** is a way of combining DCF evaluation with a minimum payback period.

- With the **IRR method** of project appraisal, the internal rate of return of the project is calculated. This is the cost of capital at which the NPV of the project would be zero, and so is the discount rate of return that the project is expected to earn. A project is financially viable if its IRR exceeds the company's target rate of return (its cost of capital).

- A major weakness of the IRR method is its failure to take account of the total value of a capital project (the project's NPV). When there are mutually exclusive investments, the IRR method might favour a project with a higher IRR but a lower NPV. In this case NPV should be used.

- The NPV method of project appraisal is consistent with the financial objective of *maximising shareholder wealth*. Given certain assumptions, the value of a company should be expected to increase by the NPV of any projects that it undertakes.

- An **asset replacement decision** is a decision as to the optimal replacement cycle for a regularly-purchased asset. There are three techniques for using the NPV method to evaluate an asset replacement decision: the lowest common multiple method, the time horizon method and the equivalent annual cost method (which is probably the easiest of the three).

Quick quiz

1   Make an investment recommendation, given the following information. Project X, an eight-year project, would be expected to earn an NPV of + $800,000. Project Y, a four-year project, would be expected to earn an NPV of + $750,000.

2   The cumulative NPV of a project is - $4,900 at the end of Year 3 and + $3,500 at the end of Year 4. Assuming that cash flows during a year occur at an even rate, what would be the estimated discounted payback period, to the nearest month?

3   The expected NPV of a project would be - $72,600 at a discount rate of 15% and + $197,300 at a discount rate of 12%. Using these figures, estimate the IRR.

4   The expected NPV of a project would be + $3,000 at a discount rate of 8% and + $1,200 at a discount rate of 10%. Using these figures, estimate the IRR.

5   A project requiring an equity investment of $100,000 in Year 0 would be expected to have an NPV of + $125,000 at a cost of capital of 9%. If the cost of finance for the company is 9%, by how much would the total value of the company's shares be expected to rise if the project is undertaken?

Answers to quick quiz

1   If the projects are not mutually exclusive, both should be undertaken. If they are mutually exclusive, Project X should be undertaken because it has a higher NPV; however, if the company requires projects to pay back within a maximum time period, Project Y might be preferred.

2   The PV of net benefits in Year 4 is $8,400, which takes the cumulative NPV from -$4,900 to + $3,500. If cash flows are assumed to occur evenly throughout the year, the positive cash flows therefore have a PV of $700 per month in Year 4. Payback will therefore take place at the end of month 7 in Year 4.

$$\text{Discounted payback} = 3 \text{ years} + \frac{4,900}{(4,900 + 3,500)} \times 12 \text{ months}$$

$$= 3 \text{ years} + 7 \text{ months.}$$

3   $$\text{IRR} = 12\% + \frac{197,300}{(197,300 + 72,600)} \times (15 - 12)\%$$

$$= 12\% + 2.2\%$$

$$= 14.2\% \text{ approx.}$$

4   In this question, both NPVs are positive. Using the interpolation method, an IRR is calculated as follows. The NPV falls by $1,800 ($3,000 - $1,200) between 8% and 10%. The IRR is above 10%, and the NPV will be zero at:

$$\text{IRR} = 8\% + \frac{3,000}{3,000 - 1,200} \times (10 - 8)\%$$

$$= 8\% + 3.3\%$$

$$= 11.3\% \text{ approx.}$$

5   $125,000, ie the NPV of the project.

Project appraisal: sensitivity analysis and capital rationing

4

Topic list	Syllabus reference
1 What is risk and uncertainty and why does it arise?	2e
2 Uncertainty and sensitivity analysis	2e
3 Risk and scenario analysis	2e
4 Causes of a shortage of capital	2d
5 Single period capital rationing: profitability index	2d

Introduction

This chapter deals with two further topics in capital investment appraisal:

(a)   The analysis of risk and uncertainty

(b)   Capital expenditure decisions when there is a shortage of capital for investment (and so a need for capital rationing)

Either of these topics could be the subject of part of or the whole of a question in the exam.

1 What is risk and uncertainty and why does it arise?

Risk and uncertainty arise from the fact that the **future cannot be predicted** accurately. The problem is particularly severe for capital expenditure appraisal, since projects might have a duration of many years, and a large amount has to be spent now to obtain uncertain future benefits.

The terms risk and uncertainty are often used interchangeably but a distinction should be made between them.

Key term

Risk can be applied to a situation where there are several possible outcomes and, on the basis of past relevant experience, probabilities can be assigned to the various outcomes that could prevail. **Uncertainty** can be applied to a situation where there are several possible outcomes but there is little past relevant experience to enable the probability of the possible outcomes to be predicted.

A risky situation is one where we can say that there is a 70% probability that returns from a project will be in excess of $100,000 but a 30% probability that returns will be less than $100,000. If, however, no information can be provided on the returns from the project, we are faced with an uncertain situation.

In general, risky projects are those whose future cash flows, and hence the projects returns, are likely to be variable - the greater the variability, the greater the risk. The problem of risk is more acute with capital investment decisions than other decisions for the following reasons.

(a) Estimates of capital expenditure might be for up to several years ahead, such as for major construction projects, and all too often with long-term projects, actual costs escalate well above budget as the work progresses.

(b) Estimates of benefits will be for up to several years ahead, sometimes 10, 15 or 20 years ahead or even longer, and such long-term estimates can at best be approximations.

1.1 Why are projects risky?

The term '**uncertainty analysis**' may be used to describe a situation where doubts about the future cash flows cannot be measured, whereas the term '**risk analysis**' might be used to describe a situation where probabilities are estimated for possible future outcomes.

A decision about whether or not to go ahead with a project is based on expectations about the future. Forecasts of cash flows (whether they be inflows or outflows) that are likely to arise following a particular course of action are made. These forecasts are made, however, on the basis of what is expected to happen given the present state of knowledge and the future is, by definition, uncertain. Actual cash flows are almost certain to differ from prior expectations. It is this uncertainty about a project's future income and costs that gives rise to risk in business generally and investment activity in particular.

2 Uncertainty and sensitivity analysis

Uncertainty can be analysed through **sensitivity analysis**. One way of analysing uncertainty is to ask '**what if...?' questions**. Another approach is to measure by how much estimates of cash flows for key variables (sales price, sales volume, running costs, capital cost, etc) would need to change for the worse before the project ceased to be financially viable.

Sensitivity analysis is one method of analysing the uncertainty surrounding a capital expenditure project and enables an assessment to be made of how the project's NPV would change if there is a change in any of the estimated costs, revenues or savings that are used to calculate that NPV.

The NPV could depend on a number of uncertain cash flow items.

    (a)   Estimated selling price
    (b)   Estimated sales volume
    (c)   Estimated cost of capital
    (d)   Estimated initial cost
    (e)   Estimated operating costs
    (f)   Estimated benefits

Question 4.1   **New information**

A project involves some initial expenditure but has positive annual net cash inflows throughout the remainder of its life. A project appraisal was carried out using both the NPV and the IRR method. However new information has been obtained and it is now known that a **lower** cost of capital should have been used.

What is the effect of using the new information?

	Delete as appropriate		
IRR	Increases	Decreases	Stays the same
NPV	Increases	Decreases	Stays the same

(For the answer to this question, see the Answer section at the end of this book.)

There are two basic approaches to sensitivity analysis when there is uncertainty about the estimates of costs or benefits.

    (a)   One method is to ask 'What if ...?' questions. For example, what if the sales price is, say, 5% lower than estimated? Or what if sales volumes are, say, 20% below estimate? Or what if the running costs are 10% per annum higher than estimated? Each cash flow item or 'variable' can be analysed in turn, and the effect on the NPV of a possible change in the cash flow estimates calculated. An indication is thus provided of those variables to which the NPV is most sensitive (critical variables).

    (b)   A second approach is to take each variable (cash flow item) in turn, and calculate by how much (in percentage terms) the cash flow estimates would have to change for the worse before the project's NPV fell to zero. Any change in cash flows in excess of this percentage amount would make the project NPV negative, so that the project would not be financially viable.

Sensitivity analysis therefore provides an indication of how a project might fail, and which cash flow items are particularly critical. Once these critical variables have been identified, management should review them to assess whether or not there is a strong possibility of events occurring that will lead to a negative NPV. Management should also pay particular attention to controlling those variables to which the NPV is particularly sensitive, once the decision has been taken to accept the investment.

Let's consider an example.

2.1 Example: sensitivity analysis

Kenney is considering a project with the following cash flows.

	Year	0	1	2
		$'000	$'000	$'000
Initial investment		(7,000)		
Variable costs			(2,000)	(2,000)
Cash inflows (650,000 units at $10 per unit)			6,500	6,500
Net cash flows		(7,000)	4,500	4,500

The cost of capital is 8%.

Year	Discount factor at 8%
1	0.926
2	0.857

Required

Measure the sensitivity of the project to changes in variables.

Solution

The NPV of the project can be calculated by first of all calculating the total PV of the cash flows for each cash flow item, ie for variable costs and sales revenues, and the capital outlay. The NPV of the project is the sum of these totals.

Year	Discount factor 8%	PV of initial investment $'000	PV of variable costs $'000	PV of cash inflows $'000	PV of net cash flow $'000
0	1.000	(7,000)			(7,000)
1	0.926		(1,852)	6,019	4,167
2	0.857		(1,714)	5,571	3,857
		(7,000)	(3,566)	11,590	1,024

The project has a positive NPV of $1,024,000 and would appear to be worthwhile. The changes in cash flows which would need to occur for the project to only just break even (NPV = 0), and hence be on the point of being unacceptable, are as follows.

(a) **Initial investment.** The initial investment can rise by $1,024,000 before the investment breaks even. The initial investment may therefore increase by 1,024/7,000 ×100% = 14.6%.

(b) **Sales volume.** The present value of the cash inflows less the present value of the variable costs is $(11,590,000 − 3,566,000) = $8,024,000. These will have to fall to $7,000,000 for the NPV to be zero, and so would have to fall by $1,024,000. Since the estimated PV of contribution is $8,024,000, sales volume would therefore need to fall by ($1,024/$8,024) × 100% = 12.8% before the NPV fell to zero.

(c) **Selling price.** The PV of sales revenue is $11,590,000. Given no change in estimated sales volume, sales revenue would need to fall by $1,024,000 before the NPV fell to zero. If there is no change in sales volume, any such fall in sales revenue would have to be due to the sales price being less than estimated, by ($1,024/$11,590) × 100% = 8.8%.

(d) **Variable costs.** The estimated PV of variable costs is $3,566,000. Given no change in sales volume, total variable costs can increase by $1,024,000, before the NPV falls to zero. This would represent an increase in variable costs above estimate by ($1,024/$3,566) × 100% = 28.7%.

(e) **Cost of capital.** We can calculate the IRR of the project. Let's try discount rates of 15% and 20%.

BPP
LEARNING MEDIA

Year	Net cash flow $'000	Discount factor 15%	PV $'000	Discount factor 20%	PV $'000
0	(7,000)	1.000	(7,000)	1.000	(7,000)
1	4,500	0.870	3,915	0.833	3,749
2	4,500	0.756	3,402	0.694	3,123
		NPV =	+ 317	NPV =	(128)

$$\text{IRR} = 15\% + \left[\frac{317}{317 + 128} \times (20 - 15)\% \right] = 18.56\%$$

The cost of capital can therefore increase from 8% to over 18% before the NPV becomes negative.

The elements to which the NPV appears to be most sensitive are the selling price followed by the sales volume, and it is therefore important for management to pay particular attention to these factors so that they can be carefully monitored.

Question 4.2 — Sensitivity

N Ure is considering a project with the following cash flows.

Year	Cost of equipment $	Annual running costs $	Annual savings $
0	(8,500)		
1		2,000	5,000
2		2,500	7,000
3		4,000	8,000

The cost of capital is 9%. Measure the sensitivity (in percentages) of the project to changes in the levels of expected costs and savings.

Year	Discount factor at 9%
1	0.917
2	0.842
3	0.772

(For the answer to this question, see the Answer section at the end of this book.)

2.2 Weaknesses of this approach to sensitivity analysis

There are some weaknesses with this approach to sensitivity analysis.

(a) The method requires that changes in each key variable are isolated but management should also be interested in the combination of the effects of changes in two or more key variables. Looking at factors in isolation is unrealistic, since they are often interdependent.

(b) Sensitivity analysis does not examine the **probability** that any particular variation in costs or revenues might occur.

(c) Sensitivity analysis does not distinguish between cash flow estimates that might be controllable by management actions and those that are uncontrollable.

(d) In itself, it does not provide a decision rule. What is a tolerable variation in cash flow estimates that would not affect an investment decision? When is a project so uncertain that it would be unacceptably risky to undertake it? Parameters defining tolerable levels of variation must be laid down by managers.

Exam focus point

Sensitivity analysis can often appear as a part of a question, as for example in the June 2004 and the December 2006 papers.

3 Risk and scenario analysis

Risk means the variability of returns from the expected value, which could be either beneficial or detrimental. As we noted earlier, the distinction between uncertainty and risk is that with risk we can determine the potential possible outcomes and their associated probability of arising.

Based on the principles of CAPM, the discount rate applied for appraisal purposes should allow for the systematic risk of the project, but how should we deal with the specific risk that the company will face? Whilst in theory this is irrelevant to diversified investors, it is not irrelevant to the company unless it is a highly internally diversified conglomerate.

To undertake risk analysis on a given project we need to go through the following stages

- **Risk identification** – Identify the risks specific to the project

- **Risk analysis** – Estimate the frequency of occurrence and the consequences of their occurrence.

- **Risk mitigation** – Consider the possibility of mitigating the downside risks, by reducing the frequency of occurrence, reducing the adverse consequences if they do occur, or both, along with the costs of any possible mitigation options, to see whether they are financially viable or not. We can then to select the best combination of mitigation options.

- **Residual risks** – The remaining or residual risks must be acceptable to the business if the project is to be undertaken.

If the project is to be undertaken we need to control these residual risks, through a series of measures which may include

- Appointment of risk custodians
- Plans for dealing with foreseeable and unforeseeable crises
- Regular monitoring of the risks
- Regular management reviews

3.1 Identifying Risks

Risks could be identified through the use of a risk matrix or table. Such a matrix would have various risk factors as column headings, e.g. Political, Business, Economic, Project, Natural, Financial and Crime. The table rows would relate to the risks inherent in the various stages of the project: Promotion of concept, Design, Contract negotiations, Project approval, Raising of capital, Construction, Operation and maintenance, Receiving revenues, and Decommissioning.

Each of these main headings would have a number of subheadings, e.g. the Natural risk column may have sub-columns headed Weather, Earthquake, Fire, Explosion and Ground conditions etc. The Design row may have sub-rows in the table covering Failure to meet specified standards, Professional negligence, etc. The matrix would act as a checklist to show that all possibilities have indeed been covered.

It may be that it is not possible to obtain realistic estimates of the probability of occurrence or likely consequences of some of the identified risks, however, it should be emphasised that risks of very serious or disastrous events, however uncertain or however low the probability of occurrence, should never be ignored. Such risks should always be the subject of searching analysis, and any which cannot be eliminated should be highlighted in the final report.

3.2 Risk and scenario analysis

The aim of risk analysis is to ascertain the frequency of occurrence and the consequences of the occurrence of any of the identified risks.

A guide to the frequency of occurrence could possibly be obtained by consulting experts in each risk. It may be possible to obtain a probability distribution for the risk. The analysis should be supplemented by a study of the statistics available, if any, from other projects. The financial consequences if the event occurs will be expressed in present value terms. The objective is to determine a distribution of possible NPVs and associated probabilities for each identified risk.

The risks will then be prioritised for further analysis, with those having a minimal impact perhaps being disregarded to be covered by a general contingency allowance later. However, any risks which may have a significant consequences should be retained for further analysis along with the risks having higher expected NPVs.

With this information we can now undertake scenario analysis on the various possible combinations of scenario that exist, taking account of their probability of occurrence and NPV consequences. This may be undertaken using decision tree type techniques to identify the various possibilities and associated probabilities whenever the possibilities are discrete in nature, i.e. the risk event either arises or does not. Where, however, the risk is continuous, e.g. a range of possible sales volumes with likelihoods perhaps following a normal distribution, computer based stochastic modelling may be necessary in order to determine a distribution of possible NPVs.

Although it may appear that the second method would be superior, practical experience has shown that the number of assumptions that have to be made in building a stochastic model is so large that it is frequently doubtful whether the results can be relied upon with sufficient confidence to justify the effort and expense involved. More seriously, there is the danger of losing sight of key factors and assumptions in looking at the output from such a model, whereas the effort of working up a scenario analysis by hand often forces the analyst to concentrate on the important risks and assumptions.

Despite this, however, a comparatively simple stochastic model may well be useful to simulate one specific project activity, where the assumptions underlying the model, and its limitations, can be kept clearly in view.

If, having now arrived at a probability distribution of NPVs for the project as a whole, we find that all the NPVs are positive then the project is clearly acceptable. If, as is more likely, we find that some of the resulting NPVs are negative then we will be aware that, under certain circumstances, the project is not viable. In either case, and more so in the latter case, we should now go on to consider methods of mitigating these downside risks to increase their NPVs and the projects viability.

3.3 Risk mitigation

For each of the major downside risks, consideration would now be given to identifying the main options for mitigating the risks, by one of:

- **Risk avoidance** – Some risks will only be contained at acceptable levels by terminating the activity. Risk avoidance means not undertaking or terminating an activity that carries risk. Examples of this would be not entering a contract with many contingencies, or not buying a business to avoid any potential tax consequences. Avoidance may seem to be the obvious answer to all risks, but avoiding risks also means losing out on the potential return or profit associated with it.

- **Risk reduction** – Risk reduction involves retaining the activity in the business whilst undertaking actions to constrain the risk to acceptable levels, establishing systems and procedures to mitigate the effects of any risk. Risk reduction examples include alarm systems to warn of a fire or sprinkler systems to reduce its effects

- **Risk transfer** – Risk transfer involves transferring the risk to a third party through either contractually or by hedging. Insurance is a contractual method of transferring risk as are many construction contracts. Financial risks, on the other hand, tend to be hedged through the use of offsetting derivatives positions

The viability or cost-effectiveness of each of these options would need to be considered and the costs factored into the NPV model/distribution. Where no viable mitigation approach exists, the only option remaining is risk retention. **Risk retention** involves tolerating the loss when it arises and all risks that are not avoided or transferred fall into this category. Many business risks are tolerable without any further action being taken. Risk retention is a viable strategy for small risks where the cost of insuring against the risk would be greater than the total losses sustained over time. It is also the only treatment for uninsurable risks such as the effects of war. In this situation, the decision to tolerate the risk may, however, be supplemented by contingency planning to mitigate its effects

The amount of work involved at this stage of the analysis can sometimes be considerable, especially in relation to the secondary risks and their mitigation, which may necessitate recycling through the whole process.

The result of risk mitigation is to

- Reduce adverse NPV effect of any downside risk
- Reduce the overall NPV as a result of the costs of any mitigation measures

As a result, the distribution of possible NPVs gets narrowed, typically with a lower mean (lower risk, lower return). In the extreme, if all risks are mitigated the company can expect no more than the risk-free return.

A decision can now need to be taken on whether the project should proceed or not. An investment submission should be prepared based on the best possible combination of mitigation options. It should show the expected NPV and the probability distribution of NPVs.

Any residual risks should be fully identified and analysed, and particular attention paid to any remaining risks which (even if they have a low or uncertain probability of occurrence) could have a serious or catastrophic effect on the outcome of the project as a whole. The project finance method should be specified and an analysis provided showing the likely effect on investors after taking account of expected price inflation, borrowing, tax, etc.

With such information, allied to business experience, the managers of the business will now be in a position to assess whether the project lies within the risk appetite or risk tolerance of the business in order to determine whether the project should proceed.

3.4 Other methods for assessing residual risks

In practice, it is common for organisations to use crude methods to try to assess investment risk, such as using pessimistic estimates, or increasing the target cost of capital. Alternatively, a maximum payback period might be applied.

Only if management know for certain what is going to happen in the future can they appraise a project in the knowledge that there is no risk. It is, of course, unlikely that such information would be available since the future is uncertain by nature. There are, however, some crude but effective steps that management can take to assess the acceptability of any residual risk in investment decision-making.

(a)   A maximum payback period can be set to reflect the fact that the longer the time period under consideration the more risk increases.

(b)   A high discount rate can be used, to make it more difficult for projects to be seen as financially acceptable.

(c)   Sensitivity analysis can be used to determine the critical factors within the decision-making process. Management effort can then be directed to those factors that are critical to the success of a particular decision.

(d)   To ensure that future events are no worse than predicted, prudence, and overly-pessimistic estimates can be applied.

As already mentioned, these methods are quite crude for risk assessments, being unscientific and subject to judgements/opinion. Some of them may, however, be useful in other circumstances, eg payback period when cash flow is a priority.

Question 4.3   Assumptions

A company is considering a new investment in a five-year project. The investment would involve the purchase of equipment costing $500,000 and an investment in working capital of $100,000. The project is expected to have a five-year life, and the expected sales revenues would be $300,000 each year for five years and the annual operating cash expenditures would be $120,000. The equipment is expected to fall in value by about 15% each year, and will have a resale value of about 20% to 30% of its original cost at the end of Year 5.

There are two matters causing some concern to management.

(a)   The equipment will be used to make and sell a new product, and the estimated selling price might be too optimistic. It is possible that the sale price might need to be reduced by 10% to achieve the planned sales volume.

(b)   There is some risk that a competitor will produce a new version of a rival product, which would take the market from the product the company proposes to launch. It is most unlikely that the competitor would be in a position to launch this rival product for at least three years.

The company's cost of capital is 12%.

Year	Discount factor at 12%
0	1.00
1	0.89
2	0.80
3	0.71
4	0.64
5	0.57

Required

(a)   Using the most optimistic assumptions, what will be the NPV of the investment?
(b)   Using the most pessimistic assumptions, what will be the NPV of the investment?

(For the answer to this question, see the Answer section at the end of this book.)

4 Causes of a shortage of capital

> **FAST FORWARD**
>
> **Capital rationing** is necessary when there is insufficient capital to undertake all projects that are available with a positive NPV. When there is capital rationing in a single period only, and projects are divisible, they should be ranked by their **profitability index**. Projects with the highest profitability indices should be selected.

The decision rule with DCF techniques is to accept all projects which result in a positive NPV when discounted at the organisation's cost of capital. If an organisation is in a **capital rationing** situation, and does not have enough capital to invest, it will not be able to enter into all projects with a positive NPV.

Key term

> **Capital rationing**: a situation in which a company has a limited amount of capital to invest in potential projects, such that the different possible investments need to be compared with one another in order to allocate the capital available most effectively.

4.1 Reasons for capital rationing

Capital rationing may arise for self-imposed reasons or for external reasons.

Self-imposed reasons, sometimes referred to as **'soft capital rationing'**, may arise for one of the following reasons.

(a)   Management might be reluctant to raise more capital for investment by issuing new shares, because of concern that this may lead to outsiders gaining control of the business.

(b)   Management might be unwilling to issue additional share capital if it will lead to a short-term dilution in earnings per share.

(c)   Management might not want to raise additional debt capital because they do not wish to be committed to large fixed interest payments.

(d)   There may be a desire within the organisation to limit investment to a level that can be financed solely from retained profits.

(e)   The capital expenditure budget might set a restriction on capital spending.

External reasons for capital rationing, sometimes known as **'hard capital rationing',** may arise for one of the following reasons.

(a)   Raising money through the stock market may not be possible if share prices are depressed.

(b)   Banks may consider the organisation to be too risky to be granted further loan capital.

5 Single period capital rationing: profitability index

The analysis in this text is mainly related to a situation where capital rationing is required in **one time period only**, and is not expected to be an ongoing problem. In other words, capital is a 'limiting factor' in Year 0 only.

The following further assumptions will be made.

(a)   If a project is not accepted and undertaken during the period of capital rationing, the opportunity to undertake it is lost. It cannot be postponed until a subsequent period when no capital rationing exists.

(b)   There is complete certainty about the outcome of each project, so that the choice between projects is not affected by considerations of risk.

(c)   Projects are divisible, so that it is possible to undertake, say, half of Project X in order to earn half of the net present value (NPV) of the whole project.

5.1 Profitability index

When there is single period capital rationing, the problem is to decide which projects to undertake now, and which will not be undertaken. Since capital in Year 0 is a limiting factor, the basic approach is to rank all investment opportunities in terms of the PV of net cash inflows per $1 of capital outlay.

Key term

> The **profitability index** of a project is the ratio of the present value of its net cash inflows to the amount of capital expenditure in Year 0, the year of the capital shortage.

The PV of net cash inflows per $1 of capital outlay is known as a **profitability index**. (For example, if you get $2 back when you spend $1 the profitability index is 2.) The organisation should undertake the projects with the highest profitability indices, starting at the top of the rankings and working down through the list of projects until all the available capital is committed.

Ranking projects in terms of their total NPVs will normally result in a sub-optimal capital rationing decision, since this method of choosing projects leads to the selection of large projects each with a high individual NPV, but with a combined total NPV lower than could be obtained by investing in a larger number of smaller projects.

5.2 Example: single period capital rationing

Hard Times is considering five projects, V, W, X, Y and Z. Relevant details are as follows.

Project	Investment required	Present value of net cash inflows	NPV
	$	$	$
V	(25,000)	28,750	3,750
W	(10,000)	10,640	640
X	(20,000)	22,801	2,801
Y	(30,000)	32,230	2,230
Z	(40,000)	43,807	3,807

The company has only $75,000 of capital available to invest. All projects are divisible. Which projects should the company undertake in order to maximise the total NPV from its investments?

Solution

Without capital rationing all five projects would be viable investments. However, there is only $75,000 available for projects that would require $125,000 of capital expenditure in total in Year 0.

The selection should be based on rankings in order of profitability index. This is derived by dividing the present value of the net cash inflows by the investment required.

Project	Present value of net cash inflows	Investment required	Profitability index	Ranking
	$	$		
V	28,750	(25,000)	1.15	1
W	10,640	(10,000)	1.06	5
X	22,801	(20,000)	1.14	2
Y	32,230	(30,000)	1.07	4
Z	43,807	(40,000)	1.10	3

The optimal project selection is as follows.

Project	Ranking		Capital outlay		NPV
			$		$
V	1		(25,000)		3,750
X	2		(20,000)		2,801
Z	3	(balance)	(30,000)	(30/40 × $3,807)	2,855
			(75,000)		9,406

There is sufficient capital to invest in three-quarters of project Z, the third-ranked project ($30,000/$40,000). The NPV of this investment in 75% of Z will be three-quarters of the NPV of all project Z, ie 75% of $3,807 = $2,855.

The maximum obtainable NPV, given the capital rationing, is $9,406.

If the company had invested in the projects with the largest absolute NPV, the total NPV would not have been as large.

Project	Ranking by size of NPV		Capital outlay $		NPV $
Z	1st		(40,000)		3,807
V	2nd		(25,000)		3,750
X	3rd	(balance)	(10,000)	(10/20 × $2,801)	1,401
			(75,000)		8,958

5.3 Problems with the profitability index method

The use of a profitability index to rank projects in order of priority has a number of problems.

(a)   The approach can only be used if projects are divisible. If the projects are not divisible a decision has to be made by examining the absolute NPVs of all possible combinations of complete projects that can be undertaken within the constraints of the capital available. The combination of projects which remains at or under the limit of available capital without any of them being divided, and which maximises the total NPV, should be chosen.

(b)   The selection criterion is fairly simplistic, taking no account of the possible strategic value of individual investments in the context of the overall objectives of the organisation.

(c)   The approach does not take into account the possibility that some of the capital projects could be deferred, and undertaken at a later date.

Question 4.4   Capital rationing

Bleak House is experiencing capital rationing in year 0, when only $60,000 of investment finance will be available. No capital rationing is expected in future periods, but none of the three projects under consideration by the company can be postponed. The expected cash flows of the three projects are as follows.

Project	Year 0 $	Year 1 $	Year 2 $	Year 3 $	Year 4 $
A	(50,000)	(20,000)	20,000	40,000	40,000
B	(28,000)	(50,000)	40,000	40,000	20,000
C	(30,000)	(30,000)	30,000	40,000	10,000

The cost of capital is 10%. You are required to decide which projects should be undertaken in year 0, in view of the capital rationing, given that projects are divisible.

Year	Discount factor at 10%
1	0.909
2	0.826
3	0.751
4	0.683

(For the answer to this question, see the Answer section at the end of this book.)

5.4 Postponing projects

We have so far assumed that projects cannot be postponed until Year 1. If this assumption is removed, the choice of projects in year 0 would be made by reference to the loss of NPV from **postponement**.

5.5 Multi-period capital rationing

When capital is expected to be in short supply for more than one period, the selection of an optimal investment programme cannot be made by ranking projects according to a profitability index. Other techniques, notably linear programming, should be used, but this is outside the scope of this syllabus.

Chapter roundup

- Risk and uncertainty arise from the fact that the **future cannot be predicted** accurately. The problem is particularly severe for capital expenditure appraisal, since projects might have a duration of many years, and a large amount has to be spent now to obtain uncertain future benefits.

- The term '**uncertainty analysis**' may be used to describe a situation where doubts about the future cash flows cannot be measured, whereas the term '**risk analysis**' might be used to describe a situation where probabilities are estimated for possible future outcomes.

- Uncertainty can be analysed through **sensitivity analysis**. One way of analysing uncertainty is to ask '**what if...?' questions**. Another approach is to measure by how much estimates of cash flows for key variables (sales price, sales volume, running costs, capital cost, etc) would need to change for the worse before the project ceased to be financially viable.

- In practice, it is common for organisations to use crude methods for reducing investment risk, such as using pessimistic estimates, or increasing the target cost of capital. Alternatively, a maximum payback period might be applied.

- **Capital rationing** is necessary when there is insufficient capital to undertake all projects that are available with a positive NPV. When there is capital rationing in a single period only, and projects are divisible, they should be ranked by their **profitability index**. Projects with the highest profitability indices should be selected.

Quick quiz

1   A project with an expected NPV of $37,000 would earn annual contributions to profits with a total present value of $500,000. By what percentage would sales volume have to fall short of the expected level before the project ceased to be viable?

2   Define profitability index.

Answers to quick quiz

1   (37,000/500,000) × 100% = 7.4%

2   The ratio, for a capital project, of the PV of its future net cash inflows to the amount of capital outlay.

5

Allowing for inflation and taxation in DCF

Topic list	Syllabus reference
1 Allowing for inflation	2a
2 Allowing for inflation in practice	2a
3 Allowing for taxation	2a

Introduction

In this analysis of investment projects so far, we have ignored the effects that inflation and taxation may have on the decision to accept or reject. This chapter considers these effects, and this concludes your study of investment appraisal in this Text.

1 Allowing for inflation

Inflation should be provided for in financial planning. In DCF, project cash flows should be increased to allow for expected inflation, and these should then be discounted at the money cost of capital. Alternatively, non-inflated cash flows should be discounted at the real cost of capital.

So far we have not considered the effect of **inflation** on the appraisal of capital investment proposals. As the inflation rate increases, so will the minimum return required by an investor. For example, you might be happy with a return of 5% in an inflation-free world, but if the rate of inflation was running at 15% you would expect a considerably greater yield.

1.1 Example: inflation

A company is considering investing in a project with the following cash flows.

Time	Actual cash flows at today's prices $	Actual cash flows, allowing for inflation at 10% per annum $
0	(18,000)	(18,000)
1	9,000	9,900
2	8,000	9,680
3	7,000	9,317

The company requires a minimum return of 20% under the present and anticipated conditions. Inflation is currently running at 10% a year, and this rate of inflation is expected to continue indefinitely. Should the company go ahead with the project?

The company's required rate of return is 20%. This is the return investors require in the expectation that inflation will be 10% per annum over the lifetime of the project. Suppose that the company invested $1,000 for one year on 1 January. On 31 December it would require a minimum return of $200. With the initial investment of $1,000, the total value of the investment by 31 December must therefore increase to $1,200. During the course of the year the purchasing value of the dollar would fall due to inflation. We can restate the amount received on 31 December in terms of the purchasing power of the dollar at 1 January as follows.

Amount received on 31 December in terms of the value of the dollar at 1 January $= \dfrac{\$1,200}{(1.10)^1} = \$1,091$

In terms of the value of the dollar at 1 January, the company would make a profit of $91 which represents a rate of return of 9.1% in 'today's money' terms. This is known as the **real rate of return**. The required rate of 20% is a **money rate of return** (sometimes called a nominal rate of return). The money rate measures the return in terms of the dollar which is, of course, falling in value. The real rate measures the return in constant price level terms.

The two rates of return and the inflation rate are linked by the equation

(1 + money rate) = (1 + real rate) × (1 + inflation rate)

where all the rates are expressed as proportions.

In our example,

(1 + 0.20) = (1 + 0.091) × (1 + 0.10) = 1.20

So **which rate** should be used for DCF appraisals, the real rate of return or the money rate of return? The rule is as follows.

(a)   If the cash flows are expressed in terms of the actual number of dollars that will be received or paid on the various future dates (**money** or **nominal** cash flows), we use the money rate for discounting.

(b)   If the cash flows are expressed in terms of the value of the dollar at time 0 (that is, in constant price level terms, real cash flows), we use the real rate.

The cash flows given in Paragraph 1.1 are expressed in terms of the actual number of dollars that will be received or paid at the relevant dates. We should, therefore, discount them using the money rate of return.

Time	Cash flow	Discount factor	PV
	$	20%	$
0	(18,000)	1.000	(18,000)
1	9,900	0.833	8,247
2	9,680	0.694	6,718
3	9,317	0.579	5,395
			2,360

The project has a positive net present value of $2,360.

Alternatively, we can use the cash flows at today's prices (real flows) and discount them using the real rate of 9.1%. The discount factors at 9.1% are:

Year	Discount factor at 9.1%
1	0.917
2	0.840
3	0.770

Time	Cash flow	Discount factor	PV
	$	9.1%	$
0	(18,000)	1.000	(18,000)
1	9,000	0.917	8,253
2	8,000	0.840	6,720
3	7,000	0.770	5,390
			2,363

Allowing for some small rounding errors, the present value of the cash flows and the NPV is exactly the same as before. In other words, the NPV of a project will be exactly the same, no matter whether it is calculated:

(a)   with actual cash flows and the money rate of return, or

(b)   non-inflated cash flows and the real rate of return.

However, this is only true if the **same rate of inflation** is applied to all cash flows and incorporated within the money rate of return - see below.

1.2 The advantages and misuses of real values and a real rate of return

Although it is recommended that companies should discount money values at the money cost of capital, there are some advantages of using real values discounted at a real cost of capital.

(a)   When all costs and benefits rise at the same rate of price inflation, real values are the same as current day values, so that no further adjustments need be made to cash flows before discounting. In contrast, when money values are discounted at the money cost of capital, the prices in future years must be calculated before discounting can begin.

(b)   The government might possibly prefer to set a real return as a target for its investments, as being more suitable to their particular situation than a commercial money rate of return.

1.3 Costs and benefits which inflate at different rates

Not all costs and benefits will rise in line with the general level of inflation. In such cases, we can apply the money rate to inflated values to determine a project's NPV, and discount at the money cost of capital.

<table>
<tr><td>Question 5.1</td><td>Costs and benefits</td></tr>
</table>

Rice is considering a project which would cost $5,000 now. The annual benefits, for four years, would be a fixed income of $2,500 a year, plus other annual savings amounting to $500 in year 1, rising by 5% each year (compound) because of inflation. Running costs will be $1,000 in the first year, but would increase at 10% each year (compound) because of inflating labour costs. The company's required money rate of return is 16%. Is the project worthwhile?

Year	Discount factor at 16%
1	0.862
2	0.743
3	0.641
4	0.552

(For the answer to this question, see the Answer section at the end of this book.)

1.4 Current market rates of return

Current market rates of return are money rates of return. Investment yields on debt capital and equity capital are therefore money yields.

1.5 Expectations of inflation and the effects of inflation

When managers evaluate a particular project, they can only guess at what the rate of inflation is going to be. Their expectations will probably be wrong, at least to some extent, because it is extremely difficult to forecast the rate of inflation accurately. The only way in which uncertainty about inflation can be allowed for in project evaluation is by risk and uncertainty analysis.

We stated earlier that costs and benefits may rise at levels different from the general rate of inflation: inflation may be **general,** affecting prices of all kinds, or **specific** to particular prices. Generalised inflation has the following effects.

(a) Since non-current assets and inventories will increase in money value, the same quantities of assets must be financed by increasing amounts of capital.

(i) If the future rate of inflation can be predicted, management can work out how much extra finance the company will need, and take steps to obtain it (for example by retaining more profits, or by borrowing).

(ii) If the future rate of inflation cannot be predicted with accuracy, management should guess at what it will be and plan to obtain extra finance accordingly. However, plans should also be made to obtain 'contingency funds' if the rate of inflation exceeds expectations. For example, a higher bank overdraft facility might be negotiated, or a provisional arrangement made with a bank for a loan.

(b) Inflation means higher costs and higher selling prices. The effect of higher prices on demand is not necessarily easy to predict. A company that raises its prices by 10% because the general rate of inflation is running at 10% might suffer a serious fall in demand.

2 Allowing for inflation in practice

In practice, it is very common to ignore inflation when carrying out capital project appraisal, and to use current market rates of interest (money rates) with non-inflated cash flows. There are probably two main reasons for this.

(a) Inflation rates are often difficult to predict, and so it is frequently assumed that inflation will not be significant, and can be ignored.

(b) It is a safety-first approach. Future cash flow estimates are often uncertain, and for most projects, longer-term annual cash flows of a project are cash inflows. By not allowing for inflation, the estimated cash inflows will be under-stated, and a project will have to justify itself financially without the benefit of inflating revenues.

3 Allowing for taxation

FAST FORWARD

Taxation also has an effect on the cash flows of a project and should be allowed for in DCF. Two main aspects of taxation must be considered: (a) If a project earns profits, there will be extra tax to pay. (b) There will be capital allowances to be claimed on the asset. These reduce the tax payable.

Exam focus point

BPP have been informed that although a broad understanding of taxation is required, capital allowances will not be tested within DCF problems.

So far, in looking at project appraisal, we have ignored **taxation**. However, payments of tax, or reductions of tax payments, are cash flows and ought to be considered in DCF analysis. Typical assumptions which may be stated in an examination question are as follows.

(a) Income tax is payable in the same year as the year in which the taxable profits are made. Thus, if a project increases taxable profits by $10,000 in year 2, there will be a tax payment, assuming tax at 30%, of $3,000 in Year 2.

This is not always the case in examination questions. Look out for questions which state that tax is payable in the year after the one in which the profits arise. In this case, an increase in profits of $10,000 in Year 2 would give rise to higher taxation of $3,000 in Year 3, assuming tax at 30%.

(b) Net cash flows from a project should be considered as the taxable profits arising from the project (unless an indication is given to the contrary).

3.1 Example: taxation

A company is considering whether or not to purchase an item of machinery costing $40,000 in 20X5. It would have a life of four years, after which it would be sold for $5,000. The machinery would create annual cost savings of $14,000.

The rate of income tax is 30%. Tax is payable in the same year as the profits arise. The after-tax cost of capital is 8%.

Should the machinery be purchased?

Solution

The net cash flows and the NPV can be calculated as follows.

Year	Equipment $	Savings $	Tax on savings $	Net cash flow $	Discount factor 8%	Present value of cash flow $
0	(40,000)			(40,000)	1.000	(40,000)
1		14,000	(4,200)	9,800	0.926	9,075
2		14,000	(4,200)	9,800	0.857	8,399
3		14,000	(4,200)	9,800	0.794	7,781
4	5,000	14,000	(4,200)	14,800	0.735	10,878
						(3,867)

The NPV is negative and so the purchase appears not to be worthwhile.

3.2 Taxation and DCF

FAST FORWARD

> When taxation is allowed for in DCF, the cost of capital used should be the company's **after-tax cost of capital**. This allows for the tax relief on the company's debt finance.

The effect of taxation on capital budgeting is theoretically quite simple. Organisations must pay tax, and the effect of undertaking a project will be to increase or decrease tax payments each year. These incremental tax cash flows should be included in the cash flows of the project for discounting to arrive at the project's NPV.

When taxation is ignored in the DCF calculations, the discount rate will reflect the pre-tax rate of return required on capital investments. When taxation is included in the cash flows, a **post-tax required rate of return** should be used.

Question 5.2   Annual net cash inflows

A company is considering the purchase of an item of equipment, which would earn profits before tax of $25,000 a year. Depreciation charges on the equipment would be $20,000 each year for six years. Income tax is at 30%.

(a)   What would be the annual net cash inflows of the project assuming that tax payments occur in the same year as the profits giving rise to them.

(b)   What is the NPV of the project, if the after-tax cost of capital is 8%?

Year	Discount factor at 8%
1	0.926
2	0.857
3	0.794
4	0.735
5	0.681
6	0.630

(For the answer to this question, see the Answer section at the end of this book.)

Chapter roundup

- **Inflation** should be provided for in financial planning. In DCF, project cash flows should be increased to allow for expected inflation, and these should then be discounted at the money cost of capital. Alternatively, non-inflated cash flows should be discounted at the real cost of capital.

- (1 + real cost of capital) × (1 + rate of inflation) = (1 + money cost of capital)

- **Taxation** also has an effect on the cash flows of a project and should be allowed for in DCF. Two main aspects of taxation must be considered: (a) If a project earns profits, there will be extra tax to pay. (b) There will be capital allowances to be claimed on the asset. These reduce the tax payable.

- When an asset is disposed of, there will be (a) a **balancing allowance** or (b) a **balancing charge**, depending on whether the sale value of the asset is (a) lower or (b) higher than the remaining balance of the asset value, after deducting cumulative capital allowances to date. The balancing allowance or charge must be multiplied by the rate of tax to obtain the effect on cash flow.

- When taxation is allowed for in DCF, the cost of capital should be the company's **after-tax cost of capital**. This allows for the tax relief on the company's debt finance.

Quick quiz

1   The money cost of capital is 11%. The expected annual rate of inflation is 5%. What is the real cost of capital?

2   A company wants a minimum real return of 3% a year on its investments. Inflation is expected to be 8% a year. What is the company's minimum money cost of capital?

3   Summarise briefly how taxation is taken into consideration in capital budgeting.

Answers to quick quiz

1    $\dfrac{1.11}{1.05} = 1.057$. The real cost of capital is 5.7%.

2    $1.03 \times 1.08 = 1.1124$. The money cost of capital is 11.24%.

3   Taxation on profits (or reduced tax payments due to losses). Capital allowances. Cost of capital = after-tax cost of capital, to reflect the fact that interest payments on debt capital are tax-allowable.

Part C
Raising finance

Sources of finance: share capital

Introduction

Previous chapters have considered investment appraisal, and for example have recommended that a company should spend $1m now in the anticipation of receiving large cash inflows in the future. But where in the $1m to come from? Companies need capital to operate and to invest for the future.

This chapter starts looking at the possible sources of finance that a company can raise to have the capital that it needs. This chapter looks at possible types of share capital, while the next chapter looks at other sources of finance, such as loans or bonds.

1 The need for finance

Companies can raise new **long-term finance** as **equity (ordinary share capital), preference share capital** or **debt capital.**

In order to operate, and to invest, businesses must have capital. Finance for a business is provided either by its owners, which in the case of a company means its shareholders, or from creditors.

Finance is also categorised as either long-term or short-term.

(a) **Short-term finance** is provided by creditors who expect to be paid in the fairly short-term, or who could demand payment at short notice. Examples of short-term finance are trade payables, a bank overdraft, and a bank loan repayable in the near future.

(b) **Long-term finance** is finance that the business could retain or expects to have for a long time. It consists of share capital and long-term debt capital.

Long-term capital can be categorised into two main types, **equity** and **debt**.

Sources of equity capital are **retained profits** and **new share issues.** It is much easier for a public company to raise new equity capital (on the stock market) than it is for a private company to raise share capital.

(a) Equity shareholders are the ordinary shareholders of a company. They invest expecting to obtain a certain return on their investment. The objective of the company should be to maximise shareholder wealth, and to prevent the value of shares from falling, the company must provide returns for its shareholders that at least meet their expectations.

(b) Providers of long-term debt are lenders or investors in bonds issued by the company. Investors in debt capital are entitled to receive interest on their investment, and to the repayment of the debt principal at maturity. They have no further claims on the company, provided the company honours its debt obligations.

If a company gets into financial difficulties, the providers of debt must be paid what they are owed before any dividends can be paid to the shareholders. Depending on how much debt capital the company has, a rise or fall in profits will result in a larger percentage rise or fall in the profits available for the shareholders. Equity investments are therefore more risky than debt investments in the same company. The higher risk in equity investments means that equity investors will expect a higher return on their investment than investors in debt.

There is a **trade off between risk and return**. The various sources of finance available to a company can be considered in terms of:

(a) the level of risk in the investment for the investor, and thus
(b) the level of return the investor will require.

This chapter describes share capital as a source of finance for companies, and the next chapter looks at other sources of finance.

2 Ordinary shares (equity)

A share issue by a public company might be to raise cash for new investment, to 'float' the company on the stock market or to finance an acquisition (or 'takeover') of another company.

A public limited company is one

- Which has a minimum issued share capital of £50,000, on which all the share premium and at least 25% of the nominal value have been paid up.

- Whose Memorandum of Association states that it is a public company.

- Which is correctly registered as public.

Such companies must have either 'plc' or 'Public Limited Company' at the end of their names.

The owners of a company are its ordinary shareholders or 'equity' shareholders. In a company's balance sheet, equity finance is represented by the nominal value of the ordinary shares plus the company's reserves.

When a company is first established, the capital to set it up is provided by ordinary shareholders. As a company grows, and requires more finance, the ordinary shareholders are an important source of additional funds.

Equity finance can be obtained from the ordinary shareholders in either of two ways:

(a) Through retained profits
(b) By issuing new shares

2.1 Retained profits as a source of equity finance

For most companies, retained profits are a major source of new finance. It is usual practice for profitable companies to pay out a proportion of their profits in the form of dividends to shareholders, and to retain the remainder within the business. In this way, a company keeps some equity capital for reinvestment, development and growth.

This means, for example, that if a company makes a profit of $10 million after tax, and pays out $4 million in dividends, it will have retained $6 million of equity capital within the business.

2.2 Issuing new shares

FAST FORWARD

The methods of issuing shares in a flotation are an **offer for sale** or **offer for subscription**, a **placing**, an **intermediaries** offer, an **introduction** or a combination of two of these. Occasionally, a company might issue shares in an **offer for sale by tender**.

For some companies, from time to time, retained profits are an insufficient source of funds. The company might be making losses, and so might require new funds to restore its financial position. Alternatively, a company might have plans for capital investment in excess of what it can finance 'internally' through retained profits. If so, it will need to raise extra finance 'externally'. If it chooses to raise the extra capital in the form of equity, it must issue new shares.

A new issue of ordinary shares might be made in a variety of circumstances. Three common reasons are:

(a) To raise more cash for investment

(b) Partly to raise more cash, but partly to 'float' the company on the stock market. When a company comes to the stock market for the first time, its existing shareholders will sell some of their shares to other investors. When existing shareholders sell their shares in a 'flotation', the money goes to the shareholders, not the company.

(c) To finance the takeover of another company. ABC might acquire the shares of another company, XYZ, by issuing new shares of its own in exchange for the shares of XYZ. The former shareholders of XYZ become shareholders of ABC, and ABC becomes the controlling shareholder of XYZ.

2.3 Pre-emption rights

Legally in the UK and many other countries, the current shareholders of a company have prior rights to subscribe for any new issues of shares **for cash** before they can be offered to anyone else. These are called their **pre-emption rights** and their purpose is to ensure that the level of influence or control that a shareholder has is not diluted by any issue without his prior knowledge and agreement.

The existence of pre-emption rights means that listed companies cannot issue equity shares, convertibles or warrants for cash other than to the current equity shareholders of the company, except with their prior approval in general meeting.

It is quite common to see the waiving of pre-emption rights as a proposed special resolution at the AGM of public companies. Under Companies Act rules shareholders can vote to forego their pre-emption rights for a period of up to five years, though the stock exchange's rules for listed companies are stricter, requiring such a resolution to be passed at each AGM.

Pre-emption rights are by no means universal and such rules do not apply in many Pacific rim countries.

The advantage of pre-emption rights is that they protect the shareholders from dilution, since they must be offered any new issues first. In countries where pre-emption rights do not apply, a shareholders interests may be substantially diluted if he simply does not hear about any issue in time.

The disadvantage of pre-emption rights is the expense in terms of money and time in observing and administrating the constraint. If a company needed to raise finance and a single willing and able investor was available this would be by far the quickest and cheapest route, but with pre-emption rights it would not be permitted.

2.4 Raising equity finance: stock market companies

FAST FORWARD

In a stock market introduction, no new shares are issued, and no shares are sold by existing shareholders to other investors (the general public).

Public companies are allowed to sell their shares to the public and are able to obtain a Stock Exchange listing, however, they do not have to be listed. The terminology here is sometimes confusing, as obtaining a listing is frequently referred to as 'going public'.

If a company does choose to go public on the London Stock Exchange (LSE) then ther are two primary markets to choose from:

- Main market
- AIM (Alternative Investment Market) – the LSE's global market for growing companies.

The main differences in the admission criteria for these two markets are as follows.

Criteria	Main market	AIM
Minimum shareholding in public hands	25%	0%
Minimum trading record	3 years	0 years
Prior shareholder approval required for substantial acquisitions and disposals	Yes	No
Pre-vetting of admission documents by UKLA	Yes	No
Minimum market capitalisation	Yes	No
Sponsor needed for certain share transactions	Yes	No (need nominated advisor)

The reasons why a company might seek to bring its shares to a stock market can be summarised as follows.

(a) **Access to a wider pool of finance.** A company that is growing fast may need to raise larger sums than is possible as a private company. A stock market listing widens the number of potential investors. It may also improve the company's credit rating, making debt finance easier and cheaper to obtain.

(b) **Improved marketability of shares.** Shares that are traded on the stock market can be bought and sold in relatively small quantities at any time. This means that it is easier for exiting investors to realise a part of their holding.

(c) **Transfer of capital to other uses.** Founder owners may wish to liquidate the major part of their holding either for personal reasons or for investment in other new business opportunities.

(d) **Enhancement of the company image.** Quoted companies are commonly believed to be more financially stable, and listing may improve the image of the company with its customers and suppliers, allowing it to gain additional business and to improve its buying power.

(e) **Facilitation of growth by acquisition.** A listed company is in a better position to make a paper offer (ie an offer in shares rather than in cash) for a target company than an unlisted one.

2.5 The issue price for shares

FAST FORWARD

The capital raised by a company in a share issue is the number of new shares issued multiplied by the price per share, minus the issue costs. Issue costs for large share issues include **underwriting commission**.

It is important to remember that the issue price for shares will be a market price, ie an amount that the company expects investors to be willing to pay. The issue price has no relationship whatsoever to the nominal value of the shares, except that the issue price cannot be lower than the nominal value. This means, for example, that if a company with ordinary shares of, say, 10c each, issues new ordinary shares, the issue price could be anything above 10c, depending on the market value of the shares.

The capital raised by a company from a new issue of shares is the number of new shares issued multiplied by the issue price, minus the costs of the issue.

3 Obtaining a listing

FAST FORWARD

A company with shares already traded on a stock market might make a new issue of shares to raise extra cash, though in many countries the company will be constrained by pre-exemption rights rules. A requirement of legislation in many countries is that unless shareholders agree to waive their rights, a new issue of shares should be in the form of a **rights issue**. In a rights issue, shareholders are offered new shares in proportion to their existing shareholding. In practice, shareholders often agree to waive their rights, particularly for small share issues. A new issue of shares by a listed company might therefore be by means of a placing.

Key term

When a company comes to a stock market for the first time, it is said to 'float' its shares on the market. Another commonly-used term to describe a flotation is to '**obtain a stock market listing**' for the shares.

A 'listed company' is therefore a company whose shares are on the official list and traded on the main stock market of the country concerned.

In practice, when a company comes to the stock market for the first time, the company is usually too small to justify a full listing. Most flotations of companies are on to a 'junior' stock market of the country concerned rather than the main market. For example, in the UK, the junior market is called the **Alternative Investment Market** or **AIM**.

3.1 Methods of obtaining a listing

There are several methods by which companies can bring their shares to listing. The methods available differ according to whether or not the company already has some equity shares listed. In other words, the method of bringing shares to listing can depend on whether:

    (a)   The company is applying for a listing for its shares for the first time, or

    (b)   The company already has some shares listed, and now wishes to issue more shares of the same class.

The most common methods of issuing shares to the public and in a stock market flotation are:

    (a)   An **offer for sale** or **offer for subscription**

    (b)   A **placing**

    (c)   An **intermediaries offer**

The various methods of bringing securities to listing can be used in tandem. For example:

    (a)   A company might make an offer in two parts or tranches, one a placing with institutional investors and the other an intermediaries offer, through which the general investing public can apply for shares.

    (b)   A company might combine an offer for sale (in which current shareholders sell existing shares) with an offer for subscription (in which the company allots new shares).

3.2 The requirement for an adequate market in the company's shares

A condition for listing is that a 'sufficient number' of the company's shares must be distributed to the public. This requirement of the listing rules will affect the method or methods selected for bringing the shares to listing.

The reason for this condition is that, as a general principle, the authorities wish to ensure, as far as it reasonably can, that there will be an 'adequate' market in the shares after admission to listing. This means that investors should readily be able to buy and sell the company's shares on the stock market without causing severe movements in the share price.

The best way of ensuring a sufficiently 'liquid' market in the shares is to make a substantial quantity available to the investing public in the flotation. The authorities take the view that an adequate market will only normally be possible if a minimum number of the shares are owned by a wide spread of the investing public.

4 Offer for sale and offer for subscription

The most common methods of obtaining a listing are by means of an offer for sale, offer for subscription or placing.

Offers for sale and offers for subscription are known collectively as '**public offers**', and are used for *large* offerings of shares when a large company is obtaining a listing for the first time.

When shares are offered to the public, offers are invited from the investing public at large, ie both institutional investors and private individual investors.

Key terms

An **offer for sale** is an invitation to the public by existing shareholders to purchase shares that are already in issue.

An **offer for subscription** is an invitation to the public by a company to subscribe for shares that are not yet in issue or allotted.

The difference between an offer for sale and an offer for subscription is therefore whether the shares are already existing and in issue, or whether they are new shares to be issued by the company. A flotation could combine an offer for sale with an offer for subscription.

Another arrangement is for a company to issue new shares and sell them to its sponsoring investment bank, and for the investment bank then to offer these new shares to the general public. Since the shares are already in issue when offered to the public by the bank, the issue is an offer for sale, although its purpose is for the company to issue new shares to raise cash.

4.1 Issuing houses and sponsoring member firms

When an unquoted company applies for a listing for its shares, and for admission to trading on the main stock exchange, it must be sponsored by a firm that is a member of the Stock Exchange. This **sponsoring member firm** has the responsibility of ensuring that the company meets the requirements for listing, and carries out the necessary procedures to apply for a listing and for admission of the shares to trading.

The company will also employ the services of an **issuing house**, which might well be the sponsoring member firm itself. An issuing house has the job of trying to ensure a successful issue for the company's shares, by advising on an issue price for the shares, and trying to interest institutional investors in buying some of the shares.

4.2 Underwriting an issue

It is usual for large share issues to be underwritten. **Underwriting** is a form of insurance, to make sure that all the shares are sold. An underwriter agrees to buy all the shares in the issue that are not subscribed for by someone else. In return, the underwriter receives a commission.

The risk for the underwriter is that some of the shares (conceivably all of them) will not be sold, leaving the underwriter to buy all the unsold shares at the issue price. The market price of the shares after the issue will be lower than the issue price, leaving the underwriter with a loss. The underwriting commission is the reward the underwriter receives in return for taking on this risk.

Although one institution will agree to underwrite an entire share issue, it will off-load some of the risk on to sub-underwriters, and share its commission with them.

4.3 The issue price and offers for sale

The offer price must be advertised a short time in advance, so it is fixed without certain knowledge of the condition of the market at the time offers to buy the shares are invited. To ensure the success of an issue, the share price is often set lower than it might otherwise be. It is common practice for an issuing house to try to ensure that a share price rises to a premium above its issue price soon after trading begins. A target premium of 20% above the issue price would be fairly typical.

Companies will be keen to avoid over-pricing an issue, so that the issue is under-subscribed, leaving underwriters with the unwelcome task of having to buy up the unsold shares. On the other hand, if the issue price is too low then the issue will be oversubscribed and the company would have been able to raise the required capital by issuing fewer shares.

The share price of an issue is usually advertised as being based on a certain P/E ratio. The P/E ratio for a company is the ratio of the share price to the most recent annual profit per ordinary share ('earnings per share'). The P/E ratio for the share issue can then be compared by investors with the P/E ratios of similar quoted companies.

4.4 Offers for sale by tender

When share prices in the stock market are rising, it might be very difficult to decide on the issue price for shares in an offer for sale or subscription. One way of trying to ensure that the issue price reflects the value of the shares as perceived by the market is to make an **offer for sale by tender**. In an offer for sale by tender, **a minimum price** is fixed for the issue, and investors are invited to tender for shares at prices equal to or above this minimum amount. The shares are then allotted to the successful bidders at the same price, which is **the highest price at which they will all be taken up**. This is known as the **striking price**.

Offers for sale by tender are much less common than offers for sale or subscription. The reasons why offers for sale by tender might not be preferred are as follows.

(a) It is sometimes felt that the decision to make an offer by tender reflects badly on the ability of the issuing house to determine the issue price.

(b) It is claimed that the use of tenders leaves the determination of prices to the 'uninformed public' rather than the City 'experts'. However, in practice, the major influence on the striking price will be the tenders of the institutional investors.

(c) An offer for sale is more certain in the amount of finance that will be raised.

(d) Some potential investors may be deterred from applying for shares as they do not wish to have to decide on a price.

4.5 Example: offer for sale by tender

Byte Henderson is a new company that is making its first public issue of shares. It has decided to make the issue by means of an offer for sale by tender. The intention is to issue up to 4,000,000 shares at a minimum price of 300 cents.

The following tenders have been received. (Each applicant has made only one offer.)

Price tendered per share $	Number of shares applied for at this price
6.00	50,000
5.50	100,000
5.00	300,000
4.50	450,000
4.00	1,100,000
3.50	1,500,000
3.00	2,500,000

(a) How many shares would be issued, and how much in total would be raised, if Byte Henderson chooses:

(i) To maximise the total amount raised?
(ii) To issue exactly 4,000,000 shares?

(b) Harvey Goldfinger, a private investor, has applied for 12,000 shares at a price of $5.50 and has sent a cheque for $66,000 to the issuing house that is handling the issue. In both cases (a)(i) and (ii), how many shares would be issued to Mr Goldfinger, assuming that any partial acceptance of offers would mean allotting shares to each accepted applicant in proportion to the number of shares applied for? How much will Mr Goldfinger receive back out of the $66,000 he has paid?

Ignore the costs of the issue.

Solution

(a)   We begin by looking at the cumulative tenders.

$	Cumulative number of shares applied for	Amount raised if price is selected $
6.00	50,000	300,000
5.50	150,000	825,000
5.00	450,000	2,250,000
4.50	900,000	4,050,000
4.00	2,000,000	8,000,000
3.50	3,500,000	12,250,000
3.00	6,000,000	12,000,000 (restricted)

(i)   To maximise the total amount raised, the issue price should be $3.50. The total raised (before deducting issue costs) would be $12,250,000.

(ii)   To issue exactly 4,000,000 shares, the issue price must be $3.00. The total raised would be $12,000,000. At an issue price of $3.00, there would be applications for a total of 6,000,000 shares.

(b)   (i)   Harvey Goldfinger would be allotted the full 12,000 shares he applied for, but at $3.50 per share (not the $5.50 per share he offered). He would receive a refund of 12,000 × $2 = $24,000 out of the $66,000 he has paid.

(ii)   If 4,000,000 shares are issued, applicants would receive two thirds of the shares they tendered for. Harvey Goldfinger would be allotted 8,000 shares at $3 per share and would receive a refund of $42,000 out of the $66,000 he has paid.

An offer for sale by tender or offer for subscription by tender would only be used when there is uncertainty about what the price for the shares should be, and the company either:

(a)   Does not want to risk a poor response to the offer because the share price is set too high, or

(b)   Believes that there could be strong demand for the shares, and wants to see what price investors might be willing to pay.

Question 6.1   Striking price

Potrill recently made a tender offer of shares, for which the following offers were received:

Share price	Number of shares tendered at this price(000)
$0.50	2,400
$0.85	1,800
$1.25	1,350
$1.70	800

Which striking price would maximise receipts from the issue?

(For the answer to this question, see the Answer section at the end of this book.)

5 Placing

When companies 'go public' for the first time, a *large* issue will probably take the form of an offer for sale or offer for subscription (or occasionally an offer for sale by tender). A smaller issue is more likely to be a placing.

In a placing, either existing shares (held by current shareholders) or new shares are offered to investors in a selective marketing process. The shares are not offered to the investing public generally.

Key term

In the context of a company bringing its shares to listing, a **placing** is:

(a) A **marketing of the shares**, which may be either shares already in issue but not yet listed, or new shares still to be allotted

(b) To **specified persons or to specified clients of the sponsor** (or to specified clients of any issuing house that assists in the placing)

(c) Which does **not involve an offer to the public**, and

(d) Does not involve an offer to the company's existing shareholders generally.

The 'placees', ie the investors to whom the shares are marketed and sold, are normally institutional investors.

A placing is used when:

(a) The quantity of shares for sale or subscription is fairly small, so that the much higher cost of an offer for sale or subscription is not justified; but

(b) The requirement of the authorities, that an adequate quantity of the company's shares will be distributed to the market, is met.

A placing can be used both when a company does not yet have any equity shares listed, and also when it has equity shares listed and is now making a new issue of shares.

6 Intermediaries offer

An intermediaries offer is a method of bringing a company's shares to listing and making some shares available to the general investing public through a selected intermediary or selected intermediaries (stock broker/dealers).

The number of shares made available to the public in an intermediaries offer is much less than in an offer for sale or offer for subscription. An intermediaries offer may therefore be used in conjunction with a placing.

Key term

In the context of a company bringing its shares to listing for the first time, an **intermediaries offer** is:

- A marketing of shares, which may be already in issue, or not yet allotted, or a combination of both
- by means of an offer to intermediaries by the issuer (or on behalf of the issuer)
- for the intermediaries to sell on/allocate to their own clients.

The intermediaries will typically be firms of broker/dealers on the Stock Exchange.

For example, ABC might seek a listing by means of an intermediaries offer for some of its shares. The corporate broker acting for ABC will market the issue to other firms of stockbrokers or securities houses ('intermediaries'). These intermediaries will then make application forms available to their own clients, investment institutions and the investing public. Any member of the public or any institution wishing to buy some of the shares on offer must apply to an intermediary, not to ABC's own broker. The intermediaries then submit applications to the company's broker (on special application forms available to them from the broker or its associates) and shares are then allotted/sold accordingly.

The UK listing of Newsquest plc in October 1997 was partly by means of an intermediaries offer, described in the prospectus as follows:

Individuals resident in the UK, the Channel Islands or the Isle of Man can apply for Ordinary Shares through Intermediaries by completing application forms distributed by Intermediaries. Up to 10% of the Ordinary Shares available under the Offer …will be available to meet demand under the Intermediaries Offer.

Applications by Intermediaries under the Intermediaries Offer must be received by SBC Warburg Dillon Read by not later than 12 noon on Wednesday 15 October 1997. Intermediaries must apply for Ordinary Shares in the Intermediaries Offer on the application forms available to Intermediaries....

The intermediaries were defined as 'member firms of the London Stock Exchange or authorised persons under the Financial Services Act 1986....'

7 Stock market introduction

An introduction is a relatively uncommon method for a company to obtain a first listing for its shares, although it might be used by an overseas company as a method of obtaining a listing and admission to trading for its existing shares on the domestic Stock Exchange.

It is an unusual method for companies to bring their shares to listing because **no new shares are issued** by the company **and no existing shares are marketed**.

The Listing Authority gives a listing to the company's existing shares (and the Stock Exchange admits the shares to trading) without a requirement to make any more of these shares available to the public. This will only occur provided that **a sufficient number of the company's shares are already in the hands of the general public**. This should ensure that an adequate market will exist in the shares after flotation.

This situation will occur when a well-established public or private company, whose shares are already widely distributed, decides to apply for a listing.

(a)   The most common use of an introduction for UK-incorporated companies is where an AIM-quoted company wishes to transfer to the main market of the London Stock Exchange, and so applies for a listing.

(b)   An introduction may also be used when a listed company demerges, and splits into two or more separate companies. The new companies created as a result of the demerger may be brought to listing by means of an introduction.

In both of these situations, a sufficient quantity of the company's shares are already in the hands of the general public. The purpose of the introduction is to gain a listing on the main Stock Exchange, in order that the shares can be traded more easily.

An introduction may be used together with another method of share issue, such as a placing. In this way, some shares will be sold/allotted to the general investing public.

8 New issues of shares by quoted companies

A company with shares in issue that are already quoted on a stock market might wish to make a new issue of shares to raise capital. Under the law of many countries, there is a requirement for new shares to be offered to existing shareholders in proportion to their existing shareholding. This is a legal right of the current shareholders, and any such share issue is therefore known as a **rights issue**.

However, shareholders might agree to forgo these 'pre-emption' rights, particularly if the number of new shares to be issued is relatively small. In such cases, the new shares might be issued in a placing.

8.1 New share issues by quoted companies: underwriting and deep discounted issues

A quoted company making a new issue of shares is unlikely to have the issue underwritten in a placing. A rights issue should in theory not require underwriting, since new shares are being offered to existing shareholders. However, the underwriting of rights issues is common practice.

With underwriting, the company making the issue is sure of receiving the funds it wants to raise, net of expenses.

As an alternative to underwriting an issue, a company could choose to issue its shares at a **deep discount**, that is, at a price a long way below the current market price, to ensure the success of the issue. This is not common. Occasionally, rights issues have been both underwritten and made at a deep discount.

9 Rights issue

Key term

> A **rights issue** is an offer to existing shareholders enabling them to buy more shares, in proportion to their existing shareholding, usually at a price lower than the current market price.

Existing shareholders have **pre-emption rights** when new shares are issued. So that existing shareholders' rights are not diluted by the issue of new shares, legislation usually requires that before any equity shares are allotted for cash they must first be offered to existing shareholders.

A **rights issue** provides a way of raising new share capital by means of an offer to existing shareholders, inviting them to subscribe cash for new shares in proportion to their existing holdings. For example, a rights issue on a one for four basis at 280c per share would mean that a company is inviting its existing shareholders to subscribe for one new share for every four shares they hold, at a price of 280c per new share. A rights issue may be made by any type of company, private or public, listed or unlisted. The analysis below, however, applies primarily to listed companies.

The major advantages of a rights issue are as follows.

   (a)   Rights issues are cheaper than offers for sale to the general public. This is partly because the administration is simpler and partly because the cost of underwriting will be less.

   (b)   Rights issues are more beneficial to existing shareholders than issues to the general public. **New shares are issued at some discount to the current market price**, to make them attractive to investors. If the shares are issued to the general public, the benefit of the discount will be enjoyed by whoever buys the shares. A rights issue secures the discount on the market price for existing shareholders, who may either keep the shares or sell them if they wish.

   (c)   Relative voting rights are unaffected if shareholders all take up their rights.

9.1 Deciding the issue price for a rights issue

When it comes to pricing a rights issue there are very few constraints. To make the **offer price** of the rights issue attractive, it will invariably be lower than the current market price of existing shares. In addition, the offer price must be at or above the nominal value of the shares, so as not to contravene company law.

Beyond that, pricing of the issue is largely irrelevant. If the issue is at a small discount then fewer shares will be issued. If the issue is at a large discount then more shares will be issued. A shareholder with 10% of the orignal shares will take up 10% of the new issue for the same total cost (regardless of the issue price) and have a 10% interest in the business after the issue.

The issue will not be affected by the issue price but by investors opinions on what the finance will be used for. If investors believe the company have an exciting project to finance, the issue will be a success (irrespective of the issue price). If not it will be a failure.

It is sometimes suggested that pricing needs to be carefully considered to prevent excessive dilution of the ETS. This is simply not true since all prior reported EPS figures will be adjusted for the effects of the issue, maintaining comparability year-on-year.

Exam focus point

This area was examined for 3 marks in the December 2006 exam.

9.2 Example: rights issue (1)

Seagull can achieve a profit after tax of 20% on the capital employed. At present its capital structure is as follows.

	$
2,000,000 ordinary shares of $1 each	2,000,000
Retained earnings	1,000,000
	3,000,000

The directors propose to raise an additional $1,260,000 from a rights issue. The current market price is $1.80.

Required

(a) Calculate the number of shares that must be issued if the rights price is:
$1.60; $1.50; $1.40; $1.20.

(b) Calculate the dilution in earnings per share (EPS) in each case.

Solution

The earnings at present are 20% of $3,000,000 = $600,000. This gives earnings per share of 30c. The earnings after the rights issue will be 20% of $4,260,000 = $852,000.

Rights price $	No of new shares ($1,260,000 ÷ rights price)	EPS ($852,000 ÷ total no of shares) Cents	Dilution Cents
1.60	787,500	30.6	+ 0.6
1.50	840,000	30.0	–
1.40	900,000	29.4	– 0.6
1.20	1,050,000	27.9	– 2.1

9.3 The market price of shares after a rights issue: the theoretical ex-rights price

After the announcement of a rights issue, there is a tendency for share prices to fall, although the extent and duration of the fall may depend on the number of shareholders and the size of their holdings. This temporary fall is due to uncertainty in the market about the consequences of the issue, with respect to future profits, earnings and dividends.

After the issue has actually been made, the market price per share will normally fall, because there are more shares in issue and the new shares were issued at a discount price.

When a rights issue is announced, all existing shareholders have the right to subscribe for new shares, and so there are **rights attached** to the existing shares. The shares are therefore described as being 'cum rights' (with rights attached) and are traded cum rights. On the first day of dealings in the newly-issued shares, the rights no longer exist and the old shares are now 'ex rights' (without rights attached).

In theory, the new market price will be the consequence of an adjustment to allow for the discount price of the new issue, and a **theoretical ex rights price** can be calculated.

9.4 Example: rights issue (2)

Fundraiser has 10,000,000 ordinary shares of $1 in issue, which have a market price on 1 September of $2.10 per share. The company decides to make a rights issue, and offers its shareholders the right to subscribe for one new share at $1.50 each for every four shares already held. After the announcement of the issue, the share price fell to $1.95, but by the time just prior to the issue being made, it had recovered to $2 per share. This market value just before the issue is known as the cum rights price. What is the theoretical ex rights price?

Solution

In theory, the market price will fall after the issue, as follows.

	$
10,000,000 shares have a 'cum rights' value of (× $2)	20,000,000
2,500,000 shares will be issued to raise (× $1.50)	3,750,000
The theoretical value of 12,500,000 shares is	23,750,000

The theoretical ex rights price is ($23,750,000/12,500,000) = $1.90 per share.

The same calculation is often shown as follows.

	$
Four shares have a cum rights value of (× $2)	8.00
One new share is issued for	1.50
The value of five shares is theoretically	9.50

The theoretical ex rights price is $9.50/5 = $1.90 per share.

9.5 The value of rights

Shareholders in a rights issue can either take up their rights and buy the shares they are entitled to, or they can sell their rights on the stock market.

The value of rights is the theoretical gain a shareholder would make by exercising his rights.

(a)   Using the above example, if the price offered in the rights issue is $1.50 per share, and the market price after the issue is expected to be $1.90, the value attaching to a right is $1.90 − $1.50 = $0.40. A shareholder would therefore be expected to gain 40 cents for each new share he buys. If he does not have enough money to buy the share himself, he could sell the right to subscribe for a new share to another investor, and receive 40 cents from the sale. This other investor would then buy the new share for $1.50, so that his total outlay to acquire the share would be $0.40 + $1.50 = $1.90, the theoretical ex rights price.

(b)   The value of rights attaching to existing shares is calculated in the same way. If the value of rights on a new share is 40 cents, and there is a one for four rights issue, the value of the rights attaching to each existing share is 40 ÷ 4 = 10 cents.

Exam focus point

Calculations of the theoretical ex-rights price and the value of the nil-paid rights was examined for 5 marks in the December 2006 exam.

9.6 The options available to shareholders

The possible courses of action open to shareholders in a rights issue are:

(a)   To **'take up' or 'exercise' the rights**, that is, to buy the new shares at the rights price. Shareholders who do this will maintain their percentage holdings in the company by subscribing for the new shares

(b)   To **sell the rights** on the market. The buyer of the rights is then entitled to subscribe for the new shares at the offer price. Shareholders who sell their rights will have a lower percentage holding in the share capital of the company after the issue. The total value of their shares will also be less after the rights issue, on the assumption that the actual market price after the issue is close to the (lower) theoretical ex-rights price.

(c)   To **do nothing**. Shareholders are protected from the consequences of their inaction because rights not taken up are sold on a shareholder's behalf by the company. The shareholder (or the company) gets the difference between the issue price and the market price after the issue.

Question 6.2   Rights issue

Gopher has issued 3,000,000 ordinary shares of $1 each, which are at present selling for $4 per share. The company plans to issue rights to purchase one new equity share at a price of $3.20 per share for every three shares held. A shareholder who owns 900 shares thinks that he will suffer a loss in his personal wealth because the new shares are being offered at a price lower than market value. On the assumption that the actual market value of shares will be equal to the theoretical ex rights price, what would be the effect on the shareholder's wealth if:

(a)   He sells all the rights
(b)   He exercises half of the rights and sells the other half
(c)   He does nothing at all?

(For the answer to this question, see the Answer section at the end of this book.)

9.7 The actual market price after a rights issue

The actual market price of a share after a rights issue may differ from the theoretical ex rights price. This will occur when the expected earnings yield from the new funds raised is different from the earnings yield from existing funds in the business. The market will take a view of how profitably the new funds will be invested, and will value the shares accordingly. An example will illustrate this point.

9.8 Example: rights issue (3)

Musk currently has 4,000,000 ordinary shares in issue, valued at $2 each, and the company has annual earnings equal to 20% of the market value of the shares. A one for four rights issue is proposed, at an issue price of $1.50. If the market continues to value the shares on a price/earnings ratio of 5, what would be the value per share if the new funds are expected to earn, as a percentage of the money raised:

(a)   15%?
(b)   20%?
(c)   25%?

How do these values in (a), (b) and (c) compare with the theoretical ex rights price? Ignore issue costs.

Solution

The theoretical ex rights price will be calculated first.

	$
Four shares have a current value (× $2) of	8.00
One new share will be issued for	1.50
Five shares would have a theoretical value of	9.50

The theoretical ex rights price is $\dfrac{\$9.50}{5} = \$1.90$.

The new funds will raise 1,000,000 × $1.50 = $1,500,000.

Earnings as a % of money raised	Additional earnings	Current earnings	Total earnings after the issue
	$	$	$
15%	225,000	1,600,000	1,825,000
20%	300,000	1,600,000	1,900,000
25%	375,000	1,600,000	1,975,000

If the market values shares on a P/E ratio of 5, the total market value of equity and the market price per share would be as follows.

Total earnings	Market value (5 × Earnings)	Price per share (5,000,000 shares)
$	$	$
1,825,000	9,125,000	1.825
1,900,000	9,500,000	1.900
1,975,000	9,875,000	1.975

If the additional funds raised are expected to generate earnings at the same rate as existing funds, the actual market value will probably be the same as the theoretical ex rights price.

If the new funds are expected to generate earnings at a lower rate, the market value will fall below the theoretical ex rights price. If this happens, shareholders will lose.

If the new funds are expected to earn at a higher rate than current funds, the market value should be above the theoretical ex rights price. If this happens, shareholders will profit by taking up their rights.

The decision by individual shareholders as to whether they take up the offer will therefore depend on:

(a)   The expected rate of return on the investment (and the risk associated with it)
(b)   The return obtainable from other investments (allowing for the associated risk)

Exam focus point

> In the June 2002 exam, there was a question on rights issues which required some explanation and discussion and also the calculation of the price of a rights issue and the number of shares to be issued.
>
> In the December 2006 exam there was a question requiring the calculation of the actual price after the rights issue in a similar manner to the above.

9.9 Rights issues or issuing shares for cash to new investors?

When shares are issued for cash to outside buyers, existing shareholders forfeit their **pre-emption rights** to shares. Companies can issue shares for cash without obtaining prior approval from shareholders for each such share issue, provided that they have obtained approval from shareholders within the past 12 months to make new issues of shares for cash which are not rights issues. (This shareholder approval could be obtained at the company's Annual General Meeting.)

Companies can therefore issue shares for cash without having to bear the high costs of a rights issue, for example by placing shares for cash at a higher price than they might have been able to obtain from a rights issue.

10 The timing of new equity issues

New equity issues in general (offers for sale and placings as well as rights issues) are more common when share prices are high and the stock market is buoyant than when share prices are low and the stock market is depressed.

(a)   When **share prices are high**, investors' confidence will also be high, and investors will be more willing to put money into companies with the potential for growth.

By issuing shares at a high price, a company will reduce the number of shares it must issue to raise the amount of capital it wants. This will reduce the dilution of earnings for existing shareholders.

(b)   If **share prices are low**, business confidence is likely to be low too. Companies may not want to raise capital for new investments until expectations begin to improve. Similarly, investors will be reluctant to subscribe for new shares when they think that the company's share price might fall still further.

11 Other methods of issuing shares

Shares are sometimes issued for other reasons. Shares offered under a **share option scheme** are to provide an incentive to the option holder. **Scrip issues** are intended to convert balance sheet reserves into nominal share capital.

There are other methods of issuing new shares. Two further methods that are worth mentioning are:

(a)   Shares issued under a share option scheme
(b)   A bonus issue (also called a scrip issue or capitalisation issue)

A share issue might also be arranged in the form of a 'book-building' operation.

11.1 Share options

Many companies have a **share option scheme** for selected employees. Under such a scheme, the company gives certain employees the right, at a future date, to subscribe for new shares in the company at a price that is determined now.

For example, suppose that the current market price per share of PQR is $4. Its chief executive might be given options to subscribe for, say, 200,000 shares in the company at a future date, at a price of, say, $3.80. If the chief executive subsequently exercises these options, he or she will buy 200,000 new shares in the company for $760,000. By this time, the share price may well have risen to, say, $6, which means that the chief executive will benefit from an instant profit of ($6 - $3.80) $2.20 per share.

Although share option schemes of this type raise new capital for a company, they are seen more as an incentive arrangement for key employees, who are able to profit from any rise in the company's share price after the options have been awarded.

11.2 Book-building

With some share issues, an investment bank is appointed as the '**book runner**', and organises the sale of the shares to targeted clients (mainly investment institutions).

The responsibility for the success of a new issue of shares might be given to an investment bank that becomes the 'book runner' for the issue. The bank obtains the assistance of a syndicate of other banks, often in a number of different countries. Each member of the syndicate then approaches its clients and attempts to interest them in investing in the issue.

Book-building is an arrangement for selling shares in an issue, rather than a method of issue.

12 Scrip dividends, scrip issues and stock splits

Scrip dividends, scrip issues and stock splits are not methods of raising new equity funds, but they *are* methods of altering the share capital structure of a company, or in the case of scrip dividends and scrip issues, increasing the issued share capital of the company.

12.1 Scrip dividends

Key term

A **scrip dividend** is a dividend payment which takes the form of new shares instead of cash.

Effectively, a scrip dividend converts retained earnings into issued share capital. When the directors of a company would prefer to retain funds within the business but consider that they must pay at least a certain amount of dividend, they might offer equity shareholders the choice of a **cash dividend** or a **scrip dividend**. Each shareholder would decide separately which to take. There is no need for all shareholders to agree on whether to have a cash dividend or a scrip dividend.

12.2 Scrip issues

Key term

A **scrip issue** (or **bonus issue**) is an issue of new shares to existing shareholders, by converting equity reserves into issued share capital.

If a company with issued share capital of 100,000 ordinary shares of $1 each made a **one for five scrip issue**, 20,000 new shares would be issued to existing shareholders, one new share for every five old shares held. Issued share capital would be increased by $20,000, and reserves (probably share premium account, if there is one) reduced by this amount.

By creating more shares in this way, a scrip issue does not raise new funds, but does have the advantage of making shares cheaper and therefore (perhaps) more easily marketable on the Stock Exchange. For example, if a company's shares are priced at $16 on the Stock Exchange, and the company makes a one for one scrip issue, we should expect the share price after the issue to fall to $8 each. Shares at $8 each might be more easily marketable than shares at $16 each.

12.3 Stock splits

The advantage of a scrip issue mentioned above is also the reason for a **stock split**. A stock split occurs where, for example, each ordinary share of $1 each is split into two shares of 50c each, thus creating cheaper shares with greater marketability. There is possibly an added psychological advantage, in that investors should expect a company which splits its shares in this way to be planning for substantial earnings growth and dividend growth in the future. As a consequence, the market price of shares may benefit. For example, if one existing share of $1 has a market value of $20, and is then split into two shares of 50c each, the market value of the new shares might settle at $11.

The difference between a stock split and a scrip issue is that a scrip issue converts equity reserves into share capital, whereas a stock split leaves balance sheet reserves unaffected. Both are popular with investors as they are seen as likely to lead to increased dividends.

12.4 Stock splits, scrip issues and changes in shareholder wealth

As we have seen, stock splits and scrip issues are not methods of raising equity finance. They are accounting adjustments, with scrip issues involving the conversion of reserves of the company (often non-distributable reserves such as share premium) into nominal share capital.

They produce no extra cash for the company, and they will therefore have no effect on the profits and cash flows produced by the company's investments. It therefore follows that stock splits and scrip issues should have no effect on total shareholder wealth.

For example, suppose that a company has 5 million shares in issue, each with a current market price of $4.20. The company makes a 2 for 5 bonus issue.

(a) The value of the company's shares before the bonus issue is $21 million (5 million × $4.20).

(b) The number of shares in issue after the bonus issue is 7 million, because 2 million new shares are issued (2/5 × 5 million).

(c) The bonus issue raises no new finance, so the total value of the shares will remain at $21 million.

(d) The share price should therefore fall to $3 ($21 million/7 million shares).

13 Repurchase of shares

A company may, with shareholder consent, **repurchase** some of its shares and cancel them. This will reduce the company's ordinary share capital. Any repurchase of shares must be made out of distributable profits (retained profits), and the nominal value of the repurchased shares must be transferred to a capital reserve account, known as a **capital redemption reserve**.

Occasionally, a company might decide that it has too much equity capital. Equity capital is generally regarded as permanent capital for a company, but a company may, **with shareholder consent**, repurchase a quantity of its existing shares and cancel them. The repurchase and cancellation of shares results in a reduction in the equity shares of the company concerned.

A company might have an excess equity capital for either of two main reasons:

(a) It has surplus capital to its needs. By repurchasing and cancelling ordinary shares, it will reduce its share capital, leaving the profits and dividends of the company to be shared by fewer shareholders.

(b) It would like to reduce its ordinary share capital and increase its debt capital funding, perhaps because interest rates have fallen and debt capital is now much cheaper than in the past.

Case Study

In October 2000, Redrow, the UK housebuilder, unveiled plans to buy back 30% of its shares via a tender offer at 170p (market price was 169.5p). This was to achieve a 'better match between debt and equity' on its balance sheet – the gearing level at the time being 4.5%.

Under the law of many countries, there are provisions to protect creditors of the company in the event of a reduction in share capital. When a company reduces its issued share capital, it is required to:

(a)   make the repurchase and cancellation of the shares out of distributable profits and

(b)   replace the nominal value of the shares that are cancelled with a 'capital reserve'. This reserve, known as a capital redemption reserve, cannot be distributed to shareholders by way of dividend. It ensures that the long-term equity capital of the company is not reduced.

13.1 Example: repurchase of shares

Bligh has 20,000,000 ordinary shares of $1 each in issue, and distributable reserves (retained profits) of $50,000,000. The company has too much ordinary share capital, and the directors obtain shareholder approval for the company to buy up to 5,000,000 of its shares on the open market and cancel them.

The company subsequently buys 5,000,000 of its shares on the open market, at a price of $12,000,000.

The company had $18 million in the bank prior to the share repurchase.

How will the company's balance sheet be affected by the share repurchase?

Solution

	Balance sheet before $		Balance sheet after $
Cash	18,000,000	(– $12,000,000)	6,000,000
Share capital	20,000,000	(– $5,000,000)	15,000,000
Capital redemption reserve	0	(+ $5,000,000)	5,000,000
Distributable profits	50,000,000	(– $12,000,000)	38,000,000

The effect of a company buying back some of its shares and cancelling them is therefore to reduce distributable profits by the price paid to repurchase the shares. The non-distributable capital of the company (share capital plus capital reserves) remains unchanged in total, with the fall in nominal share capital offset by an increase in the capital redemption reserve.

14 Preference shares

FAST FORWARD

Some companies have **preference share capital**. Preference shares are not equity, and preference shareholders are not owners of their company. Preference shares entitle their holders to dividend, with priority for payment over ordinary shareholders (and priority over ordinary shareholders to the repayment of capital, in the event of the winding up of the company and the liquidation of its assets).

Preference shares are non-equity shares. Non-equity shares are shares giving their holders the right to receive a dividend, but only up to a specific limit. Preference shareholders are entitled to a dividend before any dividend is paid to the ordinary shareholders.

An annual preference dividend is usually paid in two equal amounts every six months. This is a fixed percentage amount of the nominal value of the share. Unlike bond interest, which is paid out of pre-tax profits, preference dividend comes out of post-tax profits. It must be paid before any dividend can be paid to equity (ordinary) shareholders.

If the company is wound up, for example if it becomes insolvent, preference shareholders rank behind creditors and ahead of equity shareholders in the order of entitlement to payment from the proceeds of selling off the company's assets. The amount receivable by preference shareholders in a winding up, however, is limited to the nominal value of the shares (and possibly also any unpaid dividend).

14.1 Types of preference shares

FAST FORWARD 〉〉

Preference shares may be **cumulative, participating, redeemable** or **convertible**, although conventional shares are none of these.

Preference shares are normally irredeemable, and entitle the shareholders to a fixed annual dividend. Some preference share issues, however, have special features, and the shares may be:

(a) Cumulative
(b) Participating
(c) Redeemable, or
(d) Convertible.

Shares can be a combination of these types, for example preference shares might be cumulative redeemable shares.

14.2 Cumulative preference shares

Cumulative preference shares differ from conventional preference shares by giving the shareholders special rights in the event that the company has insufficient distributable reserves (or cash) to pay a due preference dividend. In the event that any due dividend is unpaid, the 'arrears' of dividend remain payable and accumulate. The preference shareholders must receive their arrears of dividend before any ordinary dividends can be paid to equity shareholders.

14.3 Example

A company with 40 million 5% cumulative preference shares of $1 did not pay any dividend last year to its preference or ordinary shareholders. It would like to resume dividend payments in the current year.

The company cannot pay a dividend in the current year to ordinary shareholders (equity) until it has paid the preference shareholders' their arrears of dividend from last year ($2 million) and the dividend payable to date for the current year.

If the preference shares had been non-cumulative, their holders would not be entitled to the $2 million arrears of dividend.

14.4 Participating preference shares

Participating preference shares have extra dividend rights. In addition to receiving a fixed annual dividend, holders of these shares also participate in the company's surplus profits. This extra 'participating' dividend is usually set at a specified percentage of the dividend paid on the ordinary shares.

14.5 Redeemable preference shares

Redeemable preference shares are preference shares that either will be redeemed at a specified future date, or could be redeemed at a specified future date, at the option of either the shareholders or the company.

FAST FORWARD

When redeemable preference shares are redeemed, the accounting requirements are the same as for the repurchase and cancellation of ordinary shares.

The redemption price for redeemable preference shares is either at par or above par (ie at or above the nominal value of the shares). The rules for the redemption of preference shares are similar to those for the purchase and cancellation of its own shares by a company (described above). The redemption is made out of distributable profits, and the long-term capital of the company must be maintained by transferring the nominal value of the shares redeemed to a capital redemption reserve account.

14.6 Convertible preference shares

Convertible preference shares give their holder the right to convert the preference shares into ordinary shares of the company, at a specified future date (or between specified future dates) and at a specified rate of conversion. For example, 8% preference shares of $1 each might be convertible into ordinary shares of the company at a specified future date, at the rate of four preference shares for each 50c ordinary share in the company.

Convertible preference shares are also usually redeemable. If they are not converted into equity, they will eventually be redeemed.

The advantage for a company of issuing convertible preference shares is that investors might be willing to buy them (and so provide new capital to the company) in return for a fixed annual preference dividend for a number of years and then the opportunity to convert the preference shares into equity. By the time that the date for conversion has arrived, the ordinary share price might have risen to the point where the preference shareholders can make a profit by converting their shares.

14.7 Preference share markets

On the stock market, preference shares are traded in the same way as equity shares and corporate bonds. However, the market for preference shares is very small, and new issues of preference shares are fairly uncommon, except in venture capital financing arrangements.

In the international capital markets, companies occasionally issue redeemable convertible preference shares. These are regarded as part of the 'euroconvertibles market', together with convertible bonds and equity warrant bonds. (These are described in the next chapter.)

Question 6.3   True or false?

Which of the following statements concerning share issues are true?

(i)   A bonus issue is likely to result in an increase in the share price per share
(ii)   A stock split does not affect balance sheet reserves
(iii)   An introduction does not necessarily result in a new share issue
(iv)   In a placing, a minimum number of shares must be offered to the public

(For the answer to this question, see the Answer section at the end of this book.)

Chapter roundup

- Companies can raise new **long-term finance** as **equity (ordinary share capital)**, **preference share capital** or **debt capital.**

- **Sources of equity** capital are **retained profits** and **new share issues.** It is much easier for a public company to raise new equity capital (on the stock market) than it is for a private company to raise share capital.

- A share issue by a public company might be to raise cash for new investment, to 'float' the company on the stock market or to finance an acquisition (or 'takeover') of another company.

- The methods of issuing shares in a flotation are an **offer for sale** or **offer for subscription**, a **placing,** an **intermediaries** offer, an **introduction** or a combination of two of these. Occasionally, a company might issue shares in an **offer for sale by tender**.

- In a stock market introduction, no new shares are issued, and no shares are sold by existing shareholders to other investors (the general public).

- The capital raised by a company in a share issue is the number of new shares issued multiplied by the price per share, minus the issue costs. Issue costs for large share issues include **underwriting commission**.

- A company with shares already traded on a stock market might make a new issue of shares to raise extra cash. A requirement of legislation in many countries is that unless shareholders agree to waive their rights, a new issue of shares should be in the form of a **rights issue**. In a rights issue, shareholders are offered new shares in proportion to their existing shareholding. In practice, shareholders often agree to waive their rights, particularly for small share issues. A new issue of shares by a listed company might therefore be by means of a placing.

- Shareholders in a rights issue can either take up their rights and buy the shares they are entitled to, or they can sell their rights on the stock market.

- Shares are sometimes issued for other reasons. Shares offered under a **share option scheme** are to provide an incentive to the option holder. **Scrip issues** are intended to convert balance sheet reserves into nominal share capital.

- With some share issues, an investment bank is appointed as the '**book runner**', and organises the sale of the shares to targeted clients (mainly investment institutions).

- A company may, with shareholder consent, **repurchase** some of its shares and cancel them. This will reduce the company's ordinary share capital. Any repurchase of shares must be made out of distributable profits (retained profits), and the nominal value of the repurchased shares must be transferred to a capital reserve account, known as a **capital redemption reserve**.

- Some companies have **preference share capital**. Preference shares are not equity, and preference shareholders are not owners of their company. Preference shares entitle their holders to dividend, with priority for payment over ordinary shareholders (and priority over ordinary shareholders to the repayment of capital, in the event of the winding up of the company and the liquidation of its assets).

- Preference shares may be **cumulative**, **participating**, **redeemable** or **convertible**, although conventional shares are none of these.

- When redeemable preference shares are redeemed, the accounting requirements are the same as for the repurchase and cancellation of ordinary shares.

Quick quiz

1   A public company has a market capitalisation of $180 million and its shares are traded on the Stock Exchange. It wishes to raise $10 million through a new share issue. What method of share issue is it likely to use?

2   What might be an alternative to underwriting, for a rights issue, where the company and its advisers want to ensure that the issue is a success and all the shares on offer are subscribed for?

3   A company has 600 million ordinary shares of 50 cents each in issue, currently priced at $8 per share. It is planning a 2 for 5 rights issue at 750 cents per share. Ignoring the costs of the issue, how much capital will the company expect to raise?

4   A company has ordinary share capital in issue of 100 million shares of 20 cents each (nominal value). It wishes to repurchase and cancel 5 million shares. If it repurchases these shares at a price of 350 cents each, what will be the effect on its balance sheet?

5   A company has issued a quantity of 5% convertible preference shares of $1 each. These are convertible in four years' time into ordinary shares of 50 cents each, at the rate of one ordinary share for every three preference shares. If the shares are not converted, they will be redeemed at par. The current ordinary share price is 225 cents per share. By how much must the ordinary shares rise in value to make conversion a preferable option to redemption for the preference shareholders?

Answers to quick quiz

1   A rights issue would be required by law unless the shareholders have agreed to waive their rights. In view of the fairly small size of the issue, it is likely that the shareholders will be asked to waive their rights, and for the issue to be made by way of a placing.

2   An alternative (or supplement) to underwriting would be a deep discounted rights issue. The offer price in a rights issue is always below the current market price. In a deep discounted rights issue, the size of the discount to market value would be much larger than normal.

3   240 million shares will be issued at 750 cents each, to raise $1,800 million, ignoring issue costs.

4   The cost of the repurchase is $17.5 million (5 million shares × 350 cents each). Distributable profits and the company's cash balance will both be reduced by this amount. There will also be a reduction in share capital of $1 million (5 million shares × 20 cents nominal value) and a corresponding increase in the capital redemption reserve.

5   The redemption value of 3 preference shares is $3. To make conversion a preferable option, the market price of the ordinary shares needs to rise over the next four years from 225 cents to more than 300 cents, an increase of one-third.

Other sources of finance

7

Topic list	Syllabus reference
1 Long-term and short-term finance	3a
2 Loan stock or bonds	3a
3 The market value of bonds	3a
4 Types of bonds	3a
5 Convertibles	3a
6 Bonds with share warrants attached	3a
7 Bank finance	3a
8 Leasing and hire purchase	3a
9 Invoice discounting and debt factoring	3a
10 Bills of exchange	3a
11 Bankers' acceptance (BA) credit facility	3a
12 PFI/PPP	3a
13 Finance and the small business	3g
14 Fixed versus floating rate of interest	3a
15 Internally-generated funds	3a

Introduction

An alternative to raising capital by issuing shares is to take on fresh debt, for example by taking out a bank loan, or by issuing debentures. The cost of debt is paid in an annual interest charge; while dividends can be suspended in economic hard times, the annual interest charge must always be paid each year.

After reading this chapter, you should be able to discuss all the differences between shares and debt as sources of finance.

1 Long-term and short-term finance

A company may use long-term or short-term debt capital as sources of finance. The cost of debt capital is **interest**.

Share capital is regarded as long-term finance for a company. Other sources of finance may be either long-term or short-term. Some of these finance sources, notably short-term trade credit, are obtained at no cost to the company. This chapter describes the main alternative sources of finance that involve an interest cost to the company.

Loan capital is long-term borrowing. The **cost of borrowing is interest**, which is payable on the outstanding amount of the loan principal.

Companies might borrow either from banks, or from non-bank investors. Companies might borrow from non-bank investors under a private loan agreement. However, most company borrowing from investors other than banks is in the form of loan stock or bonds.

2 Loan stock or bonds

Companies might raise debt capital from investors by issuing **bonds**, also called **loan stock** or **debenture stock**. These are debt capital issued in the form of securities (**securitised debt**), usually at a fixed rate of interest. Bonds issued by public companies are traded in a secondary bond market after issue.

The terms **loan stock**, **bonds** and **debenture stock** are often used interchangeably. They are all descriptions of debt securities issued by a company to raise long-term capital. Debt capital is issued in the form of securities, and in this respect is similar to share capital. To offer its debt capital to the general investing public, the company must be a public company. It is usual for debt securities to be listed, and admitted to trading on the Stock Exchange.

The methods of issuing debt capital are either an **offer to the public** or a **placing**. In practice, the main buyers of debt securities are institutional investors, and a new issue is placed by means of a **book-building operation**, with one or more banks organising a syndicate of banks to sell the issue and to 'run the book' for the issue. For example, if a company arranges to issue $40 million of bonds, a syndicate might be organised by the company's investment bank to sell the securities to their institutional clients.

Key terms

Loan stock is long-term debt capital raised by a company, on which interest is paid, usually at a fixed rate of interest. Holders of the loan stock are therefore long-term creditors of the company. The interest payable is based on the nominal value of the debt, which is the loan principal, and is often referred to as the 'coupon'.

It is more usual to refer to loan stock by the name '**bonds**'. This is a name used for loan stock in the international capital markets, and in the US markets, which are the main markets for issues of loan capital by companies.

Notes are debt securities with a relatively short term to maturity when they are issued. Debt securities issued with a five-year maturity are more likely to be called notes rather than bonds.

A **debenture** is a written acknowledgement of a debt incurred by a company, normally containing provisions about the term of the loan and the interest rate payable. In the UK, it is usual for bonds to be issued under a trust deed, and the trustees would be responsible for looking after the interests of the bondholders, for example ensuring that the company meets its interest payment obligations. **Debenture stock** is a name for loan stock issued as a debenture.

2.1 Interest payments

The interest rate on bonds (the **coupon**) is usually close to the current market rate when bonds are issued, therefore bonds are usually issued at a price close to their par value. Bonds, unless convertible into equity, are redeemed at maturity either at par value or (less usually) at a price above par.

It is usual in the many countries for interest on bonds to be paid in two equal six-monthly amounts each year.

For example, if a company issues $20 million of 6% loan stock, the interest cost will be $1,200,000 each year. The interest will probably be paid half-yearly, $600,000 in each payment. The 'coupon' on this loan stock is 6%.

2.2 Issue price of debt capital

Bonds are priced in the market relative to a par value of 100. A price of 101.25, for example, means that the market price of the bonds is $101.25 for each $100 nominal value of the bonds.

Unlike share capital, debt capital is usually issued at a price at or close to 'par value'. This is because when a new issue is made, the company will normally try to set the interest rate (coupon) at a level that reflects current market interest rates and the credit rating of the issue.

After an issue of bonds has been made, the market price will vary up or down, as market interest rates change. However, given no change in the credit rating for the bonds, bond market prices are more stable than share prices.

2.3 The redemption of bonds

Bonds are usually redeemable, normally at par (or possibly at a slight premium to par). For example, if a company issues $50 million of 7.5% ten-year bonds, redeemable at par, it will redeem the bonds after ten years for $50 million.

Bonds might have an earliest and a latest redemption date. For example, 8% loan stock 2009/2011 is redeemable at any time, usually at the choice of the company, between an earliest date in 2009 and a latest date in 2011. The company's decision about when to redeem the debt will probably depend on whether the coupon on the bonds is higher or lower than current market interest rates. If market interest rates are lower than the coupon, because interest rates have fallen, it will be cheaper to redeem the bonds at the earliest opportunity and make a new bond issue at a lower rate of interest.

2.4 Tax relief on bond interest

Interest payable by a company on its debt capital, including interest on bonds, is an **allowable expense for tax purposes**. Interest costs are therefore deducted from profits in calculating the amount of profit that is liable to tax.

A very important feature of corporate bonds is that the company receives tax relief on its interest payments.

Suppose for example that a company issues $20 million of 10% bonds. Interest payments will be $2,000,000 each year, but the company will receive relief from tax on these payments. If the rate of tax is 30%, this means that the company's tax payments would be reduced each year by 30% of $2,000,000, ie by $600,000. The net cost of the debt interest would therefore be just $1,400,000. The 'after-tax' cost of debt in this example is just $1,400,000/$20 million, which is 7%.

For irredeemable debt, the after-tax cost of debt is calculated simply by multiplying the gross interest rate by a factor of $(1 - t)$, where t is the tax rate as a proportion. When the rate of interest is 10% gross and the rate of tax is 30%, the after-tax cost of interest is therefore $10\% \times (1 - 0.30) = 10\% \times 0.7 = 7\%$.

The tax relief on debt interest can make debt capital a cheap source of long-term capital, and much more attractive than equity capital.

2.5 Secured and unsecured bonds

> Bonds might be **secured** on the assets of the company. However, unlike bank loans, it is quite common for bonds to be **unsecured**. International bonds (eurobonds) are unsecured. Investors assess the creditworthiness of the borrower by the **credit ratings** given to the bond issue by credit rating agencies.

An issue of bonds may be either unsecured, or secured bonds against specified assets of the company. If the company defaults on its interest payments, the bondholders (ie the trustees acting on their behalf) can take control over the secured assets, and arrange for payment to be obtained from the liquidation of these assets.

Mortgage bonds are bonds secured by a mortgage on specific property (land and buildings) of the borrower.

Many bonds issues are **unsecured**. All international bond issues, for example, are unsecured. This is the main reason why bond investors insist on credit ratings (see below).

2.6 The market for corporate bonds

> The **bond markets** are accessible only to **large companies**.

To raise capital by issuing bonds, a company must be able to attract investors willing to buy them. In the UK, for example, this is difficult for all but the largest companies (except perhaps in a venture capital arrangement, which is described in a later chapter). The UK domestic market for bonds is dominated by government securities (gilts), and a UK company wishing to issue bonds must normally use either the international bond market in Europe, or the US bond markets.

Investors in these bond markets expect bond issues to be given at least one **credit rating**, but usually two, usually by a credit rating agency. The largest rating agencies are Moody's and Standard & Poor's, which are paid by the company for giving a rating to its bond issue. 'Investment grade' credit ratings are usually only given to bond issues by large and well-established companies, and the interest rate a company must offer is strongly influenced by the credit rating given to the issue.

Bond issues on the international bond market are normally sold to investors by a syndicate of banks in a number of different countries. Although it is usual to arrange for bonds to be listed and admitted to trading on a large stock market such as the London Stock Exchange, the market for buying and selling international bonds after their issue is mainly conducted through international dealers. Transactions are arranged either by telephone or by means of an electronic dealing system of ISMA, the International Securities Markets Association.

3 The market value of bonds

> The **market value of a bond** after its issue represents the amount investors are willing to pay for the bond's future income stream (interest payments and repayment of principal at maturity). It is the **present value** of the future cash flows from the bond, discounted at a cost of capital that is the investment return required by the bond investors.

Key term

> The **market value of bonds** can be defined as the present value to bond investors of the future cash returns from their bonds, discounted at the rate of return they require from their bond investment.

This simply means that what bond investors are willing to pay 'now' for a bond is the value they place on the future income from the bonds.

3.1 Example: market price of a bond

A company issued some 6% bonds a few years ago. The bonds pay interest annually, and now have exactly five years remaining to maturity (the most recent interest payment just having been made). They will be redeemed at par. Investors in bonds of this type currently require a yield of 7% per annum.

What will be the market value of these bonds?

Year	Discount factor at 7%
1	0.935
2	0.873
3	0.816
4	0.763
5	0.713

Solution

The bond investors will receive annual interest of $6 for each $100 (nominal value) of the bonds, and $100 at the end of year 5 from the redemption of the bonds at par. The market value of the bonds is therefore as follows.

Year	Cash return	Discount factor at 7%	PV of return
1	6	0.935	5.61
2	6	0.873	5.24
3	6	0.816	4.90
4	6	0.763	4.58
5	106	0.713	75.58
	Value of bond		95.91

The market value of the bonds will be $95.91. The market value is below par because investors currently require a yield (7%) that is higher than the coupon payable on the bonds (6%).

Question 7.1
Market value

A company has issued 8% bonds that have four years remaining to maturity. Interest is payable annually, and the most recent interest payment has just been made. The bonds will be redeemed at par. Investors in these bonds require an annual return of 6% per annum.

What is the market value of these bonds?

Year	Discount factor at 6%
1	0.943
2	0.890
3	0.840
4	0.792

(For the answer to this question, see the Answer section at the end of this book.)

4 Types of bonds

There are different types of bonds, and various terms might be used to describe bonds.

4.1 Eurobonds

Eurobonds are bonds issued on the international bond market. They might be denominated in any freely-traded currency. The most common currencies for bond issues are the US dollar and the euro; however, other currencies (eg sterling, Swiss francs, yen etc.) are sometimes used, depending on conditions in the financial markets. Due to the possibility of confusion with the euro currency, it is now usual to refer to 'international bonds' rather than 'eurobonds'.

4.2 Senior debt and subordinated debt (junior debt)

FAST FORWARD

Senior debt gives its holders prior rights to payment of interest and, in the event of the liquidation of the company, to repayment of the debt capital. **Subordinated debt (junior debt)** ranks behind senior debt (but ahead of equity shareholders) in this order of priority. Senior debt, which might be a bank loan, is often secured by a charge on the company's assets.

Debt may be ranked in order of priority, in the event that the borrowing company is unable to meet its interest payment obligations, or the company goes into liquidation. **Senior debt** gives its holders a prior right, ahead of other debt capital providers, to:

(a)   The receipt of interest, and

(b)   The repayment of capital out of the proceeds of the company's liquidated assets (in the event of liquidation of the borrowing company).

Subordinated debt refers to debt capital on which the right to interest payments and, in the event of insolvency of the borrower, the right to return of capital out of the proceeds from the company's liquidated assets, ranks after other debt issues in order of priority.

4.3 Mezzanine finance

FAST FORWARD

Mezzanine finance is a form of unsecured lending that also includes an arrangement giving an equity interest to the borrower. It might be available to medium-sized companies in situations where conventional loans are not available, for example to companies subject to an MBO or MBI.

'Mezzanine finance' is a term given to a form of risk capital that combines the characteristics of conventional lending with equity funding. It may be used where a lender considers the provision of traditional finance to be too risky. In return for accepting a higher risk, a provider of mezzanine finance receives a higher rate of interest and some form of equity stake in the company.

Key term

Mezzanine finance is not easily defined, but its constituent elements are:

(a)   **Unsecured** debt, typically in the form of subordinated bonds or notes with a maturity of up to about eight years. The rate of interest on the debt is higher than for senior debt/secured debt.

(b)   An **equity feature,** whereby the lender is entitled to an equity stake in the company, or possibly to share options.

Some organisations specialise in providing mezzanine finance. Borrowers are typically 'middle market' companies with annual revenues of around US$10 million to US$100 million, and typical amounts of capital provided are around US$3 million to US$15 million.

Traditionally, mezzanine finance has been used to bridge a 'gap' in financing for companies that have just had a management buyout (MBO) or management buy-in (MBI). However, lenders are willing to provide mezzanine finance for other situations, such as providing capital for the development of the company's business, or to help finance a takeover. The providers of this type of finance look for a company with **good cash flows**, that can support the level of debt that the borrowing company is taking on.

Mezzanine finance will rank below senior debt but ahead of equity shareholders in priority for repayment of their capital in the event that the company goes into liquidation.

4.4 Junk bonds

> **FAST FORWARD**
>
> **Junk bonds** are bonds with a non-investment grade credit rating. They are high risk investments, and trade on the second hand bond markets at a significant discount to par value.

Credit rating agencies use a scale of credit ratings. Bonds with a credit rating at or above a certain level are 'investment grade' and credit ratings below this are non-investment grade.

'**Junk bond**' is a US term for bonds with a non-investment grade credit rating. Because the risk of default on interest payments is relatively high, junk bonds must offer a much higher yield to bond investors than investment-grade bonds.

Suppose for example that a company makes an issue at par of 8% ten-year bonds with an investment grade credit rating. After the issue, the credit rating might be downgraded to junk bond status. If so, depending on the extent of the downgrading, the share price of the bond will fall, usually by a substantial amount. Investors will only be prepared to buy the bonds at a price that provides them with a high yield to compensate them for the credit risk they have taken on by purchasing the bonds. A fall in junk bond prices to 50.0 or even less is not uncommon.

There is a fairly active market in the US for junk bonds, but the market is much less developed in Europe. In Europe, there is a **high-yield bond market**, which are bonds issued by medium-sized companies. Due to the comparatively high credit risk with these bonds, the coupon offered to investors is higher than with 'conventional' bond issues by large organisations. At the moment, the high-yield bond market is very small.

4.5 Asset securitisation

> **FAST FORWARD**
>
> **Asset-backed securities** are bonds issued by a specially-created company with a finite life. They are used by organisations that own income-generating assets, such as mortgages, to sell the assets to raise immediate capital. Interest is paid to the bondholders out of income generated by the underlying assets (eg from mortgage interest payments and mortgage capital redemption).

The term '**securitisation**' means converting something into a security, such as shares or bonds.

Asset securitisation is a way of raising capital by converting assets that will provide a future stream of income into bonds. The bonds are called '**asset-backed securities**'.

Suppose for example that a bank has made a large number of mortgage loans to customers, and now wants to raise capital by selling them off. It might do this by arranging for a special company to be set up. This company (a '**special purpose vehicle**' or SPV) makes an agreement to buy the mortgages from the bank. It then makes an issue of securities (a few ordinary shares, but mostly bonds). Investors subscribe for the SPV bonds on the understanding that the loan interest will be paid out of the mortgage interest payments from the mortgages purchased by the SPV, and the eventual redemption of the bonds will be made from the repayment of the mortgage loans.

The SPV uses the capital raised from issuing its securities to purchase the mortgages from the bank. The bank has therefore converted its mortgage assets into cash. Investors in the SPV bonds will continue to receive interest from the SPV until the bonds mature, when the bonds will be redeemed and the SPV wound up.

5 Convertibles

Companies might occasionally raise capital by issuing **convertible bonds or bonds with share warrants attached**. Both convertibles and warrants are forms of **delayed equity**, because they might result in a new issue of shares at some time in the future. A convertible bond is a bond that can be exchanged at a future date, at the option of the bondholder, into a fixed quantity of new shares of the company. Warrants entitle their holder to subscribe for a quantity of new shares, at some time in the future, at a fixed exercise price.

Convertible loan stock is similar to convertible preference shares, and a company might choose to raise loan capital by issuing this type of bond.

Key term

> **Convertible securities** are fixed return securities that may be converted, on pre-determined dates and at the option of the holder, into ordinary shares of the company at a predetermined conversion rate.

Conversion terms often vary over time. For example, the conversion terms of convertible stock might be that on 1 April 2008, $2 of stock can be converted into one ordinary share, whereas on 1 April 2009, the conversion price will be $2.20 of stock for one ordinary share. Once converted, convertible securities cannot be converted back into the original fixed return security.

5.1 The conversion value and the conversion premium

The current market value of ordinary shares into which a unit of stock may be converted is known as the conversion value. For example, if $100 of convertibles can be converted into 20 ordinary shares and the current market value of the shares is $4 each, the conversion value of $100 of the stock is $80.

The **conversion value** will be below the face value of the loan stock at the date of the loan stock issue, but will be expected to increase as the date for conversion approaches, on the assumption that a company's shares ought to increase in market value over time. The difference between the issue value of the stock and the conversion value as at the date of issue is the implicit **conversion premium**.

5.2 Example: Convertible bonds

A company issues $25 million of 5% convertible bonds at 102.00. The bonds are convertible in five years' time into ordinary shares of the company, at the rate of 15 shares for each $100 of bonds. The current share price is $5.60.

(a)   The **conversion value** for each $100 of bonds is $15 \times \$5.60 = \$84$.

(b)   The bonds were issued at 102.00, and so the **conversion premium** is (102 – 84) $18 for 15 shares, or $1.20 per share. As a percentage of the conversion value, the conversion premium is (1.20/5.60) 21.43%.

5.3 The issue price and the market price of convertible loan stock

A company will aim to issue convertibles with the greatest possible conversion premium as this will mean that, for the amount of capital raised, it will, on conversion, have to issue the lowest number of new ordinary shares. The premium that will be accepted by potential investors will depend on the company's growth potential and so on prospects for a sizeable increase in the share price.

Convertible loan stock issued at par normally has a lower coupon rate of interest than straight debentures. This lower yield is the price the investor has to pay for the conversion rights. It is, of course, also one of the reasons why the issue of convertible stock is attractive to a company.

When convertible loan stock is traded on a stock market, its *minimum* market price will be the price of straight debentures with the same coupon rate of interest. If the market value falls to this minimum, it follows that the market attaches no value to the conversion rights.

The actual market price of convertible stock will depend not only on the price of straight debt but also on the current conversion value, the length of time before conversion may take place, and the market's expectation as to future equity returns and the risk associated with these returns. If the conversion value rises above the straight debt value then the price of convertible stock will normally reflect this increase.

Most companies issuing convertibles expect them to be converted. They view the stock as **delayed equity**. They are often used either because the company's ordinary share price is considered to be particularly depressed at the time of issue or because the issue of equity shares would result in an immediate and significant drop in earnings per share. There is no certainty, however, that the security holders will exercise their option to convert; therefore the stock may run its full term and need to be redeemed.

5.4 Example: convertible debentures

CD has issued 50,000 units of convertible debentures, each with a nominal value of $100 and a coupon rate of interest of 10% payable yearly. Each $100 of convertible debentures may be converted into 40 ordinary shares of CD in three years time. Any stock not converted will be redeemed at 110 (that is, at $110 per $100 nominal value of stock).

Estimate the likely current market price for $100 of the debentures, if investors in the debentures now require a pre-tax return of only 8%, and the expected value of CD's ordinary shares on the conversion day is:

(a) $2.50 per share
(b) $3.00 per share

Solution

(a)   *Shares are valued at $2.50 each*

If shares are only expected to be worth $2.50 each on conversion day, the value of 40 shares will be $100, and investors in the debentures will presumably therefore redeem their debentures at 110 instead of converting them into shares.

The market value of $100 of the convertible debentures will be the discounted present value of the expected future income stream.

Year		Cash flow $	Discount factor 8%	Present value $
1	Interest	10	0.926	9.26
2	Interest	10	0.857	8.57
3	Interest	10	0.794	7.94
3	Redemption value	110	0.794	87.34
				113.11

The estimated market value is $113.11 per $100 of debentures.

(b)   *Shares are valued at $3 each*

If shares are expected to be worth $3 each, the debenture holders will convert their debentures into shares (value per $100 of stock = 40 shares × $3 = $120) rather than redeem their debentures at 110.

Year		Cash flow/value $	Discount factor 8%	Present value $
1	Interest	10	0.926	9.26
2	Interest	10	0.857	8.57
3	Interest	10	0.794	7.94
3	Value of 40 shares	120	0.794	95.28
				121.05

The estimated market value is $121.05 per $100 of debentures.

5.5 Advantages and disadvantages of convertible bonds

Convertible bonds might have potential advantages to a company as a form of bond issue to raise capital.

(a) The coupon on convertibles is usually lower than the coupon on a comparable 'conventional' bond. This is because investors are willing to accept a lower rate of interest in return for the opportunity to benefit from a rise in the company's share price, and to convert their bonds into shares.

(b) If the company has good growth prospects, investor demand for its convertible bonds should be strong.

The disadvantages of convertibles are that:

(a) The market for convertible bonds is not large, due to a restricted interest in these bonds by investors.

(b) Since convertibles are issued with a conversion premium, the share price must rise by a minimum amount between the issue date and the conversion date, to make conversion of the bonds worthwhile. For this reason, if a company's growth prospects are not good, investors will be unwilling to invest in convertibles.

6 Bonds with share warrants attached

A share warrant gives its holder the right, at a future date, to subscribe for new shares in a company at a fixed subscription price.

Warrants are usually issued as part of a package with unsecured bonds. An investor who buys the bonds will also acquire a certain number of warrants. The purpose of warrants is to make the bonds more attractive.

Key term

> A **warrant** is a right given by a company to an investor, allowing him to subscribe for new shares at a future date at a fixed, pre-determined price (the **exercise price**).

Once issued, warrants are detachable from the stock and can be sold and bought separately before or during the 'exercise period' (the period during which the right to use the warrants to subscribe for shares is allowed). The market value of warrants will depend on expectations of actual share prices in the future.

During the exercise period, the market price of a warrant should not fall below the higher of:

(a) nil, and
(b) its 'theoretical value', which equals:

(Current share price – Exercise price) × Number of shares obtainable from each warrant.

If, for example, a warrant entitles the holder to purchase two ordinary shares at a price of $3 each, when the current market price of the shares is $3.40, the minimum market value ('theoretical value') of a warrant would be ($3.40 – $3) × 2 = 80c.

If the price fell below the theoretical value during the exercise period, then 'arbitrage' would be possible. For example, suppose the share price is $2.80 and the warrant exercise price is $2.20. The warrants are priced at 50c with each entitled to one share. Ignoring transaction costs, investors could make an instant gain of 10c per share by buying the warrant, exercising it and then selling the share.

For a company with good growth prospects, warrants will usually be quoted at a premium, known as the **warrant conversion premium**, prior to the exercise period. It is sometimes expressed as a percentage of the current share price.

6.1 Example: warrant conversion premium

An investor holds some warrants that can be used to subscribe for ordinary shares on a one-for-one basis at an exercise price of $2.50 during a specified future period. The current share price is $2.25 and the warrants are quoted at 50c. What is the warrant conversion premium?

Solution

The easiest way of finding the premium is to deduct the current share price from the cost of acquiring a share using the warrant, treating the warrant as if it were currently exercisable:

	$
Cost of warrant	0.50
Exercise price	2.50
	3.00
Current share price	2.25
Premium	0.75

You may be wondering why an investor would prefer to buy warrants at 50c when this means that it will cost him more to get the ordinary shares than if he bought them directly. The attractions of warrants to the investor are:

(a)   Low initial outlay - he only has to spend 50c per share as opposed to $2.25. This means that he could buy 4½ times as many warrants as shares or, alternatively, he could invest the remaining $1.75 in other, less risky investments.

(b)   Lower downside potential - his maximum loss per share is 50c instead of $2.25. Of course the risk of the loss of 50c is much greater than the risk of losing $2.25. The share price of $2.25 is below the exercise price. If it remained at this level until the end of the exercise period, the warrants would become worthless as it would not be worthwhile exercising them, and

(c)   High potential returns - see below.

6.2 The gearing effect of warrants

Warrants offer the investor the possibility of making a high profit as a percentage of the initial investment. This is because the price of the warrants will tend to move more or less in line with the price of the shares. Thus, if the share price rises by 50c the increase in the value of the warrant will be similar. For example, when the share price of a company is $2.25 and the cost of a share warrant is 50c, a 50c increase in share price is a gain of about 22% on investment, but a 50c increase in the warrant price is a 100% gain. This illustrates the so-called gearing effect of warrants.

Continuing with the example above, we can recalculate the premium, assuming a 50c rise in the share price and a 50c rise in the warrant price:

	$
Cost of warrant (50c + 50c)	1.00
Exercise price	2.50
	3.50
Current share price ($2.25 + 50c)	2.75
Premium	0.75

The premium has stayed the same.

Note also that the share price is now above the exercise price. The warrants now have an 'intrinsic value' of 25c (ie 275c – 250c).

In the short run the warrant price and share price normally move fairly closely in line with each other. In the longer term the price of the warrant and hence the premium will depend on:

    (a)   The length of time before the warrants may be exercised

    (b)   The current price of the shares compared with the exercise price, and

    (c)   The future prospects of the company

As the exercise period approaches, the premium will reduce. Towards the end of the exercise period the premium will disappear because, if there were a premium, it would be cheaper to buy the shares directly rather than via the warrant.

6.3 Advantages of warrants

The main **advantages of warrants to the company** wanting to raise capital are as follows.

    (a)   Warrants themselves do not involve the payment of any interest or dividends. Furthermore, when they are initially attached to bonds, the interest rate on the bonds will be lower than for a comparable straight debt, because investors will accept a lower interest rate on the bonds in return for the prospect of obtaining equity shares at a favourable price.

    (b)   Warrants make a bond issue more attractive and may make an issue of unsecured bonds possible where a conventional bond issue might not succeed in attracting investors.

    (c)   Warrants are a means of raising additional equity funds in the future.

The main **advantage of warrants to the investor** is the potential for a high, though speculative, profit on a relatively low initial investment.

Question 7.2   **Share warrants**

A company has issued share warrants. Each warrant gives its holder the right to subscribe for one new share in the company, in about three years time, at an exercise price of 780c. The warrants are traded on the Stock Exchange and have a market value of 68c. The current market price of the shares is 762c.

    (a)   What is the premium on the warrants?

    (b)   Do the warrants have an intrinsic value?

    (c)   Investor A buys shares in the company at 762c. Investor B buys warrants at 68c. Suppose the share price rises by 10c. What will be the gain (as a percentage of their investment) for investors A and B respectively?

(For the answer to this question, see the Answer section at the end of this book.)

7 Bank finance

A major source of debt capital for companies is **bank finance**, in the form of an overdraft facility, term loan or revolving credit facility. The **interest rate** on bank loans is usually **variable**, ie adjusted up or down in response to changes in official rates such as the bank base rate or LIBOR. Bank loans may be either secured or unsecured.

For many companies, it is not possible to raise capital by issuing bonds. Bond investors prefer to invest in larger companies, which are seen as less risky. **Bank lending,** however, is a major source of finance for many companies of all sizes. It might be either **secured or unsecured**: it is common for bank loans to be secured by a fixed charge or by a fixed and floating charge over assets of the borrowing company. The **interest rate** on bank loans is **usually variable**, and set at a margin above either base rate (an administered rate determined by the bank itself) or the London Inter-bank Offered Rate (LIBOR) which is a money market rate of interest.

7.1 Matching the bank lending facility to the borrower's needs

A loan facility should be arranged to meet the requirements of the borrower. There are different types of loan facility, each designed to meet different requirements and circumstances.

Three important factors in deciding what type of facility might be most appropriate are:

(a)   What is the loan facility for? Why does the borrower want the money?

(b)   How does the borrower expect to repay the loan capital? Where is the money going to come from to make the repayment?

(c)   Is it important that the bank should commit the funds, and so be unable to call in the loan on demand?

7.2 Finance for day-to-day operating requirements

The borrower might want to borrow money to cover day-to-day cash deficits from trading operations. A typical trading company incurs operating expenditures, for example by purchasing inventory and paying employees their wages and salaries. It also earns income from sales, when its debtors eventually pay what they owe. As a general rule, companies have to spend money before they earn it, and so may have short-term cash shortages, especially when the business is growing. It might need to borrow money to cover its short-term cash requirements, expecting to repay the loans out of its eventual operating income. The actual amount that the company needs to borrow should fluctuate over time, with the patterns of cash receipts and payments from business operations.

Day-to-day cash requirements to cover short-term cash deficits have traditionally been financed by a **bank overdraft**. However, a bank may also be willing to provide a **term loan** for the same purpose (see later).

7.3 Finance for capital expenditure

A company might need to borrow to finance a 'lump sum' expenditure, such as capital expenditure on land and buildings, or plant and machinery. If so, it might need all the money at once. Alternatively, it might need some of the money now, and some more later, because the capital expenditure programme is scheduled over a period of time, perhaps several months or even several years.

Finance for capital expenditure will often be repaid out of the income eventually earned from the capital assets acquired with the spending. In such circumstances, the borrower might be willing to repay the loan principal gradually, over time, from its operating income. Each loan payment by the borrower will consist partly of interest and partly of some capital repayment. The outstanding amount of the loan will therefore gradually reduce over time, until it is fully paid off by the end of the loan period.

Alternatively, the borrower might wish to repay the loan capital all in one single payment, at the end of the loan term. The lending bank must be satisfied that the borrower will be able to make the repayment in this way.

Bank lending to finance capital expenditure is normally in the form of:

(a)   A term loan, when the loan money is provided in full at the start of the loan period, or

(b)   A term loan, when the loan funds can be taken out at any time, for a period not exceeding the remaining duration of the loan facility and provided the maximum lending limit is not exceeded, or

(c)   A **revolving credit facility** (see later).

7.4 Committed funds

A loan facility might be committed or uncommitted. A **committed facility** means that the lending is pre-arranged, and can be accessed by the borrower:

(a)   At any time, within the duration of the facility
(b)   Up to the maximum amount of the facility

For example, if a bank overdraft facility for $5,000,000 is committed up to 31 December 2006, the borrower can run up an overdraft of up to $5 million at any time up to 31 December 2006. The bank cannot reduce the borrowing limit or shorten the period of the lending facility, because the facility is committed.

In return for giving a commitment in advance, the bank will charge a **commitment fee**. Usually, a commitment fee is an annual charge, for each year that the facility is available.

When a facility is **uncommitted**, the bank is not obliged to advance further funds when the borrower asks for them. Instead, the bank has some discretion in deciding whether or not to lend the extra money. The bank might even be able to call in money that has already been lent, for immediate repayment (eg with an uncommitted overdraft facility).

7.5 Overdraft facility

An overdraft facility is a traditional method for a bank to finance the short-term borrowing requirements of individuals and companies. As a general rule, the understanding is that the overdraft will be repaid out of future income. (A bank may offer a **term loan** instead of an overdraft, for the same purpose.)

Bank overdrafts should be familiar to you, perhaps even from direct personal experience! The basic features of an overdraft are listed below. Check which ones you are already aware of, and which you did not know about.

(a)   When the credit balance on the customer's account is used up, the customer may overdraw on the account, provided that the bank agrees.

(b)   A bank may agree to provide a customer with an overdraft facility, up to a stated amount, for a stated period of time.

(c)   The rate of interest on an overdraft is quite high, and much higher than for a term loan.

(d)   Interest is payable only on the overdraft balance, not on the total amount of the overdraft facility. A customer with an overdraft facility whose current account is in credit will therefore not pay any interest, so long as the account remains in credit.

(e)   A customer may repay an overdraft without giving notice. This differs from a term loan, where the customer may terminate the loan early, but usually only by giving notice to the bank.

(f)   An overdraft facility may be committed for a specified period of time, but this is fairly unusual. An overdraft facility is usually 'on demand' (uncommitted).

A company using a bank overdraft may be said to be using the overdraft to 'finance its working capital requirements'. The logic behind this statement is that a company's working capital consists primarily of inventories, receivables and payables. A bank overdraft is needed when investment is tied up in inventories and trade receivables, and the credit taken from creditors is insufficient to keep the company's bank account in credit.

7.6 Term loans

A term loan is a loan of a specified amount, for a specified length of time (the 'term' of the loan). Most term loans are for a period or 'maturity' of up to five years, but depending on conditions in the banking industry, term loans may be offered to 'good' customers for periods of up to ten years or possibly even longer.

The **interest on term loans** is usually at a variable rate, at a margin above the London Inter-bank Offered Rate (LIBOR) or base rate, although some term loans are at a fixed rate. As with bond interest, **tax relief** is given to corporate borrowers on the interest payments on bank loans.

The purpose of a term loan may be to finance one or more capital expenditures, such as the purchase of new long-term assets or a business acquisition. A term loan, rather than an overdraft facility, might also be to finance the borrower's working capital requirements.

A term loan is usually a committed facility for the full term of the loan, and is not 'on demand'. The loan capital is provided either:

(a) 'up front', in a single amount of money at the start of the loan term, or

(b) over an extended period of time, in several portions or 'tranches', as and when the borrower needs the money.

The borrower will pay **interest** on the amount of the loan capital that still remains unpaid (the amount of the loan 'outstanding').

The **loan capital** must be repaid in full by the end of the term of the loan, and the borrower needs to have sources of income out of which to afford the repayment. There are different ways in which the loan capital might be repaid, and the method of repayment will be agreed between the bank and the borrower. The method that is most appropriate in a particular instance will depend on when and how the borrower anticipates having the money to afford the capital repayment.

(a) **Amortisation**. If the borrower expects to repay the loan out of regular operating income, perhaps income generated by capital expenditure financed by the loan, the loan payments may provide for amortisation of the loan. Amortisation means that the loan capital will be repaid gradually over the term of the loan. The borrower makes regular loan payments, and each payment consists partly of interest and partly of some capital repayment. (*Note.* Repayment mortgage loans to individuals work on this same principle.)

(b) **Bullet repayment**. The borrower may pay nothing except interest throughout the term of the loan. Throughout the term of the loan, the loan capital still outstanding remains unchanged, and does not reduce in size (unlike amortisation). At the end of the loan term ('maturity'), the loan capital is then repaid in full in a single amount. The borrower has to have a source of income from which to make the bullet repayment at maturity. One way of doing this might be to negotiate a new term loan, and use the new loan to pay off the old loan.

(c) **Balloon repayment**. A borrower may be able to make some repayments of loan capital during the term of the loan, but not immediately. This may be, for example, because the loan is used to finance capital expenditure, and the extra income this earns will take time to build up. The loan payments might therefore start fairly small, consisting perhaps of interest only. Over time, however, loan payments grow larger (like a balloon being blown up), and include an increasing amount of loan capital repayment. The loan capital is therefore repaid in full over the term of the loan, but not in any significant amount until nearer maturity, or even at maturity. At maturity, the final loan payment will include a small interest element and will repay the last part of the loan capital outstanding.

Term loans are available not just in sterling, but in **any freely-traded foreign currency**, notably US dollars, euros, yen and Swiss francs. Borrowers may also arrange a 'multi-currency' facility, whereby a loan of up to a maximum agreed amount can be drawn in tranches of different currencies.

7.7 Revolving credit facility

A revolving credit facility is a lending agreement whereby the bank makes available to the borrower a specified maximum amount of loan capital for a specified term.

(a) The borrower can 'draw down' the loan capital in tranches, almost as and when required during the term of the facility.

(b) There isn't an agreed repayment schedule, and the borrower can repay the loan capital at any time. The loan capital must be repaid in full by the end of the term of the facility, and the total amount borrowed at any time cannot exceed the maximum limit of the facility.

(c) The borrower can repay some loan capital and then borrow more funds subsequently. In this respect, a revolving loan facility is different from a term loan.

(d) Each tranche is borrowed for a specific term, in the same way as a term loan. A borrower may draw down a tranche for, say, three months or six months. At the maturity of a tranche of loan, the borrower doesn't have to repay the loan capital. Instead, the loan can be 'rolled over'. In other words, the tranche of capital can be borrowed for a further period. Loans can be rolled over continually, if required, right up to the end of the credit facility.

(e) Interest is payable only on the loan capital outstanding, not on the full amount of the loans available under the facility.

A revolving credit facility is usually a committed facility, and the bank charges a commitment fee for providing it.

7.8 Example

It might clarify the nature of a revolving credit facility to show an illustrative example. Suppose that a company arranges a two-year revolving credit facility for $10 million, from 1 January Year 1. The borrower might borrow in tranches and make capital repayments as follows. (Note: Interest payments are ignored here.)

Date	Capital borrowed before the transaction	Draw down of funds	Repayment of funds	Capital borrowed after the transaction
Year 1	$m	$m	$m	$m
1 January	0	4.0		4.0
30 April	4.0	3.5		7.5
5 July	7.5		2.0	5.5
9 Sept	5.5	4.0		9.5
Year 2				
16 January	9.5		3.5	6.0
28 March	6.0	2.0		8.0
17 June	8.0		3.0	5.0
31 Dec	5.0		5.0	0

During the period, the company has borrowed in excess of $10 million, but the total amount outstanding at any time never exceeds the $10 million limit of the facility.

8 Leasing and hire purchase

Another source of finance for capital expenditure is leasing. A lessee enters an agreement to rent an asset from a lessor, who is the legal owner of the asset. An **operating lease** is an asset rental agreement where the term of the lease is significantly less than the useful life of the asset. A **finance lease** is an arrangement whereby a lessee obtains an asset from a lessor, for most or all of the useful life of the asset. With an operating lease, the lease payments are regarded as straightforward rental payments. With a finance lease, the arrangement is seen, in accounting terms, as the acquisition of a non-current asset by the lessee, which is financed by the lessor. Rental payments are therefore treated as a combination of part interest on the lease finance and part repayment of the lease finance.

The nature of leasing

Rather than buying an asset outright, using either available cash resources or borrowed funds, a business might lease an asset. **Leasing** is a popular source of finance in many countries. Leasing can be defined as a contract between a lessor and a lessee for the hire of a specific asset.

(a) The **lessor** retains ownership of the asset.

(b) The **lessee** has possession and use of the asset on payment of specified rentals over a period.

Many lessors are financial intermediaries such as banks and insurance companies. These organisations buy the equipment from the manufacturer, and then lease them to a company that wants to obtain them under a leasing arrangement. The range of assets leased is wide, and includes office equipment and computers, items of machinery, cars and commercial vehicles, aircraft, ships and buildings.

8.1 Types of leasing

Leases can be **finance leases** or **operating leases**. A further type of leasing arrangement is **sale and leaseback**, an arrangement which is similar to mortgaging.

Operating leases are rental agreements between a lessor and a lessee whereby:

(a) The lessor supplies the equipment to the lessee

(b) The lessor is responsible for servicing and maintaining the leased equipment

(c) The period of the lease is fairly short, less than the expected economic life of the asset, so that at the end of one lease agreement, the lessor can either lease the same equipment to someone else, and obtain a good rent for it, or sell the equipment second-hand

Operating leases are effectively a form of equipment rental arrangement. Much of the growth in leasing business in recent years has been in operating leases.

Finance leases are lease agreements between the user of the leased asset (the lessee) and a provider of finance (the lessor) for **most or all** of the asset's expected useful life.

8.2 Example

Suppose that a company decides to obtain a company car and finance the acquisition by means of a finance lease. A car dealer will supply the car. A finance house will agree to act as lessor in a finance leasing arrangement, and so will purchase the car from the dealer and lease it to the company. The company will take possession of the car from the car dealer, and make regular payments (monthly, quarterly, six monthly or annually) to the finance house under the terms of the lease.

There are other important characteristics of a finance lease.

(a) The lessee is responsible for the upkeep, servicing and maintenance of the asset. The lessor is not involved in this at all.

(b) The lease has a **primary period**, which covers all or most of the useful economic life of the asset. At the end of this primary period, the lessor would not be able to lease the asset to someone else, because the asset would be worn out. The lessor must therefore ensure that the lease payments during the primary period pay for the full cost of the asset as well as providing the lessor with a suitable return on his investment.

(c) It is usual at the end of the primary period to allow the lessee to continue to lease the asset for an indefinite **secondary period,** in return for a very low nominal rent, sometimes called a 'peppercorn rent'. Alternatively, the lessee might be allowed to sell the asset on a lessor's behalf (since the lessor is the owner) and to keep most of the sale proceeds, paying only a small percentage (perhaps 10%) to the lessor.

Under some schemes, a lessor leases equipment to the lessee for most of the equipment's life, and at the end of the lease period sells the equipment himself, with none of the sale proceeds going to the lessee.

8.3 Example

Returning to the example of the car lease, the primary period of the lease might be three years, with an agreement by the lessee to make three annual payments of $6,000 each. The lessee will be responsible for repairs and servicing, road tax, insurance and garaging. At the end of the primary period of the lease, the lessee might be given the option either to continue leasing the car at a nominal rent (perhaps $250 a year) or to sell the car and pay the lessor 10% of the proceeds.

8.4 Attractions of leasing

The attractions of leases to the supplier of the equipment, the lessee and the lessor are as follows.

(a) The supplier of the equipment is paid in full at the beginning. The equipment is sold to the lessor, and apart from obligations under guarantees or warranties, the supplier has no further financial concern about the asset.

(b) The lessor invests finance by purchasing assets from suppliers and makes a return out of the lease payments from the lessee. Provided that a lessor can find lessees willing to pay the amounts he wants to make his return, the lessor can make good profits. He will also get capital allowances on his purchase of the equipment.

(c) Leasing might be attractive to the lessee:

    (i) If the lessee does not have enough cash to pay for the asset, and would have difficulty obtaining a bank loan to buy it, and so has to rent it in one way or another if he is to have the use of it at all, or

    (ii) If finance leasing is cheaper than a bank loan: the cost of payments under a loan might exceed the cost of a lease

Operating leases have these further advantages.

(a) The leased equipment does not have to be shown in the lessee's published balance sheet. In contrast, assets obtained under a **finance** lease arrangement must be shown in the lessee's balance sheet as a non-current asset.

(b) The equipment is leased for a shorter period than its expected useful life. In the case of high-technology equipment, if the equipment becomes out of date before the end of its expected life, the lessee does not have to keep on using it, and it is the lessor who must bear the risk of having to sell obsolete equipment second-hand.

Not surprisingly perhaps, a major growth area in operating leasing has been in computers and office equipment (such as photocopiers and fax machines) where technology is continually improving.

8.5 Hire purchase

Financing arrangements similar to finance leases are **hire purchase finance** and **instalment credit finance**. With these, however, the borrower eventually acquires ownership of the asset. With leases, the asset remains the property of the lessor.

Another form of credit finance with which leasing can be contrasted is **hire purchase**, which is a form of instalment credit. There are two basic forms of instalment credit, whereby an individual or business purchases goods on credit and pays for them by instalments.

(a)   **Lender credit** occurs when the buyer borrows money and uses the money to purchase goods outright.

(b)   **Vendor credit** occurs when the buyer obtains goods on credit and agrees to pay the vendor by instalments. Hire purchase is an example of vendor credit.

Hire purchase is similar to leasing, with the exception that ownership of the goods passes to the hire purchase customer on payment of the final credit instalment, whereas a lessee never becomes the owner of the goods.

Hire purchase agreements nowadays usually involve a finance house.

(a)   The supplier sells the goods to the finance house.
(b)   The supplier delivers the goods to the customer who will eventually purchase them.
(c)   The hire purchase arrangement exists between the finance house and the customer.

The finance house will nearly always insist that the hirer should pay a deposit towards the purchase price, perhaps as low as 10%, or as high as 33%. The size of the deposit will depend on the finance company's policy and its assessment of the hirer. This is in contrast to a finance lease, where the lessee might not be required to make any large initial payment.

An industrial or commercial business can use hire purchase as a source of finance. With **industrial hire purchase**, a business customer obtains hire purchase finance from a finance house in order to purchase a non-current asset. Goods bought by businesses on hire purchase include company vehicles, plant and machinery, office equipment and farming machinery. Hire purchase arrangements for fleets of motor cars are quite common, and most car manufacturers have a link with a leading finance house so as to offer hire purchase credit whenever a car is bought.

When a company acquires a capital asset under a hire purchase agreement, it will eventually obtain full legal title to the asset. The HP payments consist partly of 'capital' payments towards the purchase of the asset, and partly of interest charges.

8.6 Example

For example, if a company buys a car costing $10,000 under an HP agreement, the car supplier might provide HP finance over a three year period at an interest cost of 10%, and the HP payments might be, say, as follows.

	Capital element	Interest element	Total HP payment
	$	$	$
Year 0: down payment	2,540	0	2,540
Year 1	2,254	746	3,000
Year 2	2,479	521	3,000
Year 3	2,727	273	3,000
Total	10,000	1,540	11,540

The tax position on a hire purchase arrangement is as follows.

(a)   The buyer obtains whatever capital allowances are available, based on the capital element of the cost. Capital allowances on the full capital element of the cost can be used from the time the asset is acquired.

(b)   In addition, interest payments within the HP payments are an allowable expense against tax, spread over the term of the HP agreement.

(c)   Capital payments within the HP payments, however, are not allowable against tax.

It might be useful to compare both leasing and hire purchase finance with the option of buying the asset, possibly with a bank loan as finance.

Leasing	Hire purchase
It might be easier to obtain lease finance from a finance leasing company than it is to obtain a bank loan. The lessee is able to obtain the use of the asset without having to pay for it in full 'up front'.	It might be easier to obtain HP finance from a finance company than it is to obtain a bank loan. The buyer is able to obtain the use of the asset without having to pay for it in full 'up front'. However, the buyer will be required to pay a percentage of the full cost as a down payment.
Lease finance might possibly be cheaper than purchase with a bank loan.	HP finance might possibly be cheaper than purchase with a bank loan.
The lessee never owns the asset, but the asset might have a low residual value at the end of its life, in which case ownership is not a significant issue with a finance lease.	The buyer eventually acquires ownership of the asset. If the asset has a high residual value, this could be a significant benefit.
When technological change is rapid, assets can get out of date quickly. By using operating leases, a company can continually upgrade its assets to the most recent up-to-date models.	

8.7 Sale and leaseback

In a **sale and leaseback arrangement**, a company sells an asset to a bank or finance company, and then leases it back. The asset is typically a building, and the company sells the building to raise capital, and leases it back because the building is in operational use.

A business that already owns an asset, typically a building, might agree to sell the asset to a financial institution and to lease it back on terms specified in the agreement.

The business raises capital by selling the asset and so has the benefit of the funds from the sale while retaining use of the asset. However, the lessee is now required to make lease payments on the asset to the financial institution. Sale and leaseback is therefore a form of raising capital by selling valuable assets, without losing the use of those assets.

Another advantage of sale and leaseback is that the company does not have to tie up capital in assets such as buildings. Instead, it can use its money to invest in 'core assets' of the business, in order to develop and grow the business.

The main disadvantage of sale and leaseback is its potential cost. The leaseback arrangement will include a provision for rent reviews on the property. Over time, rental costs will almost certainly rise, probably by large amounts. If the company still owned its property, it would not be faced with these rising costs.

9 Invoice discounting and debt factoring

The sources of finance described above are largely long-term finance. Companies are also able to raise short-term finance, usually by obtaining 'cash up front' for debts that it is owed.

9.1 Factoring

A **factor** or factoring organisation specialises in trade debts, and manages the debts owed to a client (a business customer) on the client's behalf.

> **Factoring** is an arrangement to have debts collected by a factor company, which advances a proportion of the money it is due to collect.

The main aspects of factoring are as follows.

(a)   Administration of the client's invoicing, sales accounting and debt collection service are carried out by the factor. The factor collects the debts in its own name, which means that the client's customers are aware that a factor is involved in the debt collection process.

(b)   The factor provides credit protection for the client's debts. It takes over the risk of loss from bad debts and so 'insures' the client against such losses. (This service is also referred to as 'debt underwriting' or the 'purchase of a client's debts'.) The factor usually purchases these debts 'without recourse' to the client, which means that if the client's debtors do not pay what they owe, the factor will not ask for his money back from the client.

(c)   The factor also provides finance to the client, by making payments to the client in advance of collecting the debts. This is sometimes referred to as 'factor finance' because the factor is providing cash to the client against outstanding debts.

9.2 The debts administration service of factoring companies

A company might be struggling just to do the administrative tasks of recording credit sales, sending out invoices, sending out monthly statements and reminders, and collecting and recording payments from customers. If the company's sales revenue is growing rapidly, or if its sales are changing from largely cash sales to largely credit sales, the accounting administration might be unable to cope with the extra work. A factoring organisation can help.

The administration of a client's debts by the factor covers:

(a)   Keeping the books of account for sales
(b)   Sending out invoices to customers
(c)   Collecting the debts
(d)   Credit control (ensuring that customers pay on time) and chasing late payers

For the client, the advantages are that the factor takes on a job of administration, thereby saving staff costs for the client. The factor can take advantage of economies of scale for a large debts administration organisation. This should enable the factor to price his services reasonably.

The factor's service **fee for debt administration** varies according to the size of the client's operation, but it is typically between 0.75% and 2% of the book value of the client's debts. A factor is unlikely to agree to provide a service to **small firms**, firms which have only recently been established, firms in a high-risk market or with a history of bad debts, or businesses selling small value items to the general public (such as mail order firms). A business might be considered too small for factoring if its annual revenue were less than US$250,000.

9.3 Credit protection (debt underwriting) and factoring

Many companies do not have the information or the capability to assess credit risks properly. Factors, however, do have this capability, and can therefore carry out the **credit control function** for a client, vetting individual customers and deciding whether to grant credit and how much credit to allow. Because they control credit in this way, they will also underwrite their client's debts. However, **a factor is not a debt collection agency** in the sense that he can be relied on to get money out of customers when no one else can. Factors are involved in normal receivables administration (bookkeeping, invoicing and credit management as well as collecting money) and do not want to get involved with problem customers.

Most factors provide a debts administration service in which **credit protection** is an integral part. This is because the service is usually without recourse to the client in the event of non-payment by the customer. Without recourse factoring or **non-recourse** factoring effectively means that the factor buys the client's debts from him and so the client is guaranteed protection against bad debts.

Under a **without recourse** arrangement, the factor assumes full responsibility for credit control, because he now bears the credit risk. The factors will approve the amount of credit to be allowed to individual customers by the client. The factor will keep a continuous watch over customers' accounts. If a payment becomes overdue, the factor will consult the client. The client may decide to take over the bad debt risk from the factor, rather than incur bad will from the customer if the factor were to take legal action to recover the debt. Otherwise the factor is free to take non-payers to court to obtain payment. Not every factoring organisation will purchase approved debts **without recourse** and **'with recourse'** factoring might be provided, for example for very large debts.

9.4 Making advances on debts (factor finance)

Some companies have difficulty in financing their trade receivables. **If a company's sales revenue is rising rapidly**, its total receivables will rise quickly too. Selling more on credit will put a strain on the company's cash flow. The company, although making profits, might find itself in difficulties because it has too many receivables and not enough cash. **If a company grants long credit to its customers**, it might run into cash flow difficulties for much the same reason. Exporting companies must often allow long periods of credit to foreign buyers. Factors offer their clients a debt financing service to overcome these problems, and will be prepared to advance cash to the client against the security of the client's receivables. The client will assign his receivables to the factor.

A factoring organisation might be asked by a client to advance funds to the client against the debts which the factor has purchased, up to 80% of the value of the debts. For example, if a client makes credit sales of $100,000 a month, the factor might be willing to advance up to 80% of the invoice value (here $80,000) in return for a commission charge, and interest will be charged on the amount of funds advanced. The rate of interest will be tied to bank base rate, and may be a little higher than the client would pay a bank for an overdraft. The balance of the money will be paid to the client when the customers have paid the factor, or after an agreed period.

Advances from factors should be used in order to finance the extra inventory and receivables required for growth. The funds should not be used to finance non-current assets, and should not be a long-term source of funds. Factor financing might help a company to adjust to growth, but growth does not continue indefinitely, and when business settles down at a steady level, the need for money in advance ought to disappear.

9.5 Advantages and disadvantages of factoring

The **advantages of factoring** for a business customer include the following.

(a) The business can pay its suppliers promptly, and so be able to take advantage of any early payment discounts that are available.

(b) Optimum inventory levels can be maintained, because the business will have enough cash to pay for the inventories it needs.

(c) Growth can be financed through sales rather than by injecting fresh external capital.

(d) The business gets finance linked to its volume of sales. In contrast, overdraft limits tend to be determined by historical balance sheets.

(e) The managers of the business do not have to spend their time on the problems of slow-paying debtors.

(f) The business does not incur the costs of running its own invoicing and debt collection department.

The disadvantages of factoring include

(a) Costs involved, debts are normally factored at a discount or for a fee, the scale of this fee should be assessed in comparison to the cost of other short-term finances. For example a 2.5% fee for debtors that normally settle within one month represents a significant annualised cost, and even if competitively priced there is still a cost.

(b) It may reduce the scope for borrowing since these debts will not be available as security.

(c) The direct link between the business and its customers is lost with the result that

   – queries and disputes have to be referred on

   – how the factor deals with customers impacts on how they view the company

   – some customers do not like this removed, third party, involvement and take their custom elsewhere

(d) Ending a debt factoring arrangement is similar to repaying debt as a company will need to effectively buy back any unsettled debts.

Exam focus point

In the December 2006 exam a question required a discussion of those advantages and disadvantages for 7 marks.

9.6 Factoring and bank finance

If a company arranges with a factor for advances to be made against its debts, the debts will become the security for the advance. This may require the consent of any bank which has a charge over the company's debts as part of a bank lending agreement. The bank may therefore wish to reduce the company's overdraft limit. Certainly, a company should inform its bank when it makes an agreement with a factor for advances against debts.

9.7 Example: factoring

A company makes annual credit sales of $1,500,000. Credit terms are 30 days, but its debt administration has been poor and the average collection period has been 45 days with 0.5% of sales resulting in bad debts which are written off.

A factor would take on the task of debt administration and credit checking, at an annual fee of 2.5% of credit sales. The company would save $30,000 a year in administration costs. The payment period would be 30 days.

The factor would also provide an advance of 80% of invoiced debts at an interest rate of 14% (3% over the current base rate). The company can obtain an overdraft facility to finance its receivables at a rate of 2.5% over base rate.

Should the factor's services be accepted? Assume a constant monthly sales revenue.

Solution

It is assumed that the factor would advance an amount equal to 80% of the invoiced debts, and the balance 30 days later.

(a)   The *current situation* is as follows, using the company's debt collection staff and a bank overdraft to finance all debts, at an interest rate of 14% - 3% + 2.5% = 13.5%.

Credit sales $1,500,000 pa
Average credit period   45 days

The annual cost is as follows:

	$
Finance/holding cost: $\dfrac{45}{365} \times \$1,500,000 \times 13.5\%$	24,966
Bad debts: 0.5% × $1,500,000	7,500
Total cost	32,466

(b)   *The cost of the factor.* 80% of credit sales financed by the factor would be 80% of $1,500,000 = $1,200,000. For a consistent comparison, we must assume that 20% of credit sales would be financed by a bank overdraft. The average credit period would be only 30 days. The annual cost would be as follows.

			$
Factor's finance:	$\dfrac{30}{365}$	× $1,200,000 × 14%	13,808
Overdraft:	$\dfrac{30}{365}$	× $300,000 × 13.5%	3,329
			17,137
Cost of factor's services: 2.5% × $1,500,000			37,500
Less savings in company's administration costs			(30,000)
Net cost of the factor			24,637

(c)   *Conclusion.* The factor is cheaper. In this case, the factor's fees exactly equal the savings in bad debts ($7,500) and administration costs ($30,000). The factor is then cheaper overall because it will be more efficient at collecting debts. The advance of 80% of debts is not needed, however, if the company has sufficient overdraft facility because the factor's finance charge of 14% is higher than the company's overdraft rate of 13.5%.

Exam focus point

> In the December 2006 exam you were required to determine the net financial cost/benefit of employing a debt factor for 10 marks.

9.8 Invoice discounting

Invoice discounting is related to factoring and many factors will provide an invoice discounting service. It is the purchase of a selection of invoices, at a discount. The invoice discounter does not take over the administration of the client's sales ledger, and the client is responsible for collecting the debt. The customer (debtor) whose debt has been sold is unaware of the invoice discounting arrangement.

A company should only want to have some invoices discounted when it has a temporary cash shortage, and so invoice discounting tends to consist of one-off deals.

Key term

> **Invoice discounting**: the purchase (by the provider of the discounting service) of trade debts at a discount. Invoice discounting enables the company from which the debts are purchased to raise working capital.

If a client needs to generate cash, he can approach a factor or invoice discounter, who will offer to purchase selected invoices and advance up to 75% of their value. At the end of each month, the factor will pay over the balance of the purchase price, less charges, on the invoices that have been settled in the month. (Receipts from the paid invoices belong to the invoice discounter or factor).

There is an element of credit protection in the invoice discounting service, but its real purpose is to **improve the client's cash flow**. Since the invoice discounter does not control debt administration, and relies on the client to collect the debts for him, it is a more risky operation than normal factoring and so a factor might only agree to offer an invoice discounting service to reliable, well-established companies.

9.9 Foreign trade and debt management: export factoring

Foreign debts raise the following special problems.

(a) When goods are sold abroad, the customer might ask for credit. The period of credit might be 30 days or 60 days, say, after receipt of the goods; or perhaps 90 days after shipment. Exports take time to arrange, and there might be complex paperwork. Transporting the goods can be slow, if they are sent by sea. These delays in foreign trade mean that exporters often build up large investments in inventories and receivables. These working capital investments have to be financed somehow.

(b) The risk of bad debts can be greater with foreign trade than with domestic trade. If a foreign debtor refuses to pay a debt, the exporter must pursue the debt in the debtor's own country, where procedures will be subject to the laws of that country.

The functions performed by an **overseas factor** or **export factor** are essentially the same as with the factoring of domestic trade debts. Many overseas factors are subsidiaries of banks or their agents, normally offering facilities to companies with annual export credit sales in excess of US$£250,000.

Small firms without a major overseas presence may gain from the provision of advice on the creditworthiness of overseas customers. Agents acting on their behalf in pursuing overseas debts may have useful expertise that can be tapped. However, export factoring is more expensive than the factoring of domestic debts.

10 Bills of exchange

Bills of exchange are a form of IOU, although they are perhaps described more accurately as a 'you owe me'. When A sells goods to B, the settlement of the debt might be arranged by means of a bill of exchange (called a **trade bill** as B is a trader). A will draw a bill on B, asking B to pay a certain sum of money on a certain date in the future, such as 90 days after the date of the bill. B then acknowledges the debt by **accepting** the bill. Acceptance involves signing the bill, and returns it to the drawer, A. By accepting the bill, B is acknowledging its debt to A and is giving a promise to pay. After the credit period (the term of the bill) has expired, B will pay A the money owed. A trade bill is therefore a form of trade credit.

A trade bill arrangement is therefore as follows.

(a) A company is owed money, and draws a bill on the organisation required to pay the debt (the 'drawee'). The bill is a 'you owe me'.

(b) The drawee acknowledges the debt by accepting it.

(c) The drawee must pay the amount owed on the date specified. A bill will specify the bank where the drawer should collect the payment.

10.1 Trade bills

When a company obtains payment from its customers through **trade bills**, it can arrange to obtain finance from its bank against the security of the bill. For example, if A sells goods to B for $50,000, the terms of payment might be agreed so that A draws a 90 day bill of exchange on B for $50,000, which B 'accepts'. A can then ask its bank to 'discount the bill'. A will then receive payment now from the bank of an amount that is less than the full face value of the debt, ie the payment is at a discount, instead of receiving full payment in 90 days from B. After 90 days, B must pay the holder of the bill, who might still be the bank.

The rate of discount on the bill, which is the cost to A of discounting, will depend on the 'quality' of the bill. A higher discount applies to trade bills (bills drawn on and accepted by companies such as B) than to bank bills (bills drawn on and accepted by a bank). A lower discount is called a 'finer' discount.

10.2 Bank bills

Banks might agree to accept a bill on a customer's behalf, provided that arrangements are made for the customer to reimburse the bank. For example, if C is owed money by D for a trade debt, the bank of D might agree to an arrangement whereby C draws a bill on the bank. The bank will accept the bill, and so give a promise to pay. C can then discount the bill (sell it at a discount). Banks are generally regarded as less of a payment risk than non-bank companies. The size of the discount will be lower for the bank bill than it would if the bill had been drawn on and accepted by D. (Bank bills can be discounted 'at finer rates', and are easier to find buyers for.)

Both trade bills and **bank bills** are used quite commonly in international trade. For example, suppose that Bulldog in the UK sells goods to a company in Singapore. The terms of payment might be for Bulldog to draw a bill of exchange on the Singapore company's bank (in the UK or Singapore). The bank bill could then be used by Bulldog to raise finance, with the bill attracting a finer rate of discount because it has been accepted by a reputable bank.

11 Bankers' Acceptance (BA) credit facility

Acceptance **credits** are a source of finance from banks for large companies, which are an alternative to bank overdrafts, but which make use of bank bills. Whereas a bank bill is normally drawn by another person on the bank, in a bankers' acceptance facility arrangement, the bills are drawn on the bank **by the customer**.

An acceptance credit facility, which is offered by clearing banks as well as merchant banks, operates as follows.

(a)   A bank and a large corporate customer agree a facility which allows the customer to draw bills of exchange on the bank, which the bank will accept. The bills are normally payable after 60 or 90 days, but might have a term as long as 180 days. They can be denominated in any required currency.

(b)   The accepted bills are then sold (discounted) by the bank in the discount market on behalf of the customer, and the money obtained from the sale, minus the bank's acceptance commission, is made available to the customer. Because of the bank's standing and reputation, bills accepted by it can be sold in the market at a low rate of discount.

(c)   When a bill matures, the company will pay the bank the value of the bill and the bank will use the money in turn to pay the bill holder.

A bank will only agree to provide an acceptance credit facility to a corporate customer of good standing, because the bank must be confident that its money is safe. The length of time over which the acceptance credit facility is available will be subject to agreement between the bank and the customer, but may be as long as five years. The customer can draw bills on the bank throughout this period, up to the credit limit.

Acceptance credits are attractive to customers for the following reasons.

(a)   They provide companies with alternative finance to a bank overdraft, with the money being obtained from a source outside the bank (the purchaser of the discounted bills).

(b)   The amount of credit is promised to the customer for a stated period of time.

(c) There may be a cost advantage to the customer, because the rate of discount on bank bills in the discount market might be lower than the interest rate on a bank loan, or overdraft, which is related to the bank base rate or LIBOR (London Inter-bank Offered Rate). The reason for this is mainly that the interest rate on a discounted bill is fixed for the life of the bill (typically 90 days) because this rate is inherent in the discounted sale price of the bill. If market interest rates are rising during this period, and overdraft rates are going up, it would be more costly to maintain an overdraft than to have an acceptance credit facility.

(d) The company can assess the cost of its credit facility with more certainty, because costs are fixed over the life of a bill.

12 PFI/PPP

The UK government has programmes to finance public service projects with private sector finance. Private sector companies become involved in the financing, construction and operation/management of the public services. The programmes are known as the **Private Finance Initiative (PFI)** and **Public-Private Partnership (PPP)**. These might be used to finance projects such as hospitals, schools and the upgrading of the London Underground service.

The **Private Finance Initiative (PFI)** and **Public-Private Partnership scheme (PPP)** are initiatives by the UK government for raising private capital for major public works programmes. PPP is seen by the government as an extension of its original PFI policy.

The aims of both PFI and PPP are to:

(a) Obtain private sector involvement in the design and operation of public services that require heavy capital investment

(b) Encourage competition between private sector firms or consortia, thereby obtaining this involvement at a competitive price

(c) Obtain private sector capital to finance projects, either in whole or in part, so that the private sector takes on some of the finance risk of the projects

(d) Obtain private sector involvement in the long term management and operation of the project.

The current UK government has pursued a policy of using private sector finance to undertake public sector investments, through the PFI and the PPP. Critics of PFI argue that using the private sector to finance schools, hospitals and other public sector investments is a way of making tomorrow's generation pay for today's government decisions. It might be useful to think about the stated aims of government economic policy in this area. In June 1998, the newly-elected UK Labour government issued a paper, *Stability and Investment for the Long Term*, setting out two new rules for fiscal policy.

(a) The first rule, known as the 'golden rule' was that over the business cycle, the government would only borrow to invest, and would not borrow to finance 'current' spending. This golden rule was based on the idea of 'inter-generational equity'. 'Those generations that benefit from public spending should also meet the cost.' Investment spending creates assets that will support services and benefit taxpayers in future generations as well as now, and so it has been deemed appropriate that future generations should help to pay the bill. Government policy in this area would help 'to match the cost and benefits of public spending across generations.'

(b) The second rule is the 'sustainable investment rule', that 'net public debt, as a proportion of GDP, will be held over the economic cycle at a stable and prudent level.' The government appears to intend that the debt level will be stable and at a prudent level if tax revenues allow the government to carry out its spending policies and also meet its interest payment obligations. A key control variable is now that the government should, over the economic cycle, balance its current spending budget (the public sector current budget or PSCB).

12.1 Private Finance Initiative (PFI)

The Private Finance Initiative is an arrangement whereby private sector organisations provide the capital for the construction of major public service assets, such as hospitals or schools.

The successful bidder for a PFI project will raise the capital to finance the project, build the asset and, when the asset has been built, manage and operate it for an agreed period of time, which may be 30 years or so.

Under a PFI arrangement, for example, a private sector firm might undertake to build a new hospital to agreed specifications, and when the hospital has been built and becomes operational, to manage the hospital's operations (ie provide facilities management) in return for agreed payments from the State.

Since PFI projects are still relatively new, it is not clear whether they will be a cost-effective way of financing public service projects, or whether they are merely an arrangement to defer large costs for the 'next generation' to finance.

PFI projects are undertaken by either a single firm, often a construction firm, or a consortium of construction firms. These firms do not have the capital to support a large number of different projects at the same time, because of the huge investments required. A feature of financing PFI projects has therefore been that a consortium of contractors might set up a special company and sell rights to future income from the project to this new company. The new company then issues securities, mainly bonds, to raise money from investors. The money raised from issuing the bonds is used to pay the consortium for the future income rights, and the consortium uses this money to finance the project. The bond investors will be paid interest out of the future project income, with any surplus going to the consortium.

Case Study

Jarvis, a quoted facilities management company, has a subsidiary that specialises in building and running schools under PFI deals with local authorities, and has signed at least 11 such contracts. This subsidiary accounts for 27% of the total group profits. For example, Barnhill Community School, in west London, cost £20m to build and the local council has contracted to make 25 annual payments of £1.6m to cover both building and operating costs. Jarvis takes both the asset and liability into its balance sheet for the 25-year contract. The company feels such deals are 20% cheaper than traditional funding, taking account of the high value of the school at the end of the PFI contract.

12.2 Public-Private Partnership

Public-private partnership (PPP) is a development from PFI. As its name implies, it is another type of arrangement for the financing of major public service projects, whereby both the government and consortia of private sector firms provide finance. Ownership of the projects is through shareholdings in specially-established companies.

Case Study

An example of a PPP arrangement is the UK government's arrangements for the London Underground system.

When a PPP project is completed, responsibility for management and operations lies with the companies providing the finance.

13 Finance and the small business

Despite the wide range of sources of finance, both equity and debt, **small companies** find it **very difficult to raise finance** to develop their business. Capital providers regard them as too much of an investment risk or credit risk.

This chapter has described a variety of sources of debt finance for companies. Most of these finance sources are much more easily-accessible to large and well-established companies than they are to small companies. Reasons for this include:

(a)   Private companies find it difficult to raise large amounts of new equity capital, because they cannot offer their shares to the public. Unlike public companies, they cannot issue shares on a stock exchange. The most important source of new equity is therefore retained profit. However, small companies are unlikely to earn large amounts of profit to retain.

(b)   Lenders will not be prepared to lend much money to companies that do not have a reasonable amount of equity capital. When a company relies too heavily on debt capital, the debt providers in effect take on too much of the financing risk.

(c)   Only large public companies are able to issue bonds in the market. Even medium-to-large companies are likely to find it difficult to raise capital by issuing junk bonds, because the market for these bonds is very small.

(d)   A traditional source of finance for all companies has been bank lending. However, banks will not lend to risky companies, except at high interest rates. If banks do agree to lend to small companies, the lending will probably be secured on assets of the company, or even on the personal assets of the company's owner-director. Owner-directors are often unwilling to allow a bank to take their personal property (eg private home) as security for a loan, or to provide a personal guarantee for a loan.

(e)   Mezzanine finance might be available to medium-sized companies with annual revenue of US$10 million or more, but not to smaller companies.

(f)   Due to the difficulty small companies have in obtaining finance, many small businesses rely on operating leases to acquire non-current assets.

The problems for small businesses in raising finance are due to a number of causes.

(a)   **Lack of information**. A potential lender has very little information about the business on which to make a credit assessment and base a lending decision. In contrast, larger companies must file annual accounts at Companies House. A potential lender might refuse to consider a request for finance unless the borrower is prepared to provide the required financial information. A bank, for example, might insist on obtaining extensive financial information about a potential borrower, including a budget.

(b)   **Inadequate security**. Lenders, particularly banks, might insist on security for any finance they provide. Bank loans are often secured by a fixed charge over one or more specific assets of the borrower's business, or by a fixed and floating charge over the entire business undertaking. Small businesses might not have sufficient assets of value to offer as security for a loan of the required amount.

(c)   **Funding gap**. A funding gap refers to the difference between the amount of funds that are available and the amount of funds that are needed. A small business might be able to obtain some finance from external sources, and to retain some profits for reinvestment. However, a small business often needs more new finance than it can obtain in order to grow at the rate it has the potential to achieve.

In certain situations, a small business might be able to raise **venture capital** (VC), either via a VC organisation or an individual (business angel). Venture capital is described in a later chapter.

A Government funded **Small Firms Loan Guarantee scheme** might guarantee loans from banks and other financial institutions for small firms that have viable business proposals but who have tried and failed to get a conventional loan because of a lack of security.

Exam focus point	A question in the December 2002 exam considered the problems that small businesses face in raising long-term finance, and asked for three examples of sources of long-term finance and/or assistance available specifically for such businesses.

14 Fixed versus floating rate of interest

> **FAST FORWARD**
>
> Bank finance is normally provided at a **floating** rate of interest, and bonds are usually issued at a fixed rate or 'coupon'.

For small companies wishing to borrow, a bank is normally the only source of funds. Interest on bank loans is charged at a **floating** (variable) rate of interest, and the rate charged will be a margin or 'spread' above either the bank's base rate or a LIBOR rate. The size of the spread will depend on the perceived creditworthiness of the borrower. 'Weak' applicants will be required to pay a higher spread.

Borrowing at a **fixed rate** of interest is usually only possible in the bond markets, which are accessible only to companies above a certain size. (However, if you have studied the Risk Management syllabus, you might be aware that it is possible to pay a fixed rate of interest by borrowing at a floating rate and arranging an **interest rate swap** in order to become a net payer of fixed interest.)

> **FAST FORWARD**
>
> **Fixed** rate borrowing can be preferable when interest rates are low and likely to rise. Floating rate borrowing is preferable when interest rates are expected to fall.

Large companies that have the choice of borrowing at a floating rate or a fixed rate have to decide which rate is preferable.

(a) Fixed rate borrowing has a known cost, and a company can budget its interest costs knowing exactly what they will be. Floating rate loans have an uncertain future cost, because the interest charge will rise or fall with changes in the base rate or LIBOR rate.

(b) If a company expects interest rates to go up in the future, it might decide to borrow at a fixed rate, in order to secure a low interest cost. If interest costs do rise, fixed rate borrowing will turn out to be cheaper than floating rate borrowing.

(c) On the other hand, if interest rates are expected to fall in the future, a company might choose to borrow at a floating rate, in order to benefit from lower interest charges when the rate does fall.

It is difficult to predict future movements in interest rates with certainty, and in practice companies that do have a choice between fixed and floating rate borrowing will often arrange a mixture of each. However, when interest rates are thought to be at their lowest point in the economic cycle, fixed rate borrowing in the bond markets will probably be cheaper, and when interest rates are thought to have reached their peak in the cycle, fixed rate borrowing will probably be avoided.

15 Internally-generated funds

The main source of new finance for most profitable companies, but especially small and medium-sized companies, is **retained profits.**

It is important to remember that for most profitable companies, retained profits are the major source of funding. For example, if a company maintains a dividend cover of two times (which is not particularly high in practice), this means that 50% of its after-tax profits are retained in the business. It is very unusual for a company to pay out all its profits in dividends, and the proportion of profits retained to provide long-term finance is typically in the region of 33% to 67%.

Small companies in particular rely on retained profits for new funding, because they often have difficulty in raising finance from any other source other than bank borrowing.

Generating retaining profits each year can represent a significant ongoing source of new finance for a business, each year that profits are retained is a new source.

Another source of internally generated funds comes from improvements in working capital management. Chasing receivables, delaying payables and minimising inventory holdings and holding times can provide a one-off boost to business funds, but this can only be one-off. While a company may contrive to generate profits indefinitely, there will always be a limit to the improvements it can make to the management of working capital.

In addition, there are few adverse effects to a business of generating profits, whereas any action to improve the control of working capital may have some unwanted adverse effects. For example chasing receivables can alienate customers, driving them away from the company. Delaying payables may alienate suppliers and, if this is overdone, they may refuse to sell to the business. Minimising stock holdings presents the risk of running out of stock, resulting in customers viewing the company as unreliable. In addition there will be the costs of the credit controllers and stock controllers needed to operate this policy.

In conclusion, ongoing profit generation is the primary internal source of funds. Improvements in the control of working capital can be used as a one-off measure but there are limits to what can be achieved and significant business risks from going too far.

Irrespective of the concerns noted in respect of working capital improvements, internal sources of finance are very much favoured by businesses as they are the easiest and cheapest sources. There is no extra cost involved in retaining profits, whereas there are extra costs involved in arranging bank borrowings or issuing debt, and issuing new equity represents the highest cost alternative. This, in essence, is the pecking order theory of finance, that a company should raise finance thought the cheapest/easiest route.

Chapter roundup

- A company may use long-term or short-term debt capital as sources of finance. The cost of debt capital is **interest**.

- Companies might raise debt capital from investors by issuing **bonds**, also called **loan stock** or **debenture stock**. These are debt capital issued in the form of securities (**securitised debt**), usually at a fixed rate of interest. Bonds issued by public companies are traded in a secondary bond market after issue.

- The interest rate on bonds (the **coupon**) is usually close to the current market rate when bonds are issued, therefore bonds are usually issued at a price close to their par value. Bonds, unless convertible into equity, are redeemed at maturity either at par value or (less usually) at a price above par.

- **Interest** payable by a company on its debt capital, including interest on bonds, is an **allowable expense for tax purposes**. Interest costs are therefore deducted from profits in calculating the amount of profit that is liable to tax.

- Bonds might be **secured** on the assets of the company. However, unlike bank loans, it is quite common for bonds to be **unsecured**. International bonds (eurobonds) are unsecured. Investors assess the creditworthiness of the borrower by the **credit ratings** given to the bond issue by credit rating agencies.

- The **bond markets** are accessible only to **large companies**.

- The **market value of a bond** after its issue represents the amount investors are willing to pay for the bond's future income stream (interest payments and repayment of principal at maturity). It is the **present value** of the future cash flows from the bond, discounted at a cost of capital that is the investment return required by the bond investors.

- **Senior debt** gives its holders prior rights to payment of interest and, in the event of the liquidation of the company, to repayment of the debt capital. **Subordinated debt (junior debt)** ranks behind senior debt (but ahead of equity shareholders) in this order of priority. Senior debt, which might be a bank loan, is often secured by a charge on the company's assets.

- **Mezzanine finance** is a form of unsecured lending that also includes an arrangement giving an equity interest to the borrower. It might be available to medium-sized companies in situations where conventional loans are not available, for example to companies subject to an MBO or MBI.

- **Junk bonds** are bonds with a non-investment grade credit rating. They are high risk investments, and trade on the second hand bond markets at a significant discount to par value.

- **Asset-backed securities** are bonds issued by a specially-created company with a finite life. They are used by organisations that own income-generating assets, such as mortgages, to sell the assets to raise immediate capital. Interest is paid to the bondholders out of income generated by the underlying assets (eg from mortgage interest payments and mortgage capital redemption).

- Companies might occasionally raise capital by issuing **convertible bonds or bonds with share warrants attached**. Both convertibles and warrants are forms of **delayed equity**, because they might result in a new issue of shares at some time in the future. A convertible bond is a bond that can be exchanged at a future date, at the option of the bondholder, into a fixed quantity of new shares of the company. Warrants entitle their holder to subscribe for a quantity of new shares, at some time in the future, at a fixed exercise price.

- A major source of debt capital for companies is **bank finance**, in the form of an overdraft facility, term loan or revolving credit facility. The **interest rate** on bank loans is usually **variable**, ie adjusted up or down in response to changes in official rates such as the bank base rate or LIBOR. Bank loans may be either secured or unsecured.

BPP
LEARNING MEDIA

- Another source of finance for capital expenditure is leasing. A lessee enters an agreement to rent an asset from a lessor, who is the legal owner of the asset. An **operating lease** is an asset rental agreement where the term of the lease is significantly less than the useful life of the asset. A **finance lease** is an arrangement whereby a lessee obtains an asset from a lessor, for most or all of the useful life of the asset. With an operating lease, the lease payments are regarded as straightforward rental payments. With a finance lease, the arrangement is seen, in accounting terms, as the acquisition of a non-current asset by the lessee, which is financed by the lessor. Rental payments are therefore treated as a combination of part interest on the lease finance and part repayment of the lease finance.

- Financing arrangements similar to finance leases are **hire purchase finance** and **instalment credit finance**. With these, however, the borrower eventually acquires ownership of the asset. With leases, the asset remains the property of the lessor.

- In a **sale and leaseback arrangement**, a company sells an asset to a bank or finance company, and then leases it back. The asset is typically a building, and the company sells the building to raise capital, and leases it back because the building is in operational use.

- The UK government has programmes to finance public service projects with private sector finance. Private sector companies become involved in the financing, construction and operation/management of the public services. The programmes are known as the **Private Finance Initiative (PFI)** and **Public-Private Partnership (PPP)**. These might be used to finance projects such as hospitals, schools and the upgrading of the London Underground service.

- Despite the wide range of sources of finance, both equity and debt, **small companies** find it **very difficult to raise finance** to develop their business. Capital providers regard them as too much of an investment risk or credit risk.

- Bank finance is normally provided at a **floating** rate of interest, and bonds are usually issued at a **fixed** rate or 'coupon'.

- **Fixed** rate borrowing can be preferable when interest rates are low and likely to rise. Floating rate borrowing is preferable when interest rates are expected to fall.

- The main source of new finance for most profitable companies, but especially small and medium-sized companies, is **retained profits**.

Quick quiz

1   What is a eurobond?

2   A company issues 7.5% loan stock at par. The rate of tax is 30%. What is the after-tax cost of the debt capital for the company?

3   What is junior debt?

4   A construction company enters an agreement with a health authority to finance the building of a new hospital, and to be responsible both for its construction and for the management of the hospital for 30 years after it has been built. What is the name given to this type of government financing arrangement?

5   What are the two main differences between leasing an asset and acquiring an asset under a hire purchase arrangement?

6   X is owed $12,000 by a customer, C. X draws a bill of exchange, payable after 90 days, on C. How can this arrangement be used to raise immediate finance for X?

7   FGH arranges a bankers' acceptance facility with its bank. How will this enable FGH to raise short-term finance?

8   What are the three main elements of factoring?

9   A difference between factoring and invoice discounting is that with one arrangement, the debtors are aware of its existence, and with the other type of arrangement, they are not. Which is which?

Answers to quick quiz

1 A bond issued in the international bond market, and marketed to investors in more than one country. It may be denominated in any freely-convertible currency, such as US dollars or euros.

2 $7.5\% \times (1 - 0.3) = 7.5\% \times 0.7 = 5.25\%$.

3 Subordinated debt. This is debt that ranks behind other debt capital in terms of rights to payment of interest and rights to repayment of capital in the event of the winding up of the company and the liquidation of its assets.

4 A Private Finance Initiative (PFI) programme.

5 With a leasing arrangement, the asset remains the property of the lessor. With HP, the buyer eventually acquires ownership of the asset, when the final payment has been made. Secondly, with a leased asset, the capital allowances for tax purposes are claimed by the lessor. The lessee claims the lease payments as an expense for tax purposes. With HP, the buyer claims the capital allowances, and also tax relief on the interest element of the HP payments.

6 X draws the bill on C. C accepts the bill, and so acknowledges that it will pay the amount due on the date stipulated. On receipt of the accepted bill, X can arrange for its bank to discount the bill, ie sell it at a discount to its face value, in the 'discount market' for bills. The size of the discount reflects an interest rate to the provider of the finance (the buyer of the bill) for the period up to the payment date for the bill.

7 FGH can raise finance by drawing bills on its bank, which the bank will accept and then sell on the discount market. The proceeds from the sale are given to FGH, thereby providing short-term finance. When the bills mature, FGH must provide its bank with the money for the bank to meet its payment obligations on the bills.

8 Administration of the client's debts (invoicing, debt collection). If there is non-recourse factoring, credit insurance. Finally, the factor provides finance, by paying a percentage of the face value of the debts to the client before the money has been collected.

9 Factoring: the client's customers are aware of the factor and make their payments to the factor. With invoice discounting, the client is unaware of the arrangement, and makes payment to the company in the normal way.

Financing options

8

Introduction

Each company must choose an appropriate capital structure, ie the balance of the various possible sources of finance such as ordinary shares, preference shares, bonds and so on.

This chapter starts to consider how a company should set about making such a decision, looking at both long-term sources of finance and short-term sources of finance.

1 Capital structure and sources of finance

Financial strategy issues relating to **capital structure** are deciding from which source to raise new capital. Decisions include choosing a suitable balance between debt capital and equity capital (gearing level), and deciding to what extent current assets can safely be financed by current liabilities.

Capital structure refers to the way in which an organisation is financed, by a combination of long-term capital (equity capital, preference shares, bonds, bank loans, convertible loan stock and so on) and short-term liabilities, such as a bank overdraft and trade payables. It refers in particular to:

(a)   The balance between equity and debt capital, and

(b)   The balance between long-term and short-term finance.

The sources of new finance chosen by a company will affect its capital structure. Raising new debt capital, for example, will increase the proportion of debt in the capital structure, whereas retaining profits will increase the proportion of equity.

Equally, a financial policy of maintaining a particular capital structure (eg a target debt: equity ratio) will affect a company's choices about where any new finance should come from.

The purpose of this chapter is to look at:

(a)   How a company might forecast its total new funding requirements

(b)   How a company might assess its capital structure

(c)   How changes in capital structure might affect the perceived risk of investing in the company, and the return required by investors

(d)   How a company might choose sources of finance to close its funding gap

We shall begin by looking at total funding requirements and estimating the funding gap, and then go on to consider the choice between equity and debt capital for new finance. We shall then look at the balance between long-term and short-term capital, and the problems of under-capitalisation and overtrading.

1.1 Principles of capital structure

The assets of a business must be financed somehow, and when a business is growing, the additional assets must be financed by additional capital.

As a general rule, assets that yield profits over a long period of time should be financed by long-term funds. In this way, the returns made by the asset will be sufficient to pay either the interest cost of the loans raised to buy it, or dividends on its equity funding. If, on the other hand, a long-term asset is financed by short-term funds, the company cannot be certain that when the loan becomes repayable, it will have enough cash (from profits) to repay it.

It is usually prudent for a company not to finance all of its short-term assets with short-term liabilities, but instead to finance short-term assets partly with short-term funding and partly with long-term funding.

1.2 Long-term capital requirements for replacement and growth

A distinction can be made between long-term capital that is needed to finance the replacement of worn-out assets, and capital that is needed to finance growth. If a company is not growing and only needs finance to maintain its current level of operations, including the replacement of non-current assets, its main sources of funding are likely to be internally-generated, provided that the rate of inflation is reasonably low. In contrast, when a company is seeking to **grow**, it will need extra finance.

1.3 Debt and financial risk

A high level of debt creates financial risk. **Financial risk** can be seen from different points of view.

(a) **The company** as a whole. If a company builds up debts that it cannot pay when they fall due, it will be forced into liquidation.

(b) **Creditors**. If a company cannot pay its debts, the company will go into liquidation owing creditors money that they are unlikely to recover in full.

(c) **Ordinary shareholders**. A company will not make any distributable profits unless it is able to earn enough profit before interest and tax to pay all its interest charges, and then tax. The lower the profits or the higher the interest-bearing debts, the less there will be, if there is anything at all, for shareholders. When a company has *preference shares* in its capital structure, ordinary shareholders will not get anything until the preference dividend has been paid.

1.4 Debt v preference shares

Legally, preference shares are part of the share capital of a business. Commercially, however, there is little difference between preference shares and unsecured debt (especially subordinated debt). Both preference shares and debt

- normally pay a fixed annual return (interest or dividends)
- may be irredeemable, redeemable at a pre-set value or convertible.

For a profitable going concern there is no commercial difference, and as a result it is normal to treat preference shares effectively as debt when considering gearing ratios.

The only true difference that arises is in respect of the risk to investors. In particular

- If profitability is low a company can cut any preference dividend, but it cannot avoid interest on debt.

- If a company becomes insolvent, preference shareholders rank below all debt holders, even subordinated debt.

To compensate for this additional risk, preference shareholders are liable to receive a higher return than long-term debt holders.

Within our consideration of capital structure, however, it would be best to consider the true commercial substance and treat any preference shares as a form of debt.

2 Using financial forecasts

FAST FORWARD

> **Balance sheet projections** and **forecast cash flow statements** can be used to estimate the size of future funding gaps. These forecasts can be used as a starting point for deciding how much new finance might be required, and from what sources they should be obtained.

Raising new finance can be a fairly lengthy process. A company should therefore try to anticipate its funding requirements in advance, and keep them under continual review. One technique for forecasting finance requirements is to make projections of financial statements.

A financing deficit can be anticipated by preparing either a projected balance sheet or a projected cash flow statement, based on:

(a) Estimates of future profits

(b) A forecast of asset requirements, and

(c)   Financial policy targets, such as the company's intended dividend policy, the debt: equity ratio in the capital structure, and working capital targets, for example, for inventory turnover and debt collection periods.

The forecast balance sheet or cash flow statement might reveal a funding gap. A **funding gap** is simply the difference between the funds (finance) that a company thinks it will need, and the finance that will be available, based on the assumptions in the forecast. If a funding gap is expected, the company should then consider the most appropriate ways of closing it.

2.1 Financial targets

In addition to setting financial objectives for growth in earnings and earnings per share, and in dividend per share, a company might set **other financial targets**, such as:

(a)   A restriction on the company's level of **gearing**, or debt. For example, a company's management might decide that:

(i)   The ratio of long-term debt capital to equity capital should never exceed, say, 1:1

(ii)   The cost of interest payments should never be higher than, say, 25% of total profits before interest and tax

(b)   A target for **profit retentions**. For example, management might set a target that dividend cover (the ratio of the annual profit available for distribution to the dividends actually distributed) should not be less than, say, 2.5 times.

(c)   A target for **operating profitability**. For example, management might set a target for the profit/sales ratio (say, a minimum of 10%) or for a return on capital employed (say, a minimum ROCE of 20%).

These financial targets are not primary financial objectives, but they can act as subsidiary targets or constraints which should help a company to achieve its main financial objective without incurring excessive risks.

A major problem with setting a number of different financial targets, either primary targets or supporting secondary targets, is that they might not all be consistent with each other, and so might not all be achievable at the same time. When this happens, some compromises will have to be accepted.

2.2 Example: forecast balance sheet

Lion Grange has recently introduced a formal scheme of long range planning. Sales in the current year reached $10,000,000, and forecasts for the next five years are $10,600,000, $11,400,000, $12,400,000, $13,600,000 and $15,000,000. The ratio of net profit after tax to sales is 10%, and this is expected to continue throughout the planning period. Net asset turnover, currently 0.8 times, will remain more or less constant. Net asset turnover is the ratio of sales revenue in the year to the amount of net assets the company needs to sustain these sales.

It was suggested at a recent board meeting that:

(a)   If profits rise, dividends should rise by at least the same percentage

(b)   An earnings retention rate of 50% should be maintained. This is the ratio of retained profits to distributable profits. Dividends should therefore also be just 50% of distributable profits

(c)   The ratio of long-term borrowing to long-term funds (debt plus equity) is limited (by the market) to 30%, which happens also to be the current long term borrowing: long-term funds ratio ('gearing ratio') of the company

You are required to prepare a financial analysis of the draft long range plan.

Solution

The draft financial plan, for profits, dividends, assets required and funding, can be drawn up in a table, as follows.

	Current year $m	Year 1 $m	Year 2 $m	Year 3 $m	Year 4 $m	Year 5 $m
Sales	10.00	10.60	11.40	12.40	13.60	15.00
Net profit after tax (10%)	1.00	1.06	1.14	1.24	1.36	1.50
Dividends (50% of profits after tax)	0.50	0.53	0.57	0.62	0.68	0.75
Net assets (125% of sales)	12.50	13.25	14.25	15.50	17.00	18.75
Equity (increased by retained earnings)	* 8.75	9.28	9.85	10.47	11.15	11.90
Maximum debt (30% of net assets)	3.75	3.97	4.28	4.65	5.10	5.63
Funds available	12.50	13.25	14.13	15.12	16.25	17.53
Shortfall in funds **	0	0	(0.12)	(0.38)	(0.75)	(1.22)

* Equity. In the current year, the equity figure is the balancing figure, equal to the difference between total net assets and the amount of debt capital. In subsequent years, the equity rises by the amount of retained profits, on the assumption that there will be no new issue of shares.

** Shortfall in funds. This is the difference each year between the net assets required and the funds available, assuming that debt capital will not exceed 30% of net assets.

The forecast reveals an increasing funding gap, starting in Year 2. The company's management will have to consider ways of closing this gap.

(a) The company could plan a new share issue, or decide to allow the ratio of debt capital to net assets to rise above 30%.

(b) In Years 2 and 3, the shortfall can be eliminated by retaining a greater percentage of profits, but this may have a serious adverse effect on the share price. In year 4 and year 5, the shortfall in funds cannot be removed even if dividend payments are reduced to nothing.

(c) The net asset turnover might be lower than it could be. The situation would be eased if investments were able to generate a higher volume of sales, so that fewer non-current assets and less working capital would be required to support the projected level of sales. For example, a reduction in the requirement for net assets by $1.22 million in Year 5 would close the Year 5 funding gap. This would reduce net assets from $18.75 million to $17.53 million. The net asset turnover would have to improve from 0.8 times to (15.00/17.53) about 0.86 times.

(d) If asset turnover cannot be improved, it may be possible to increase the profit to sales ratio by reducing costs or increasing selling prices. Higher profits would help to reduce the funding gap, because retained profits would be higher.

(e) If a new issue of shares is proposed to make up the shortfall in funds, the amount of funds required must be considered very carefully. Total dividends would have to be increased in order to pay dividends on the new shares. The company seems unable to offer prospects of suitable dividend payments, and so raising new equity might be difficult.

(f) It is conceivable that extra funds could be raised by issuing new debt capital, so that the level of gearing would be over 30%. It is uncertain whether investors would be prepared to lend money so as to increase gearing. If more funds were borrowed, profits after interest and tax would fall so that the share price might also be reduced.

Question 8.1 Funding gap

A company has the following current balance sheet.

	$
Non-current assets	100,000
Current assets minus current liabilities (working capital)	20,000
	120,000
Equity, capital	90,000
Long-term debt	30,000
	120,000

The company has made the following forecasts of profitability over the next three years

Profits after tax

	$
Year 1	60,000
Year 2	75,000
Year 3	75,000

These profit forecasts are based on the assumption that assets will be increased as follows.

End of:	Non-current assets $	Working capital $
Year 1	120,000	30,000
Year 2	140,000	40,000
Year 3	160,000	50,000

The company intends to pay two-thirds of profits after tax as dividends to shareholders.

Required

(a) Assuming these estimates and targets are applied, calculate the funding gap in each year.
(b) Suggest briefly how the funding gap might be eliminated

(For the answer to this question, see the Answer section at the end of this book.)

2.3 Using financial forecasts to evaluate financing proposals

Financial forecasts can be used to assess the effect on the company's financial position of a proposal to finance a capital expenditure by one method or another.

2.4 Example

A summarised draft balance sheet of Rufus is as follows.

	$ million
Assets less current liabilities	150
Debt capital	(70)
	80
Share capital (20 million shares of $1)	20
Reserves	60
	80

The company's profits in the year just ended are as follows.

	$ million
Profit before interest and tax	21.0
Interest	6.0
Profit before tax	15.0
Taxation at 30%	4.5
Profit after tax (earnings)	10.5
Dividends	6.5
Retained profits	4.0

The company is now considering an investment of $25 million. This will add $5 million each year to profits before interest and tax.

(a) There are two ways of financing this investment. One would be to borrow $25 million at a cost of 8% per annum in interest. The other would be to raise the money by means of a 1 for 4 rights issue.

(b) Whichever financing method is used, the company will increase dividends per share next year from 32.5c to 35c.

(c) The company does not intend to allow its gearing level, measured as debt finance as a proportion of equity capital plus debt finance, to exceed 55% as at the end of any financial year. In addition, the company will not accept any dilution in earnings per share.

Assume that the rate of taxation will remain at 30% and that debt interest costs will be $6 million plus the interest cost of any new debt capital.

Required

(a) Produce a profit forecast for next year, assuming that the new project is undertaken and is financed (i) by debt capital or (ii) by a rights issue.

(b) Calculate the earnings per share next year, with each financing method.

(c) Calculate the effect on gearing as at the end of next year, with each financing method.

Solution

Current earnings per share are $10.5 million/20 million shares = 52.5 cents.

If the project is financed by $25 million of debt at 8%, interest charges will rise by $2 million. If the project is financed by a 1 for 4 rights issue, there will be 25 million shares in issue.

	Finance with debt	Finance with rights issue
	$m	$m
Profit before interest and tax (+ 5.0)	26.0	26.00
Interest	8.0	6.00
	18.0	20.00
Taxation (30%)	5.4	6.00
Profit after tax	12.6	14.00
Dividends (35p per share)	7.0	8.75
Retained profits	5.6	5.25
Earnings (profits after tax)	$12.6 m	$14.0 m
Number of shares	20 million	25 million
Earnings per share	63 c	56 c

The projected balance sheet as at the end of the year will be:

	Finance with debt $m	Finance with rights issue $m
Assets less current liabilities	180.6	180.25
(150 + new capital 25 + retained profits)		
Debt capital	(95.0)	(70.00)
	85.6	110.25
Share capital	20.0	25.00
Reserves	65.6	* 85.25
	85.6	110.25

* The rights issue raises $25 million, of which $5 million is represented in the balance sheet by share capital and the remaining $20 million by share premium. The reserves are therefore the current amount ($60 million) plus the share premium of $20 million plus retained profits of $5.25 million.

	Finance with debt	Finance with rights issue
Debt capital	95.0	70.0
Debt capital plus equity finance	(95.0 + 85.6)	(70.0 + 110.25)
Gearing	53%	39%

Either financing method would be acceptable, since the company's requirements for no dilution in EPS would be met with a rights issue as well as by borrowing, and the company's requirement for the gearing level to remain below 55% is (just) met even if the company were to borrow the money.

Exam focus point

There was a 20 mark question on using financial forecasts to evaluate financing proposals in the June 2007 exam.

2.5 Using forecasts of cash flow

Instead of forecasting a funding gap by drawing up forecast balance sheets, a company could forecast its funding requirements by preparing forecast cash flow statements. This is a statement that sets out:

(a)   Cash flows from operating profits. These can be estimated as operating profits before interest and taxation, plus depreciation charges

(b)   Interest payments

(c)   Taxation payments

(d)   Payments to acquire non-current assets (or receipts from the sale of non-current assets)

(e)   Dividend payments

(f)   Cash flows from financing activities

2.6 Example: forecast cash flow statement

A company has a current cash balance of $30,000. It has made the following estimates for the next three years:

	Year 1 $	Year 2 $	Year 3 $
Operating profit before interest and tax	25,000	35,000	50,000
Depreciation charges	35,000	63,000	63,000
Payments of:			
Interest	10,000	10,000	10,000
Taxation	9,000	12,000	16,000
Dividends	8,000	12,000	20,000

The company's forecasts of growth in profits are based on an assumption that there will be spending on capital equipment of $120,000 in Year 1 and $150,000 in Year 3.

The company does not anticipate any change in its working capital requirements.

Required

On the basis of these assumptions, calculate the cash shortage (funding shortage) that the company might anticipate over the next three years.

Solution

	Year 1	Year 2	Year 3
	$	$	$
Operating profit before interest and tax	25,000	35,000	50,000
Depreciation charges	35,000	63,000	63,000
Cash flows from operations	60,000	98,000	113,000
Payments of:			
Interest	(10,000)	(10,000)	(10,000)
Taxation	(9,000)	(12,000)	(16,000)
Capital expenditure	(120,000)		(150,000)
Dividends	(8,000)	(12,000)	(20,000)
Cash surplus/(deficit) for the year	(87,000)	64,000	(83,000)
Cash at start of year	30,000	(57,000)	7,000
Cash at end of year	(57,000)	7,000	(76,000)

This forecast shows a cash deficit in Year 1 and Year 3. The deficit is quite large in proportion to the company's profits, and it seems likely that the funding gap will have to be closed by raising long-term capital.

3 Financial ratios for assessing capital structure

FAST FORWARD

Financial ratios for assessing the balance between debt capital and equity capital in a company's capital structure are the **interest cover ratio**, the **debt ratio** and the **gearing ratio**.

Several financial ratios can be used to assess capital structure. Three ratios are used to assess the balance between debt capital and equity in the capital structure. These are:

(a)   The interest cover ratio
(b)   The debt ratio
(c)   The gearing ratio

Each of these ratios looks at the level of debt in a company's capital structure, and can be used to assess the financial risk in that amount of debt. Financial risk refers to the possibility that the company might be unable to meet all its debt obligations, and might default on the payment of interest or the repayment of loan principal. The higher the proportion of debt in the capital structure, the greater is the financial risk, particularly when interest rates are high. (In contrast, when interest rates are low and falling, a company should be able to support a larger amount of debt.)

3.1 Interest cover

Interest cover is a measure of financial risk that is designed to show the financial risk in terms of profit. The basic question is: 'Are the company's profits sufficient to meet its interest payment obligations, bearing in mind that profits might possibly fall in the future?'

The interest cover ratio is simply the ratio of annual profits before interest to the amount of annual interest payments.

$$\text{Interest cover} = \frac{\text{Profit before interest and tax}}{\text{Interest}}$$

The reciprocal of this, the interest to profit ratio, is also sometimes used.

As a general guide, an interest cover of **less than three times** (3.0) is considered low, indicating that profitability is too low given the debt level of the company. An interest cover ratio below two times (2.0) would be considered dangerously low, suggesting that the company should either increase operating profits, or consider reducing its debts and replacing debt capital with new equity.

3.2 The debt ratio

The **debt ratio** is another measure of financial risk. It is the ratio of a company's total debts, long-term and short-term, to its total assets. Total assets are defined as net non-current assets plus total current assets. (Long-term provisions and liabilities, such as deferred taxation, are ignored.)

Another way of looking at the amount of debt is the ratio of debt to equity (the **debt/equity ratio**).

There is no firm rule on the maximum safe debt ratio, but as a general guide, you might regard 50% as a safe limit to debt. In practice, many companies operate successfully with a higher debt ratio than this, but 50% is a helpful benchmark. If the debt ratio is over 50% and getting worse, the company's debt position will be worth looking at more closely, and management should consider ways of reducing the debt burden.

4 Gearing

Gearing is the ratio of prior charge capital to either equity capital or total capital. It is a term that is used to refer to the balance between debt capital and equity capital.

The term '**gearing**' (or '**leverage**') is used to refer to the proportion of debt capital in a company's capital structure. The actual definition of **financial gearing** is the relationship between 'prior charge capital' and equity capital. Prior charge capital is any form of long-term capital that has a prior right to payment of interest or dividends, ahead of equity shareholders (and a prior right to the return of capital in the event of a winding up of the company). It therefore includes preference share capital as well as debt capital.

There are two ways of defining the financial gearing ratio.

$$\text{Gearing} = \frac{\text{Prior charge capital}}{\text{Equity capital}} \times 100\%$$

$$\text{Gearing} = \frac{\text{Prior charge capital}}{\text{Total capital employed}} \times 100\%$$

Prior charge capital = long-term debt capital (including lease finance) + preference share capital, and it might also include short-term debt (bank overdraft and loans repayable within 12 months). **Equity capital** is the total of ordinary share capital plus balance sheet reserves. **Total capital employed** is the sum of prior charge capital and equity capital.

With the first definition of gearing above, a company is low geared if the gearing ratio is less than 100%, highly geared if the ratio is over 100% and neutrally geared if it is exactly 100%. With the second definition, a company is neutrally geared if the ratio is 50%, low geared below that, and highly geared above that.

Suppose the balance sheet of a company is as follows.

	$
Non-current assets at cost	750,000
Less accumulated depreciation	180,000
Non-current assets at net book value	570,000
Current assets	290,000
	860,000

Ordinary share capital	160,000
Reserves	270,000
	430,000
Long-term debt	310,000
Current liabilities	120,000
	860,000

The current liabilities consist of a bank overdraft of $50,000, a bank loan of $60,000 that is repayable in six months' time, and trade payables.

When gearing is measured as prior charge capital as a proportion of equity capital, the gearing ratio is:

(a) (310,000/430,000) × 100% = 72%, if the definition of debt capital is to exclude short-term interest-bearing debt; or

(b) (310,000 + 50,000 + 60,000)/430,000 = 0.98 or 98%, if the definition of debt capital is to include short-term interest-bearing debt.

This company is fairly low-geared, and there is no reason to suspect that there is too much debt in its capital structure.

Question 8.2 — Financial gearing ratio

From the following balance sheet, compute the company's financial gearing ratio.

	$'000	$'000
Non-current assets		12,400
Current assets		1,000
		13,400
Capital and reserves		
Called up share capital		
Ordinary shares		1,500
Preference shares		500
		2,000
Share premium account		760
Revaluation reserve		1,200
Retained earnings		2,810
		6,770
Non-current liabilities		
Debentures	4,700	
Bank loans	500	
Deferred tax	300	
Deferred income	250	
		5,750
Current liabilities		
Loans	120	
Bank overdraft	260	
Trade payables	430	
Bills of exchange	70	
		880
		13,400

(For the answer to this question, see the Answer section at the end of this book.)

4.1 Gearing ratios based on market values

An alternative method of calculating a gearing ratio is one based on **market values**:

$$\frac{\text{Market value of debt (including preference shares)}}{\text{Market value of equity} + \text{Market value of debt}} \times 100\%$$

The **advantage** of this method is that potential investors in a company are able to judge the further debt capacity of the company more clearly by reference to market values than they could by looking at balance sheet values. A company with high asset values in its balance sheet might have poor profits after tax and low dividends, so that the gearing ratio based on market values might be high (with debt capital worth more than equity) whereas the gearing ratio based on balance sheet values would be lower. The company should find the task of raising new debt capital fairly difficult, because of its low profitability and consequent high gearing ratio based on market values.

The **disadvantage** of a gearing ratio based on market values is that it disregards the value of the company's assets, which might be used to secure further loans. A gearing ratio based on balance sheet values arguably gives a better indication of the security for lenders of fixed interest capital.

5 The effect of gearing on earnings

FAST FORWARD

When a company has debt capital (ie is geared), changes up or down in the company's profits before interest and tax have a greater (percentage) effect on earnings per share. The change in earnings per share for a given percentage change in PBIT is greater in higher-geared companies than in lower-geared companies. This potential variability in earnings per share is the major reason why the financial risk for equity investors increases as the gearing level increases.

The level of gearing in a company's capital structure has a considerable effect on the amount of earnings attributable to the ordinary shareholders.

A highly geared company must earn enough profits to cover its interest charges before anything is available for equity. On the other hand, if borrowed funds are invested in projects which provide returns in excess of the cost of debt capital, then shareholders will enjoy increased returns on their equity.

Provided that a company can generate returns on capital in excess of the interest payable on debt, introducing financial gearing into the capital structure will enable **earnings per share** to be raised. If the company fails to generate such returns, earnings per share will be reduced, and so gearing increases the **variability of shareholders' earnings**. Gearing, however, also increases the probability of **financial failure** occurring through a company's inability to meet interest payments in poor trading circumstances.

A further important aspect of gearing is the effect on equity returns as a result of a rise or fall in profitability. When the profits of a company rise or fall, the change in the return on equity capital is greater for a higher-geared company than for a lower-geared company.

5.1 Example

Suppose that there are two identical companies, X and Y, earning exactly the same amount of profit before interest and tax (PBIT). PBIT in each company is $10,000, and the rate of tax is 30%. The only difference between the two companies is that X is all-equity, financed by 100,000 shares of $1 each (no reserves) and Y is financed by a mixture of 50,000 shares of $1 each (no reserves) and $50,000 of fixed rate 10% debt.

When profit before interest and tax is $10,000, the earnings per share is 7c in each company.

	X $	Y $
Profit before interest and tax	10,000	10,000
Interest	-	5,000
Profit before tax	10,000	5,000
Tax at 30%	3,000	1,500
Profit after tax (earnings)	7,000	3,500
Number of shares	100,000	50,000
Earnings per share	$0.07	$0.07

If PBIT rises, the earnings per share will rise by a larger percentage amount in the geared company Y than in the ungeared company X.

Suppose PBIT rises by 20% to $12,000. EPS will rise in the ungeared company by 20% to 8.4c. In the geared company, EPS will rise by more than 20%.

	X $	Y $
Profit before interest and tax	12,000	12,000
Interest	-	5,000
Profit before tax	12,000	7,000
Tax at 30%	3,600	2,100
Profit after tax (earnings)	8,400	4,900
Number of shares	100,000	50,000
Earnings per share	$0.084	$0.098
Increase in EPS	20%	40%

On the other hand, if PBIT falls, the earnings per share will fall by a larger percentage amount in the geared company Y than in the ungeared company X.

Suppose PBIT falls by 20% to $8,000. EPS will fall in the ungeared company by 20% to 5.6c. In the geared company, EPS will fall by more.

	X $	Y $
Profit before interest and tax	8,000	8,000
Interest	-	5,000
Profit before tax	8,000	3,000
Tax at 30%	2,400	900
Profit after tax (earnings)	5,600	2,100
Number of shares	100,000	50,000
Earnings per share	$0.056	$0.042
Fall in EPS	20%	40%

This example illustrates a key aspect of financial risk and gearing. The risk with gearing is not simply the risk that a company might be unable to meet its interest payment obligations when it is highly-geared. There is, more significantly, the risk of a sharp fall in earnings per share if the company's profits were to fall. The effect on EPS would be greater for shareholders in a higher-geared company than for shareholders in a lower-geared company. An investor in shares who does not want a significant financial risk in his investment would therefore prefer to invest in a low-geared company than in a high-geared company.

It is also important to recognise that the financial risk from high gearing is a two-way risk, in the sense that there is an 'up side' for investors as well as a downside. The downside risk is that earnings per share could fall sharply if profits fall. The up side is that earnings per share could rise sharply if profits rise. Even so, equity investors in high-geared companies will expect a higher return, to compensate them for the higher financial risk.

5.2 Breakeven point in PBIT

Exam focus
point

An examination question might ask you to calculate the level of PBIT at which earnings per share will be the same for two companies that are identical in every respect except for their gearing. A method of calculating the PBIT breakeven is illustrated in the example below.

5.3 Example

Two companies A and B are identical in every respect except for their gearing. A is financed by 150,000 shares of $1 each and $150,000 of 8% debt. B is financed by 200,000 shares of $1 each and $100,000 of 8% debt.

The tax rate is 30%. If both companies earn exactly the same profit before interest and tax, at what level of PBIT will earnings per share be exactly the same in each company?

Solution

Let the PBIT, in $000, be $P

	A $'000	B $'000
Profit before interest and tax	P	P
Interest	12	8
Profit before tax	(P – 12)	(P – 8)
Tax	30%	30%
Earnings	0.7 (P – 12)	0.7 (P – 8)
Number of shares (in 000s)	150	200
EPS	$\dfrac{0.7 (P - 12)}{150}$	$\dfrac{0.7 (P - 8)}{200}$

The EPS will be the same in each company when:

$$\frac{0.7\,(P - 12)}{150} = \frac{0.7\,(P - 8)}{200}$$

$$140\,(P - 12) = 105\,(P - 8)$$

$$140P - 1{,}680 = 105P - 840$$

$$35P = 840$$

$$P = 24$$

Breakeven PBIT is $24,000.

You can check this if you are not sure. The EPS is 5.6c in each company when PBIT is $24,000.

6 Factors influencing the choice of financing methods

FAST FORWARD

Factors influencing the choice of financing method, other than gearing, include the company's **profitability**, the **relative cost** of different sources of finance, **ease of access** to different sources of finance, **dilution of ownership** with some forms of equity issue, maximum **borrowing limits**, other loan covenants and the **restrictions on management decision-making** these might cause, the **security** required for borrowing and whether adequate security can be provided, whether a particular method of raising finance can be 'sold' to investors, **conditions in the capital markets** and the **purpose** for which the finance is required.

The selection of financing methods for raising new capital will be influenced by a variety of factors.

Profitability. Retained profits are an important source of new funding, but these are available only to profitable companies.

The cost of capital. Companies should try to raise new finance at the lowest marginal cost. When there is a choice between debt and equity, one is likely to be a cheaper option than the other. The after-tax cost of debt finance is usually lower than the cost of equity, and it might therefore be supposed that companies will always prefer to raise new capital in the form of debt rather than equity. However, as the gearing ratio increases, existing equity investors might require higher returns to justify the increasing financial risk, and the overall effect of higher gearing might therefore be to increase the company's cost of capital (its WACC). The relationship between financial risk and returns is explored in more depth later in this chapter.

The cost of raising funds. There are expenses involved in raising capital, such as fees to financial advisers and solicitors, and underwriting fees (for share issues). Some methods of raising finance are cheaper than others. For example, it is cheaper to raise new equity through a placing than through an offer for sale.

Dilution of ownership. Dilution of ownership occurs when the existing shareholders in a company suffer a reduction in the proportion of the total equity capital in the company that they own. A dilution of ownership will occur when new shares are issued to investors other than the existing shareholders. With the exception of rights issues, new issues of shares therefore result in a dilution of ownership. If existing shareholders are reluctant to support a rights issue, they might prefer their company to raise new capital by borrowing, so that dilution does not occur.

Maximum loan limits. When companies borrow from a bank, the lending bank will insist on various covenants being written into the loan agreement. A covenant is an undertaking by the borrower, and breach of a covenant will put the borrower in default. (Similarly, when a company makes a bond issue, there will be covenants.)

A common type of covenant is one that places restrictions on a company's ability to raise new debt capital, or that sets a borrowing limit on the total debt capital the company is permitted to have. If a company has an existing bank loan or bond issue that restricts its total borrowings, and it is nearing the permitted borrowing limit, the company might be unable to raise new capital by borrowing, without breaching its covenant. In such a situation, the company would have to consider equity capital as its only funding option (unless it can redeem the loan or bond issue to which the restrictive covenant applies, and so free itself from the restriction).

Interference in decision-making. Loan covenants given by a borrower might have the effect of restricting the borrower's freedom of action. If a bank insists on excessively harsh covenants, a company might decide against obtaining a bank loan. Examples of restrictive covenants are listed below.

Covenant	Purpose
Not to dispose of any non-current assets of substantial value, unless new assets are purchased to replace them.	A company needs to maintain its non-current assets in order to carry on getting sales revenue and making profits, out of which the loan interest will be paid. Substantial asset disposals could reduce the borrower's profit-making capability.
Not to dispose of any substantial non-current assets, nor any business operation of the company, unless the proceeds from the disposal are used to pay back some or all of the loan.	The purpose of this covenant is the same as the one above, except that the company is allowed to make disposals provided the money is used to pay back some or all of the loan.

Covenant	Purpose
Not to acquire another business during the term of the loan or facility.	The purpose of this covenant would be to prevent the company from taking an excessive risk by purchasing a new business that might turn out to be a bad acquisition. A bad acquisition would damage the company's profitability and affect its ability to meet its loan payment obligations.
Not to lend any money to a third party (unless it is in the normal course of the borrower's business).	This covenant would prevent the borrower from using its cash to make a loan to someone, thus converting a no-risk asset (ie cash) into an asset (ie the loan to the third party) where the risk of non-payment could be high.
Not to pay any dividends to ordinary shareholders, and not to buy back any shares from shareholders, except with the consent of the bank.	This covenant might be included in a loan agreement to a small company, where the loan is part of a venture capital funding arrangement. The covenant does not ban payments to shareholders, but calls for prior approval by the bank.

Security required. With debt finance, the lender often requires security, in the form of a charge over assets of the company. A company might be unable to borrow if it has insufficient assets to offer as security.

Persuading investors to provide the capital. When a company wants to raise new capital in the market, by issuing shares or bonds, it has to make the issue attractive. The issue therefore needs to be 'marketable'. Investors will want to know why the capital is required, and what returns are expected from investing it. If the reasons for wanting the capital are unconvincing, investors are unlikely to subscribe to the issue.

Conditions in the market. Conditions in the capital markets change over time. The international bond markets go through periods when particular types of bond issue are in demand, and other times when investors are unwilling to buy particular types of bond, or even any bonds at all. For example, the market for convertible bonds, or for sterling-denominated bonds go through periods of strong demand from investors and weak demand. A company might be advised to make a particular type of bond issue to take advantage of a window of opportunity.

In the same way, the demand for new share issues goes through cycles. When share prices are rising and the economic outlook is good, investors are keen to buy shares. When share prices are falling, or when companies in a particular industrial sector are doing badly, raising capital through share issues might be impossible (unless the shares are issued at a very large discount to the current market price, an option that the company is unlikely to take).

Purpose. The choice of financing method will be affected by the purpose for which the capital is required. Short-term finance, such as factor finance, should be used to finance day-to-day operations ('working capital'). Similarly, a bank overdraft should be used to finance day-to-day operations, and should not be used to acquire long-term assets.

7 Short-term financing and capital structure

In addition to deciding the optimal balance between debt and equity, a company should also consider the balance between long-term and short-term capital. There are different ways in which a balance between long-term and short-term funds might be achieved. Short-term funding includes:

(a)   A bank overdraft
(b)   Trade payables (ie buying supplies on credit)
(c)   Factor finance and invoice discounting

BPP
LEARNING MEDIA

(d)   Bill finance

(e)   Acquiring equipment under operating lease agreements

The diagram below illustrates three alternative types of policy A, B and C. The dotted lines A, B and C are the cut-off levels between short-term and long-term financing for each of the policies A, B and C respectively. Assets above the relevant dotted line are financed by short-term funding while assets below the dotted line are financed by long-term funding.

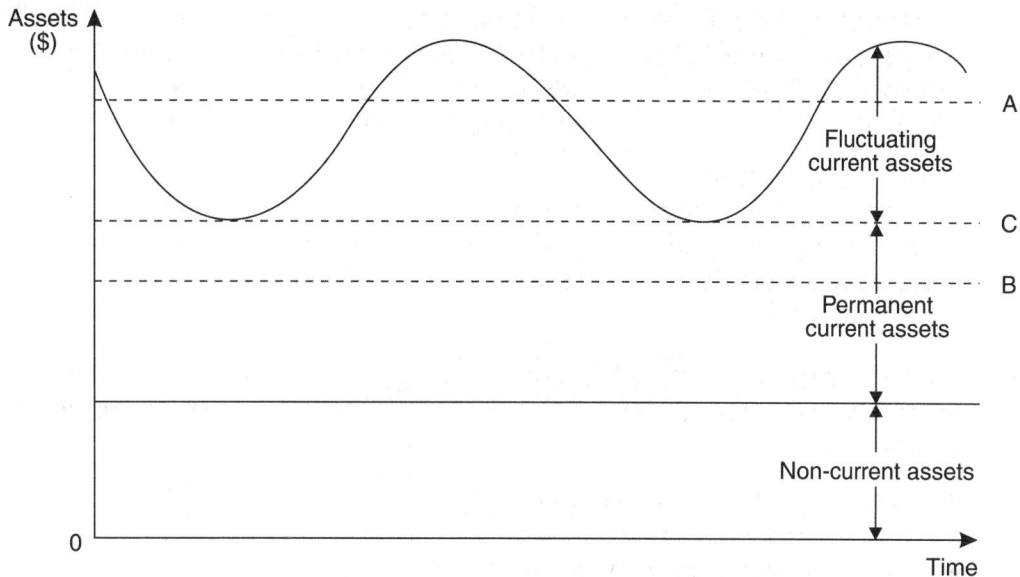

Fluctuating current assets together with permanent current assets form part of the working capital of the business. These assets may be financed by either long-term funding (including equity capital) or by current liabilities (short-term funding). This can be seen in terms of policies A, B and C.

(a)   Policy A can be characterised as **conservative**. All non-current assets and permanent current assets, as well as part of fluctuating current assets, are financed by long-term funding. There is only a need to call upon short-term financing at times when fluctuations in current assets push total assets above the level of dotted line A. At times when fluctuating current assets are low and total assets fall below line A, there will be surplus cash which the company will be able to invest in marketable securities.

(b)   Policy B is more **aggressive** in its approach to financing working capital. Not only are fluctuating current assets all financed out of short-term sources, but also a part of the permanent current assets. This policy presents an increased risk of liquidity and cash flow problems, although potential returns will be increased if short-term financing can be obtained more cheaply than long-term finance.

(c)   A **balance** between risk and return might be best achieved by policy C, in which long-term funds finance permanent assets while short-term funds finance non-permanent assets.

8 Working capital ratios

You should already be familiar with the financial ratios that are used to analyse a company's working capital management. Brief reminders of the ratios are given below.

8.1 What is working capital?

Key term

> The **net working capital** of a business can be defined as its current assets minus its current liabilities.
>
> (a) **Current assets** are mainly cash, inventories of raw materials, work in progress and finished goods, and amounts receivable from debtors.
>
> (b) **Current liabilities** may include amounts owed to trade creditors, taxation payable, dividend payments due, short-term loans, long-term payables maturing within one year, and so on.

The items of working capital that are particularly relevant to the amount of capital a company needs to maintain are inventories, receivables and trade payables.

(a) A company needs to acquire inventories. A retail business needs to acquire inventories for resale. A manufacturing business has to acquire raw materials, and has to pay employees to convert these into finished goods. It must also hold inventories of finished goods until they can be sold.

(b) A company must usually sell goods on credit, and will not receive payment from customers until some time after the sale has been made.

A company's investment in inventories and receivables represents the expenditures it must incur on operational items before it can make money back from its sales. To some extent, a business can finance its investment in inventories and receivables by delaying payments to its own suppliers.

Supermarkets provide an extreme example of this. A supermarket chain buying goods for resale from a supplier will often sell the goods in its stores and receive cash from customers long before it has to pay suppliers for the goods. In this situation, inventories are entirely financed by the trade creditors of the business.

However, a company must be sure that its cash flows are adequate, and that it always has the money coming in from customers to meet its payment obligations to suppliers.

8.2 What is working capital management?

Ensuring that sufficient liquid resources are maintained is a matter of working capital management. This involves achieving a balance between the requirement to minimise the risk of insolvency and the requirement to maximise the return on assets.

Working capital management can often best be assessed with the aid of ratios, however working capital management ratios, as with all ratios, need to be treated with caution. For example the current ratio and the quick ratio compare the scale of the current assets or the more liquid current assets to the scale of the current liabilities.

The number that comes out from a ratio calculation is, however, largely irrelevant and sense can only be made from it in comparison to the same ratio for a prior period, a competitor or a budget.

A current ratio of 1 tells you nothing on its own. What ratios are useful for is identifying trends and discontinuities. For example.

- If the current ratio this year is 1, the same as it has been for the last 10 years, then this appears to be normal for this business and is not a matter for concern.

- If the current ratio this year is 1, but has been 0.5 for the last 10 years then something has changes and this change warrants investigation. It is not necessarily a problem, for example it may be a temporarily large cash balance from the sale of excess property, but the cause needs investigating.

With working capital management, ongoing trends are generally positive, whilst discontinuities warrant investigation.

8.3 The current ratio and the quick ratio

A standard test of liquidity is the **current ratio**.

$$\text{Current ratio} = \frac{\text{Current assets}}{\text{Current liabilities}}$$

Companies are not able to convert all their current assets into cash very quickly. In particular, some manufacturing companies might hold large quantities of raw material inventories, which must be used in production to create finished goods. Finished goods might be warehoused for a long time, or sold on lengthy credit. In such businesses, where inventory turnover is slow, most inventories are not very liquid assets. For these reasons, we calculate an additional liquidity ratio, known as the quick ratio or acid test ratio.

The **quick ratio** or **acid test ratio** is:

$$\text{Quick ratio} = \frac{\text{Current assets less inventories}}{\text{Current liabilities}}$$

8.4 The receivables collection period

A rough measure of the average length of time it takes for a company's debtors to pay what they owe is the '**receivables days**' ratio, or **receivables collection period**.

$$\text{Receivables days} = \frac{\text{Trade receivables}}{\text{Credit sales turnover}} \times 365 \text{ days}$$

This estimate of receivables days is only approximate.

(a)   The balance sheet value of receivables might be abnormally high or low compared with the 'normal' level the company usually has.

(b)   Sales revenue in the income statement excludes sales tax, but the receivables' figure in the balance sheet includes sales tax. We are not strictly comparing like with like.

8.5 The inventory turnover period

Another ratio worth calculating is the inventory turnover period, or inventory holding period days. This is another estimated figure, obtainable from published accounts, which indicates the average number of days that items of inventory are held for. As with the average debt collection period, it is only an approximate figure, but one which should be reliable enough for finding changes over time.

The inventory turnover period, or number of inventory days, is:

$$\text{Inventory turnover period} = \frac{\text{Average inventory}}{\text{Cost of sales}} \times 365 \text{ days}$$

Adding together the inventory days and the receivables days gives us an indication of how soon inventory is convertible into cash, thereby giving a further indication of the company's liquidity.

9 Funding the investment in current assets

FAST FORWARD

Current assets are financed either by short-term sources (current liabilities, such as trade payables) or by long-term sources of finance. The relationship between current assets and current liabilities is a measure of the relative extent to which current assets are financed from each of these sources. The relationship is also a measure of the liquidity of the company, and its ability to meet its payment obligations to short-term creditors, when they fall due, out of cash flows from operations (sale of inventories and payments by debtors). The commonly-used measures of liquidity are the **current ratio** and **quick ratio** (also called the acid test ratio).

9.1 The volume of current assets required

The volume of current assets required will depend on the nature of the company's business. For example, a manufacturing company may require more inventories than a company in a service industry. As the volume of output by a company increases, the volume of current assets required will also increase.

Even assuming efficient inventory holding, debt collection procedures and cash management, there is still a certain degree of choice in the total volume of current assets required to meet output requirements. Policies of low inventory-holding levels, tight credit and minimum cash holdings may be contrasted with policies of high inventories (to allow for safety or buffer levels of inventory), easier credit and sizeable cash holdings (for precautionary reasons).

9.2 Over-capitalisation and working capital

FAST FORWARD

A company will be over-capitalised when it holds excessive quantities of inventories, allows debtors excessive time to pay their debts, and take less time to pay creditors than is necessary. Problems of **over-capitalisation** can be overcome by better working capital management (ie management of inventories, receivables and payables).

If there are excessive inventories, receivables and cash, and very few payables, there will be an **over-investment** by the company in current assets. Working capital will be excessive and the company will be in this respect over-capitalised. The return on investment (return on capital employed) will be lower than it should be, and long-term funds will be unnecessarily tied up when they could be invested elsewhere to earn profits.

Over-capitalisation with respect to working capital should not exist if there is good management, but the warning signs of excessive working capital would be unfavourable accounting ratios, including the following.

(a)   **Sales/working capital.** The volume of sales as a multiple of the working capital investment should indicate whether, in comparison with previous years or with similar companies, the total volume of working capital is too high.

(b)   **Liquidity ratios.** A sudden increase in a current or quick ratio may indicate over-investment in working capital.

(c)   **Turnover periods**. Excessive turnover periods for inventories and receivables, or a short period of credit taken from suppliers, might indicate that the volume of inventories or receivables is unnecessarily high, or the volume of payables too low.

10 Overtrading

FAST FORWARD

Overtrading occurs when a company tries to finance its inventories and receivables largely out of current liabilities, and with an insufficient investment of long-term funds in working capital. Overtrading gives rise to cash flow difficulties (liquidity problems).

In contrast with over-capitalisation, overtrading happens when a business tries to do too much too quickly with too little long-term capital, so that it is trying to support too large a volume of trade with the capital resources at its disposal. A company that is **overtrading** is therefore **under-capitalised**.

Even if an overtrading business operates at a profit, it could easily run into serious trouble because it is short of money. Such liquidity troubles stem from the fact that it does not have enough capital to provide the cash to pay its debts as they fall due.

Key term

> **Overtrading** is excessive trading by a business with insufficient long-term capital at its disposal, raising the risks of inadequate liquidity and operational cash flows.

10.1 Example: overtrading

Great Ambition appoints a new managing director who has great plans to expand the company. He wants to increase revenue by 100% within two years, and to do this he employs extra sales staff. He recognises that customers do not want to have to wait for deliveries, and so he decides that the company must build up its inventory levels. There is a substantial increase in the company's inventories. These are held in additional warehouse space which is now rented. The company also buys new cars for its extra sales representatives.

The managing director's policies are immediately successful in boosting sales, which double in just over one year. Inventory levels are now much higher, but the company takes longer credit from its suppliers, even though some suppliers have expressed their annoyance at the length of time they must wait for payment. Credit terms for debtors are unchanged, and so the volume of receivables, like the volume of sales, rises by 100%.

In spite of taking longer credit, the company still needs to increase its overdraft facilities with the bank, which are raised from a limit of $40,000 to one of $80,000. The company is profitable, and retains some profits in the business, but profit margins have fallen. **Gross profit margins** are lower because some prices have been reduced to obtain extra sales. **Net profit margins** are lower because overhead costs are higher. These include sales representatives' wages, car expenses and depreciation on cars, warehouse rent and additional losses from having to write off out-of-date and slow-moving inventory items.

The balance sheet of the company might change over time from (A) to (B).

	Balance sheet (A)		Balance sheet (B)	
	$	$	$	$
Non-current assets		160,000		210,000
Current assets				
Inventory	60,000		150,000	
Receivables	64,000		135,000	
Cash	1,000		–	
		125,000		285,000
		285,000		495,000
Share capital		10,000		10,000
Retained earnings		200,000		205,000
		210,000		215,000
Current liabilities				
Bank overdraft	25,000		80,000	
Payables	50,000		200,000	
		75,000		280,000
		285,000		485,000
Sales		$1,000,000		$2,000,000
Gross profit		$200,000		$300,000
Net profit		$50,000		$20,000

In situation (B), the company has reached its overdraft limit and has four times as many payables as in situation (A) but with only twice the sales revenue. Inventory levels are much higher, and inventory turnover is lower.

The company is overtrading. If it had to pay its next trade creditor, or salaries and wages, before it received any income, it could not do so without the bank allowing it to exceed its overdraft limit. The company is profitable, although profit margins have fallen, and it ought to expect a prosperous future. But if it does not sort out its cash flow and liquidity, it will not survive to enjoy future profits.

Suitable **solutions to the problem** would be measures to reduce the degree of overtrading.

(a)   Overtrading is a form of under-capitalisation. The company should improve the balance between its long-term and short-term capital, and should finance a greater proportion of its current assets with long-term capital. For example, cash could be raised and injected into the business by issuing new equity capital.

(b)   The company could abandon ambitious plans for increased sales and more fixed asset purchases until the business has had time to consolidate its position, and build up its capital base with retained profits.

10.2 Symptoms of overtrading

Symptoms of overtrading are as follows.

(a)   There is a rapid increase in sales revenue.

(b)   There is a rapid increase in the volume of current assets and possibly also non-current assets. Inventory turnover and receivables turnover might slow down, in which case the rate of increase in inventories and receivables would be even greater than the rate of increase in sales.

(c)   There is only a small increase in proprietors' capital (perhaps through retained profits). Most of the increase in assets is financed by credit, especially:

(i)   Trade payables - the payment period to creditors is likely to lengthen

     (ii)   A bank overdraft, which often reaches or even exceeds the limit of the facilities agreed by the bank

(d)   Some debt ratios and liquidity ratios alter dramatically.

     (i)   The proportion of total assets financed by proprietors' capital falls, and the proportion financed by credit rises

     (ii)   The current ratio and the quick ratio fall

     (iii)   The business might have a liquid deficit, that is, an excess of current liabilities over current assets.

Emphasis has been given so far to the danger of overtrading when a business seeks to increase its revenue too rapidly without an adequate capital base. In other words, overtrading is brought upon the business by the ambition of management. This is not the only **cause of overtrading**, however. **Other causes** are as follows.

(a)   When a business repays a loan, it often replaces the old loan with a new one. However a business might repay a loan without replacing it, with the consequence that it has less long-term capital to finance its current level of operations.

(b)   A business might be profitable, but in a period of inflation, its retained profits might be insufficient to pay for replacement non-current assets and inventories, which now cost more because of inflation. The business would then rely increasingly on credit, and find itself eventually unable to support its current volume of trading with a capital base that has fallen in real terms.

Chapter roundup

- Financial strategy issues relating to **capital structure** are deciding from which source to raise new capital. Decisions include choosing a suitable balance between debt capital and equity capital (gearing level), and deciding to what extent current assets can safely be financed by current liabilities.

- **Balance sheet projections** and **forecast cash flow statements** can be used to estimate the size of future funding gaps. These forecasts can be used as a starting point for deciding how much new finance might be required, and from what sources they should be obtained.

- Financial ratios for assessing the balance between debt capital and equity capital in a company's capital structure are the **interest cover ratio**, the **debt ratio** and the **gearing ratio**.

- **Gearing** is the ratio of prior charge capital to either equity capital or total capital. It is a term that is used to refer to the balance between debt capital and equity capital.

- When a company has debt capital (ie is geared), changes up or down in the company's profits before interest and tax have a greater (percentage) effect on earnings per share. The change in earnings per share for a given percentage change in PBIT is greater in higher-geared companies than in lower-geared companies. This potential variability in earnings per share is the major reason why the financial risk for equity investors increases as the gearing level increases.

- Factors influencing the choice of financing method, other than gearing, include the company's **profitability**, the **relative cost** of different sources of finance, **ease of access** to different sources of finance, **dilution of ownership** with some forms of equity issue, maximum **borrowing limits**, other loan covenants and the **restrictions on management decision-making** these might cause, the **security** required for borrowing and whether adequate security can be provided, whether a particular method of raising finance can be 'sold' to investors, **conditions in the capital markets** and the **purpose** for which the finance is required.

- Higher gearing increases the financial risk for equity investors in a company, and they will require a higher return to compensate them for the higher risk. (Higher returns means either expectations of higher profits and dividends in the future, otherwise the share price will fall.) At high gearing levels, a further increase in gearing will increase the financial risk for existing lenders and bondholders, as well as equity shareholders. This is because the risk will increase that the company might be unable to meet its interest payment and debt repayment obligations. In principle, the optimum gearing level is where the company minimises the average total cost of all its finance, from all sources.

- **Current assets are financed** either by short-term sources (current liabilities, such as trade payables) or by long-term sources of finance. The relationship between current assets and current liabilities is a measure of the relative extent to which current assets are financed from each of these sources. The relationship is also a measure of the liquidity of the company, and its ability to meet its payment obligations to short-term creditors, when they fall due, out of cash flows from operations (sale of inventories and payments by debtors). The commonly-used measures of liquidity are the **current ratio** and **quick ratio** (also called the acid test ratio).

- A company will be over-capitalised when it holds excessive quantities of inventories, allows debtors excessive time to pay their debts, and take less time to pay creditors than is necessary. Problems of **over-capitalisation** can be overcome by better working capital management (ie management of inventories, receivables and payables).

- **Overtrading** occurs when a company tries to finance its inventories and receivables largely out of current liabilities, and with an insufficient investment of long-term funds in working capital. Overtrading gives rise to cash flow difficulties (liquidity problems).

Quick quiz

1   What is financial risk? What effect does it have on investors?

2   How does financial risk differ from business risk?

3   A company currently makes profits before interest and tax (PBIT) of $900,000. It is financed by 3,000,000 ordinary shares of $1 and 6% debt capital of $10 million. Tax on profits is 30%.

   (a)   What is the current earnings per share?

   (b)   By what percentage amount would EPS fall if PBIT fell by 10%?

   (c)   By how much would PBIT need to fall before the company is unable to meet its interest payment obligations out of its profits?

4   A company's gearing level, measured as the ratio of debt capital to total capital, is currently 60%, and its weighted average cost of capital is 7.6%. It needs to raise an extra $20 million. If it raises the money by issuing more debt capital, the weighted average cost of the company's total capital would rise to 8%. If it raises the money by making a new share issue, the weighted average cost of its capital would fall to 7.5%. Which method of funding should the company choose, assuming both options are available to it?

5   A company has current assets of $870,000 and current liabilities of $580,000. How much of its investment in current assets is financed by long-term capital?

Answers to quick quiz

1   Financial risk arises from uncertainty or variability in the expected returns to investors due to the method of finance and the capital structure of the company. It is caused by the risk of non-payment of interest or dividends, and by the risk of loss of capital due to insolvency of the company. In the case of equity, financial risk is also created by the possibility of large variations in annual earnings, due to changes in the company's profits. Risk for equity investors is greater as gearing increases.

2   In contrast to financial risk (described above), business risk arises from the possibility of rises or falls in the company's profitability due to business/operational factors.

3   (a)   Interest = £600,000 per annum. Profits after interest but before tax are $300,000, and so profits after tax are $210,000. There are 3,000,000 shares, so the earnings per share are 7 cents.

   (b)   PBIT falls to $810,000, and profits before tax therefore fall to $210,000. Profits after tax will be $147,000, and EPS will be 4.9c. This is a fall of 2.1c or 30%.

   (c)   If PBIT falls by more than $300,000 from its current level of $900,000, ie by more than one-third, the company will be unable to meet its obligations out of profits to pay the annual interest charges of $600,000.

4   Raise the capital through an equity issue, since the weighted average cost of capital will fall.

5   $870,000 – $580,000 = $290,000.

9

The cost of capital

Topic list	Syllabus reference
1 What is the cost of capital?	3f
2 The cost of equity capital	3f
3 The cost of debt capital and preference share capital	3f
4 Special problems	3f
5 The weighted average cost of capital (WACC)	3f
6 The NPV of new projects and shareholder wealth	2a, 3f
7 The capital asset pricing model (CAPM)	3f

Introduction

In earlier chapters it was stated that a company should appraise possible investment projects using the NPV method and the cost of capital as the discount rate. This chapter explains how a company can calculate its own cost of capital, particularly the weighted average cost of capital (WACC).

1 What is the cost of capital?

The **cost of capital** is the rate of return that a business must pay to satisfy the providers of funds, and it reflects the riskiness of the funding transaction.

When a company evaluates an investment, and possibly decides how the investment should be financed if it goes ahead, it might carry out a DCF analysis and estimate the NPV of the project. Calculating an NPV involves discounting future cash flows at a cost of capital. To do this, the company must first of all establish what its cost of capital is.

Key term

> The **cost of capital** has two aspects to it.
>
> (a)   It is the **cost of funds** that a company raises and uses.
>
> (b)   It is also the return that investors expect to be paid for putting funds into the company. It is therefore the **minimum return** that a company should make on its own investments, to earn the cash flows out of which investors can be paid their return.

The cost of capital can therefore be measured by studying the returns required by investors, and then used to derive a discount rate for DCF analysis and investment appraisal.

1.1 The cost of capital as an opportunity cost of finance

The cost of capital, however it is measured, is an opportunity cost of finance, because it is the minimum return that investors require. If they do not get this return, they will transfer some or all of their investment somewhere else. Here are two examples.

(a)   If a bank offers to lend money to a company, the interest rate it charges is the yield that the bank wants to receive from investing in the company, because it can get just as good a return from lending the money to someone else. In other words, the interest rate is the opportunity cost of lending for the bank.

(b)   When shareholders invest in a company, the returns that they can expect must be sufficient to persuade them not to sell some or all of their shares and invest the money somewhere else. The yield on the shares is therefore the opportunity cost to the shareholders of not investing somewhere else.

1.2 The cost of capital and risk

The cost of capital has three elements. It consists of a premium over a risk-free rate to compensate the investor for the business risk and for the finance risk in the investment.

(a)   The **risk-free rate of return** is the return which would be required from an investment if it were completely free from risk. Typically, a risk-free yield would be the yield on government securities.

(b)   The **premium for business risk** is an increase in the required rate of return due to the existence of uncertainty about the future and about a firm's business prospects. The actual returns from an investment may not be as high as they are expected to be. Business risk will be higher for some firms than for others, and some types of project undertaken by a firm may be more risky than other types of project that it undertakes.

(c)   The **premium for financial risk** relates to the danger of high debt levels (high gearing). For ordinary shareholders, financial risk is evident in the variability of earnings after deducting payments to holders of debt capital. The higher the gearing of a company's capital structure, the greater will be the financial risk to ordinary shareholders, and this should be reflected in a higher risk premium and therefore a higher cost of capital.

Because different companies are in different types of business (varying business risk) and have different capital structures (varying financial risk) the cost of capital applied to one company may differ radically from the cost of capital of another.

1.3 The costs of different sources of finance

Where a company uses a mix of equity and debt capital, its overall cost of capital might be taken to be the weighted average of the cost of each type of capital. The weighted average cost of capital, and whether it is the appropriate cost of capital to use, is considered later. First of all, we must look at the cost of each separate source of capital: equity, preference shares and forms of debt capital.

2 The cost of equity capital

New funds from equity shareholders are obtained either from new issues of shares or from cash deriving from retained earnings. Both of these sources of funds have a cost. Shareholders will not be prepared to provide funds for a **new issue of shares** unless the return on their investment is sufficiently attractive. **Retained earnings** also have a cost. This is an opportunity cost, the dividend forgone by shareholders.

Shareholders put a value on their shares. In the case of shares traded on a stock market, this value is represented by the market price of the shares. The market price shows how much investors are currently willing to pay for the shares, in return for the future benefits they expect to obtain. A term sometimes used is the **dividend payout ratio**, which is simply the proportion of total post-tax profits that is paid out in total as a dividend (for example, if profits are $100,000 and $25,000 in total is paid out in dividends the dividend payout ratio is 25%).

2.1 The dividend valuation model

FAST FORWARD

> The **dividend valuation model** can be used to estimate a cost of equity, on the assumption that the market value of shares is directly related to the expected future dividends on the shares.

The cost of equity, both for new issues and retained earnings, could be estimated by means of a **dividend valuation model**, on the assumption that the market value of shares is directly related to expected future dividends on the shares. If the future annual dividend per share (D_1) is expected to be *constant* in amount 'in perpetuity', the share price (P_0) can be calculated by the following formula:

$$P_0 = \frac{D_1}{r}$$

where r is the cost of equity, expressed as a proportion (eg 12% = 0.12).

The share price is 'ex dividend', which means that it excludes the value of any current dividend that has just been paid or is currently payable. The next annual dividend is receivable in one year's time.

The share price is the present value of a constant annual dividend forever, ie in perpetuity. The mathematical formula is quite simple because **the PV of a constant annual cash flow $C in perpetuity, discounted at a cost of capital r, is $C/r.**

Re-arranging this formula, we get a formula for the cost of equity.

$$r = \frac{D_1}{P_0}$$

where r   is the shareholders' cost of capital

       D_1 is the annual dividend per share, starting at Year 1 and then continuing annually in perpetuity

The following assumptions are made in the dividend valuation model.

(a)   The dividends from projects for which the funds are required will be of the same risk type or quality as dividends from existing operations.

(b)   There would be no increase in the cost of capital, for any other reason besides (a) above, from a new issue of shares.

(c)   All shareholders have perfect information about the company's future, there is no delay in obtaining this information and all shareholders interpret it in the same way.

(d)   Taxation can be ignored.

(e)   All shareholders have the same marginal cost of capital.

(f)   There would be no issue expenses for new shares.

Suppose that ABC is a company with no dividend growth prospects, which has just paid an annual dividend of 16c per share. The share price is 200c. Applying the dividend valuation model, the cost of equity can be calculated as 16/200 = 0.08, ie 8%.

2.2 The dividend growth model

Expected **growth in dividends** can be allowed for in calculating a cost of equity, using Gordon's growth model.

Shareholders will normally expect dividends to increase year by year and not to remain as a constant amount every year. The so-called 'fundamental theory of share values' states that the market price of a share is the present value of the expected future revenue cash flows from the share, discounted at the cost of equity capital. Given an expected **constant annual growth in dividends**, the share price formula would be:

$$P_0 = \frac{D_0(1+g)}{(r-g)}$$

where:

D_0 is the current year's annual dividend (ie the Year 0 dividend)
P_0 is the current ex-dividend share price
r is the cost of equity, expressed as a proportion
g is the annual growth rate, in dividends, expressed as a proportion (eg 4% = 0.04)

This formula assumes a constant growth rate in dividends, but it can be adapted for uneven growth.

Re-arranging the formula, we get a formula for the ordinary shareholders' cost of capital.

$$r = \frac{D_0(1+g)}{P_0} + g$$

This is equivalent to the following equation

$$r = \frac{D_1}{P_0} + g$$

where D_1 is the dividend in year 1, so that $D_1 = D_0 (1 + g)$.

This dividend growth model is sometimes called **Gordon's growth model**.

       Cost of equity capital

A share has a current market value of 96c, and the last dividend was 12c. If the expected annual growth rate of dividends is 4%, calculate the cost of equity capital.

(For the answer to this question, see the Answer section at the end of this book.)

2.3 Estimating growth rates

The value of g may be estimated in two ways:

    (i)   by extrapolation of growth in **past** dividends
    (ii)   by analysis of the **future** earnings rate and retention policy

These are illustrated in the following example.

2.4 Example: cost of equity capital

The dividends and earnings of Hall Shores over the last five years have been as follows.

Year	Dividends $	Earnings $
20X1	150,000	400,000
20X2	192,000	510,000
20X3	206,000	550,000
20X4	245,000	650,000
20X5	262,350	700,000

The company is financed entirely by equity and there are 1,000,000 shares in issue, each with a market value of $3.35 ex div.

What is the cost of equity?

What implications does dividend growth appear to have for earnings retentions?

Solution

The dividend growth model will be used. The dividend per share in the current year is $262,350/1,000,000 = $0.26235.

(a)   Dividends have risen from $150,000 in 20X1 to $262,350 in 20X5. The increase represents four years growth. (Check that you are aware that there are four years' growth, and not five years' growth, in the table.) The average growth rate, g, may be calculated as follows.

$$\text{Dividend in 20X1} \times (1+g)^4 \quad = \quad \text{Dividend in 20X5}$$

$$(1+g)^4 \quad = \quad \frac{\text{Dividend in 20X5}}{\text{Dividend in 20X1}}$$

$$= \quad \frac{\$262,350}{\$150,000} = 1.749$$

$$1 + g \quad = \quad \sqrt[4]{1.749} = 1.15$$

$$g \quad = \quad 0.15 = 15\%$$

(b)   The growth rate over the last four years is assumed to be expected by shareholders into the indefinite future, so the cost of equity, r, is:

$$\frac{d_0(1+g)}{P_0} + g = \frac{0.26235(1.15)}{3.35} + 0.15 = 0.24 = 24\%$$

(c)   Retained profits will earn a certain rate of return and so growth will come from the yield on the retained funds. It might be assumed that g = bR where b is the yield on new investments and R is the proportion of profits retained for reinvestment. In our example, if we applied this assumption the future annual growth rate would be 15% if bR continued to be 15%. If the rate of return on new investments averages 24% (which is the cost of equity) and if the proportion of earnings retained is 62.5% (which it has been, approximately, in the period 20X1 – 20X5) then g = bR = 24% × 62.5% = 15%.

3 The cost of debt capital and preference share capital

The **cost of debt** is the return an enterprise must pay to its lenders.

- For **irredeemable debt**, this is the (post-tax) interest as a percentage of the ex div market value of the loan stock (or preference shares).

- For **redeemable debt**, the cost is given by the internal rate of return of the cash flows involved. The same technique is used to calculate either the pre-tax or the post-tax cost of redeemable debt.

3.1 Cost of irredeemable debt or irredeemable preference shares

Estimating the cost of fixed interest or fixed dividend capital is much easier than estimating the cost of ordinary share capital because the interest received by the holder of the security is fixed by contract and will not fluctuate.

The cost of debt capital already issued is the rate of interest (the **internal rate of return**) which equates the current market price with the discounted future cash receipts from the security.

Ignoring taxation for the moment, in the case of **irredeemable debt** (or **preference shares**) the future cash flows are the interest (or dividend) payments in perpetuity so that:

$$P_0 = \frac{I}{K_d}$$

where

P_0 is the current market price of debt capital after payment of the current interest (dividend)
I is the annual interest (dividend in the case of irredeemable preference shares)
K_d is the cost of debt (preference share) capital

This formula can be re-arranged:

$$K_d = \frac{I}{P_0}$$

3.2 Cost of redeemable debt or redeemable preference shares

If the debt is **redeemable,** then in the year of redemption the interest payment will be received by the investor/lender as well as the amount payable on redemption, so:

$$P_0 = \frac{I}{(1 + K_d)} + \frac{I}{(1 + K_d)^2} + ... + \frac{I + P_n}{(1 + K_d)^n}$$

where P_n = the amount payable on redemption in year n.

The above equation cannot be simplified so 'K_d' will have to be calculated by trial and error, as an **internal return of return (IRR)** for the cash flows.

The best trial and error figure to start with in calculating the cost of redeemable debt is to take the cost of debt capital as if it were irredeemable and then add the annualised capital profit that will be made from the present time to the time of redemption.

3.3 Example: cost of debt capital

Owen Allot has in issue 10% debentures of a nominal value of $100. The market price is $90 ex interest. Ignoring taxation, calculate the cost of this capital if the debenture is:

(a)   Irredeemable
(b)   Redeemable at par after 10 years

Solution

(a)   The cost of irredeemable debt capital is:

$$\frac{I}{P_0} = \frac{\$10}{\$90} \times 100\% = 11.1\%$$

(b)   The cost of debt capital is 11.1% if irredeemable. The capital profit that will be made from now to the date of redemption is $10 ($100 − $90). This profit will be made over a period of ten years which gives an annualised profit of $1 which is about 1% of current market value. The best trial and error figure to try first is, therefore, 12%.

Year		Cash flow $	Discount factor 12%	PV $	Discount factor 11%	PV $
0	Market value	(90)	1.000	(90.00)	1.000	(90.00)
1-10	Interest	10	5.650	56.50	5.889	58.89
10	Capital repayment	100	0.322	32.20	0.352	35.20
				(1.30)		4.09

The approximate cost of debt capital is therefore:

$$(11 + \frac{4.09}{(4.09 - -1.30)} \times 1) = 11.76\%$$

The cost of debt capital estimated above represents the cost of continuing to use the finance rather than redeem the securities at their current market price. It would also represent the cost of raising additional fixed interest capital if we assume that the cost of the additional capital would be equal to the cost of that already issued. If a company has not already issued any fixed interest capital, it may estimate the cost of doing so by making a similar calculation for another company which is judged to be similar as regards risk.

3.4 Cost of debt capital and taxation

The interest on debt capital is an allowable deduction for purposes of taxation and so the cost of debt capital and the cost of share capital are not properly comparable costs. This tax relief on interest ought to be recognised in DCF computations. One way of doing this is to include tax savings due to interest payments in the cash flows of every project. A simpler method, and one that is normally used, is to allow for the tax relief in computing the cost of debt capital, to arrive at an 'after-tax' cost of debt. The **after-tax cost of irredeemable debt capital** is:

$$K_d = \frac{I}{P_0}(1-t)$$

where K_d is the cost of debt capital

   I is the annual interest payment

   P_0 is the current market price of the debt capital ex interest (that is, after payment of the current interest)

   t is the rate of tax.

Therefore if a company pays $10,000 a year interest on irredeemable debenture stock with a nominal value of $100,000 and a market price of $80,000, and the rate of tax is 30%, the cost of the debentures would be:

$$\frac{10,000}{80,000}(1-0.30) = 0.0875 = 8.75\%$$

The higher the rate of tax is, the greater the tax benefits in having debt finance will be compared with equity finance. In the example above, if the rate of tax had been 40%, the cost of debt would have been, after tax:

$$\frac{10,000}{80,000}(1-0.40) = 0.075 = 7.5\%$$

In the case of **redeemable debentures**, the capital repayment is not allowable for tax. To calculate the cost of the debt capital to include in the weighted average cost of capital, it is necessary to calculate an internal rate of return that takes account of tax relief on the interest.

3.5 Example: after-tax cost of redeemable debt capital

(a)   A company has outstanding $660,000 of 8% debenture stock on which the interest is payable annually on 31 December. The stock is due for redemption at par on 1 January 20X6. The market price of the stock at 28 December 20X2 was 95.00 ex interest. Ignoring taxation, what do you estimate to be the current market rate of interest?

(b)   If the effective rate of tax is 30% what would be the cost to the company of the debenture stock in (a) above? Assume that tax relief on interest payments arises in the same year as the interest payment.

Solution

(a)   The current market rate of interest is found by calculating the pre-tax internal rate of return of the cash flows shown in the table below. A discount rate of 10% is chosen for a trial-and-error start to the calculation.

Item and date		Year	Cash flow $	Discount factor 10%	Present value $
Market value (ex int)	28.12.X2	0	(95)	1.000	(95.00)
Interest	31.12.X3	1	8	0.909	7.28
Interest	31.12.X4	2	8	0.826	6.61
Interest	31.12.X5	3	8	0.751	6.01
Redemption	1.1.X6	3	100	0.751	75.10
				NPV	0

By coincidence, the market rate of interest is 10% since the NPV of the cash flows above is zero.

(b)   Again we must identify the current interest payable and use ex interest figures.

At a market value of 95.00

Item and date	Year	Cash flow ex int $	Discount factor at 5%	PV 5% $	Discount factor at 8%	PV 8% $
Market value	0	(95.00)	1.000	(95.00)	1.000	(95.00)
Interest less tax saved	1	5.60	0.952	5.33	0.926	5.19
Interest less tax saved	2	5.60	0.907	5.08	0.857	4.80
Interest less tax saved	3	5.60	0.864	4.84	0.794	4.45
Redemption	3	100.00	0.864	86.40	0.794	79.40
NPV				6.65		(1.16)

The estimated cost of debt is:

$$5\% \; + \; \left(\frac{6.65}{(6.65+1.16)} \right) \times (8-5)\%$$

= 7.6% approx

3.6 The cost of floating rate debt

If a firm has **floating rate debt**, then the cost of an equivalent fixed interest debt should be substituted. 'Equivalent' usually means fixed interest debt with a similar term to maturity in a firm of similar standing, although if the cost of capital is to be used for project appraisal purposes, there is an argument for using debt of the same duration as the project under consideration.

3.7 The cost of short-term funds

The cost of short-term funds such as bank loans and overdrafts is the current interest being charged on such funds.

4 Special problems

4.1 Private companies and the cost of equity

The cost of capital cannot be calculated from market values for **private companies** in the way that has been described so far, because the shares in a private company do not have a quoted market price. Since private companies do not have a cost of equity that can be readily estimated, it follows that a big problem for private companies which want to use DCF for evaluating investment projects is how to select a cost of capital for a discount rate.

Suitable approaches might be: to estimate the cost of capital for similar public companies, but then add a further premium for additional business and financial risk; or to build up a cost of capital by adding estimated premiums for business risk and financial risk to the risk-free rate of return.

4.2 Government organisations and the cost of capital

The same problem faces government organisations. Government organisations do not have a market value, and most of them do not pay interest on much or all of the finance they receive. Government activities do not involve business risk, and there is no financial risk either for the investor, which is mainly the government itself. In practice, the problem can be overcome by using a target 'real' rate of return set by the Treasury rather than a market cost of capital.

5 The weighted average cost of capital (WACC)

FAST FORWARD

The **weighted average cost of capital** can be used to evaluate a company's investment projects if:

- The project is small relative to the company
- The existing capital structure will be maintained (same financial risk)
- The project has the same business risk as the company
- New investments are financed by new sources of funds, and a marginal cost of capital approach is used

5.1 Computing a discount rate

We have now looked at the costs of individual sources of capital for a company. But how does this help us to work out the cost of capital as a whole, or the discount rate to apply in DCF investment appraisals?

In many cases it will be difficult to associate a particular project with a particular form of finance. A company's funds may be viewed as a **pool of resources**. Money is withdrawn from this pool of funds to invest in new projects and added to the pool as new finance is raised or profits are retained. Under these circumstances it might seem appropriate to use an average cost of capital as the discount rate.

The correct cost of capital to use in investment appraisal is the **marginal cost** of the funds raised (or earnings retained) to finance the investment. This is the additional cost to the company of obtaining the funds to invest in the project.

The weighted average cost of capital (WACC) might be considered the most reliable guide to the marginal cost of capital, but only on the assumption that the company continues to invest in the future:

   (a)   in projects of a standard level of business risk, and
   (b)   by raising funds in the same equity/debt proportions as its existing capital structure.

5.2 General formula for the WACC

A general formula for the weighted average cost of capital is:

$$WACC = K_{eg} \frac{E}{E+D} + K_d \frac{D}{E+D}$$

where K_{eg} is the cost of equity
       K_d is the cost of debt
       E is the market value of equity in the firm
       D is the market value of debt in the firm

The above formula ignores taxation. Bringing in tax, we should calculate the cost of debt net of tax, where the tax rate is t, as follows.

$$WACC = K_{eg} \left(\frac{E}{E+D}\right) + K_d(1-t) \left(\frac{D}{E+D}\right)$$

If you need to calculate WACC where debt is redeemable, you should calculate the after-tax cost of debt using the techniques set out earlier in this chapter and substitute this into the formula in place of $K_d(1-t)$.

5.3 Example: weighted average cost of capital

Prudence is financed partly by equity and partly by debentures. The equity proportion is always kept at two thirds of the total. The cost of equity is 18% and that of debt 12%. A new project is under consideration which will cost $100,000 and will yield a return before interest of $37,500 a year for four years. Should the project be accepted? Ignore taxation.

Solution

Since the company will maintain its gearing ratio unchanged, it is reasonable to assume that its marginal cost of funds equals its WACC. The weighted average cost of capital is as follows.

	Proportion	Cost		Cost × proportion
Equity	$\frac{2}{3}$	18%		12%
Debt	$\frac{1}{3}$	12%		4%
			WACC	16%

Year	Cash flow $	Discount factor at 16%	PV $
0	(100,000)	1.000	(100,000)
1	37,500	0.862	32,325
2	37,500	0.743	27,863
3	37,500	0.641	24,038
4	37,500	0.552	20,700
NPV			4,926

The NPV of the investment is $4,926. Subject to sensitivity analysis, it therefore appears financially justifiable.

5.4 Weighting

In the last example, we simplified the problem of **weighting the different costs of capital** by giving the proportions of capital. Two methods of weighting could be used.

(a) Weights could be based on market values (by this method, the cost of retained earnings is implied in the market value of equity).

(b) Weights could be based on balance sheet values ('book values').

Although balance sheet values are often easier to obtain they are of doubtful economic significance. It is therefore appropriate to use market values. However, for unquoted companies estimates of market values are likely to be extremely subjective and consequently book values may be used.

When using market values it is not possible to split the equity value between share capital and reserves and only one cost of equity can be used. This removes the need to estimate a separate cost of retained earnings.

5.5 Example: WACC

PLZ has equity share capital of 100 million shares with a current market price of 500c each, bonds with a current market value of $100 million and $150 million of bank loans. The company expects to maintain its current capital structure (the proportion of equity to bonds to bank loans) into the foreseeable future. The cost of equity is 12%, the after tax cost of the bonds is 7% and the after tax cost of the bank loans is 6%.

What is the company's weighted average cost of capital?

Solution

The WACC can be calculated as follows.

	Market value (MV) $m	Cost	MV × Cost $m
Equity	500	0.12	60
Bonds	100	0.07	7
Bank loans	150	0.06	9
	750		76

$$\text{WACC} = \frac{76}{750} = 0.101, \text{ ie } 10.1\%$$

Question 9.2

The management of Custer Ackers are trying to decide on a cost of capital to apply to the evaluation of investment projects. The company has an issued share capital of 500,000 ordinary $1 shares, with a current market value cum div of $1.17 per share. It has also issued $200,000 of 10% debentures, which are redeemable at par in two years time and have a current market value of $105.30 per cent, and $100,000 of irredeemable 6% preference shares, currently priced at 40c per share. The preference dividend has just been paid, and the ordinary dividend and debenture interest are due to be paid in the near future.

Management consider the current capital structure of the company to be similar to their plans for its longer-term capital structure.

The ordinary share dividend will be $60,000 this year, and the directors have publicised their view that earnings and dividends will increase by 5% a year into the indefinite future.

Required

Calculate the WACC. Assume a tax rate of 30%. Assume also that tax savings occur in the same year as the interest payments to which they relate.

Note. The cost of capital of a security is the IRR which equates the current market value of the security with its expected future cash flows.

Year	Discount factor at 10%	Discount factor at 8%
1	0.909	0.926
2	0.826	0.857

(For the answer to this question, see the Answer section at the end of this book.)

5.6 Arguments for using the WACC

The weighted average cost of capital can be used in investment appraisal if we make the following assumptions.

(a)   The project is small relative to the overall size of the company.

(b)   The weighted average cost of capital reflects the company's long-term future **capital structure**, and capital costs. If this were not so, the current weighted average cost would become irrelevant because eventually it would not relate to any actual cost of capital.

(c)   The project has the same degree of **business risk** as the company has now.

(d)   New investments must be financed by new **sources of funds**: retained earnings, new share issues, new loans and so on.

(e)   The cost of capital to be applied to project evaluation reflects the **marginal cost of new capital** (see below).

Key term

> **Business risk** (or **systematic risk**) is risk arising from the existing operations of an enterprise (eg relating to macroeconomic factors) which cannot be reduced by diversification of investments.

5.7 Arguments against using the WACC

The arguments against using the WACC as the cost of capital for investment appraisal (as follows) are based on criticisms of the assumptions that are used to justify use of the WACC.

(a) New investments undertaken by a company might have different **business risk** characteristics from the company's existing operations. As a consequence, the return required by investors might go up (or down) if the investments are undertaken, because their business risk is perceived to be higher (or lower).

(b) The finance that is raised to fund a new investment might substantially change the capital structure and the perceived **financial risk** of investing in the company. Depending on whether the project is financed by equity or by debt capital, the perceived financial risk of the entire company might change. This must be taken into account when appraising investments.

(c) Many companies raise **floating rate** debt capital as well as fixed interest debt capital. With floating rate debt capital, the interest rate is variable, and is altered every three or six months or so in line with changes in current market interest rates. The cost of debt capital will therefore fluctuate as market conditions vary. Floating rate debt is difficult to incorporate into a WACC computation, and the best that can be done is to substitute an 'equivalent' fixed interest debt capital cost in place of the floating rate debt cost.

5.8 Marginal cost of capital approach

The **marginal cost of capital approach** involves calculating a marginal cut-off rate. This is the cost to the company of raising the additional capital to finance the project.

It can be argued that the current weighted average cost of capital should be used to evaluate projects where a company's capital structure changes only very slowly over time. In such a situation, the marginal cost of new capital should be roughly equal to the weighted average cost of current capital. If this view is correct, then by undertaking investments that offer a return in excess of the WACC, a company will increase the market value of its ordinary shares in the long run. This is because the excess returns would provide surplus profits and dividends for the shareholders.

However, where gearing levels fluctuate significantly, or the finance for a new project carries a significantly different level of risks from that of the existing company, there is good reason to seek an alternative marginal cost of capital to establish the incremental financing costs of the new project.

6 The NPV of new projects and shareholder wealth

Using the **dividend valuation model**, it can be illustrated that the total wealth of a company's shareholders will increase by the NPV of any project that is undertaken, provided that there is no change in the company's WACC. This is an important concept, and helps to explain why the NPV method of project appraisal is the most appropriate to use, in cases where the financial objective of the organisation is to increase shareholder wealth.

We begin considering this argument for companies financed entirely by equity, so that the WACC and the cost of equity are the same.

Suppose that a company relying on equity as its only source of finance wishes to invest in a new project. The money will be raised by issuing new share capital to the existing shareholders. For simplicity, it will be assumed that the cash inflows generated by the new project will be used to increase dividends. The project will have to show a positive net present value (NPV) at the shareholders' marginal cost of capital, because otherwise the shareholders would not agree to provide the new capital.

The gain to the shareholders after acceptance of the new project will be the difference between:

(a) The market value of the company before acceptance of the new project and

(b) The market value of the company after acceptance of the new project, less the amount of funds raised from the shareholders to finance the project.

The market value of the shares will increase by the present value of the extra future dividends generated by the project. In formula terms, this is:

$$\frac{A_1}{(1+K_e)} + \frac{A_2}{(1+K_e)^2} + \frac{A_3}{(1+K_e)^3} + \dots$$

where A_1, A_2 ..... are the additional dividends at years 1, 2 and so on

K_e is the shareholders' marginal cost of capital

Thus if the shareholders have financed the project, their net gain will be

PV (additional dividends) − cost of project

This is the NPV of the project. In other words, shareholder wealth will increase by the NPV of the project.

6.1 Investments financed by retained profits

A similar analysis applies if a project is financed by retained profits. To make the capital available for investment, current dividends would have to be reduced. However, even though in the short term dividends will be reduced, this will be more than compensated for in the long term by the fact that extra cash inflows generated by the investments will increase dividends in the future. (Indeed, it can be argued in theory that no dividends should be paid until all projects with positive net present values have been financed.)

6.2 Conclusions for ungeared companies

If an all equity company undertakes a project, and it is financed in such a way that its cost of capital remains unchanged, the total wealth of the ordinary shareholders will increase by the amount of the NPV of the project.

6.3 Geared companies

Although the mathematics are more complex, a similar conclusion can be applied to companies with debt finance in their capital structure. Provided that the stock market is aware of the expected future cash flows from new investments, and shares management's expectations of what these will be, share prices should rise to reflect the expected NPV of new investments. In other words, shareholder wealth will increase by the NPV of new investments, possibly as soon as those investments are undertaken.

7 The capital asset pricing model (CAPM)

FAST FORWARD

An alternative method of calculating the cost of equity is to use the **capital asset pricing model**. This states that the cost of equity is at a premium above the risk-free rate. The size of this premium is the difference between the average stock market returns and the risk-free rate of return, multiplied by a **beta factor**.

Key term

The **Capital Asset Pricing Model (CAPM)** is a formula for predicting the required rate of return for an investment, based upon its level of systematic risk relative to that of the market as a whole.

The capital asset pricing model is a formula for calculating the cost of equity capital. It is an alternative to the dividend valuation model and dividend growth model. The uses of the capital asset pricing model (CAPM) include:

(a) Establishing the 'correct' equilibrium market value of a company's shares

(b) Establishing the cost of a company's equity (and the company's average cost of capital), taking account of both the business and financial risk characteristics of a company's investments

It is useful to try to understand the logic underlying the CAPM. A starting point is the difference between systematic risk and unsystematic risk in investments.

7.1 Systematic risk and unsystematic risk

Whenever an investor invests in some shares, or a company invests in a new project, there will be some risk involved. The actual return on the investment might be better or worse than that hoped for. To some extent, risk is unavoidable, unless the investor settles for risk-free securities such as gilts. Investors must take the rough with the smooth and for reasons outside their control, returns might be higher or lower than expected.

Provided that the investor diversifies his investments in a suitably wide portfolio, the investments which perform well and those which perform badly should tend to cancel each other out, and much risk can be diversified away. In the same way, a company which invests in a number of projects will find that some do well and some do badly, but taking the whole portfolio of investments, average returns should turn out much as expected.

Risks that can be diversified away are referred to as **unsystematic risk**.

However, not all risk can be diversified away. All securities will be affected to some extent by the underlying risks of the market - **changes** in the **economy**, unexpected global events (e.g. September 11 2001), general elections etc - which will cause variations in the returns of the most diversified of portfolios.

This inherent risk, known as the **systematic risk** or **market risk**, **cannot be diversified away**.

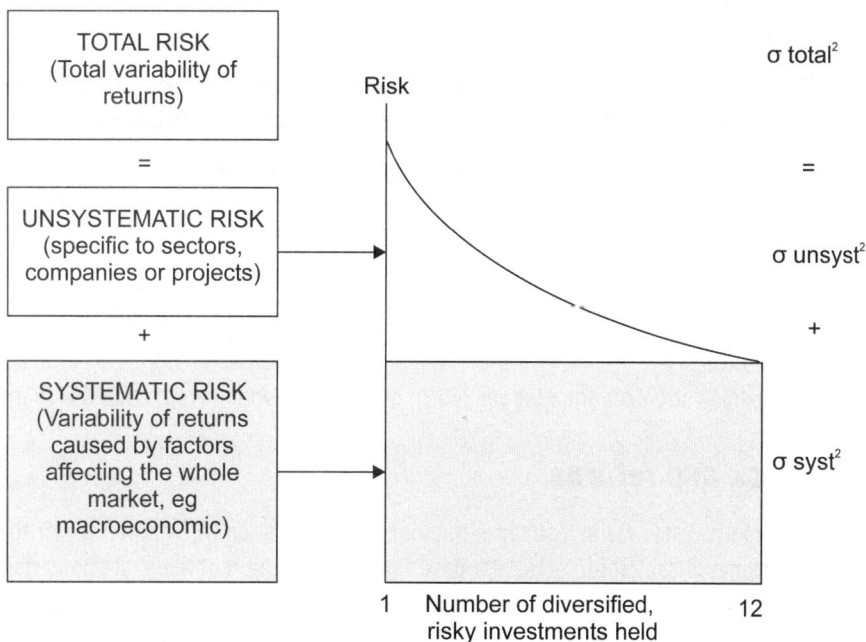

Systematic risk must be accepted by any investor, unless he invests entirely in risk-free investments. In return for accepting systematic risk, an investor will expect to earn a return which is higher than the return on a risk-free investment. **The amount of systematic risk in an investment varies between different types of investment.**

(a) The systematic risk in the operating cash flows of a tourism company which will be highly sensitive to consumers' spending power might be greater than the systematic risk for a company which operates a chain of supermarkets.

(b) Some individual projects will be more risky than others and so the systematic risk involved in an investment to develop a new product would be greater than the systematic risk of investing in a replacement asset.

Systematic risk and unsystematic risk: implications for investments

If an investor wants to avoid risk altogether, he must invest entirely in **risk-free securities**. If an investor holds shares in just a few companies, there will be some unsystematic risk as well as systematic risk in his portfolio, because he will not have spread his risk enough to diversify away the unsystematic risk. To eliminate unsystematic risk, he must build up a well-diversified portfolio of investments.

If an investor holds a **balanced portfolio** of all the stocks and shares on the stock market, he will incur systematic risk which is exactly equal to the average systematic risk in the stock market as a whole.

Shares in **individual companies will have systematic risk characteristics which are different to this market average**. Some shares will be less risky and some will be more risky than the stock market average. Similarly, **some investments will be more risky and some will be less risky than a company's 'average' investments**.

7.2 Systematic risk and the CAPM

The capital asset pricing model is mainly concerned with how systematic risk is measured (using **beta factors**) and with how systematic risk affects required returns and share prices.

CAPM theory includes the following propositions.

(a)   Investors in shares require a return in excess of the risk-free rate, to compensate them for systematic risk.

(b)   Investors should not require a premium for unsystematic risk, because this can be diversified away by holding a wide portfolio of investments.

(c)   Because systematic risk varies between companies, investors will require a higher return from shares in those companies where the systematic risk is greater.

The same propositions can be applied to **capital investments by companies**.

(a)   Companies will want a return on a project to exceed the risk-free rate, to compensate them for systematic risk.

(b)   Unsystematic risk can be diversified away, and so a premium for unsystematic risk should not be required.

(c)   Companies should want a bigger return on projects where systematic risk is greater.

7.3 Market risk and returns

The CAPM was first formulated for investments in stocks and shares on the market, rather than for companies' investments in capital projects. It is based on a comparison of the systematic risk of individual investments (shares in a particular company) and the risk of all shares in the market as a whole. Market risk (systematic risk) is the average risk of the market as a whole. Taking all the shares on a stock market together, the total expected returns from the market will vary because of systematic risk. The market as a whole might do well or it might do badly.

7.4 Risk and returns from an individual security

Similarly, an individual security may offer prospects of a return of x%, but with some risk (business risk and financial risk) attached. The return (the x%) that investors require from the individual security will be higher or lower than the market return, depending on whether the security's systematic risk is greater or less than the market average. A major assumption in CAPM is that there is a **linear relationship** between the return obtained from an individual security and the average return from all securities in the market.

7.5 Example: CAPM (1)

The following information is available about the performance of an individual company's shares and the stock market as a whole.

	Individual company	Stock market as a whole
Price at start of period	105.0	480.0
Price at end of period	110.0	490.0
Dividend during period	7.6	39.2

The return on the company's shares (r_j) and the return on the 'market portfolio' of shares (r_m) may be calculated as:

$$\frac{\text{Capital gain (or loss)} + \text{dividend}}{\text{Price at start of period}}$$

$$r_j = \frac{(110 - 105) + 7.6}{105} = 0.12 \qquad\qquad r_m = \frac{(490 - 480) + 39.2}{480} = 0.1025$$

A statistical analysis of 'historic' returns from a security and from the 'average' market may suggest that a linear relationship can be assumed to exist between them. A series of comparative figures could be prepared (month by month) of the return from a company's shares and the average return of the market as a whole. The results could be drawn on a scattergraph and a 'line of best fit' drawn (using linear regression techniques) as shown in the following diagram.

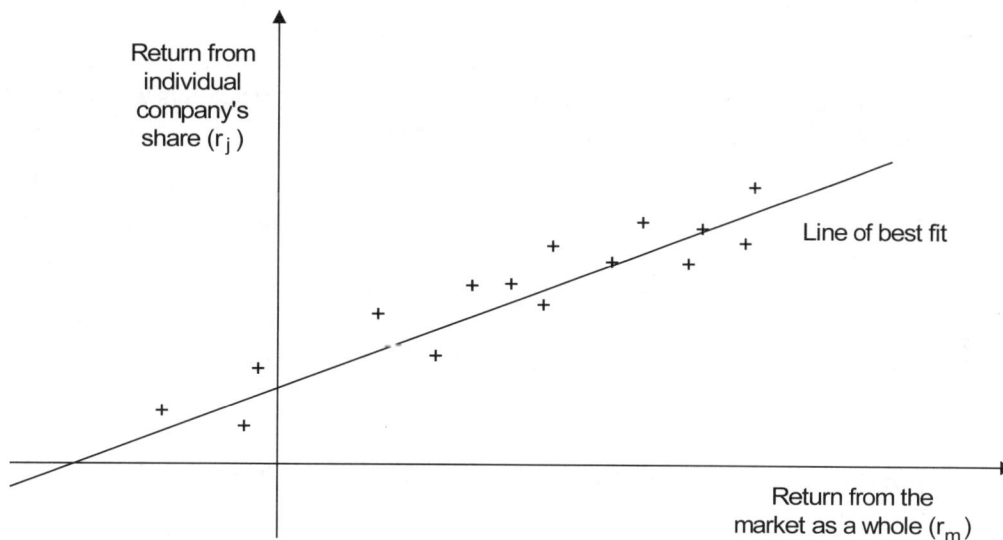

This analysis would show three things. (Note that returns can be negative. A share price fall represents a capital loss, which is a negative return.)

(a) The return from the security (r_j) and the return from the market as a whole will tend to rise or fall together.

(b) The scattergraph may not give a good line of best fit, unless a large number of data items are plotted, because actual returns are affected by unsystematic risk as well as by systematic risk.

(c) What is of interest here, however, is the angle or gradient of the line of best fit. Here it is less than 45°, indicating that a given change in market return generally corresponds to a smaller change in share return. This indicates that the share's returns are less susceptible to market risk factors than market average, i.e. its systematic risk element is lower than market average.

The conclusion from this analysis is that individual securities will be either more or less risky than the market average in a fairly predictable way. The measure of this relationship between market returns and an individual security's returns, reflecting differences in systematic risk characteristics, can be developed into a **beta factor for the individual security**.

7.6 The beta factor

Each company's equity has its own beta factor. A higher beta indicates higher (non-diversifiable) systematic risk. When a company has a beta factor in excess of 1.0, its expected returns are higher than the average returns for the market as a whole. A beta factor of less than 1.0 indicates systematic risk lower than the market average, and so expected returns are also lower than the market average.

Key term

A share's **beta factor** or **beta coefficient** is the measure of its volatility in terms of market risk. The beta factor of the **market as a whole** is **1.0**. Market risk makes market returns volatile and the beta factor is simply a basis or yardstick against which the risk of other investments can be measured.

Suppose that returns on shares in XYZ tend to vary twice as much as returns from the market as a whole, so that if market returns went up 3%, say, returns on XYZ shares would be expected to go up by 6% and if market returns fell by 3%, returns on XYZ shares would be expected to fall by 6%. The beta factor of XYZ shares would be 2.0.

Thus if the average market return rises by, say, 2%, the return from a share with a beta factor of 0.8 should rise by 1.6% in response to the *same conditions* which have caused the market return to change. The *actual* return from the share might rise by, say, 2.5%, or even fall by, say, 1%, but the difference between the actual change and a change of 1.6% due to general market factors would be attributed to unsystematic risk factors unique to the company or its industry.

It is an essential principle of CAPM theory that unsystematic risk can be cancelled out by diversification. In a well-balanced portfolio, an investor's gains and losses from the unsystematic risk of individual shares will tend to cancel each other out. In other words, if shares in X do worse than market returns and the beta factor of X's shares would predict, shares in Y will do better than predicted, and the net effect will be self-cancelling elimination of the specific (unsystematic) risk from the portfolio, leaving the average portfolio return dependent only on **changes in the average market return** and **the beta factors of shares in the portfolio**.

7.7 Excess returns over returns on risk-free investments

The CAPM also makes use of the principle that returns on shares in the market as a whole are expected to be higher than the returns on risk-free investments. The difference between market returns and risk-free returns is called an **excess return** or **market risk premium**. For example, if the return on British Government stocks is 5% and market returns are 9%, the excess return on the market's shares as a whole is 4%.

The difference between the risk-free return and the expected return on an individual security can be measured as the excess return for the market as a whole multiplied by the security's beta factor.

7.8 Example

Thus, if shares in DEF have a beta of 1.5 when the risk-free return is 9% and the expected market return is 13%, then the expected return on DEF shares would exceed the risk-free return by $(13 - 9) \times 1.5\% = 6\%$ and the total expected return on DEF shares would be $(9 + 6)\% = 15\%$. If the market returns fall by 3% to 10%, say, the expected return on DEF shares would fall by $1.5 \times 3\% = 4.5\%$ to 10.5%, being $9\% + (10 - 9) \times 1.5\% = 10.5\%$.

7.9 The CAPM formula

The CAPM can be used to calculate a cost for equity, to go into the calculation of WACC. A beta factor can also be applied to individual capital projects, so that high-risk projects should be expected to provide a higher return than lower-risk projects.

The capital asset pricing model is a statement of the principles explained above. It can be stated as follows.

$$E(r_j) = r_f + (E(r_m) - r_f)\beta_j$$

where $E(r_j)$ is the expected return from an individual security

      r_f is the risk-free rate of return

      $E(r_m)$ is the expected return from the market as a whole

      β_j is the beta factor of the individual security

7.10 Example: CAPM (2)

ABC's shares have a beta value of 1.2. The market return is 10% and the risk-free rate of return is 6%.

The expected return on ABC's equity is:

6% + ((10 − 6) × 1.2) % = 10.8%.

7.11 The CAPM and share prices

The CAPM can be used not only to estimate expected returns from securities with differing risk characteristics, but also to **predict the values of shares**.

7.12 Example: CAPM (3)

Company X and Company Y both pay an annual cash return to shareholders of 34.5 cents per share and this is expected to continue in perpetuity. The risk-free rate of return is 8% and the current average market rate of return is 12%. Company X's β coefficient is 1.8 and Company Y's is 0.8. What is the expected return from Companies X and Y respectively, and what would be the predicted market value of each company's shares?

Solution

(a)   The expected return for X is 8% + (12% − 8%) × 1.8 = 15.2%

(b)   The expected return for Y is 8% + (12% − 8%) × 0.8 = 11.2%

The dividend valuation model can now be used to derive expected share prices.

(c)   The predicted value of a share in X is $\dfrac{34.5c}{0.152}$ = 227 cents

(d)   The predicted value of a share in Y is $\dfrac{34.5c}{0.112}$ = 308 cents

The actual share prices of X and Y might be higher or lower than 227c and 308c. If so, CAPM analysis would conclude that the share is currently either overpriced or underpriced.

The risk-free rate of return is 7%. The average market return is 11%.

(a) What will be the return expected from a share whose β factor is 0.9?

(b) What would be the share's expected value if it is expected to earn an annual dividend of 5.3c, with no capital growth?

(For the answer to this question, see the Answer section at the end of this book.)

7.13 The CAPM and project appraisal

The CAPM can be used instead of the dividend valuation model to establish an equity cost of capital to use in project appraisal.

The cost of equity is $K_{eg} = r_f + (E(r_m) - r_f) \times \beta_e$

where β_e is the beta value for the company's equity capital.

7.14 Example: CAPM (4)

A company is financed by a mixture of equity and debt capital, whose market values are in the ratio 3:1. The debt capital, which is considered risk-free, yields 10% before tax. The average stock market return on equity capital is 16%. The beta value of the company's equity capital is estimated as 0.95. The tax rate is 30%.

What would be an appropriate cost of capital to be used for investment appraisal of new projects with the same systematic risk characteristics as the company's current investment portfolio?

Solution

An appropriate cost of capital to use, assuming no change in the company's financial gearing, is its WACC. The CAPM can be used to estimate the cost of the company's equity.

K_{eg} = 10% + (16 − 10) × 0.95% = 15.7%

The after tax cost of debt is $0.70 \times 10\% = 7.0\%$.

The WACC is therefore:

$(\frac{3}{4} \times 15.7\%) + (\frac{1}{4} \times 7.0\%) = 13.5\%$.

The cost of capital to use in project appraisal is 13.5%.

7.15 How is the WACC different using the CAPM?

You might be wondering how the weighted average cost of capital (WACC) is different when we use the CAPM compared to the method of calculating the WACC which was described earlier in this chapter. The only difference is the method used to calculate the cost of the firm's equity: the dividend valuation model (DVM) or the CAPM. Using the different techniques for measuring the cost of equity should, in theory, produce the same results, however differences may arise as a result of the differing assumptions and limitations of the two models.

A contrast of the assumptions of the two model shows the following

DVM	CAPM
Investors are rational and risk averse	Investors are rational and risk averse
Capital markets are perfect	Capital markets are perfect
Capital markets are efficient, hence prices are in equilibrium	Capital markets are efficient, hence prices are in equilibrium
Dividends are paid regularly (or will be in the future)	N/A
Dividend growth is known/stable	N/A
N/A	Investors are diversified
N/A	Investors can freely invest or borrow at the risk-free rate
N/A	All investors have the same expectations regarding future returns

A contrast of the limitations of the two model shows the following

DVM	CAPM
Can only be applied to dividend paying stocks	N/A
Difficulty in establishing stable values for growth rates	N/A
N/A	CAPM is a single period model, i.e. the results are only valid so long as the inputs (risk-free rate, market return, beta) remain constant.
N/A	Only applicable for diversified investors
N/A	Ability to establish a relevant, reliable and stable beta factor

Whilst there is some overlap of assumptions, it is clear that they are not completely consistent, hence differences will arise.

7.16 The usefulness and limitations of the CAPM for capital investment decisions

The CAPM produces a required return based on the expected returns on the stock market as a whole, expected project returns, the risk-free interest rate and the variability of project returns relative to the market returns.

Its main advantage when used for investment appraisal is that it produces a discount rate based on the systematic risk of the individual investment. It can be used to compare projects of all different risk classes and is therefore superior to a DCF approach that uses only one discount rate for all projects, regardless of their risk.

The model was developed with respect to securities. By applying it to an investment within the firm, the company is assuming that the shareholder wishes investments to be evaluated as if they were securities in the capital market and thus assumes that all shareholders will hold diversified portfolios and will not look to the company to achieve diversification for them.

Chapter roundup

- The **cost of capital** is the rate of return that a business must pay to satisfy the providers of funds, and it reflects the riskiness of the funding transaction.

- The **dividend valuation model** can be used to estimate a cost of equity, on the assumption that the market value of shares is directly related to the expected future dividends on the shares.

- Expected **growth in dividends** can be allowed for in calculating a cost of equity, using Gordon's growth model.

- The **cost of debt** is the return an enterprise must pay to its lenders.

  - For **irredeemable debt**, this is the (post-tax) interest as a percentage of the ex div market value of the loan stock (or preference shares).

  - For **redeemable debt**, the cost is given by the internal rate of return of the cash flows involved. The same technique is used to calculate either the pre-tax or the post-tax cost of redeemable debt.

- The **weighted average cost of capital** can be used to evaluate a company's investment projects if:

  - The project is small relative to the company

  - The existing capital structure will be maintained (same financial risk)

  - The project has the same business risk as the company

  - New investments are financed by new sources of funds, and a marginal cost of capital approach is used

- An alternative method of calculating the cost of equity is to use the **capital asset pricing model**. This states that the cost of equity is at a premium above the risk-free rate. The size of this premium is the difference between the average stock market returns and the risk-free rate of return, multiplied by a **beta factor**.

- Each company's equity has its own beta factor. A higher beta indicates higher (non-diversifiable) systematic risk. When a company has a beta factor in excess of 1.0, its expected returns are higher than the average returns for the market as a whole. A beta factor of less than 1.0 indicates systematic risk lower than the market average, and so expected returns are also lower than the market average.

- The CAPM can be used to calculate a cost for equity, to go into the calculation of WACC. A beta factor can also be applied to individual capital projects, so that high-risk projects should be expected to provide a higher return than lower-risk projects.

Quick quiz

1   A cost of capital can be said to consist of three elements. What are they?

2   A company has just paid an annual dividend of 15c per share, and the share price is 600c. What is its cost of equity, using the dividend valuation formula, if it expects future annual dividends per share (a) to be constant for the foreseeable future or (b) to grow by 5% per annum for the foreseeable future?

3   Why is it not possible to calculate the after-tax cost of redeemable debt capital as the pre-tax cost of debt capital multiplied by the factor $(1 - t)$?

4   Why should a weighted average cost of capital be used as the discount rate, instead of the cost of the funds that are specifically used to finance each new investment?

5   What is the name given to risk that can be diversified away by investing in a wide portfolio of shares or a wide portfolio of capital projects?

6   A company's share capital has an estimated beta value of 0.88. The risk-free rate of return is 6% and the market rate of return is 9.5%. What is the company's cost of equity, using the CAPM?

7   A company's cost of equity, as measured by the CAPM, is 10%. The company proposes to raise a large amount of debt capital, and so alter its capital structure by increasing its gearing. Will the cost of equity remain the same, will it rise or will it fall?

8   A company's beta factor is 1.0. The risk-free rate of return is 5% and the market rate of return is 9%. The actual return earned by the company's shareholders last year was 7.8%. How is this explained, in the context of the CAPM?

Answers to quick quiz

1   A risk-free rate of return, a premium for business risk and a premium for financial risk

2   (a)   Cost of equity = 15/600 = 0.025, ie 2.5%
    (b)   Cost of equity =[(15 × 1.05)/600] + 0.05 = 0.02625 + 0.05 = 0.07625, ie 7.625%

3   Because there is no tax implication of the change in capital value (current v redemption), which is one of the elements contributing towards the cost of redeemable debt capital.

4   Use of the WACC is based on the idea that a company has a pool of finance to invest, and all projects are financed from this common pool. It is assumed that specific sources of finance are not raised for individual projects. It is also assumed that the capital structure of the company will continue unchanged, and new sources of finance will be obtained accordingly, to keep the current equity/debt balance.

5   Unsystematic risk

6   6% + 0.88 (9.5 – 6)% = 9.08%

7   A change in the gearing ratio will change the financial risk element of the dividends' systematic risk. The risk will be higher, due to the higher gearing, and the company's cost of equity will therefore rise.

8   The expected return, applying the CAPM, should have been 9% (same as the market return for a beta of 1.0). The actual return was only 7.8%. The difference of 1.2% would be attributable to factors that can be diversified away (ie unsystematic risk factors) and possibly also some statistical error in the calculation of the beta factor.

Part D
Capital markets

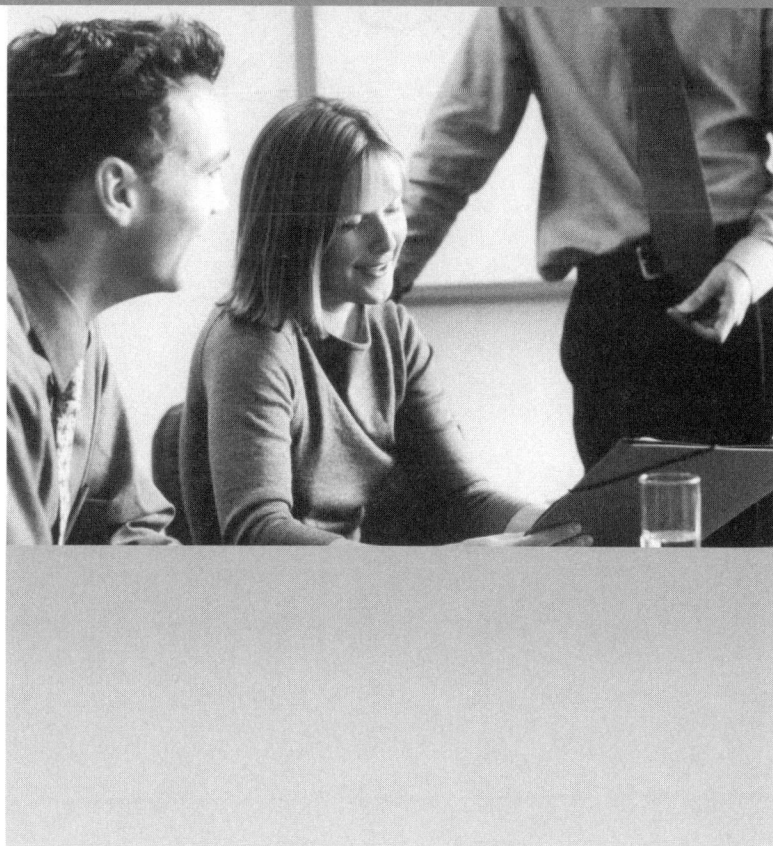

10

Capital markets

Topic list	Syllabus reference
1 The nature and purpose of stock exchanges	4a
2 Stock exchanges and stock markets	4a
3 The secondary market	4a
4 Obtaining a listing	4b
5 The international capital markets	4e
6 Stock market ratios	4f
7 Venture capital	4g

Introduction

A private company (one that is not listed on a stock exchange) may struggle to raise all the capital it needs as it becomes larger. Therefore, it might decide to become a public company and obtain a listing on a stock exchange.

This chapter looks at the nature of stock exchanges in their role as a primary market (raising new finance) and as a secondary market (trading existing shares between investors).

1 The nature and purpose of stock exchanges

The main purposes of a stock market are to enable organisations to raise new capital (**primary market**) and to allow investors to buy and sell securities after they have been issued (**secondary market**). They also enable investors to invest in securities, such as company shares, and to benefit from the investor protection provided by the Listing Rules and the trading rules of the market.

The **capital markets** are the markets for raising and investing long-term finance. Organisations wishing to raise capital must find some way of attracting investments, and to do this, they must be brought into contact with potential investors. A function of stock markets is to provide an organised and regulated market place in which raisers of capital and capital investors can come together, and in which capital transactions can take place.

Stock markets serve two main purposes.

(a)   As **primary markets** they enable organisations to raise new finance, by issuing new shares or new debentures. In most countries, a company must have public company status to be allowed to raise finance from the public on a capital market.

Capital markets make it easier for companies to raise new long-term finance than if they had to raise funds privately by contacting investors individually.

The markets also provide a way for investors to invest in companies, by buying shares or bonds.

(b)   As **secondary markets** they enable existing investors to sell their investments, should they wish to do so. In other words, the stock markets provide an 'exit route' for an investor who wants to cash in his investment in shares. A shareholder in a 'listed' company can sell his shares whenever he wants to on the Stock Exchange. The marketability of securities is a very important feature of the capital markets, because investors are more willing to buy stocks and shares if they know that they could sell them easily, should they wish to.

The secondary markets also enable investors to alter their investment portfolio, by selling some shares and purchasing others. For example, an investor can switch out of telecommunications, media and technology stocks and into, say, finance and banking, by selling shares in 'TMT' companies and buying shares of banks.

Most trading of stocks and shares on the capital markets is in existing securities, rather than new issues.

These are the main functions of a stock market, but we can add three more important ones.

(a)   When a company comes to the stock market for the first time, and 'floats' its shares on the market, the owners of the company can realise some of the value of their shares in cash, because they will offer a proportion of their personally-held shares for sale to new investors.

(b)   When one company wants to take over another, it is common to do so by issuing shares to finance the takeover. For example, if ABC wants to take over XYZ, it might offer XYZ shareholders three new shares in ABC for every two shares held in XYZ. Takeovers by means of a share exchange are only feasible if the shares that are offered can be readily traded on a stock market, and so have an identifiable market value.

(c)   The market price of shares, and the total market value of a company, provides direct information to investors and company management on shareholder returns and shareholder wealth. If the main financial objective of a company is to increase the wealth of its shareholders, the success of management in achieving this objective can be monitored continually through stock market prices.

1.1 Over the counter (OTC) markets

Shares and other financial instruments are sometimes bought and sold outside the supervised and regulated official exchanges in the **'over the counter' (OTC) markets**. If the shares of a public company are not traded on any stock exchange, they may be traded 'off exchange', ie over-the-counter. In addition, investment institutions will often arrange to buy shares from another institution, or sell to another institution, without going through the stock exchange to make the transaction. Shares are traded 'off the market' in this way both to reduce transaction costs as well as to maintain secrecy.

1.2 Participants in the stock markets

The participants in the stock markets can be divided into four broad groups:

    (a)   Organisations that use the primary markets to raise capital
    (b)   Investors
    (c)   Intermediaries
    (d)   The stock market organisers and regulators

1.3 Institutional investors

Institutional investors are institutions that have large amounts of funds to invest. They are the biggest investors on the stock market but they might also invest venture capital, or lend directly to companies. The major institutional investors are **pension funds**, **insurance companies, investment trusts**, **unit trusts** and venture capital organisations. Of these, pension funds and insurance companies have the largest amounts of funds to invest.

Pension funds are funds set aside to provide for retirement pensions. They are financed from pension contributions paid into a fund by a company and its employees or by private individuals. Pension funds are continually receiving large amounts of money from pension contributions and as dividends and interest on their existing investments. They are also continually paying out money for pensions, as lump sums and regular pension payments to beneficiaries. Money coming in can be diverted to meet payment obligations, but there will usually be an excess of contributions coming in over pensions going out, and this excess must be invested.

A **fund manager** is the person who makes the investment decisions on behalf of institutional investors, buying and selling securities.

1.4 Intermediaries

Intermediaries are the organisations bringing companies and investors together in the primary markets, and buyers and sellers together in the secondary markets. Intermediaries have three main functions.

    (a)   They act in the primary markets, advising and assisting companies and other organisations to issue securities and raise funds.

    (b)   They act on behalf of clients in the secondary markets, buying and selling securities on the client's instructions. This function is carried out by **brokers** (or 'stockbrokers').

    (c)   They create a secondary market in securities, buying and selling securities on their own behalf to make a profit. Intermediary organisations that create and maintain a secondary market play an important role in helping to give the markets 'liquidity'. Stock markets are liquid when investors can buy or sell shares readily, at a fair market price. These intermediaries are known either as **market makers** or **broker-dealers**.

2 Stock exchanges and stock markets

FAST FORWARD

> When shares are traded on a stock market, the market price can be used to measure the total **market value** of the company and changes in **shareholder wealth**.

Key term

> A **stock exchange** organises a stock market. Intermediaries are members of the exchange, and agree to operate within the rules of the exchange. The exchange therefore provides an organised and regulated market, protecting investors against unfair or improper dealings by other participants in the market.

There is a distinction between a stock exchange and a stock market. A **stock exchange** is a formal stock market, with a central location (stock exchange building), systems for trading in shares, rules of conduct, and systems for disseminating information to investors. Companies whose shares are traded on a stock exchange must also comply with the rules of the exchange.

In the past, stock exchanges provided a trading floor, where transactions in securities were made. Some exchanges, particularly in the US, still have a trading floor. Outside the US, however, stock exchanges provide trading systems where shares are bought and sold by telephone, or through an electronic dealing system. There is a central stock exchange building, but no trading floor.

A **stock market** is a more general term for an organised market in securities, but without a central stock exchange building. Examples of organised stock markets that are not stock exchanges are Nasdaq, the international capital markets and some electronic share trading systems.

2.1 Tiered markets

Smaller companies can often have difficulty issuing shares on a major stock market, due to the high costs of obtaining a listing and the reluctance of many investors to buy shares in companies below a certain size. Small companies might also consider the regulatory and compliance requirements of the stock exchange to be too much of a burden.

In some countries, 'junior' stock markets have been established for smaller companies. The regulations and compliance requirements of the **junior market** are less strict than for the senior market, and the issue costs of entering the market are less than for a 'main market' listing. The junior market provides a stock market for institutions and individuals interested in investing in small (and growing) companies. Companies whose shares are traded on a junior market might eventually become large enough to progress to a main market listing.

Examples of junior markets are AIM, the Alternative Investment Market, which is a junior market operated by the London Stock Exchange, and the Neuer Markt, a junior market in Germany which is part of the German stock exchange, the Deutsche Börse. Nasdaq also differentiates between its market for large company shares (its 'National Market'), and its market for 'small cap' companies.

3 The secondary market

The secondary market is the market for trading in shares and other securities after they have been issued. To operate successfully, a secondary market must:

(a) Be liquid
(b) Provide an efficient and cheap system for trading in shares
(c) Provide a share price information system for investors and companies
(d) Provide an efficient system for the clearing and settlement of transactions

3.1 Liquidity

Liquidity refers to the relative ease with which an investor can find a buyer or seller for his shares, who is willing to pay a fair market price. A liquid market is therefore one in which large amounts of shares are traded, and no individual investors dominate the market to the point where they can manipulate the share price. An illiquid market is one in which an investor might have difficulty in finding any buyer for his shares. Liquidity varies considerably between stock markets, and can vary over time within the same stock market.

Investors prefer to deal in liquid markets, where they can find willing buyers or sellers whenever they wish to make a share transaction. The most liquid stock markets are the largest, such as the New York Stock Exchange, Nasdaq, London and Tokyo.

Some shares are more liquid than others. As a general rule, shares in large companies, where the shares are widely held by a large number of investors, are the most liquid. In contrast, shares in smaller companies tend to be less liquid, and the volume of trading in these shares is much lower than for liquid stocks.

3.2 Importance of share price information

The efficiency of trading in a secondary market depends on investors having ready access to current price information. In all the major stock markets share price information, for example details of prices at which recent share transactions have been made, is fed instantly to participants in the market.

4 Obtaining a listing

If a company wants its shares to be traded on the main market of a Stock Exchange, it must obtain a listing for the shares. When shares are listed, they are included in an 'official list' that is maintained by the relevant Listing Authority.

In order to obtain a listing for shares, a company and its advisers must comply with certain listing requirements. Many of these requirements relate to the information and documents that must be submitted for approval to the Listing Authority, and information that must be made available to investors. Another condition of being accepted for listing is that the shares must be accepted for trading by the relevant Stock Exchange.

The Stock Exchange will accept shares for trading only if the company complies with certain requirements, and the shares must also be listed. Obtaining a listing and gaining admission to trading must therefore happen at the same time.

4.1 The implications of obtaining a listing

FAST FORWARD

It is important to understand the **implications of a stock market listing**. These are set out in the text of this chapter.

For a company, the implications of obtaining a listing for its shares are as follows.

(a) The shares can be traded on the main market of the Stock Exchange. Current shareholders can therefore sell their shares on the market, should they wish to do so, and new investors can buy shares.

(b) The **value of the shares** is likely to be higher than if they were not listed, because their marketability should add to their value.

(c)   The company should find it easier to raise new capital, and might be able to issue new shares to finance takeovers of other companies. The **strategic options** of the company are therefore widened, and its **growth potential** is increased.

(d)   The shares will be held by a larger number of investors. This increases the possibility that the company will itself become **vulnerable to a takeover** by another company.

(e)   Since the shares have a market value, it will be possible to set up incentive schemes for directors or employees, whereby these individuals are rewarded with the granting of **share options**.

(f)   The company must **comply with the Listing Rules** of the Listing Authority, in order for the shares to be accepted for listing. The company must then comply with the 'continuing obligations' rules, normally including the requirement to publish interim accounts for the first six months of each year, in addition to accounts for the full year.

(g)   Listed companies are required to comply with guidelines on '**corporate governance**'. These may not be compulsory, but they are typically included in the Listing Rules, and companies are put under heavy pressure by the authorities to follow the guidelines. The guidelines include requirements for the appointment of non-executive directors to the boards of listed companies, and guidelines on directors' remuneration. In the UK the guidelines are known as the Combined Code.

(h)   A listing is likely to bring the company more to the **attention of the public**. Companies might therefore become more accountable to the public, in matters relating to social responsibility and environmental issues.

The advantages and disadvantages of obtaining a listing might be summarised briefly as follows.

Advantages	Disadvantages
Access to capital markets for raising new capital	Cost of obtaining and maintaining a listing (fees etc)
Marketability of shares. 'Exit route' for shareholders to cash in their investment	Requirement to comply with Listing Rules and the rules of the Stock Exchange
Shares can be used to make takeovers	Requirement to apply the corporate governance guidelines
Increase in the value of the company	Wider share ownership could make the company vulnerable to a takeover
Share incentive schemes for executives can be set up	Possibly, greater public accountability
Company's value easily measured by the share price	

Exam focus point

> This area was examined in June 2005 with a straightforward question asking for discussion of the nature and purpose of a Stock Exchange and the advantages and disadvantages of obtaining a listing.

5 The international capital markets

FAST FORWARD

Companies might use the **international capital markets** to raise capital. Large companies can issue bonds or shares through the international bond and equities markets. These markets are self-regulated, by the ICMA. Non-US companies can also obtain a listing on a US exchange (in particular, either the New York Stock Exchange or Nasdaq) but must first be registered with the Securities and Exchange Commission (SEC). Non-US companies can also issue shares and bonds, without the requirement for registration, in the US 'private placement' market. European company equities traded in the US markets are normally in the form of American Depository Receipts (ADRs).

The London Stock Exchange is one of the largest stock exchanges in the world, and many UK companies wanting their shares to be traded on a stock market apply for admission to either the main market or AIM.

However there are many other stock markets on which securities can be traded.

(a) Large companies can raise debt capital by issuing bonds in either the **international bond market** or in the **domestic US bond markets**. International bonds might be listed in the UK, and admitted to trading on the London Stock Exchange, but trading in the international bond market is through international banks specialising as dealers in this market. In the US, non-US companies are able to issue bonds in a 'private placement' market. This is a stock market in which investors are restricted to investment institutions, and the wider general public cannot invest. UK companies might therefore choose to issue bonds or shares in this market, to gain exposure to US investors and a more international investor base.

(b) Equity of large non-US companies might be traded on **US stock markets** in a special form known as **American Depository Receipts**, or ADRs. An ADR is a security denominated in US dollars, that is backed by a number of shares in the non-US company. A UK company wanting to raise capital in the US might therefore place a number of new shares in the custody of a bank, and a US bank will issue ADRs backed by these shares. The ADRs are registered in the US, and accepted to trading on a US stock market, such as the New York Stock Exchange or Nasdaq. When the UK company pays dividends on the shares, it makes the dividend payment in sterling, but ADR holders receive their dividends in US dollars from the US bank.

(c) Large companies might arrange an **international equity issue**. The issue is marketed through an international syndicate of banks. After the issue, the shares might be traded on the international equities market. The shares will also be listed on one or more stock exchanges (eg on the London Stock Exchange) and, in ADR form, on the New York Stock Exchange.

When the bonds or shares (ADRs) of a UK company are traded in the US, the company must comply with US market regulations. In the US, shares cannot be offered for sale to the general public unless they have been registered with the Securities and Exchange Commission (SEC). UK companies not wanting to go through the costly and time-consuming procedures for obtaining registration can opt instead for the private placement market (for which registration is not required) but they must comply with the rules of that market.

When the bonds or shares of a UK company are traded on the international capital market, it must comply with the market rules of ICMA, the International Capital Market Association, based in Zurich. ICMA was formed in 2005 by the merger of ISMA (the International Securities Market Association) and IPMA (the International Primary Market Association).

Issuing shares or bonds in the international capital markets was described in the earlier chapters on sources of finance.

6 Stock market ratios

FAST FORWARD

Investors in equities assess their returns and the performance of their investments with a number of stock market ratios. The most important of these are **dividend yield, earnings per share, price-earnings ratio** and **dividend cover**.

A company will only be able to raise finance if investors think that the returns they can expect are satisfactory in view of the risks they are taking. Investors in stock market companies can measure and assess their returns using stock market ratios.

The main stock market ratios are the **dividend yield**, **earnings per share**, the **price/earnings ratio** and the **dividend cover**.

6.1 Dividend yield

The **dividend yield** is the annual dividend received by a shareholder expressed as a percentage of the current share price.

$$\text{Dividend yield} = \frac{\text{Dividend per share}}{\text{Market price per share}} \times 100\%$$

The market price per share should be the 'ex div' price, ie the price excluding any dividend payable in the near future.

6.2 Example: dividend yield

A company pays a dividend of 15c per share. The market price is 240c. What is the dividend yield?

$$\text{Dividend yield} = \frac{15}{240} \times 100\% = 6.25\%$$

Sometimes the dividend yield is quoted **gross** in order to make it more directly comparable with gross interest rates etc. This means that the dividend as quoted and paid by a company has to be grossed up for the imputed tax credit. For example, the tax credit might be at a rate of 10% - ie the 'net' dividend paid by a company represents 90% of the gross dividend.

Thus in the above example, the gross dividend yield would be:

$$\text{Gross dividend yield} = \frac{\text{Gross dividend per share}}{\text{Market price per share}} \times 100\%$$

$$= \frac{15 \times 100/90}{240} \times 100\%$$

$$= 6.94\%$$

6.3 Interest yield

The dividend yield applies to dividend returns to shareholders. Interest yield is a similar measure of return for bondholders.

$$\text{Interest yield} = \frac{\text{Gross interest}}{\text{Market value of loan stock}} \times 100\%$$

The 'gross yield' is the interest received by the investor. Tax relief for the company on its interest payments should be ignored.

6.4 Example: interest yield

An investor buys $1,000 (nominal value) of XYZ bonds with a coupon of 8%, for the current market value of $750.

Interest yield $= \dfrac{1,000 \times 8\%}{750} \times 100\% = 10.67\%$

6.5 Dividend yield and interest yield

In practice, it is usual for the dividend yield on shares to be less than the interest yield on loan stock. The share price often rises each year, giving shareholders capital gains. In the long run, shareholders will want the return on their shares, in terms of dividends received plus capital gains, to exceed the return that investors get from fixed interest securities.

6.6 Earnings per share (EPS)

Earnings per share (EPS) is widely-used as a measure of a company's performance and is of particular importance in comparing results over a period of several years. A company must be able to sustain its earnings in order to pay dividends and re-invest in the business so as to achieve future growth. Investors also look for *growth* in the EPS from one year to the next.

Key term

> **Earnings per share (EPS)** is the profit in cents attributable to each equity (ordinary) share, calculated as:
>
> (a)   The profit for the year attributable to ordinary shareholders (profits after taxation and preference dividends)
>
> (b)   Divided by the number of equity shares in issue

Question 10.1   EPS

Walter Wall Carpets made profits before tax in 20X8 of $9,320,000. Tax amounted to $2,800,000.

The company's share capital is as follows.

	$
Ordinary shares (10,000,000 shares of $1)	10,000,000
8% preference shares	2,000,000
	12,000,000

Calculate the EPS for 20X8.

(For the answer to this question, see the Answer section at the end of this book.)

EPS on its own does not tell us anything. It must be seen in the context of several other matters.

(a)   EPS is used for the comparing of results of a company over time. Is its EPS growing? What is the rate of growth? Is the rate of growth increasing or decreasing?

(b)   Is there likely to be a significant dilution of EPS in the future, perhaps due to the exercise of share options or warrants, or the conversion of convertible loan stock into equity?

(c)   EPS should not be used blindly to compare the earnings of one company with another. For example, if A has an EPS of 12c for its 10,000,000 10c shares and B has an EPS of 24c for its 50,000,000 25c shares, we must take account of the numbers of shares. When earnings are used to compare one company's shares with another, this is done using the P/E ratio or perhaps the earnings yield.

(d)   If EPS is to be a reliable basis for comparing results, it must be calculated consistently. The EPS of one company must be directly comparable with the EPS of others, and the EPS of a company in one year must be directly comparable with its published EPS figures for previous years. Changes in the share capital of a company during the course of a year cause problems of comparability.

6.7 The price earnings ratio

The **price earnings (P/E) ratio** is the most important yardstick for assessing the relative worth of a share. It is:

$$\text{P/E ratio} = \frac{\text{Market price of share in cents}}{\text{EPS in cents}}$$

This is the same as:

$$\frac{\text{Total market value of equity}}{\text{Total earnings}}$$

The **value of the P/E ratio** reflects the market's appraisal of the share's future prospects. In other words, if one company has a higher P/E ratio than another it is because investors either expect its earnings to increase faster than the other's or consider that it is a less risky company or in a more secure industry. The P/E ratio is a measure of the relationship between the market value of a company's shares and the earnings from those shares. It is an important ratio because it relates two key considerations for investors, the market price of a share and its earnings capacity.

6.8 Example: price earnings ratio

A company has recently declared a dividend of 12c per share. The share price is $3.72 cum div and earnings for the most recent year were 30c per share. Calculate the P/E ratio.

Solution

$$\text{P/E ratio} = \frac{\text{MV ex div}}{\text{EPS}} = \frac{\$3.60}{30c} = 12$$

6.9 Changes in EPS: the P/E ratio and the share price

The dividend valuation model or fundamental theory of share values is the theory that share prices are related to expected future dividends on the shares. Another approach to assessing what share prices ought to be, which is often used in practice, is a P/E ratio approach. It is a 'common sense' approach to share price assessment (although not as well founded in theory as the dividend valuation model), which is that:

(a)   The relationship between the EPS and the share price is measured by the P/E ratio

(b)   There is no reason to suppose, in normal circumstances, that the P/E ratio will vary much over time

(c)   So if the EPS goes up or down, the share price should be expected to move up or down too, and the new share price will be the new EPS multiplied by the constant P/E ratio

For example, if a company had an EPS last year of 30c and a share price of $3.60, its P/E ratio would have been 12. If the current year's EPS is 33c, we might expect that the P/E ratio would remain the same, 12, and so the share price ought to go up to $12 \times 33c = \$3.96$.

6.10 Example: effects of a rights issue

Annette Cord Sports Goods has 6,000,000 ordinary shares in issue, and the company has been making regular annual profits after tax of $3,000,000 for some years. The share price is $5. A proposal has been made to issue 2,000,000 new shares in a rights issue, at an issue price of $4.50 per share. The funds would be used to redeem $9,000,000 of 12% debenture stock. The rate of tax is 30%.

What might be the predicted effect of the rights issue on the share price, and would you recommend that the issue should take place?

Solution

The share price might change on announcement of the rights issue, in anticipation of the change in EPS. The current EPS is 50c per share, and so the current P/E ratio is 10.

	$	$
Current annual earnings		3,000,000
Increase in earnings after rights issue		
Interest saved (12% × $9,000,000)	1,080,000	
Less tax on extra profits (30%)	324,000	
		756,000
Anticipated annual earnings		3,756,000
Number of shares (6,000,000 + 2,000,000)		8,000,000
EPS		46.95 cents
Current P/E ratio		10

The anticipated P/E ratio is assumed to be the same.

Anticipated share price   469.5 cents

The proposed share issue is a one for three rights issue, and we can estimate the theoretical ex rights price.

	$
Current value of three shares (× $5)	15.00
Rights issue price of one share	4.50
Theoretical value of four shares	19.50

Theoretical ex rights price $\frac{\$19.50}{4} = \$4.875$

The anticipated share price after redeeming the debentures would be 469.5 cents per share, which is less than the theoretical ex rights price. If the rights issue goes ahead and the P/E ratio remains at 10, shareholders should expect a fall in share price below the theoretical ex rights price, which indicates that there would be a capital loss on their investment. The rights issue is for this reason not recommended.

6.11 Changes in the P/E ratio over time

Changes in the P/E ratios of companies over time will depend on several factors.

(a) If interest rates go up, investors might be attracted away from shares and into debt capital. Share prices would fall, and so P/E ratios would also fall. Similarly, if interest rates go down, shares might become relatively more attractive to invest in, so share prices and P/E ratios would go up.

(b) If prospects for company profits improve, share prices will go up, and P/E ratios will rise. Share prices depend on expectations of future earnings, not historical earnings, and so a change in prospects, perhaps caused by a substantial rise in international trade, or an economic recession, will affect prices and P/E ratios.

(c)   Investors' confidence might be changed by a variety of circumstances, such as:

   (i)   The prospect of a change in government
   (ii)   The prospects for greater exchange rate stability between currencies

6.12 Dividend cover

The **dividend cover** is the number of times the actual dividend could be paid out of current profits.

$$\text{Dividend cover} = \frac{\text{Maximum possible equity dividend that could be paid out of current profits}}{\text{Actual dividend for ordinary shareholders}}$$

It is therefore a ratio of earnings to dividends.

The dividend cover shows the proportion of distributable profits for the year that is being retained by the company. It also indicates whether the company should be able to maintain the same dividend payments in future years (ie dividends per share), should earnings fall. A high dividend cover means that a high proportion of profits are being retained, which might indicate that the company is re-investing a large amount of profits to achieve earnings growth in the future.

Shareholders are unlikely to be satisfied with high earnings retention but low profits and dividend growth.

6.13 Example: dividend cover

The EPS of York is 20c. The dividend was 20% on the 25c ordinary shares. Calculate the dividend cover.

Solution

$$\text{Dividend cover} = \frac{20c}{20\% \times 25c} = 4$$

A dividend cover of 4 means that the company is retaining 75% of its earnings for reinvestment.

Question 10.2   **Current market price**

The earnings per share of Chard in the previous year were 30c. The dividend yield is 4% and the dividend cover is 1.5 times. What is the current market price per share?

(For the answer to this question, see the Answer section at the end of this book.)

---

7 Venture capital

FAST FORWARD

> Small companies that cannot obtain capital from any other source might be able to arrange **venture capital finance**, provided they have a strong business plan and good operational cash flows. The finance package provided by venture capitalists could be a mixture of equity, mezzanine finance, redeemable securities and subordinated loans. The venture capitalist will also want an **exit route** for the investment, such as a stock market launch or a trade sale.

7.1 Sources of capital for smaller companies

Small and unquoted companies do not have ready access to new long-term funds, except for any **cash from retained earnings** or improvements in working capital management. Extra finance might be obtained by **issuing more shares** to private shareholders, and to some extent from **bank borrowing**. When there are insufficient profits to retain, and banks are unwilling to lend, how can a company obtain new capital for investment?

In some situations, a company might be able to obtain **'venture capital'**. Many governments give some encouragement by offering tax incentives to individuals providing venture capital.

Key term

> **Venture capital**: risk capital, normally provided in return for an equity stake.

7.2 Venture capital organisations

Venture capital organisations have been operating for many years. There are now quite a large number of such organisations, particularly in the US and UK. The British Venture Capital Association is a regulatory body for all the institutions that have joined it as members. The **3i Group** is the biggest and oldest of the venture capital organisations in the UK. It was owned by the clearing banks and the Bank of England until its flotation on the stock market during 1994.

The role of venture capital organisations is to:

(a)   Obtain venture capital finance to invest

(b)   Identify companies that need finance and in which an investment of venture capital seems worth the risk

(c)   Negotiate a venture capital financing agreement with the company, and then

(d)   Provide the capital to the company

Venture capitalists want to invest in companies that will be successful. 3i Group publicity material states that successful investments have three common characteristics:

(a)   A good basic idea, a product or service which meets real customer needs
(b)   Finance, in the right form, to turn the idea into a solid business
(c)   Commitment and drive of an individual or group, and determination to succeed

The types of venture in which a venture capital organisation might invest include the following.

(a)   **Business start-ups**. When a business has been set up by individuals who have already put time and money into getting it started, a venture capital organisation might be willing to provide finance to enable the company to be grown. With start-ups, venture capitalists might prefer to be one of several financial institutions putting in the venture capital.

(b)   **Business development**. A venture capital organisation might be willing to provide development capital for a company which wants to invest in new products or new markets or to make a business acquisition, and so which needs a major capital injection.

(c)   **Management buyouts**. A management buyout is the purchase of all or parts of a business from its owners by its managers.

(d)   Helping a company where one of its owners wants to **realise all or part of his investment**. A venture capitalist might be prepared to buy some of the company's equity.

7.3 Venture capital funds

Some venture capital organisations are either public companies or subsidiaries of a large bank. These venture capitalists use either their own finance or obtain finance for investing from their parent company.

Wealthy individuals might be prepared to invest directly in small companies. Such individuals are known as **business angels** and in the UK can be controlled by the British Business Angels Association (BBAA).

Another way for individuals or organisations to invest venture capital is to put money into a **venture capital fund**.

Some organisations specialise in setting up venture capital funds, whereby the organisation raises venture capital funds from investors and invests the capital in the fund in management buyouts or expanding companies. The venture capital fund managers usually reward themselves by taking a percentage of the portfolio of the fund's investments.

Venture capital trusts are a special type of fund giving individual investors relief from income tax.

7.4 Finding venture capital

When a company's directors look for help from a venture capital institution, they must recognise that:

(a)   The institution will want an equity stake in the company

(b)   It will need convincing that the company can be successful (management buyouts of companies which already have a record of successful trading have been increasingly favoured by venture capitalists in recent years)

(c)   It may want to have a representative appointed to the company's board (perhaps as non-executive chairman), to look after its interests

The directors of the company must then contact venture capital organisations, to try to find one or more which would be willing to offer finance. Typically, a venture capitalist will consider offering finance of £500,000 upwards. A venture capital organisation will only give funds to a company that it believes can succeed, and before it will make any definite offer, it will want from the company's management:

(a)   A business plan

(b)   Details of how much finance is needed and how it would be used

(c)   The most recent trading figures of the company, a balance sheet, a cash flow forecast and a profit forecast

(d)   Details of the management team, with evidence of a wide range of management skills

(e)   Details of major shareholders

(f)   Details of the company's current banking arrangements and any other sources of finance

(g)   Any sales literature or publicity material that the company has issued

In practice, most requests for venture capital are rejected on an initial screening, and only a small percentage of all requests survive both this screening and further investigation and result in actual investments.

7.5 Business angels

Business angels are high net worth individuals who invest on their own, or as part of a syndicate. They invest across most industry sectors and stages of business development, but especially in early- and expansion-stage businesses that they perceive offer high growth potential. In addition to money, business angels often make their own skills, experience and contacts available to the company.

Business angels rarely have a connection with the company before they invest but often have experience of its industry or sector. The majority of business angels make investments for financial reasons. However, there are also other motives for investment, for example, taking an active part in the entrepreneurial process. The commitment in this respect is often very strong and offers the advantage of quick decision-making based on past business experience. For this reason, however they prefer to invest in reasonably local businesses.

Typically in the UK, business angels invest between £10,000 and £750,000 in an investment, filling what is known as the financing gap between what family and friends may be prepared to invest and the minimum investment level for venture capitalists. Where larger amounts are invested in a business, this may be as part of a syndicate organised through personal contacts or a business angel network. The lead investor is sometimes referred to as the "archangel".

The methods used by business angels to decide which businesses to invest in varies greatly, however, the following issues are all taken into consideration:

- The expertise and track record of the founders and management

- The businesses competitive edge or unique selling point

- The characteristics and growth potential of the market

- Compatibility between the management, business proposal and the business angel's skills and investment preferences

- The financial commitment of the entrepreneur

7.6 The business plan

FAST FORWARD

Financial projections in the business plan are used by a venture capitalist to decide whether or not an investment might be worthwhile.

A company wanting to raise finance from a venture capitalist will be required to submit a business plan. The venture capital organisation ('VC' below) will take account of various factors, as follows, in deciding whether to not to invest.

(a) **The nature of the company's product.** The VC will consider whether the company's product or service can be financially viable and has good sales potential, in the light of any market research that the company has carried out.

(b) **Operational cash flows**. The VC will need to be satisfied that the company is capable of earning sufficient cash flows from its operations, and will not require continual refinancing. Expected operational cash flows should therefore be large enough to cover all operating expenses and interest costs on debt finance.

(c) **Scope for cost cutting**. Ideally, the company should have some scope for improving efficiency and reducing its operating costs.

(d) **Expertise in production**. The VC will want to be sure that the company has the necessary technical ability to implement production plans with efficiency.

(e) **Expertise in management**. Venture capitalists pay much attention to the quality of management, since they believe that this is crucial to the success of the enterprise. Not only should the management team be committed to the enterprise; they should also have appropriate skills and experience.

(f) **The market and competition**. The nature of the market for the product will be considered including the threat which rival producers or future new entrants to the market may present.

(g) **Future prospects**. The VC will want to be sure that the possible prospects of profits in the future compensate for the risks involved in the enterprise. The VC will expect the company to have prepared a detailed business plan detailing its future strategy.

(h) **Board membership.** The VC is likely to require a place on the board of directors. It is quite common for the appointee to be made the non-executive chairman of the company. Board representation will ensure that the VC's interests will be taken account of, and that the VC has a say in matters relating to the future strategy of the business.

(i) **The risk borne by the existing owners.** The VC is likely to wish to ensure that the existing owners of the business bear a significant part of the investment risk relating to the expansion. If they are owner-managers, bearing part of the risk will provide an incentive for them to ensure the success of the venture. Although the VC may be providing most of the investment, the amounts provided by the owners should be significant in relation to their overall personal wealth.

The VC will want to negotiate a finance package that offers the prospect of good returns on the investment, in both the short and longer terms. The finance package agreed could be a combination of:

- (a)   Equity
- (b)   Mezzanine finance
- (c)   Convertible bonds or convertible preference shares
- (d)   Subordinated loans, probably at a high rate of interest

Venture capital organisations try to choose their investment carefully. Even so there is a high risk of business failure amongst the companies they finance. The high-risk nature of venture capital finance means that venture capitalists expect high returns from their investments. The high returns from successful investments compensate for losses on investments in businesses that subsequently collapse.

7.7 Exit routes

The ways in which the venture capitalist can eventually realise its investment are called **exit routes**. Ideally the VC will want to be reasonably satisfied that there will be a suitable exit route for its investment within a given period of time. Possible exit routes are as follows.

- (a)   **Admission of shares to trading on AIM** (or its equivalent in other countries). The venture capitalist can then sell its shares to members of the investing public.

- (b)   A **trade sale**. This is sale of its shares to another business in a takeover. The greatest problem for the management of a company financed by venture capital is that the venture capitalist might insist on a trade sale of the entire company.

- (c)   The **sale of shares to the original owners**, if they later have the resources to make such a purchase. The original owners might arrange a new finance package, in order to buyout the original venture capitalist and avoid a trade sale of their business.

- (d)   **Refinancing**. A company might find another venture capital organisation that is willing to provide new finance to buyout the original venture capitalist.

A venture capitalist might want an exit route for its investment within as little as three to four years.

7.8 Financial projections in the business plan

The financial projections in the business plan will be scrutinised very closely, and the assumptions in the forecasts will be assessed for reasonableness. The projections will probably consist of:

- (a)   Profit forecasts for the new few years
- (b)   Balance sheet forecasts as at the end of each year
- (c)   Cash flow forecasts

Assumptions that might be queried by the venture capitalist include:

- (a)   Forecasts of sales volume (quantity and price) and growth in sales

- (b)   Operating expenditures

- (c)   Non-current asset capital investment requirements

- (d)   Working capital requirements (eg inventory levels and inventory turnover, the speed of debt collection, bad debts, etc)

- (e)   Finance costs (dividends, interest, etc)

7.9 Evaluating a venture capital proposal

From the point of view of a venture capital provider, there are two issues to consider.

(a) Is the proposed venture likely to succeed? If the venture fails, the venture capitalist risks losing its entire investment. The venture capitalist cannot make a suitable return on its investment unless the business is successful.

(b) If the venture becomes a successful business, will the expected return on the venture capitalist's investment be sufficient to justify making the investment in the first place? Because of the high risk involved in venture capital financing, the venture capitalist is likely to demand a very high return on investment.

Each of these questions must be addressed. The likely success of a venture will depend on a variety of factors, such as the experience and ability of the management team, and the likely commitment of the team to making the venture a success. This is why venture capitalists usually demand a significant capital investment in the venture by the individual members of the management team, in return for a generous award of equity shares.

The assessment of a venture will also involve a thorough study of the business plan, and its financial projections. The following example indicates an approach that might be taken.

7.10 Example: evaluating a VC proposal

A group of managers of Brix, a wholly-owned subsidiary of a large trading group, have been offered an opportunity to buy their company from the group for $20.5 million. They believe that the company has excellent prospects, provided that an investment programme is undertaken to acquire new equipment and provide additional working capital. They have approached a venture capital company.

A proposal under consideration is that the management team should invest $2 million and receive 20% of the ordinary shares, and the venture capital firm should invest $15 million to acquire the other 80%. The rest of the finance required would be obtained by borrowing from a bank at an interest rate expected to be 10% per annum.

The business plan for the venture includes the following estimates for sales. Cash operating profits before interest (ie cash flows from operations, ignoring working capital changes) should be about 30% of sales revenue.

Year	Sales revenue
	$m
1	14.5
2	16.5
3	18.5
4	21.0
5	26.0

The business plan also provides for the following investment programme.

Year	Equipment purchases	Additional working capital
	$m	$m
0	5.0	0.5
1	3.5	0.4
2	3.5	0.4
3	3.0	0.4
4	3.0	0.3
	18.0	2.0

The equipment will be depreciated by the straight-line method over 10 years, to a residual value of nil.

The company will not pay any dividends for the first five years, but will use its cash from operations to finance the investment programme. If there is any surplus cash, this will be held to ensure that the company can maintain its liquidity.

The venture capital firm would look for an exit route for its investment after five years, and thinks that a trade sale for its 80% shareholding would be possible. The market value of the company after five years is estimated at 10 times the year 5 operating profits. The firm would want to make a return of at least 25% per annum on its investment.

For the purpose of this illustrative example, taxation is ignored.

How might the venture capital firm assess the proposal? (Risk analysis is not required.)

The present value of $1 at the end of Year 5, discounted at 25% per annum, is $0.33.

Solution

The venture capital firm will need to decide whether or not the company has a sound business plan. There are no plans to pay dividends in the first five years, but the company needs to generate sufficient cash flows to remain solvent over this time. A five-year cash flow analysis should be prepared.

(a)   The purchase cost of the shares will be $20.5 million, and there will be an immediate investment requirement of $5.5 million in equipment and working capital. At least $26 million is therefore needed. If the management team and the venture capital firm together invest $17 million in buying the shares, this leaves a funding shortfall of $9 million to be financed by a 10% bank loan.

Due to the cost of interest, it is unlikely that $9 million will be sufficient to cover cash requirements in year 1, and in the analysis below, it is assumed that an initial bank loan of $10 million might be needed.

If a bank loan of $10 million can be obtained, and the investors in the shares put in $17 million, the company will have $6.5 million at the start of year 0 to invest in the business.

In the table below, the cash profit is 30% of the annual sales revenue. Bank interest is calculated as 10% of $10 million in each year. The investment is the sum of the new equipment purchases and the additional working capital investment.

	Year 0 $m	Year 1 $m	Year 2 $m	Year 3 $m	Year 4 $m	Year 5 $m
Opening cash	6.5	1.00	0.45	0.50	1.65	3.65
Investment	(5.5)	(3.90)	(3.90)	(3.40)	(3.30)	–
Cash profit		4.35	4.95	5.55	6.30	7.80
Interest		(1.00)	(1.00)	(1.00)	(1.00)	(1.00)
Closing cash	1.0	0.45	0.50	1.65	3.65	10.45

(*Note.* The closing cash balance at the end of each year becomes the opening cash balance at the start of the next year.)

These forecasts suggest that the company will have sufficient liquidity if it borrows $10 million, and that some of the bank loan can probably be repaid from about year 3 onwards. Repaying some of the bank loan will reduce the cost of the annual interest charge, and so improve the cash flow still further.

(b)   If the venture capital firm is satisfied with the cash flow projections for the business, it must then go on to consider whether its investment in the company would provide a suitable return.

The company's value at the end of year 5 is expected to be ten times the year 5 operating profit. The cash operating profit is expected to be (30% of $26 million) $7.8 million. The annual depreciation charge will be 10% of the total capital equipment expenditure, $18 million, ie $1.8 million. The operating profit in Year 5 is therefore expected to be $6.0 million ($7.8 million – $1.8 million).

This suggests a value for the company of 10 × $6 million = $60 million, of which the venture capital firm will own 80% or $48 million.

The venture capitalist must assess whether an investment of $15 million in Year 0 will justify an expected return of $48 million at the end of Year 5, when a minimum return of 25% per annum is required.

The present value of $48 million in Year 5, discounted at 25% per annum, is $48 million × 0.33 = $15.84 million.

The net present value of the investment would therefore be + $0.84 million.

Ignoring all other matters (eg risk, the quality of the management team, etc), the investment would appear to be a worthwhile undertaking.

Exam focus point

> The subject of venture capital was thoroughly covered in a December 2004 exam question. Candidates were required to explain what is meant by venture capital, the main types of business likely to be attractive to a venture capitalist, the main issues the directors of a company should take into account when considering the use of venture capital and the main factors a venture capitalist will consider when assessing an investment proposal. In this sort of question you should read the requirement very carefully, as here you were required to consider venture capital from two different perspectives.

Chapter roundup

- The main purposes of a stock market are to enable organisations to raise new capital (**primary market**) and to allow investors to buy and sell securities after they have been issued (**secondary market**). They also enable investors to invest in securities, such as company shares, and to benefit from the investor protection provided by the Listing Rules and the trading rules of the market.

- When shares are traded on a stock market, the market price can be used to measure the total **market value** of the company and changes in **shareholder wealth**.

- It is important to understand the **implications of a stock market listing**. These are set out in the text of this chapter.

- Companies might use the **international capital markets** to raise capital. Large companies can issue bonds or shares through the international bond and equities markets. These markets are self-regulated, by the ICMA. Non-US companies can also obtain a listing on a US exchange (in particular, either the New York Stock Exchange or Nasdaq) but must first be registered with the Securities and Exchange Commission (SEC). Non-US companies can also issue shares and bonds, without the requirement for registration, in the US 'private placement' market. European company equities traded in the US markets are normally in the form of American Depository Receipts (ADRs).

- Investors in equities assess their returns and the performance of their investments with a number of stock market ratios. The most important of these are **dividend yield, earnings per share, price-earnings ratio** and **dividend cover**.

- Small companies that cannot obtain capital from any other source might be able to arrange **venture capital finance**, provided they have a strong business plan and good operational cash flows. The finance package provided by venture capitalists could be a mixture of equity, mezzanine finance, redeemable securities and subordinated loans. The venture capitalist will also want an **exit route** for the investment, such as a stock market launch or a trade sale.

- Financial projections in the business plan are used by a venture capitalist to decide whether or not an investment might be worthwhile.

Quick quiz

1   What is the difference between a primary and a secondary market for shares?

2   Name two US stock exchanges.

3   Which organisation regulates the international bond and equities market?

4   The share price of a company is $4.50. The P/E ratio is 15 and the dividend per share last year was 24p. What is the dividend cover?

5   Name three exit routes for a venture capitalist.

Answers to quick quiz

1   New share issues are made in a primary market. In a secondary market, shares are traded between investors after they have been issued.

2   US exchanges include the New York Stock Exchange ('Wall Street') and Nasdaq.

3   The International Capital Market Association, ICMA.

4   Share price 450c, P/E ratio 15, therefore EPS 30 cents.

    Dividend per share 24 cents, therefore dividend cover (30/24) 1.25 times.

5   Three from trade sale, stock market flotation, refinancing, sale to other directors/shareholders of the company.

11

Stock market efficiency

Topic list	Syllabus reference
1 Share prices and market efficiency	4c
2 Different forms of efficiency	4c
3 Weak form efficiency	4c
4 Semi-strong form efficiency	4c
5 Strong form efficiency	4c
6 How efficient are stock markets?	4c
7 The efficient market hypothesis and its implications	4d

Introduction

'Efficiency' of stock markets refers to the way in which the market channels funds towards the most deserving companies, and quotes fair prices for share prices. We are most concerned in this chapter with information processing efficiency, ie how quickly and how fairly a stock market prices its shares, particularly when new information about the company becomes available.

1 Share prices and market efficiency

The **efficiency** of a market refers to the extent to which share prices react to information about a company and its profitability. A market can be described as showing one of three forms of efficiency: weak form, semi-strong form and strong form.

1.1 The fundamental theory of share values

There is a theory of share prices, known as the **fundamental theory of share values**, which states:

The current market price of a share represents the present value of all future expected returns from the share, discounted at the shareholders' cost of capital (required rate of investment return).

This theory of share values is the basis of the dividend valuation model and the dividend growth model, which were explained in the chapter on cost of capital.

If the fundamental theory of share values is correct, it has implications for changes in share prices and so changes in shareholder wealth. If a company undertakes a capital project with a positive NPV, and shareholders are aware of the future cash flows arising from the project, the total value of the company's shares should rise immediately by the amount of the project's NPV.

This is a *theory* of share values. It raises the question of whether it has validity in practice, and if so, to what extent.

1.2 Market efficiency

Efficiency of a stock market, in the context of this chapter, relates to the extent to which:

    (a)   Information about a company is available to investors and

    (b)   Shareholders use this information to re-assess the value of the shares, and buy shares that seem under-priced and sell shares that seem over-priced, so that the market price rises or falls to a new level.

If a stock market is very efficient, share prices should vary in a rational way.

    (a)   If a company makes an investment with a positive net present value (NPV), shareholders will get to know about it and the market price of its shares will rise in anticipation of future dividend increases.

    (b)   If a company makes a bad investment shareholders will find out and so the price of its shares will fall.

    (c)   If interest rates rise, shareholders will want a higher return from their investments, so market prices will fall.

Capital markets are not necessarily 'efficient' or 'inefficient' but there are differing 'forms' and degrees of efficiency.

2 Different forms of efficiency

2.1 Allocative efficiency, operational efficiency and information processing efficiency

Different types of efficiency can be distinguished in the context of the operation of financial markets.

(a) If financial markets allow funds to be directed towards companies that will make the most productive use of them, then there is **allocative efficiency** in these markets.

(b) Transaction costs are incurred by participants in financial markets, for example commissions on share transactions and loan arrangement fees. Financial markets have **operational efficiency** if transaction costs are kept as low as possible. Transaction costs are kept low where there is open competition between brokers, and between dealers and market makers.

(c) The **information processing efficiency** of a stock market means the ability of a stock market to price stocks and shares fairly and quickly. An efficient market in this sense is one in which the market prices of all the securities traded on it reflect all the available information. There is no possibility of 'speculative bubbles' in which share prices are pushed up or down, by speculative pressure, to unrealistically high or low levels.

2.2 Degrees of information processing efficiency

There are three degrees of this 'information processing' efficiency:

(a) Weak form efficiency
(b) Semi-strong form efficiency and
(c) Strong form efficiency.

Tests can be carried out on the workings of a stock market to establish whether the market operates with a particular form of efficiency. **Weak form tests** are made to assess whether a stock market shows at least weak form efficiency. **Semi-strong form tests** are made to assess whether a market shows at least semi-strong form efficiency. **Strong form tests** are made to assess whether a market shows strong form efficiency.

3 Weak form efficiency

FAST FORWARD

Where efficiency is **weak form**, investors react only to historical information about a company when it is made publicly available, for example through formal announcements. A share price might therefore react, for example, to the publication of a company's annual report and accounts. Share price movements are random, and it is impossible to detect patterns or trends.

Key term

When a stock market displays **weak form efficiency**, share prices only change when historical information about a company and its profits have become publicly available, for example with the publication of a company's financial results for the previous year. Share prices do not change in anticipation of new information being announced.

Since new information about a company arrives without having been anticipated, changes in share prices should occur in a random fashion. It should be impossible to detect trends or patterns in share prices. (Some share price analysts, often referred to as **chartists**, claim to be able to identify patterns and trends in share price movements over time, and can use this knowledge of past trends to predict future price movements. Chartists would therefore claim to be able to make profits by buying or selling shares in anticipation of the price movements they have predicted.)

Once the information has been made available, individual investors can study it, and make decisions to buy or sell the shares on the basis of their analysis of the information.

Tests to prove that a stock market displays weak form efficiency is based on the tests that:

(a) **Share price changes are random** and occur in response to historical information about the company when it is released and becomes available.

(b) There is no connection between past price movements and new share price changes, and **trends in prices cannot be detected**.

4 Semi-strong form efficiency

FAST FORWARD

Where efficiency is **semi-strong form**, share prices react not only to historical information, but also to other information about the company's future prospects.

Key term

When a stock market displays **semi-strong form efficiency**, current share prices reflect **both**:

(a) All relevant information about past price movements and their implications, and

(b) All knowledge that is available publicly. This includes information about the *future prospects* of the company, even if the information has not yet been officially released.

Tests to prove semi-strong efficiency have concentrated on the ability of the market to anticipate share price changes before new information is formally announced. For example, if two companies plan a merger, the share prices of the two companies will inevitably change once the merger plans are formally announced. The market would show semi-strong efficiency, however, if it were able to *anticipate* such an announcement, so that the share prices of the companies concerned would change in advance of the merger plans being confirmed.

Research in both the UK and the USA has suggested that **market prices anticipate mergers** several months before they are formally announced, and the conclusion drawn is that the stock markets in these countries *do* exhibit semi-strong efficiency. It has also been argued that the market displays sufficient efficiency for investors to see through **'creative accounting'** or **'window dressing'** of accounts by companies which use accounting conventions to overstate profits.

Suppose that a company is planning a rights issue of shares in order to invest in a new project. If the market displays semi-strong form efficiency, the market price of the shares will change to reflect the expected consequences of the issue before it is announced.

5 Strong form efficiency

FAST FORWARD

Where efficiency is **strong-form**, share prices react to all publicly-available information, and also to information before it is made publicly available. The information reaches the market from individuals with inside knowledge.

Key term

In a market that displays **strong form efficiency**, share prices will reflect all information available:

(a) From past price changes

(b) From public knowledge or anticipation of public announcements, and

(c) From insider knowledge available to specialists or experts (such as investment managers), which is then made available to the market as a whole.

Investors in the market will be aware of all significant future changes affecting the company and its future profits and dividends. Investors will make allowances for low profits or dividends in the current year if higher profits or dividends are expected in the future.

It would then follow that in order to maximise the wealth of shareholders, management should concentrate simply on maximising the net present value of its investments. A company's management need not worry, for example, about the effect on the share price of poor reported financial results in the published accounts. This is because investors will accept low profits and dividends now if the consequence is higher profits and dividends in the future.

A market with strong-form efficiency would be consistent with the fundamental theory of share values.

6 How efficient are stock markets?

Evidence so far collected suggests that stock markets show efficiency that is at least weak form, but tending more towards a semi-strong form. In other words, current share prices reflect all or most publicly-available information about companies and their shares. (However, it is very difficult to assess market efficiency in relation to shares that are not usually actively traded.)

Financial analysts and investment managers play an important role in creating an efficient stock market. This is because an efficient market depends on the widespread availability of cheap information about companies, their shares and market conditions, and this is what the firms of market makers and other financial institutions **do** provide for their clients and for the general investing public.

7 The efficient market hypothesis and its implications

The efficient market hypothesis is that changes in share prices can be explained by the efficiency of a particular stock market. The hypothesis is not concerned with small, random fluctuations in the price of shares from day to day, and even during the course of a day. It is concerned with the underlying value of shares.

The efficient market hypothesis states that if a market displays **strong form efficiency**, a company's real financial position will be reflected in its share price. Its real financial position includes both its current position and its expected future profitability. Making profits from insider dealing would not be possible, since all information is available to the market. If the management of a company attempts to maximise the net present value of their investments and to make public any relevant information about those investments, then current share prices will in turn be maximised.

The hypothesis also states that if a market displays **semi-strong form efficiency**, it will not be possible for investors to make a speculative gain on the basis of publicly-available information. This is because share prices will already reflect this information.

Studies have shown that not even fund managers can consistently 'beat the market', suggesting that the markets do indeed have some reasonably strong efficiency. If the semi-strong form of the efficient market hypothesis is correct, then the directors of a company should 'manage' both the underlying capital investment projects and also information made publicly available concerning the company and its projects. Such information will 'signal' important facts that might be used by analysts and investors to predict future cash flows (dividends) for the equity shareholders.

A further implication for an investor is that if the market shows **strong form or semi-strong form efficiency**, he can rarely spot shares at a bargain price that will soon rise sharply in value. This is because the market will already have anticipated future developments, and will have reflected these in the share price. All the investor can do, instead of looking for share bargains, is to concentrate on building up a good spread of shares (a portfolio) in order to achieve a satisfactory balance between risk and return.

FAST FORWARD

An implication of strong-form and semi-strong form efficiencies is that it is not possible to 'beat the market' by identifying over-valued or under-valued shares (except when markets are semi-strong form efficient, and use insider knowledge to carry out insider dealing in shares).

If a market has only weak form efficiency, it will be impossible to identify patterns of share price movements and share price trends. Weak-form efficiency is therefore inconsistent with the claims of chartists.

FAST FORWARD

The implication for management is that they must be aware of the effects of information about the company on its share price. Particularly when a market has strong-form efficiency, they should invest in all capital projects with a positive NPV, and make this information available to the market. The total value of the company's shares (and shareholder wealth) will increase by the expected NPV of the projects.

7.1 Example: efficient market hypothesis

Company X has 3,000,000 shares in issue and Company Y has 8,000,000 shares.

(a)   On day 1 the market value per share is $3 for X and $6 for Y.

(b)   On day 2 the management of Y decide, at a private meeting, to make a takeover bid for X at a price of $5 per share. The takeover will produce large operating savings with a present value of $8,000,000.

(c)   On day 5 Y publicly announces an unconditional offer to purchase all shares of X at a price of $5 per share (in cash) with settlement on day 20. Details of the large savings are not announced and are not public knowledge.

(d)   On day 10 Y announces details of the savings which will be derived from the takeover.

Ignoring tax and the time value of money between days 1 and 10, and assuming the details given are the only factors having an impact on the share price of X and Y, determine the day 2, day 5 and day 10 share price of X and Y if the market is:

(a)   Semi-strong form efficient
(b)   Strong form efficient

Solution

(a)   *Semi-strong form efficient market*

With a semi-strong form of market efficiency, shareholders know all the relevant historical data and publicly available current information.

(i)   Day 1   Value of X shares: $3 each, $9,000,000 in total.
                  Value of Y shares: $6 each, $48,000,000 in total.

(ii)   Day 2   The decision at the *private* meeting does not reach the market, and so share prices are unchanged.

(iii) Day 5   The takeover bid is announced, but no information is available yet about the savings.

(1)   The value of X shares will rise to their takeover bid price of $5 each, $15,000,000 in total.

(2)   The value of Y shares will be as follows.

	$
Previous value (8,000,000 × $6)	48,000,000
Add value of X shares to be acquired, at previous market worth (3,000,000 × $3)	9,000,000
	57,000,000
Less purchase consideration for X shares	15,000,000
New value of Y shares	42,000,000
Price per share	$5.25

The share price of Y shares will fall on the announcement of the takeover, from $6 to $5.25.

(iv)   Day 20 The market learns of the potential savings of $8,000,000 (present value) and the price of Y shares will rise accordingly to:

$$\frac{\$42,000,000 + \$8,000,000}{8,000,000 \text{ shares}} = \$6.25 \text{ per share}$$

The share price of X shares will remain the same as before, $5 per share.

(b)   *Strong form efficient market*

In a strong form efficient market, the market would become aware of *all* the relevant information when the private meeting takes place. The value per share would change as early as *day 2* to:

(i)   X: $5
(ii)   Y: $6.25

The share prices would then remain unchanged until day 20.

The different characteristics of a semi-strong form and a strong form efficient market affect the **timing** of share price movements, because the relevant information affecting the share price will become available to the market eventually. The difference between the two forms of market efficiency concerns when the share prices change, not by how much prices eventually change.

You should notice, however, that in neither case (a strong form or semi-strong form efficient market) would the share prices remain unchanged until day 20.

In a **weak form** efficient market, the price of Y's shares would not reflect the expected savings until after the savings had been achieved and reported. The announcement of the takeover bid would result in a fall in the value of Y's shares for a considerable time to come.

Question 11.1   Efficient market hypothesis

Comment upon the popularity of index tracker funds – where funds are invested in a replica of a stock market index - in the light of the efficient market hypothesis.

Question 11.2   Effect on share price

Z is a company with 100 million shares in issue, currently valued at $3 each in the stock market. What might be the effect on the share price of the following events, assuming that the market displays either strong-form or semi-strong form efficiency?

(a)   The company issues a profit warning, stating that its profit for the first six months of the financial year will be $10 million below the market's expectation

(b)   The company invests $25 million in a new project that management believes will bring returns valued at $45 million

(For the answers to these questions, see the Answer section at the end of this book.)

Exam focus point | A question in June 2002 required an explanation of the efficient market hypothesis and its implications for a listed company.

7.2 Practical implications for company managers

The reason that managers should be aware of the efficiency of the stock market is that company announcements might affect the share price. Since the objective of a company is to maximise shareholder wealth, the effect of announcements on the share price needs to be considered.

(a)   If the markets display weak form efficiency, the share price will not respond immediately to announcements about the expected future profitability of new investment projects.

(b)   If the market displays semi-strong form efficiency, announcements by management about the future profitability of new investments will affect the share price.

(c)   If the market displays strong form efficiency, the share price will respond to events before they are publicly announced.

The practical implications of market efficiency for the directors of listed companies are that information about the company and both its past performance and future prospects should be carefully 'managed'. A company cannot ignore the fact that information about its prospects circulate in the market.

Factors affecting the share price that a company's management ought to be aware of include:

(a)   The announcement of its annual and interim (half-yearly) results, companies invariably announce a very positive outlook for the future but may also indulge in window dressing or more creative accounting in order to flatter their position.

(b)   Other information about its prospects, products and management (for example, the announcement of major new capital projects or major contracts)

(c)   Information about industry prospects

(d)   Takeover speculation

(e)   The state of the economy

(f)   Exchange rate changes

(g)   Interest rate changes

(h)   New legislation affecting the company

This information management is especially critical when

- The business is looking to raise new finance, especially if it is in the form of shares, warrants or hybrid securities.

- The business has attracted the attention of potential acquirers and wishes to either fight a takeover approach or to maximise shareholder benefit from such an approach.

7.3 Explaining share price movements

Events such as the 'crash' of October 1987, in which share prices fell suddenly by 20% to 40% on the world's stock markets, raised serious questions about the validity of the efficient market hypothesis. If the theory is correct, how can shares that were valued at one level on one day suddenly be worth 40% less the next day, without any change in expectations of corporate profits and dividends?

Various anomalies in share price movements appear to support the view that 'irrationality' often drives the stock market. These anomalies include:

(a)   Seasonal month-of-the-year effects, day-of-the-week effects and also hour-of-the-day effects seem to occur, so that share prices might tend to rise or fall at a particular time of the year, week or day.

(b)   There may be a short-run overreaction to recent events.

(c)   Individual shares or shares in small companies may be neglected.

There are differing views about the efficiency of the stock markets, but recent evidence suggests that the markets are less efficient than some analysts had supposed. The stock market boom of the late 1990s, followed by the collapse in share prices in 2000 and 2001, is difficult to reconcile with the proposition that the markets show semi-strong form efficiency and that share prices are therefore priced efficiently.

Chapter roundup

- The **efficiency** of a market refers to the extent to which share prices react to information about a company and its profitability. A market can be described as showing one of three forms of efficiency: weak form, semi-strong form and strong form.

- Where efficiency is **weak form**, investors react only to historical information about a company when it is made publicly available, for example through formal announcements. A share price might therefore react, for example, to the publication of a company's annual report and accounts. Share price movements are random, and it is impossible to detect patterns or trends.

- Where efficiency is **semi-strong form**, share prices react not only to historical information, but also to other information about the company's future prospects.

- Where efficiency is **strong-form**, share prices react to all publicly-available information, and also to information before it is made publicly available. The information reaches the market from individuals with inside knowledge.

- An implication of strong-form and semi-strong form efficiencies is that it is not possible to 'beat the market' by identifying over-valued or under-valued shares (except when markets are semi-strong form efficient, and use insider knowledge to carry out insider dealing in shares).

- The implication for management is that they must be aware of the effects of information about the company on its share price. Particularly when a market has strong-form efficiency, they should invest in all capital projects with a positive NPV, and make this information available to the market. The total value of the company's shares (and shareholder wealth) will increase by the expected NPV of the projects.

Quick quiz

1   What are the key features of market efficiency?

2   What is likely to be the effect on market efficiency of a change from floor-based trading in stock exchanges and manual settlement of share transactions to electronic trading and settlement systems?

3   What type of stock market efficiency is inconsistent with the belief of chartists that future share price movements can be predicted from patterns and trends?

Answers to quick quiz

1   Funds in the capital markets flow to the companies that can make the most wealth-creating use of them. Transaction costs for dealing and settlement are low. Information is made available to the market and is processed efficiently, so that share prices reflect the information that is available to the market.

2   Transaction costs should fall, making the market efficiency stronger.

3   Weak form market efficiency, which is associated with the view that share price movements are random, reacting to unexpected events and announcements.

Part E
Working capital

12

Introduction to working capital management

Topic list	Syllabus reference
1 The nature and scope of working capital management	5a
2 A reminder: working capital ratios	5b, 5d
3 Working capital needs of different businesses	5a
4 Working capital and cash flow	5a
5 The working capital requirement	5a

Introduction

Working capital is a company's net current assets, ie its inventories, receivables and cash, less its current liabilities such as trade payables. A business must maintain appropriate levels of each of these elements that comprise the working capital. The purpose of this and the following chapters is to consider how an 'appropriate' level should be determined.

1 The nature and scope of working capital management

1.1 What is working capital?

As previously defined, the working capital of a business is its **current assets less its current liabilities**.

1.2 Working capital management as cash flow management

The amount tied up in **working capital** is equal to the value of raw materials, work-in-progress, finished goods and receivables less payables. The size of this net figure has a direct effect on the **liquidity** of an organisation.

Current assets are either cash or assets that should soon generate cash for the business. Inventories of goods for resale will soon be sold. Inventories of raw materials in a manufacturing business will soon be converted into finished goods, and the finished goods will be sold. Cash sales generate cash as soon as the sale is made. Sales on credit result in receivables, and the cash will come into the business when the debtors eventually pay.

Current liabilities are debts of the business that must be paid fairly soon. A business should normally be able to pay its payable balances out of money coming in from its cash sales and receivables.

Every business needs adequate **liquid resources** to maintain day-to-day cash flow. It needs enough to pay wages and salaries as they fall due and enough to pay creditors if it is to keep its workforce and ensure its supplies. Maintaining adequate working capital is not just important in the short term. Sufficient liquidity must be maintained in order to ensure the survival of the business in the long term as well. Even a profitable company may fail if it does not have adequate cash flow to meet its liabilities as they fall due.

Working capital management can therefore be seen as the **management of operational cash flows**, to ensure that sufficient cash comes in from day-to-day business operations to meet the payment obligations of the business.

A further aspect of working capital management is to decide what amounts of cash the business should hold, and what should be done with any temporary surplus.

1.3 Avoiding over-capitalisation and overtrading

Working capital management can also be seen as the task of keeping the total investment in working capital at a level where there is neither over-capitalisation nor overtrading.

(a)   Over-capitalisation occurs when a business has a larger investment in working capital than it ought to require, given the scale of its operations. It might be evident in excessive inventory levels and slow-moving inventory items, or in an excessively high volume of receivables. The problem can be prevented by controlling inventory levels, and efficient debt collection, and by taking credit from suppliers when this is available.

(b)   Overtrading was described in an earlier chapter. This occurs when a business tries to operate with insufficient working capital, with the result that there is a high risk of cash flows into the business being insufficient to meet its payment obligations when they fall due.

1.4 Return on working capital investment

The financial objective of a company might be to make a target return on capital employed. Capital employed consists of working capital as well as long-term assets. A larger investment in working capital should therefore require a larger profit. Any changes in working capital policies should be justifiable in terms of profitability and return on capital.

1.5 Consequences of ineffective working capital management

The consequences of ineffective working capital management might be:

(a) An excessive investment in working capital, which reduces the return on capital employed

(b) Excessive inventory levels, which could lead to high costs of storage, and losses due to deterioration of inventories or obsolescence

(c) Excessive levels of receivables, which could lead to high levels of bad debts if late payers are not chased for the debts they owe

2 A reminder: working capital ratios

FAST FORWARD

Liquidity ratios may help to indicate whether a company is **over-capitalised**, with excessive working capital, or if a business is likely to fail. A business which is trying to do too much too quickly with too little long-term capital is **overtrading**.

Turnover ratios for inventory, debt collection (receivables days) and payment of creditors (payables days) can be used to assess the working capital investment required by a company, defining working capital narrowly as inventories plus trade receivables minus trade payables.

One method of monitoring and controlling working capital is through the use of working capital ratios. If you have forgotten what these are, you should return to Chapter 8, Section 8 and revise them. The most important ratios you need to know are:

(a) The current ratio (current assets: current liabilities)
(b) The acid test ratio or quick ratio (current assets excluding inventories: current liabilities)
(c) Inventories turnover
(d) Receivables days
(e) Payables days

Question 12.1
Closing stock value

The financial position of Reconstruct for the forthcoming year is to be projected on the basis of the following balance sheet relationships:

Quick assets: current liabilities	1.9:1
Non-current assets : current assets	1:1
Sales: total assets	2.2:1
Current assets: current liabilities	2.5:1

If sales are forecast at $44m for the forthcoming year, what will be the expected closing inventory value?

(For the answer to this question, see the Answer section at the end of this book.)

3 Working capital needs of different businesses

Working capital ratios can be used to monitor the control of inventories, receivables, payables and liquidity. However, they should be used with care. The amount of working capital needed by a company depends on the type of business or industry it is in.

(a) Some companies, particularly in **manufacturing** or **construction**, might have to invest heavily in inventories. If the manufacturing process is slow, a large amount of investment is required in work-in-progress, ie in the cost of producing items for sale. A construction firm might have to spend a lot of money on a contract before receiving any payments from the customer.

(b) In contrast, some companies, particularly in some **service industries**, are able to operate with very low inventory levels. Software companies, for example, need relatively small inventories. However, in some service industries, it might be quite common for extensive credit to be provided to customers, so that the investment in receivables is high.

(c) The example of **supermarkets** was referred to in an earlier chapter. Large supermarket chains have small levels of receivables, because most of their sales are cash sales. When they sell goods with a rapid turnover, such as fresh food, the supermarket companies will receive cash from their sales before they have to pay their suppliers for the goods. These companies can therefore finance a large proportion of their inventories with trade credit, and so need only a fairly low investment in working capital.

3.1 The volume of current assets required

> **FAST FORWARD**
>
> Working capital requirements vary according to the circumstances of the business and also its working capital policies.

The amount of working capital a company needs depends to some extent on its working capital policies. There is a certain degree of choice in the total investment required in inventories, receivables and cash, to support a given volume of business. Policies of low inventory holding levels, tight credit and minimum cash holdings may be contrasted with policies of high inventories (to allow for safety or buffer inventories), easier credit and sizeable cash holdings (for precautionary reasons).

4 Working capital and cash flow

4.1 The cash cycle

> **FAST FORWARD**
>
> The **cash cycle** is the average inventory turnover period plus average receivables days minus average days to pay trade payables.

The relationship between working capital management and cash flow can be seen in the **cash cycle** (also called the **working capital cycle, operating cycle** or **trading cycle**).

The cash cycle is the average time between paying creditors for supplies of materials or services, and eventually receiving payment in cash for the sale of goods made from them. It is only an approximate measure, but changes in the cash cycle over time can provide useful information to management as to whether working capital management might be improving or getting worse.

> **FAST FORWARD**
>
> **A longer cash cycle means a higher investment in working capital.** An important aspect of working capital management is therefore the control of the turnover periods for inventory, receivables and paybles.

			Days
Cash cycle	=	Average inventory turnover period	A
	Plus	Average debt collection period	B
			A + B
	Minus	Average time to pay creditors	(C)
			(A + B) - C

In a manufacturing business, this equals:

The average time that raw materials remain in inventory
less the period of credit taken from suppliers
plus the time taken to produce the goods
plus the time taken by customers to pay for the goods

4.2 The cash cycle of a retailer

It might be useful to think of a simple example of a retailer. Suppose that a retailer buys an item from a supplier, and holds it in inventory for 20 days. It pays the supplier 15 days after the purchase. The item is then sold on credit to a customer, who pays for it 18 days later. The cash cycle is the time between paying the supplier on day 15 and receiving payment from the customer, on day 38 (20 + 18). This is 23 days.

4.3 Example

ZZ is a manufacturing group serving the construction industry. Extracts from its income statements for 20X3 and the previous year 20X2, together with end-of-year balance sheet extracts, are as follows.

	20X3 $m	20X2 $m
Sales revenue	2,065.0	1,788.7
Cost of sales	1,478.6	1,304.0
Gross profit	586.4	484.7
Current assets		
Inventories	119.0	109.0
Receivables (see note 1)	400.9	347.4
Short-term investments	4.2	18.8
Cash at bank and in hand	48.2	48.0
	572.3	523.2
Current liabilities		
Loans and overdrafts	49.1	35.3
Income tax payable	62.0	46.7
Dividend payable	19.2	14.3
Other (see note 2)	370.7	324.0
	501.0	420.3
Net current assets	71.3	102.9

Notes

		20X3 $m	20X2 $m
1	Trade receivables	329.8	285.4
2	Trade payables	236.2	210.8

Required: Calculate the cash cycle in each year, using the information available.

Solution

	20X3	20X2
Receivables collection period	$\frac{329.8}{2,065.0} \times 365 = 58$ days	$\frac{285.4}{1,788.7} \times 365 = 58$ days
Inventory turnover period	$\frac{119.0}{1,478.6} \times 365 = 29$ days	$\frac{109.0}{1,304.0} \times 365 = 31$ days

Payables payment period	$\dfrac{236.2}{1,478.6} \times 365 = 58$ days	$\dfrac{210.8}{1,304.0} \times 365 = 59$ days
Cash cycle	$(58 + 29 - 58) = 29$ days	$(58 + 31 - 59) = 30$ days

The company is a manufacturing group serving the construction industry, and so might be expected to have a comparatively lengthy receivables' collection period, because of the relatively poor cash flow in the construction industry. It is clear that the company compensates for this by ensuring that they do not pay for raw materials and other costs before they have sold their inventories of finished goods (hence the similarity of receivables and payables turnover periods).

Payables' turnover is best calculated by the formula:

$$\frac{\text{Average payables}}{\text{Purchases}} \times 365$$

However, it is rare to find purchases disclosed in published accounts and so cost of sales serves as an approximation. The payables' turnover ratio often helps to assess a company's liquidity; an increase in payables days is often a sign of lack of long-term finance or poor management of current assets, resulting in the use of extended credit from suppliers, increased bank overdraft and so on.

Question 12.2   Cash cycle

Suppose that in the example above, the trade receivables days of ZZ in 20X3 had been 70 days, average inventory turnover had been 50 days and the payment period to creditors had been 25 days.

(a)   What would the cash cycle have been?

(b)   Defining working capital narrowly as inventories plus trade receivables minus trade payables, what would the company's investment in working capital have been?

(c)   How does your answer in (b) compare with the investment in working capital given the cash cycle of 29 days in the example above?

(For the answer to this question, see the Answer section at the end of this book.)

Exam focus point

In the June 2002 exam there was a question on the operating cash cycle, requiring both explanations and calculations in a specific situation. In the December 2004 exam, there was a question which required an explanation of the operating cash cycle, calculation and suggestions as to how it could be reduced.

5 The working capital requirement

Computing the working capital requirement is a matter of calculating the value of current assets less current liabilities, perhaps by taking averages over a one-year period. Study the following example carefully.

5.1 Example: working capital requirement

The following data relate to Corn, a manufacturing company.

Sales revenue for the year	$1,500,000
Costs as percentages of sales	%
Direct materials	30
Direct labour	25
Variable overheads	10
Fixed overheads	15
Selling and distribution	5

On average:

(a)   Debtors take 2.5 months before payment

(b)   Raw materials are in inventory for three months

(c)   Work-in-progress represents two months' worth of half-produced goods

(d)   Finished goods represents one month's production

(e)   Credit is taken as follows:

(i)	Direct materials	2 months
(ii)	Direct labour	1 week
(iii)	Variable overheads	1 month
(iv)	Fixed overheads	1 month
(v)	Selling and distribution	0.5 months

Work-in-progress and finished goods are valued at material, labour and variable expense cost.

Compute the working capital requirement of Corn assuming the labour force is paid for 50 working weeks a year. Working capital is defined for the purpose of this exercise as inventories (raw materials, work in progress and finished goods) plus receivables minus current liabilities.

Note that in this example, turnover periods are given in months rather than days, and the turnover ratios therefore use '× 12' (months) rather than '× 365' (days).

Solution

(a)   The annual costs incurred will be as follows.

		$
Direct materials	30% × $1,500,000	450,000
Direct labour	25% × $1,500,000	375,000
Variable overheads	10% × $1,500,000	150,000
Fixed overheads	15% × $1,500,000	225,000
Selling and distribution	5% × $1,500,000	75,000

(b)   The average value of current assets will be as follows.

		$	$
Raw materials	3/12 × $450,000		112,500
Work-in-progress			
Materials (50% complete)	1/12 × $450,000	37,500	
Labour (50% complete)	1/12 × $375,000	31,250	
Variable overheads (50% complete)	1/12 × $150,000	12,500	
			81,250
Finished goods			
Materials	1/12 × $450,000	37,500	
Labour	1/12 × $375,000	31,250	
Variable overheads	1/12 × $150,000	12,500	
			81,250
Receivables	2.5/12 × $1,500,000		312,500
			587,500

(c) Average value of current liabilities will be as follows.

		$	$
Materials	2/12 × $450,000	75,000	
Labour	1/50 × $375,000	7,500	
Variable overheads	1/12 × $150,000	12,500	
Fixed overheads	1/12 × $225,000	18,750	
Selling and distribution	0.5/12 × $75,000	3,125	
			116,875

(d) Working capital required is ($(587,500 − 116,875)) =   470,625

Longer turnover periods for inventories or receivables mean a higher investment in these items. A shorter period of credit taken from suppliers means lower trade payables. Lower trade payables means that a larger proportion of inventories and receivables must be financed by the long-term capital of the company.

An important point to understand is that the investment in working capital is largely dependent on the length of the cash cycle. Management of working capital therefore involves controlling the turnover cycles and avoiding excessively slow inventory turnover and allowing debtors an excessive amount of time to pay.

Chapter roundup

- The amount tied up in **working capital** is equal to the value of raw materials, work-in-progress, finished inventories and receivables less payables. The size of this net figure has a direct effect on the **liquidity** of an organisation.

- **Liquidity ratios** may help to indicate whether a company is **over-capitalised**, with excessive working capital, or if a business is likely to fail. A business which is trying to do too much too quickly with too little long-term capital is **overtrading**.

- **Turnover ratios** for inventory, debt collection (receivables days) and payment of creditors (payables days) can be used to assess the working capital investment required by a company, defining working capital narrowly as inventories plus trade receivables minus trade payables.

- Working capital requirements vary according to the circumstances of the business and also its working capital policies.

- The **cash cycle** is the average inventory turnover period plus average receivables days minus average days to pay trade payables.

- **A longer cash cycle means a higher investment in working capital**. An important aspect of working capital management is therefore the control of the turnover periods for inventory, receivables and payables.

Quick quiz

1   A company has a current ratio of 2.0 times and a cash cycle of 43 days. What would you expect to happen to the current ratio if the cash cycle increased to 50 days?

2   A company sells half its goods on credit and half for cash. Annual sales are $50 million. Average receivables are $4 million. What is the average debt collection period?

3   Last year, a company's annual sales revenue was $730 million, and the average debt collection period was 30 days. It earns a contribution of 20% on sales. The company believes that if it pursued a more lenient debt collection policy, so that average receivables days went up to 40 days, it could increase sales by 10%. What would be the effect of this new policy on the investment in working capital and on profit?

Answers to quick quiz

1   Inventories and receivables will increase and/or trade payables will be reduced. The current ratio should therefore be higher.

2   Taking credit sales only, the average debt collection period is $(4/25) \times 365 = 58.4$ days. Taking cash sales and credit sales together, the average debt collection period would be calculated as $(4/50) \times 365 = 29.2$ days.

3   Current average receivables = $(30/365) \times \$730$ million = $60 million.

Proposed investment in receivables = $(40/365) \times (110\%$ of $730 million) = $88 million.

Presumably, inventories and trade payables will increase by 10%, but there is no information in the question to calculate an amount.

Sales will increase by $73 million per annum, and contribution/profit (20% of sales) will therefore increase by $14.6 million.

Management of inventories and receivables

Introduction

Central to the control of working capital balances is the management of inventories and receivables. This chapter considers each of these: what are the advantages and disadvantages of holding large balances of inventories and receivables? A balance must be struck between the costs and benefits in order to identify the optimum amount to hold.

1 The management of receivables

1.1 Elements of credit control

Several factors should be considered by management when a policy for **credit control** is formulated. These include:

(a) The administrative costs of debt collection

(b) The procedures for controlling credit to individual customers and for debt collection

(c) The amount of extra capital required to finance an extension of total credit - there might be an increase in receivables, inventories and payables, and the net increase in working capital must be financed

(d) The cost of the additional finance required for any increase in the volume of receivables (or the savings from a reduction in receivables) - this cost might be bank overdraft interest, or the cost of long-term funds (such as loan stock or equity)

(e) Any savings or additional expenses in operating the credit policy, for example the extra work involved in pursuing slow payers

(f) The ways in which the credit policy could be implemented - for example:

    (i) Credit could be eased by giving debtors a longer period in which to settle their accounts - the cost would be the resulting increase in receivables

    (ii) A discount could be offered for early payment - the cost would be the amount of the discounts taken

(g) The effects of easing credit, which might be to encourage a higher proportion of bad debts, and an increase in sales volume. Provided that the extra gross contribution from the increase in sales exceeds the increase in fixed cost expenses, bad debts, discounts and the finance cost of an increase in working capital, a policy to relax credit terms would be profitable.

Exam focus point

> This area was examined for 6 marks in the June 2006 exam.

1.2 The debt collection policy

The overall **debt collection policy** of the firm should be such that the administrative costs and other costs incurred in debt collection do not exceed the benefits from incurring those costs. Some extra spending on debt collection procedures might reduce bad debt losses, and reduce the average collection period, and therefore the cost of the investment in receivables. Beyond a certain level of spending, however, additional expenditure on debt collection would not have enough effect on bad debts or on the average collection period to justify the extra administrative costs.

2 Assessing creditworthiness

FAST FORWARD

> In managing **receivables,** the **creditworthiness** of customers needs to be assessed. The risks and costs of a customer defaulting will need to be balanced against the profitability of the business provided by that customer.

A new customer might want to be given credit. The application for credit may be dealt with informally. Alternatively, a company might have formal credit assessment procedures, in order to decide:

(a)   Whether or not the customer should be given credit

(b)   If the customer is given credit, what the total credit limit should be, and

(c)   The terms of payment, ie what length of credit period should be allowed. This is usually a matter of company policy, and the same payment terms are applied to all credit customers.

Existing customers might ask for a larger amount of credit. A credit assessment of existing customers is easier than for new customers, because the customer is already known, and already has a record of making payments. The customer's record will be taken into consideration when deciding the reply to the credit application.

2.1 Assessing new customers for credit

Giving credit is a normal aspect of business and essential to make sales. Allowing too much credit will increase the risk of bad debt losses. Credit assessment should therefore be carried out with some care.

Providing credit to a customer is, in effect, offering them an interest free loan and, like all loans, needs to be properly assessed. Before making an advance, lenders should always consider the five Cs of credit ie.

(a)   **Character** – What is the customer's reputation in the industry? The preference is to only advance credit to those with impeccable credentials and references. There are a number of sources of information that can be drawn on here.

A potential corporate customer asking for credit should be asked to provide a **credit reference** from its bank. A bank reference does not guarantee that the customer will have the funds to pay its debts on time, but it should at least provide some reassurance that the customer does not already have serious cash flow problems. Even so, the bank is likely to word any reference very cautiously, and will also charge a fee (which either the company or the customer will be required to pay).

A second source of a reference would be one or more of the customer's **existing suppliers**. A trade reference should confirm that the customer has a good track record of complying with its credit terms, and so is likely to be trustworthy. The customer might even invite the company to contact one or two of its existing suppliers directly, to discuss its credit standing.

The company might also check the **register of debt judgments** by County Courts, to find out whether there have been any judgments against the customer. However, if a credit agency is used, the agency will make this check.

(b)   **Capacity** – What is the customer's history and track record of repayment? Will it be able to honour the debt. Again, these are a number of sources of information that could be drawn on here and bank references and the references of existing suppliers would once more be important considerations.

The company might also decide to obtain (and pay for) a status report from a **credit agency**. For a fee, a credit agency will report on the apparent creditworthiness of a business, basing the report upon an analysis of its financial accounts and other information about the business that is held on its database. The status report will give some sort of 'credit rating' to the customer, that can then be used as a basis for deciding what credit terms, if any, to offer.

(c)   **Capital** – How well capitalised is the customer, since this clearly impacts on their ability to repay any debt.

If the potential customer is a limited company, a copy of its **financial accounts** can be obtained from the Registrar of Companies. However, the company would need to have someone with the skills (and the time) to carry out a credit analysis of these accounts.

Where the potential new customer intends to enter into a long-term trading relationship, the company's sales manager should arrange a **site visit** to the customer's premises. The value of a site visit is to see at first hand the nature, scale and efficiency of the customer's operations and systems. The impressions obtained from such visits are often a reliable indicator of a customer's business strength and financial reliability.

(d) **Collateral** – Will the customer be prepared to offer any collateral to support any debt. This is unlikely in most receivables situations and is more relevant in the context of advancing a formal loan.

(e) **Conditions** – How sensitive is the customer to economic conditions and can it cope with an economic downturn. This will most probably have been covered by various references obtained, examination of the customer's accounts and any site visits.

A new customer's credit limit should be fixed at a low level and only increased if his payment record subsequently warrants it.

For **large value customers**, a file should be maintained of any available financial information about the customer. This file should be reviewed regularly. Such information will include analyses of the company's annual report and accounts, as well as relevant press reports about the customer and its financial position.

An organisation might devise a **credit-rating system** for new individual customers (as distinct from business customers) that is based on characteristics of the customer, such as whether the customer is a home owner, and the customer's age and occupation. Points would be awarded according to the characteristics of the customer, and the amount of credit that is offered would depend on his or her credit score.

2.2 Assessing existing customers for an extension of credit

The credit limit for an existing customer should be periodically reviewed, but it should only be raised if the customer's credit standing is good.

Lists of 'aged debts' should be produced and reviewed at regular intervals. These are lists of customer debts that are still unpaid, and for how long. Overdue payments are flagged for action, and chasing up for payment. Customers who appear on the aged debts list as overdue with payments might not be given extra credit.

There should be procedures for ensuring that further orders are not accepted from a customer (nor goods sent to a customer) who is in difficulties. If a customer has exceeded his credit limit, or has not paid debts despite several reminders, or is otherwise known to be in difficulties, sales staff and warehouse staff must be notified immediately.

Exam focus point

> The June 2006 exam featured a 10 mark question on the main sources of information that a company may use to assess customer credit worthiness.

3 Terms of sale

FAST FORWARD

> The **terms of sale** include total credit allowed, maximum time allowed for payment, and possibly terms for a settlement discount.

When a customer is given credit, the terms of sale will state:

(a) The total amount of credit allowed to the customer (ie the credit limit)

(b) The period of time within which invoices must be paid (eg invoices must be paid within 30 days of the invoice date) and

(c)   Any early payment discount (or '**settlement discount**') allowed for payment within a specified time. For example, a discount of 2% might be offered for cash payment, or for payment within, say, 14 days of the invoice date.

FAST FORWARD

> **Changing the credit period allowed** to customers will affect the size of the investment in inventories, receivables and trade payables, and might also affect total sales volume and profitability.

To decide whether it would be profitable to extend the level of total credit, it is necessary to assess:

(a)   The extra sales that a more generous credit policy would stimulate
(b)   The profitability of the extra sales
(c)   The extra length of the average debt collection period
(d)   The required rate of return on the investment in additional receivables

3.1 Example: receivables management (1)

Barred is considering a change of credit policy which will result in an increase in the average collection period from one to two months. The relaxation in credit is expected to produce an increase in sales in each year amounting to 10% of the current sales volume.

Selling price per unit	$10
Variable cost per unit	$7
Current annual sales	$2,400,000

The required rate of return on investments is 20%. Assume that the 10% increase in sales would result in additional inventories of $100,000 and additional payables of $20,000.

Advise the company on whether or not to extend the credit period offered to customers, if:

(a)   All customers take the longer credit of two months

(b)   Existing customers do not change their payment habits, and only the new customers take a full two months credit

Solution

The change in credit policy is justifiable if the rate of return on the additional investment in working capital would exceed 20%.

Extra profit

Contribution per unit ($10 – $7)	$3
Contribution/sales ratio ($3/$10)	30%
Increase in sales revenue	$240,000
Increase in contribution and profit (30% of $240,000)	$72,000

(a)   *Extra investment, if all debtors take two months credit*

	$
Average receivables after the sales increase (2/12 × $2,640,000)	440,000
Less current average receivables (1/12 × $2,400,000)	200,000
Increase in receivables	240,000
Increase in inventories	100,000
	340,000
Less increase in payables	20,000
Net increase in working capital investment	320,000

Return on extra investment $\dfrac{\$72,000}{\$320,000} = 22.5\%$

(b)   *Extra investment, if only the new debtors take two months credit*

	$
Increase in receivables (2/12 of $240,000)	40,000
Increase in inventories	100,000
	140,000
Less increase in payables	20,000
Net increase in working capital investment	120,000

Return on extra investment $\dfrac{\$72,000}{\$120,000} = 60\%$

In both case (a) and case (b) the new credit policy appears to be worthwhile.

Question 13.1

Credit policy

Vale has an annual sales revenue of $60 million, all on credit. Its average inventory level is $11 million and its average trade payables are $4.5 million. The company's average debt collection period is one month. It is considering a change to a more generous credit policy, that would result in an increase in the average debt collection period to one-and-a-half months. As a result, sales would increase by 20%. However, it has been estimated that bad debts, which have been negligible in the past, would rise to 2% of total sales.

The company earns a contribution of 20c for every $1 of sales that it makes. Its target return on capital employed is 17%.

Is the new credit policy financially justified, on the basis of the information available?

(For the answer to this question, see the Answer section at the end of this book.)

3.2 Settlement discounts

FAST FORWARD

Settlement discounts may be employed to shorten average credit periods, and to reduce the investment in receivables and therefore **interest costs**. The benefit in interest cost saved should exceed the cost of the discounts allowed.

To see whether the offer of a **settlement discount** (for early payment) is financially worthwhile we must compare:

(a)   The cost of the discount with
(b)   The benefit of a reduced investment in receivables.

Varying the discount allowed for early payment of debts affects the **average collection period** and affects the **volume of demand** (and possibly, therefore, indirectly affects bad debt losses). We shall begin with examples where the offer of a discount for early payment does not affect the volume of demand.

3.3 Example: receivables management (2)

Lowe and Price has annual credit sales of $12,000,000, and three months are allowed for payment. The company decides to offer a 2% discount for payments made within ten days of the invoice being sent, and to reduce the maximum time allowed for payment to two months. It is estimated that 50% of customers will take the discount. If the company requires a 20% return on investments, what will be the effect of the discount? Assume that the volume of sales will be unaffected by the discount.

Solution

The required approach is to calculate:

(a)   The profits forgone by offering the discount

(b)   The interest charges saved or incurred as a result of the changes in the cash flows of the company

Thus:

(a)   The annual cost of the discounts will be 2% × (50% × $12 million) = $120,000

(b)   The volume of receivables, if the company policy remains unchanged, would be:

3/12 × $12,000,000 = $3,000,000.

(c)   If the policy is changed the volume of receivables would be:

$$(\frac{10}{365} \times 50\% \times \$12,000,000) + (\frac{2}{12} \times 50\% \times \$12,000,000)$$

= $164,384 + $1,000,000 = $1,164,384.

(d)   There will be a reduction in receivables of $1,835,616.

(e)   The costs of the discount will be $120,000 per annum, but the reduction in investment will be $1,835,616. Put another way, not offering the discount will save $120,000, but there will be an additional investment in receivables of $1,835,616. Not offering the discount therefore makes a return on investment of ($120,000/$1,835,616), ie just 6.5%. The target return on investment is 20%, which means that a policy of not offering the settlement discount is not worthwhile.

(f)   *Summary*

Another way of presenting this analysis is as follows.

Reduction in receivables by offering settlement discount	$1,835,616
Return on capital	20%
	$
Value of reduction in receivables each year (20% of $1,835,616)	367,123
Less cost of discounts allowed each year	120,000
Net benefit of new discount policy each year	247,123

Question 13.2   Settlement discount

Enticement currently expects sales of $36,500 a month. It is considering a policy of allowing a discount of 3% for cash settlement. It has been estimated that one-third of customers would take up the offer and that the average debt collection period would therefore fall from 30 days to 10 days. It has also been estimated that sales volume would increase by 25%. The company makes a contribution of 10% on its sales.

The increase in sales volume would require an additional investment of $25,000 in inventories, but trade payables would increase by $15,000.

Evaluate the proposal to offer the settlement discount.

(For the answer to this question, see the Answer section at the end of this book.)

Exam focus point

In December 2002 there was a 20 mark question devoted entirely to the effects of the introduction of a receivables discount policy on profits and investment in working capital. The computations were relatively straightforward – it was a question of translating the information given in the question into profit or working capital figures. 5 marks were then given over to discussing the implications of the results of the computations.

3.4 Bad debt risk

Different credit policies are likely to have differing levels of bad debt risk. The higher sales revenue resulting from easier credit terms should be sufficiently profitable to exceed the cost of:

(a)   Bad debts, and

(b)   The additional investment necessary to achieve the higher sales

3.5 Example: receivables management (3)

Grabbit Quick achieves current annual sales of $1,800,000. The cost of sales is 80% of this amount, but bad debts average 1% of total sales, and the annual profit is as follows.

	$
Sales	1,800,000
Less cost of sales	1,440,000
	360,000
Less bad debts	18,000
Profit	342,000

The current debt collection period is one month, and the management consider that if credit terms were eased (option A), the effects would be as follows.

	Present policy	Option A
Additional sales (%)	–	25%
Average collection period	1 month	2 months
Bad debts (% of sales)	1%	3%

The company requires a 20% return on its investments. The costs of sales are 75% variable and 25% fixed. Assume there would be no increase in fixed costs from the extra revenue; and that there would be no increase in average inventories or payables. Which is the preferable policy, Option A or the present one?

Solution

The increase in profit before the cost of additional finance for Option A can be found as follows.

		$
(a)	Increase in contribution from additional sales	
	25% × $1,800,000 × 40% *	180,000
	Less increase in bad debts	
	(3% × $2,250,000) – $18,000	49,500
	Increase in annual profit	130,500
	* The Contribution/Sales ratio is 100% – (75% × 80%) = 40%	

		$
(b)		
	Proposed investment in receivables	
	$2,250,000 × 1/6	375,000
	Less current investment in receivables	
	$1,800,000 × 1/12	150,000
	Additional investment required	225,000
	Cost of additional finance at 20%	$45,000

(c)   As the increase in profit exceeds the cost of additional finance, Option A should be adopted.

4 Debt collection policies

FAST FORWARD

A business must have policies and procedures in place for **debt collection**. Some businesses use the services of a **factor** for the administration of its debts.

BPP
LEARNING MEDIA

4.1 Collecting money owed

Debt collection can be a time-consuming process. Many companies fail to apply as much effort to collecting debts as they should, with the result that customers often take a lengthy period of credit, the receivables level is much too high, and bad debts are also high.

Debt collection procedures should include:

(a) Sending invoices to customers that specify the payment terms

(b) Sending a reminder at regular intervals, perhaps every two weeks after the invoice has been sent out. Reminders are sent in the form of a **statement** to the customer. A statement itemises all the unpaid invoices payable by the customer, and the total amount of all his debts

(c) Producing regular lists of 'aged receivables', which identify overdue payments

(d) Chasing overdue payments, by e-mail or telephone

(e) Where a customer still fails to pay amounts owed, reviewing the customer's credit limits and refusing any further credit until the existing debts have been paid.

Most customers will pay, given sufficient pressing. However, a policy of pressing customers for payment should reap its rewards in the longer term, as regular customers get into the habit of paying on time.

A company might also consider a policy of hiring a debt collection agency to collect overdue debts, or a policy of taking non-payers to court. Legal action should be a last resort, for use only when the company decides that the business relationship with the customer is not worth continuing.

4.2 Receivables age analysis

An **aged analysis of receivables** will probably look very like the schedule illustrated below. The analysis splits up the total balance on the account of each customer across different columns according to the dates of the transactions which make up the total balance. Thus, the amount of an invoice which was raised 14 days ago will form part of the figure in the column headed 'up to 30 days', while an invoice which was raised 36 days ago will form part of the figure in the column headed 'up to 60 days'. (In the schedule below, 'up to 60 days' is used as shorthand for 'more than 30 days but less than 60 days'.)

HEATH - AGE ANALYSIS OF RECEIVABLES AS AT 31.1.X2						
Account number	*Customer name*	*Balance*	*Up to 30 days*	*Up to 60 days*	*Up to 90 days*	*Over 90 days*
B004	Brilliant	804.95	649.90	121.00	0.00	34.05
E008	Easimat	272.10	192.90	72.40	6.80	0.00
H002	Hampstead	1,818.42	0.00	0.00	724.24	1,094.18
M024	Martlesham	284.45	192.21	92.24	0.00	0.00
N030	Nyfen	1,217.54	1,008.24	124.50	0.00	84.80
T002	Todmorden College	914.50	842.00	0.00	72.50	0.00
T004	Tricorn	94.80	0.00	0.00	0.00	94.80
V010	Volux	997.06	413.66	342.15	241.25	0.00
Y020	Yardsley Smith & Co	341.77	321.17	20.60	0.00	0.00
Totals		6,745.59	3,620.08	772.89	1,044.79	1,307.83
Percentage		100%	53.6%	11.5%	15.5%	19.4%

An age analysis of receivables can be prepared manually or, more easily, by computer.

The age analysis of receivables may be used to help decide what action to take about older debts. Going down each column in turn starting from the column furthest to the right and working across, we can see that there are some rather old debts which ought to be investigated. Correspondence may of course already exist on some of these items. Perhaps some older invoices are still in dispute. Perhaps some debtors are known to be in financial difficulties. (If there are newer invoices also for customers who could be in financial difficulties, we should perhaps be asking whether we ought to be continuing to supply goods to these customers.)

A number of refinements can be suggested to the aged receivables listing to make it easier to use.

(a)   A report can be printed in which **overdue accounts** are seen first: this highlights attention on these items.

(b)   It can help to aggregate data by **class of customer**. In this case, a report would be printed containing, for debtors aggregated into regions, type of customer, industry sectors etc, the sales revenue, outstanding amount owed, broken down into age and days' sales outstanding.

4.3 Receivables' ageing and liquidity

Also of interest to the credit controller is the *total* percentage figure calculated at the bottom of each column. In practice the credit controller will be concerned to look at this figure first of all. A change in the ageing of debts can quickly have a significant impact on company's cash position. From working comfortably within its agreed overdraft limit, a company might find itself carrying an overdraft that could be expensive. Its own creditworthiness could then suffer, and it will also have to pay more in overdraft fees and interest.

The credit controller should try and avoid situations when a customer owing a significant amount of money starts to delay payment. He or she should review information from:

(a)   Sales staff regarding how the customer is doing
(b)   The press for any stories relevant to the customer
(c)   Competitors
(d)   The trade 'grapevine'

These can supply early warning signals.

If there is a persistent problem, the credit controller might have to insist on a refusal of further credit. This is likely to be resented by the company's sales staff who will possibly receive less commission as a result of lower sales. However, if there is a strong possibility of bad debt, the loss of a potential sale is probably more acceptable than the failure of actual money to arrive.

Additional ratios which might be useful in receivables management, in addition to days' sales outstanding, are as follows.

(a)   **Overdues as a percentage of total debt**. For example, suppose that a company's total receivables are $100,000 and of these, $24,000 are overdue payments. Overdues as a percentage of total debt would be 24%. The credit controller might be required to keep this ratio under a maximum limit, or might be set a target to reduce the ratio to a lower amount within a given period of time.

(b)   If debts are **disputed,** it is helpful to see what proportion these are of the total receivables and the total debts overdue. For example, let's return to the example of the company with outstanding receivables of $100,000, of which $24,000 are overdue. If $16,000 of debts are overdue because they are disputed, reported ratios might be:

(i)   Disputed invoices as a percentage of total debts outstanding: 16%
(ii)   Disputed invoices as a percentage of overdue debts: 67%

An increasing disputes ratio can indicate **invoicing problems**, or **operational problems**.

<table>
<tr><td>Exam focus
point</td><td>In June 2005, a question was set which required calculations of the effect on profit of an increase in sales. The calculations required concerned fixed and variable costs and levels of bad debts. The question then required discussion of the steps to take to ensure that credit customers pay on time.</td></tr>
</table>

4.4 Using factors

In an earlier chapter on sources of finance, factoring was described as a way of raising short-term finance against the receivables of the business. It is also a way of collecting debts. A business might decide to enter an agreement with a factor whereby the factor takes on the administration of the debts of the business, ie invoicing, keeping accounting records of receivables, issuing statements and debt collection.

<table>
<tr><td>Exam focus
point</td><td>A question in the June 2004 exam tested debt factoring and invoice discounting, two very practical aspects of debt collection.</td></tr>
</table>

5 Debt collection procedures

Collecting debts is a two-stage process.

(a) Having agreed credit terms with a customer, a business should issue an invoice and expect to receive payment when it is due. **Issuing invoices** and **receiving payments** is the task of sales ledger staff. They should ensure that:

    (i) The customer is fully aware of the terms of sale
    (ii) The invoice is correctly drawn up

(b) If payments become overdue, they should be 'chased'. **Chasing late payers** might be a responsibility of credit control staff. Procedures for pursuing overdue debts must be established, for example:

    (i) Issuing reminders or final demands

    (ii) Chasing payment by telephone

    (iii) The credit manager or a sales representative making a personal approach to the customer for payment

    (iv) Notifying the debt collection section about what debts are overdue so that further credit will not be given to the customer until he has paid the due amounts

    (v) Handing over the task of debt collection from the sales ledger staff to a specialist debt collection section

    (vi) Instituting legal action to recover a debt

    (vii) Hiring an external debt collection agency to collect the debt

Sales **paperwork** should be dealt with promptly and accurately.

(a) Invoices should be sent out immediately after delivery of goods.
(b) Checks should be carried out to ensure that invoices are accurate.
(c) Investigation of queries and complaints and issue of credit notes should be prompt.
(d) Monthly statements should preferably be issued early.

5.1 Customer awareness of terms of sale

Many larger companies and public sector organisations have a reputation for being slow payers. Small businesses in particular appear to suffer at the hands of larger companies which take as long a time to pay as possible. This practice can severely damage a small business, especially if the value of the invoice, in relation to the small business's expected cash flow, is large. A small business can be thrown on to the mercy of its bankers if its bills are not paid. Any business can increase its chances of getting paid by ensuring, at various stages, that the customer has **no right to plead ignorance** of the due date, or that the seller attaches no importance to it.

(a) Payment dates and terms should be discussed during the initial negotiations as to the price on the grounds that, for the supplier, payment terms can be costed into pricing calculations.

(b) When the order is confirmed in writing, payment terms should be clearly stated, not left to the small print.

(c) When a customer account is set up, the credit agreement should contain a clause whereby a customer acknowledges agreement to the supplier's terms and conditions.

(d) The invoice should state boldly the payment terms.

(e) Payment terms should also be prominently displayed on the final statement.

5.2 Proper invoicing

Slip-ups in invoicing by a supplier might create delays in payment by a customer, because the internal controls in the customer's procedures for paying the debt prevent the debt from being paid because of the discrepancies or faults. So, when issuing an invoice, sales ledger staff should check the following.

(a) The customer's name and address: are they correct and current?

(b) Is the invoice being sent to the right place? Many companies have a central purchasing area and central purchases ledger area. Invoices, if they are to get to the purchase ledger staff, must be sent to where the customer asks for them to be sent.

(c) Is the invoice recognisable and how is it to be sent? An invoice sent with the goods that is not immediately recognisable might sit on an advice note file of the stores and never get to the staff responsible for paying the invoice.

(d) Does the invoice have the customer's authorisation reference on it? If it is to be matched with a purchase order, then it must quote the purchase order number.

(e) Are the details on the invoice correct as to quantities, descriptions and details, and arithmetic total? The customer organisation's staff will be authorised to reject the invoice if the details are not correct.

(f) Finally, prompt invoicing. Having delivered the goods, the invoice should be submitted to the customer promptly.

5.3 Knowledge of customer payment systems

It helps to have some idea as to how customers pay.

(a) Some customers have an invoice run on a monthly basis. There is an inevitable cut-off point after which data cannot be input to the system. Delays might be caused by a bureaucratic backlog.

(b) Other customers, regardless of their actual obligations, ration the amount paid out per month. Personal customers with financial problems have to ration scarce resources, paying essentials (ie food, mortgage) before servicing other debts (especially non-secured loans like credit cards). Many businesses need to conserve cash and act in a similar way.

(c) Some customers will only pay when sent a reminder or when specifically asked by suppliers. Other customers will not pay until threatened with legal action.

5.4 Statements, reminders and final demands

Invoices are usually followed by a **monthly statement** to customers which will:

(a)   List the new invoices during the month
(b)   Indicate the cash received
(c)   Indicate the outstanding balance due
(d)   Analyse the debts by age, and
(e)   Serve as a reminder to the customer about payment

Instead of statements, a business might issue **reminder notices** to slow payers. The reminder would be intended to prompt the customer into making the payment. **Final demands** are sent when an invoice is overdue for payment, warning the customer that unless payment is received within a certain period of time, steps will be taken to pursue the debt by 'legal methods'. The threat of legal action should then persuade the customer to pay (if he can afford to!).

5.5 Credit insurance, third party guarantees, Romalpa clauses

A company might also consider ways of recovering a debt, or the goods, after an unpaid debt has become overdue.

(a)   For some debts, it might be worth arranging **credit insurance**, from an invoice discounting company or from an insurance company specialising in credit insurance.

(b)   In some cases, it might be possible to obtain a guarantee of payment from a third party, who will undertake to make the payment if the debtor fails to do so. The third party might be the parent company of the customer, or possibly the customer's bank.

(c)   In some cases, it might also be possible to supply goods under a 'Romalpa clause' agreement, whereby the goods remain the property of the supplier until they have been paid for.

5.6 Debt collection and small businesses

Credit management is a **particular problem for small businesses** because they usually do not have enough staff or resources to justify a full-time debt collection section. Issuing invoices and collecting debts is often just a part of the job of one or more individuals, who are therefore unable to devote all their time to the task of collecting debts. They are also unlikely to have sufficient training or experience in the work.

Small businesses also lack the money, as well as the time or resources, to carry out routine credit checks on new customers. As a result, decisions on granting credit are often based on trust. The problem might be compounded by the fact that many small businesses have a limited number of clients. If any of these becomes non-creditworthy, the financial implications for the small business could be severe.

Exam focus point

The particular problems for small businesses were examined for 4 marks in the June 2006 exam.

6 The management of inventories

Almost every company carries inventories of some sort, even if they are only inventories of consumables such as stationery. For a manufacturing business, inventories (sometimes called stocks), in the form of raw materials, work in progress and finished goods, may amount to a substantial proportion of the total assets of the business.

Inventory turnover is an element in the cash cycle. With most businesses, inventories have to be paid for before they are consumed or sold, and holding inventories therefore ties up working capital.

Inventory turnover is an element in the cash cycle, and inventory levels should be optimised.

Some businesses attempt to control inventories on a scientific basis by balancing the costs of inventory shortages against those of inventory holding. The 'scientific' control inventories may be analysed into three parts.

(a) The **economic order quantity (EOQ) model** can be used to decide the optimum order size for inventories which will minimise the costs of ordering inventories plus holding costs.

(b) If **discounts for bulk purchases** are available, it may be cheaper to buy inventories in large order sizes so as to obtain the discounts.

(c) Uncertainty in the demand for inventories and/or the supply lead time may lead a company to decide to hold **buffer goods** (thereby increasing its investment in working capital) in order to reduce or eliminate the risk of running out of inventory.

6.1 Inventory costs

An aim of inventory management should be to keep the cost of inventory holding, including the cost of the capital tied up, to a minimum consistent with efficient inventory management.

Inventory costs can be classified into four groups.

(a) **Holding costs** comprise the **cost of capital tied up**, warehousing and handling costs, deterioration, obsolescence, insurance and pilferage.

(b) **Procuring costs** depend on how the inventory is obtained but will consist of **ordering costs** for goods purchased externally, such as clerical costs, telephone charges and delivery costs.

(c) **Shortage costs** may be:

(i) The loss of a sale and the contribution which could have been earned from the sale

(ii) The extra cost of having to buy an emergency supply of inventories at a high price

(iii) The cost of lost production and sales, where the running out of goods brings an entire process to a halt

(d) The **cost of the inventory** itself, the supplier's price or the direct cost per unit of production, will also need to be considered when the supplier offers a discount on orders for purchases in bulk.

6.2 Approaches to inventory management

There are several different approaches to managing the level of inventories. Two particular issues to consider are:

(a) When to re-order new supplies of inventory items, ie deciding the **re-order level** for inventories

(b) When inventory is re-ordered from a supplier, what quantity to order, ie the **order size**.

Three systems for deciding when to re-order inventory are as follows.

(a) A **periodic review system** in which the requirement for inventory is reviewed at fixed time intervals, and varying quantities are ordered on each occasion, according to the current level of goods remaining.

(b)   A **re-order level system** in which a fixed quantity is ordered at irregular intervals, when inventory levels have fallen to a re-order level specified on the store-keeper's records or 'bin card'.

(c)   **Just in time** (JIT) procurement

(d)   material requirements planning (MRP) procurement.

6.3 Just-in-time (JIT) procurement

A just-in-time approach to inventory ordering seeks to minimise inventory levels. **Just-in-time procurement** is a term describing a policy of obtaining goods from suppliers at the latest possible time (ie when they are needed) and so avoiding the need to carry any materials or components inventory. JIT can also be applied by a manufacturing company to producing items only when they are needed, and so holding minimal inventories of finished goods.

JIT procurement relies on having suppliers capable of delivering new supplies quickly, on demand, and the ability of the organisation to manage the flow of production, so that customer orders can be processed and satisfied quickly.

Introducing JIT might bring the following potential benefits.

(a)   Reduction in inventory holding costs
(b)   Increased flexibility – spot buying
(c)   Increased quality – fresh stock
(d)   Reduced manufacturing lead times
(e)   Improved labour productivity
(f)   Reduced scrap/rework/warranty costs
(g)   Simplified stock holding systems

Reduced inventory levels mean that a lower level of investment in working capital will be required.

JIT systems do, however, have the following disadvantages

(a)   Given real world practicalities, JIT puts the company at risk of not receiving the inventory at the due date.

(b)   JIT can raise prices since, unless the whole supply chain is operating the same system, someone somewhere must be holding the inventory.

(c)   JIT excludes the possibility of making opportunities purchases arising from, say, supplier sales or competitor closures, as a result of the lack of stock holding capacity.

As a result of the first noted disadvantage JIT will not be appropriate in some cases largely because with a JIT procurement system, there is a risk that a supplier will be unable to deliver an item when it is ordered, resulting in a running out of the goods. In a hospital, for example, this could quite literally be fatal and so JIT would be quite unsuitable.

6.4 Materials requirement planning

Where JIT systems can be used in retail businesses, they are not adequate alone for manufacturing businesses where many products are made using a range of materials that may be needed at a particular time during the manufacturing process, and where each of the input materials may have differing lead times and impacts in the event of a stock-out.

MRP systems aim to deal with these more complex circumstances and aim to

- Ensure materials and products are available for production and delivery to customers.
- Maintain the lowest possible level of inventory.
- Plan manufacturing activities, delivery schedules and purchasing activities.

The starting point for any MRP system is the Master Production Schedule (MPS) that is designed to fulfil the order book or anticipated demand, and the Bill of Materials (BOM) or parts list for each product.

From the MRP we will know what needs to be produced and by when. From the BOM and knowledge on the production process we will be able to determine what material inputs are required and when they are required. From the supplier lead times we will then be able to determine when these items need to be ordered in order to satisfy production needs if using JIT procurement, or establish a purchase schedule for all the materials required.

Within this process provision needs to be made for the likelihood that a small number of the items received may be sub-standard and hence of no use to production. In addition, provision needs to be made for the possibility of late delivery on any order and the consequences that would have on production.

The primary outputs of MRP systems are the purchasing schedule for future orders and the rescheduling report highlighting any requirement to cancel, delay, speed up or increase any existing orders.

One problem with MRP systems relate to the complexity of the production and manufacturing process and the reliability and integrity of the associated data. Another is their lack of flexibility to easily deal with changes in lead times, or manufacturing times or changes to customer orders.

MRP systems are highly complex and require a lot of effort and care to maintain and run effectively. The cost savings from minimising stock holding levels through such a system needs to be carefully weighed up against the costs of maintaining the system.

6.5 The order quantity

FAST FORWARD

An **economic order quantity** for an inventory item is the re-order quantity for the item that minimises the combined costs of inventory holding and inventory ordering.

In a JIT procurement system, the quantity ordered of any inventory item should be the quantity of the item that is currently required. Where JIT is not applied, a different approach to deciding an inventory order quantity is required. One such approach is the economic order quantity system.

The **economic order quantity (EOQ)** is the optimal ordering quantity for an item of inventory. This is the order quantity that will minimise the combined costs of inventory holding and inventory ordering.

Let $d =$ usage in units for one period (the 'demand')

$P =$ purchase price **per item**

$c =$ cost of placing one order

$h =$ holding cost per unit of inventory for one period $\Big\}$ relevant costs only

$Q =$ reorder quantity

Assume that demand is constant, the lead time is constant or zero and purchase costs per unit are constant (ie there are no bulk purchase discounts).

(a)   The total annual cost of holding inventory is the average inventory level multiplied by the annual cost of holding one unit of the inventory item, ie $(Q/2)\,h$.

(b)   The total ordering costs per annum are the cost per order multiplied by the number of orders. The number of orders is (d/Q) and the total ordering costs per annum are therefore $(d/Q)\,c$

The order quantity, Q, which will minimise these total costs is:

$$Q = \sqrt{\frac{2cd}{h}}$$

You need to learn this formula, and be able to explain what each item in the formula represents.

BPP
LEARNING MEDIA

6.6 Example: economic order quantity

The demand for a commodity is 40,000 units a year, at a steady rate. It costs $20 to place an order, and 40c to hold a unit for a year. Find the order size to minimise inventory costs, the number of orders placed each year, and the length of the inventory cycle.

Solution

$Q = \sqrt{\dfrac{2 \times 20 \times 40,000}{0.4}}$ = 2,000 units. This means that there will be

$\dfrac{40,000}{2,000}$ = 20 orders placed each year, so that the inventory cycle is once every 52 ÷ 20

= 2.6 weeks. Total costs will be (20 × $20) + $(\dfrac{2,000}{2} \times 40c)$ = $800 a year.

6.7 Uncertainties in demand and lead times: a re-order level system

When the volume of demand is uncertain, or the supply lead time is variable, there are problems in deciding what the re-order level should be. By holding a 'safety' level of inventory, a company can reduce the likelihood that inventories run out during the re-order period (due to unexpected high demand or an unusually long lead time before the new supply is delivered). The average annual cost of such a safety inventory would be:

| Quantity of safety inventory (in units) | × | Inventory holding cost per unit per annum |

6.8 Re-order level

When a company holds inventories, and does not use JIT procurement methods, it might use the EOQ formula to decide the batch size for new orders. A second aspect of inventory management is to decide *when* to re-order.

The re-order level for a particular inventory item depends on the extent to which an organisation is prepared to accept running out of goods. If running out is not tolerated, inventory items have to be re-ordered in sufficient time to ensure delivery before the current inventories run out.

To avoid running out of goods:

Re-order level = Maximum supply lead time in weeks (or days) x Maximum consumption each week (or day).

For example, suppose that when new supplies of item 12345 are ordered, it usually takes the supplier 10 working days to deliver, but deliveries are sometimes made in 5 working days and sometimes take as long as 20 days. Daily consumption of the item is 4 units on average, but can be as low as one unit and as high as six units.

Inventory item 12345	Minimum	Average	Maximum
Supply lead time	5 days	10 days	20 days
Daily consumption	1 unit	4 units	6 units

To avoid all risk of running out, the re-order level should be 20 days x 6 units per day = 120 units.

A problem with a policy of never running out is that the organisation will hold excess inventories or 'buffer inventories' most of the time, and excess inventory-holding can be expensive and wasteful, particularly when items held in inventory are subject to losses through damage or deterioration. In the example above, a re-order level of 120 units will ensure no running out, in the event that it takes 20 days to obtain a new supply of the item and daily consumption is six units on each of the 20 days. However:

(a)   If the re-supply of the item takes the average period of 10 days, and consumption during this time is 4 units each day, total consumption will be just 40 units during the supply lead time. There will still be 80 units in inventory when the fresh supply arrives. This suggests that the average size of the buffer inventory is 80 units.

(b)   If the re-supply of the item takes the minimum period of 5 days, and consumption during this time is one unit each day, total consumption will be just 5 units during the supply lead time. There will still be 115 units in inventory when the fresh supply arrives.

Since holding buffer inventories can be expensive, an organisation might consider tolerating some incidences of running out, and setting the re-order levels lower, provided that the savings from lower buffer inventories are greater than the expected cost of the incidences of running out that do occur.

Question 13.3   Avoiding running out of inventory

The economic order quantity for inventory item 6789 is 500 units. The cost of holding one unit in inventory is $12 per annum. The supply lead time for this item and the daily consumption rate are as follows.

Inventory item 6789	Minimum	Average	Maximum
Supply lead time	4 days	8 days	15 days
Daily consumption	6 units	10 units	16 units

The company has a policy of avoiding running out of inventories entirely.

Required

(a)   What should the re-order level be?

(b)   What is the average size of the buffer inventory for the item, and what is the cost to the company of holding this inventory?

(c)   What is the maximum inventory level that should never be exceeded?

(For the answer to this question, see the Answer section at the end of this book.)

Exam focus point

A question in the December 2003 exam was on costs of inventory, just in time and order size.

7 Bulk purchase discounts

The simple EOQ formula is not applicable when bulk purchase discounts (also called quantity discounts) are available on order quantities above a certain size. When bulk purchase discounts are available, the cheapest order quantity is that which minimises the total of **total purchase costs, ordering costs** and **inventory holding costs**.

The total cost will be minimised:

(a)   At an order level equal to the EOQ, so that a discount is not worthwhile, or
(b)   If it is a larger amount than the EOQ, at the minimum order size necessary to earn the discount.

7.1 Example: bulk discounts

The annual demand for an item of inventory is 45 units. The item costs $200 a unit, the holding cost for one unit for one year is 15% of the unit cost and ordering costs are $300 an order. The supplier offers a 3% discount for orders of 60 units or more, and a discount of 5% for orders of 90 units or more. What is the cost-minimising order size?

Solution

(a) The EOQ ignoring discounts is:

$$\sqrt{\frac{2 \times 300 \times 45}{15\% \times 200}} = 30 \text{ units}$$

	$
Purchases (no discount) 45 × $200	9,000
Holding costs 15 units × $30	450
Ordering costs 1.5 orders × $300	450
Total annual costs	9,900

(b) The minimum order size to earn a 3% discount is 60 units, which is higher than the EOQ. With a discount of 3% and an order quantity of 60 units costs are as follows.

	$
Purchases $9,000 × 97%	8,730
Holding costs 30 units × (15% × 97% × $200)	873
Ordering costs 0.75 orders × $300	225
Total annual costs	9,828

(c) The minimum order size to earn a 5% discount is 90 units. With a discount of 5% and an order quantity of 90 units costs are as follows.

	$
Purchases $9,000 × 95%	8,550.0
Holding costs 45 units × (15% × 95% × $200)	1,282.5
Ordering costs 0.5 orders × $300	150.0
Total annual costs	9,982.5

The cheapest option is to order 60 units at a time.

Question 13.4   Discount

A company uses an item of inventory as follows.

Purchase price:	$96 per unit
Annual demand:	4,000 units
Ordering cost:	$300
Annual holding cost:	10% of purchase price
Economic order quantity:	500 units

Should the company order 1,000 units at a time in order to secure an 8% discount?

(For the answer to this question, see the Answer section at the end of this book.)

Chapter roundup

- In managing **receivables,** the **creditworthiness** of customers needs to be assessed. The risks and costs of a customer defaulting will need to be balanced against the profitability of the business provided by that customer.

- The **terms of sale** include total credit allowed, maximum time allowed for payment, and possibly terms for a settlement discount.

- **Changing the credit period allowed** to customers will affect the size of the investment in inventories, receivables and trade payables, and might also affect total sales volume and profitability.

- **Settlement discounts** may be employed to shorten average credit periods, and to reduce the investment in receivables and therefore **interest costs**. The benefit in interest cost saved should exceed the cost of the discounts allowed.

- A business must have policies and procedures in place for **debt collection**. Some businesses use the services of a **factor** for the administration of its debts.

- **Inventory turnover** is an element in the cash cycle, and inventory levels should be optimised.

- An **economic order quantity** for an inventory item is the re-order quantity for the item that minimises the combined costs of inventory holding and inventory ordering.

BPP
LEARNING MEDIA

Quick quiz

1   What factors should be considered by management in formulating a policy for credit control?

2   How might the creditworthiness of a potential new customer be checked?

3   What is credit insurance?

4   Your company offers a customer the following credit terms: 'Payment 60 days after the invoice date, or an early payment discount of 2% for payment within 10 days.' What is the return on capital for the customer from taking the discount?

5   The average inventory turnover time in a company is 43 days. How many times per annum is inventory turned over?

6   A company uses 800 units of an inventory item each month. It costs $200 per unit, and the cost of holding inventory is 12% of the item's cost. The cost of placing an order has been estimated as $800 per order. What is the economic order quantity for the item?

Answers to quick quiz

1   Administrative costs of debt collection, procedures for controlling credit to individual customers (eg assessing creditworthiness), procedures for debt collection, credit policy and its effect on total receivables and profits, early settlement discount policy.

2   Bank reference, reference from another firm, eg another supplier to the customer, report from a credit assessment agency, analysing the accounts of a business customer, using a credit rating system to assess individual customers, payment history for existing customers.

3   A form of insurance in which the insurance provider undertakes to reimburse the policy holder in the event of non-payment of a debt by a customer. When a factoring organisation provides credit insurance, it will insist on collecting the debt itself.

4   The customer will save $2 for every $100 spent by paying (60 – 10) 50 days earlier, ie by investing $98 now, the customer will save $2 in 50 days. This represents a return on capital of $(2/98) \times (365/50) \times 100\% = 14.9\%$.

5   $365/43 = 8.5$ times. This means that on average the company uses up its inventory 8.5 times every year, so that on average, there will be 8.5 orders for inventory items each year.

6   c = $800, d = (800 \times 12) = 9,600$, h = 12% of $200 = $24.

$$\sqrt{\frac{2 \times 800 \times 9,600}{\$24}} = 800 \text{ units, ie order every month.}$$

14

Management of cash and payables

Introduction

We conclude our coverage of working capital management by looking at the management of cash balances (including overdrafts) and trade payables.

Small businesses can experience particular problems in managing their working capital; these problems are described at the end of this chapter.

1 The management of cash

Cash flow management calls for the efficient management of inventories, receivables and trade payables. Cash management is concerned with using cash received, and having access to another source of finance (eg an overdraft facility), in the event that cash flows from operations are insufficient to meet payment obligations.

The cash cycle of a business generates cash from trading operations. The cycle starts with payments to suppliers of goods or services, and ends with the receipt of cash payments from receivables (or from cash sales).

One aspect of cash management is to decide how to use the money received.

(a) Cash from operations should be used to pay the **creditors** of the business, such as trade creditors, interest charges on loans and payments of taxation.

(b) Surplus cash might be used to make other payments, such as the **repayment of loans**, or the **purchase of new non-current assets**.

(c) A company might use cash to pay **dividends** to its shareholders.

(d) Surplus cash might be put on **deposit with a bank** or other financial institution, or **invested**. Cash might be invested in government bills or bonds, in other 'money market instruments', or in shares of other companies.

Cash is needed to pay creditors. Any surplus cash can then be used to purchase business assets, invest in financial assets or make payments to the business owners (shareholders).

Deciding what to do with spare cash will depend to a large extent on whether the surplus is only temporary, and whether it might be needed at some time in the future to meet payment obligations. A temporary cash surplus may be kept on hand (earning no interest), placed on 'short call' with a bank where it will earn some interest, or invested in readily-realisable securities such as UK government bonds (gilts).

The more cash which is on hand, the easier it will be for the company to meet its bills as they fall due and to take advantage of discounts. However, holding cash or near equivalents to cash has a cost - the loss of earnings which would otherwise have been obtained by using the funds in another way. The financial manager must try to **balance liquidity with profitability.**

2 Potential cash flow problems

Cash flow problems can arise for loss-making businesses, businesses that are growing and investing more in working capital and non-current assets, businesses with a seasonal trading pattern and businesses facing large one-off expenditures.

Cash flow problems can arise in various ways.

(a) **Making losses**. If a business is continually making losses, it will eventually have cash flow problems. Just how long it will take before a loss-making business runs into cash flow trouble will depend on how big the losses are, and on the size of the depreciation charge. (As a rough guide, cash flows from operations can be estimated as the profit or loss before interest and taxation, plus the depreciation charge. This is because depreciation is a non-cash expense.) If a company's losses are less than its depreciation charges, it will still be cash positive in its trading operations. In such a situation, the cash flow troubles might only begin when the business needs to replace non-current assets.

(b)   **Inflation**. In a period of inflation, a business needs ever-increasing amounts of cash just to replace used-up and worn-out assets. A business can be making a profit in historical cost accounting terms, but still not be receiving enough cash to buy the replacement assets it needs.

(c)   **Growth**. When a business is growing, it needs to acquire more non-current assets, and to support higher amounts of inventories and receivables. These additional assets must be paid for somehow (or financed by trade payables). The problems of overtrading have been described earlier.

(d)   **Seasonal business**. When a business has seasonal or cyclical sales, it may have cash flow difficulties at certain times of the year, when (i) cash inflows are low, but (ii) cash outflows are high, perhaps because the business is building up its inventories for the next period of high sales.

(e)   **One-off items of expenditure**. There might occasionally be a single non-recurring item of expenditure that creates a cash flow problem, such as the repayment of loan capital on maturity of the debt or the purchase of an exceptionally expensive item. A small or medium-sized business might decide to buy a freehold property which then stretches its cash resources for several months or even years.

2.1 Methods of easing cash shortages

The steps that are usually taken by a company when a need for cash arises, and when it cannot obtain resources from any other source such as a loan or an increased overdraft, are as follows.

(a)   **Postponing capital expenditure.** It might be imprudent to postpone expenditure on non-current assets that are needed for the development and growth of the business, but some capital expenditures might be postponable without serious consequences. Replacement of company motor vehicles is an example. If a company's policy is to replace company cars every two years, but the company is facing a cash shortage, it might decide to replace cars every three years.

(b)   **Accelerating cash inflows which would otherwise be expected at a later time**, eg by pressing debtors for earlier payment. Often, this policy will result in a loss of goodwill and problems with customers. There will be little scope for speeding up payments when the credit period currently allowed to debtors is no more than the norm for the industry. It might be possible to encourage debtors to pay more quickly by offering discounts for earlier payment.

(c)   **Reversing past investment decisions by selling assets previously acquired.** Some assets are less crucial to a business than others and so if cash flow problems are severe, the option of selling investments or property might have to be considered.

(d)   **Negotiating a reduction in cash outflows, so as to postpone or even reduce payments**. There are several ways in which this could be done.

(i)   Longer credit might be taken from suppliers. Such an extension of credit would have to be negotiated carefully: there would be a risk of having further supplies refused.

(ii)   Loan repayments could be rescheduled by agreement with a bank.

(iii)   A deferral of the payment of tax might be agreed with the tax authorities. These authorities will charge interest on the outstanding amount of tax.

(iv)   Dividend payments could be reduced. Dividend payments are discretionary cash outflows, although a company's directors might be constrained by shareholders' expectations, so that they feel obliged to pay dividends even when there is a cash shortage.

A company is earning insufficient cash flows from its operating activities to cover the interest payments to its lending bank. What effects might you expect to see in the company's balance sheet if this situation persists?

(For the answer to this question, see the Answer section at the end of this book.)

3 Monthly cash flow statements and forecasts

A monthly cash flow statement is simply a statement of cash receipts and cash payments during a given month. The statement also shows the cash balance at the start of the month and the cash balance at the end of the month.

The total monthly cash flows might be broken down into weekly cash flows, to provide more management detail.

Benefits of forecast cash flow statements are that they allow management to:

(a) Monitor the cash position, and identify any likely cash shortage or cash surplus during a future period.

(b) Check that the company is likely to operate within its bank overdraft limits.

(c) Identify any unusual cash movements during the month.

(d) Take measures to ensure that there will be sufficient cash available, where the original forecast suggests a cash shortage in the period.

Cash flow statements can be used either as a forecasting tool or as a means of monitoring actual cash flows. (Actual cash flows might be compared with budgeted or forecast cash flows for the month.)

Actual monthly cash flows might also be compared with the monthly profit. Differences will arise between cash flow and profit because of depreciation charges against profit, which are not cash flows. In addition, any change in working capital levels will affect cash flow. A cash flow statement might therefore help to identify any unusual build-up or reduction in inventories, receivables or payables.

3.1 Cash flow forecasts

FAST FORWARD

Cash flow forecasts show the expected receipts and payments during a forecast period and are a vital management control tool, especially during times of recession.

Key term

A **cash flow forecast** is a detailed forecast of cash inflows and outflows incorporating both revenue and capital items.

A cash flow forecast is thus a statement in which estimated future **cash receipts** and **payments** are tabulated in such a way as to show the forecast **cash balance** of a business at defined intervals. For example, in December 20X2 an accounts department might wish to estimate the cash position of the business during the three following months, January to March 20X3. A cash flow forecast might be drawn up in the following format.

	Jan	Feb	Mar
	$	$	$
Estimated cash receipts			
From credit customers	14,000	16,500	17,000
From cash sales	3,000	4,000	4,500
Proceeds on disposal of non-current assets		2,200	
Total cash receipts	17,000	22,700	21,500
Estimated cash payments			
To suppliers of goods	8,000	7,800	10,500
To employees (wages)	3,000	3,500	3,500
Purchase of fixed assets		16,000	
Rent and rates			1,000
Other overheads	1,200	1,200	1,200
Repayment of loan	2,500		
	14,700	28,500	16,200
Net surplus/(deficit) for month	2,300	(5,800)	5,300
Opening cash balance	1,200	3,500	(2,300)
Closing cash balance	3,500	(2,300)	3,000

In the example above (where the figures are purely for illustration) the accounts department has calculated that the cash balance at the beginning of the flow forecast period, 1 January, will be $1,200. Estimates have been made of the cash which is likely to be received by the business (from cash and credit sales, and from a planned disposal of non-current assets in February). Similar estimates have been made of cash due to be paid out by the business (payments to suppliers and employees, payments for rent, rates and other overheads, payment for a planned purchase of non-current assets in February and a loan repayment due in January).

From these estimates it is a simple step to calculate the excess of cash receipts over cash payments in each month. In some months cash payments may exceed cash receipts and there will be a **deficit** for the month; this occurs during February in the above example because of the large investment in non-current assets in that month.

The last part of the cash flow forecast above shows how the business's estimated cash balance can then be rolled along from month to month. Starting with the opening balance of $1,200 at 1 January a cash surplus of $2,300 is generated in January. This leads to a closing January balance of $3,500 which becomes the opening balance for February. The deficit of $5,800 in February throws the business's cash position into overdraft and the overdrawn balance of $2,300 becomes the opening balance for March. Finally, the healthy cash surplus of $5,300 in March leaves the business with a favourable cash position of $3,000 at the end of the flow forecast period.

Exam focus point	When preparing cash flow forecasts, it is vital that your work is clearly laid out, and referenced to workings where appropriate.

3.2 The usefulness of cash flow forecasts

The cash flow forecast is one of the most important planning tools that an organisation can use. It shows the cash effect of all plans made within the flow forecastary process and hence its preparation can lead to a modification of flow forecasts if it shows that there are insufficient cash resources to finance the planned operations.

It can also **give management an indication of potential problems that could arise and allows them the opportunity to take action to avoid such problems**. A cash flow forecast can show four positions. Management will need to take appropriate action depending on the potential position.

Cash position	Appropriate management action
Short-term surplus	Pay accounts payable early to obtain discount Attempt to increase sales by increasing accounts receivable and inventories Make short-term investments
Short-term deficit	Increase accounts payable Reduce accounts receivable Arrange an overdraft
Long-term surplus	Make long-term investments Expand Diversify Replace/update non-current assets
Long-term deficit	Raise long-term finance (such as via issue of share capital) Consider shutdown/disinvestment opportunities

3.3 Example

A company has made the following cash flow estimates for March.

Week commencing	1 March $000	8 March $000	15 March $000	22 March $000	29 March $000
Cash from debtors	10	20	15	18	16
Sale of non-current asset					5
Cash in	10	20	15	18	21
Salaries				(23)	
Capital expenditure			(17)		
Tax payment		(8)			
Advertising spend				(5)	
Other expenses	(5)	(9)	(3)	(4)	(7)
Cash out	(5)	(17)	(20)	(32)	(7)
Cash surplus/(deficit)	5	3	(5)	(14)	14
Cash at start of week	1	6	9	4	(10)
Cash at end of week	6	9	4	(10)	4

This forecast shows that the company should start the month with a small cash surplus, and end it with a slightly larger cash surplus, but that a deficit of $10,000 will arise during the fourth week. If the company does not have a bank overdraft facility, it could consider any of the following measures.

(a) Deferring some expenditure that does not have to be made as early as originally planned. In this example, payment of salaries and tax should not be deferred, but some or all of the capital expenditure, and the advertising spend, might be deferred by one or two weeks.

(b) Bringing forward some income. In this example, the company might be able to bring forward the sale of the non-current asset by one week. However, selling the asset earlier would only affect weekly cash flows by $5,000, not enough on its own to eliminate the cash deficit of $10,000 in week 4.

(c) If necessary, discussing an overdraft facility with the company's bank.

Suppose that in this example, the company decides that it can defer $6,000 of the capital expenditure from week 3 to week 5, and can bring forward the sale of the non-current asset from week 5 to week 4. The revised monthly cash flow statement will now be as follows.

Week commencing	1 March	8 March	15 March	22 March	29 March
	$000	$000	$000	$000	$000
Cash from debtors	10	20	15	18	16
Sale of non-current asset				5	
Cash in	10	20	15	23	16
Salaries				(23)	
Capital expenditure			(11)		(6)
Tax payment		(8)			
Advertising spend				(5)	
Other expenses	(5)	(9)	(3)	(4)	(7)
Cash out	(5)	(17)	(14)	(32)	(13)
Cash surplus/(deficit)	5	3	1	(9)	3
Cash at start of week	1	6	9	10	1
Cash at end of week	6	9	10	1	4

Taken together, the two measures will eliminate the cash deficit.

3.4 Preparing a cash flow forecast

A cash flow forecast question could ask you to prepare the cash flow forecast and then recommend appropriate action for management. Ensure your advice takes account both of whether there is a surplus or deficit and whether the position is long or short term.

A cash flow forecast is prepared to show the **expected receipts of cash and payments of cash** during a budget period.

It should be obvious that the **profit or loss made by an organisation during an accounting period does not reflect its cash flow position for the following reasons.**

    (a)   Not all cash receipts affect income statement income.

    (b)   Not all cash payments affect income statement expenditure.

    (c)   Some costs in the income statement such as profit or loss on sale of non-current assets or depreciation are not cash items but are costs derived from accounting conventions.

    (d)   The timing of cash receipts and payments may not coincide with the recording of income statement transactions. For example, a dividend might be declared in the results for 20X6 and shown in the income statement for that year, but paid in 20X7.

To ensure that there is sufficient cash in hand to cope adequately with planned activities, management should therefore prepare and pay close attention to a cash flow forecast rather than a income statement.

Clear workings and assumptions are very important in a cash flow forecast.

3.5 Example: A month by month cash flow forecast

From the following information which relates to George and Zola Co you are required to prepare a month by month cash flow forecast for the second half of 20X5 and to append such brief comments as you consider might be helpful to management.

    (a)   The company's only product, a vest, sells at $40 and has a variable cost of $26 made up of material $20, labour $4 and overhead $2.

    (b)   Fixed costs of $6,000 per month are paid on the 28th of each month.

(c)   Quantities sold/to be sold on credit

May	June	July	Aug	Sept	Oct	Nov	Dec
1,000	1,200	1,400	1,600	1,800	2,000	2,200	2,600

(d)   Production quantities

May	June	July	Aug	Sept	Oct	Nov	Dec
1,200	1,400	1,600	2,000	2,400	2,600	2,400	2,200

(e)   Cash sales at a discount of 5% are expected to average 100 units a month.

(f)   Customers settle their accounts by the end of the second month following sale.

(g)   Suppliers of material are paid two months after the material is used in production.

(h)   Wages are paid in the same month as they are incurred.

(i)   70% of the variable overhead is paid in the month of production, the remainder in the following month.

(j)   Corporation tax of $18,000 is to be paid in October.

(k)   A new delivery vehicle was bought in June. It cost $8,000 and is to be paid for in August. The old vehicle was sold for $600, the buyer undertaking to pay in July.

(l)   The company is expected to be $3,000 overdrawn at the bank at 30 June 20X5.

(m)   No increases or decreases in raw materials, work in progress or finished goods are planned over the period.

(n)   No price increases or cost increases are expected in the period.

Solution

Cash flow forecast for 1 July to 31 December 20X5

	July $	Aug $	Sept $	Oct $	Nov $	Dec $	Total $
Receipts							
Credit sales	40,000	48,000	56,000	64,000	72,000	80,000	360,000
Cash sales	3,800	3,800	3,800	3,800	3,800	3,800	22,800
Sale of vehicle	600	–	–	–	–	–	600
	44,400	51,800	59,800	67,800	75,800	83,800	383,400
Payments							
Materials	24,000	28,000	32,000	40,000	48,000	52,000	224,000
Labour	6,400	8,000	9,600	10,400	9,600	8,800	52,800
Variable overhead (W)	3,080	3,760	4,560	5,080	4,920	4,520	25,920
Fixed costs	6,000	6,000	6,000	6,000	6,000	6,000	36,000
Corporation tax				18,000			18,000
Purchase of vehicle		8,000					8,000
	39,480	53,760	52,160	79,480	68,520	71,320	364,720
Receipts less payments	4,920	(1,960)	7,640	(11,680)	7,280	12,480	18,680
Balance b/f	(3,000)	1,920	(40)	7,600	(4,080)	3,200	(3,000)
Balance c/f	1,920	(40)	7,600	(4,080)	3,200	15,680	15,680

Working

	June $	July $	Aug $	Sept $	Oct $	Nov $	Dec $
Variable overhead production cost	2,800	3,200	4,000	4,800	5,200	4,800	4,400
70% paid in month		2,240	2,800	3,360	3,640	3,360	3,080
30% in following month		840	960	1,200	1,440	1,560	1,440
		3,080	3,760	4,560	5,080	4,920	4,520

Comments

(a) There will be a small overdraft at the end of August but a much larger one at the end of October. It may be possible to delay payments to suppliers for longer than two months or to reduce purchases of materials or reduce the volume of production by running down existing inventory levels.

(b) If neither of these courses is possible, the company may need to negotiate overdraft facilities with its bank.

(c) The cash deficit is only temporary and by the end of December there will be a comfortable surplus. The use to which this cash will be put should ideally be planned in advance.

Exam focus point

You may be asked to prepare a cash flow forecast, and also consider the effects on the flow forecast or particular figures in it of the original assumptions changing.

In the June 2007 exam there was a 20 mark question requiring the preparation of and commentary on a monthly forecast cash flow statement.

3.6 Cash flow forecasts and an opening balance sheet

You might be given a cash flow forecast question in which you are required to analyse an opening balance sheet to decide how many outstanding accounts receivable will pay what they owe in the first few months of the cash flow forecast period, and how many outstanding accounts payable must be paid.

Suppose that a balance sheet as at 31 December 20X4 shows accounts receivable of $150,000 and trade accounts payable of $60,000. The following information is also relevant.

- Accounts receivable are allowed two months to pay
- $1^{1}/_{2}$ months' credit is taken from trade accounts payable
- Sales and materials purchases were both made at an even monthly rate

Let's try to ascertain the months of 20X5 in which the accounts receivable will eventually pay and the accounts payable will be paid.

(a) Since accounts receivable take two months to pay, the $150,000 of accounts receivable in the balance sheet represents credit sales in November and December 20X4, who will pay in January and February 20X5 respectively. Since sales in 20X4 were at an equal monthly rate, the cash flow forecast should plan for receipts of $75,000 each month in January and February from the accounts receivable in the opening balance sheet.

(b) Similarly, since accounts payable are paid after $1^{1}/_{2}$ months, the balance sheet accounts payable will be paid in January and the first half of February 20X5, which means that flow forecasted payments will be as follows.

	$
In January (purchases in 2nd half of Nov. and 1st half of Dec.20X4)	40,000
In February (purchases in 2nd half of December 20X4)	20,000
Total accounts payable in the balance sheet	60,000

(The balance sheet accounts payable of $60,000 represent $1^{1}/_{2}$ months' purchases, so that purchases in 20X4 must be $40,000 per month, which is $20,000 per half month.)

4 Banking procedures and cash management

FAST FORWARD

Cash management procedures should include procedures for banking receipts (cheques and cash) promptly, encouraging regular business customers to pay by BACS, and possibly arranging for regular payments from customers to be made by direct debit or standing order.

A business should have procedures for ensuring that receipts of cash or cheques are banked as soon as possible. Banking cash receipts on the day of receipt might seem a matter of common sense, but it is not uncommon for an overworked employee to put cheques received in the post into a desk drawer and forget about them.

4.1 Float

The term **float** is sometimes used to describe the amount of money tied up between the time when a payment is initiated (for example, when a debtor sends a cheque in payment, probably by post), and the time when the funds become available for use in the recipient's bank account.

There are three reasons why there might be a lengthy float.

(a) **Transmission delay**. When payment is sent through the post, it will take a day or longer for the payment to reach the payee.

(b) **Delay in banking the payments received (lodgement delay).** The payee, on receipt of a cheque or cash, might delay presenting the cheque or the cash to his bank. The length of this delay will depend on administrative procedures in the payee's organisation.

(c) **The time needed for a bank to clear a cheque (clearance delay).** A payment is not available for use in the payee's bank account until the cheque has been cleared. This will usually take two or three days for cheques payable in the UK. For cheques payable abroad, the delay may be longer. However, the UK now has a longer clearing cycle than any other G10 nation and the UK banks are under pressure from the Office of Fair Trading to speed up the clearing cycle. A Payment Systems Task Force has been set up and legislation is likely if there are no significant improvements by 2008.

There are several measures that a business could take to reduce the float.

(a) The payee should ensure that the lodgement delay is kept to a minimum. **Cheques** received should be presented to the bank on the day of receipt.

(b) The payee might, in some cases, arrange to **collect cheques** from the payer's premises. This would only be practicable, however, if the payer is local. The payment would have to be large to make the extra effort worthwhile.

(c) The payer might be asked to pay through his own branch of a bank, using the **bank giro system.**

(d) **BACS** (Bankers' Automated Clearing Services) is a banking system which provides for the computerised transfer of funds between banks. In addition, BACS is available to corporate customers of banks for making payments. The customer must supply payment details to BACS in electronic form, and payment will be made in two days. BACS is now commonly used by companies for salary payments and payments to regular suppliers.

(e) For regular payments, **standing orders** or **direct debits** might be used.

(f) **CHAPS** (Clearing House Automated Payments System) is a computerised system for banks to make same-day clearances (that is, immediate payment) between each other. Each member bank of CHAPS can allow its own corporate customers to make immediate (ie same-day) transfers of funds through CHAPS.

What are the potential benefits to cash flow management from Internet banking?

(For the answer to this question, see the Answer section at the end of this book.)

4.2 Other aspects of inefficient cash management

A lengthy float suggests inefficient cash management. But there are other types of delay in receiving payment from debtors, which might also suggest inefficient cash management.

(a)   There is the delay created by the length of credit given to customers. There is often a 'normal' credit period for an industry, and companies might be unable to grant less time for payment than this. However, a sign of inefficient cash management and an inadequate credit policy might be allowing longer credit to customers than is usual in the industry.

(b)   There are avoidable delays caused by poor administration (in addition to lodgement delay), such as:

(i)   Failure to notify the invoicing department that goods have been despatched, so that invoices are not sent promptly

(ii)   Cheques from debtors being made out incorrectly, to the wrong company perhaps, because invoices do not contain clear instructions.

5 Managing a bank overdraft

FAST FORWARD

An **overdraft** should be closely monitored and controlled, to minimise the interest cost and ensure that the borrowing limit is not exceeded.

Many businesses arrange an overdraft facility with their bank, which allows them to make payments to creditors when they do not have cash of their own for the payment. The interest rate on a bank overdraft is usually quite high, and an overdraft should be managed carefully, to keep the cost under control.

The measures that should be taken to manage an overdraft are as follows.

(a)   The overdraft should be negotiated with the bank in advance of the need to be overdrawn. The bank might ask to see a cash flow budget before agreeing to provide the facility.

(b)   Having agreed an overdraft limit, the limit should not be breached. Any required increase in the overdraft limit should be negotiated in advance with the bank.

(c)   Payments received should be banked immediately, to minimise the size of the overdraft.

(d)   Payments to creditors should be made at the required time, but should not be made earlier than necessary (unless an early settlement discount is available).

(e)   An overdraft facility is intended to be a temporary borrowing facility. A business should not be permanently in overdraft. A permanent overdraft indicates that some of the overdraft finance should be converted into longer-term borrowing.

Overdraft interest is charged by the day on the amount of the current overdrawn balance. If the overdraft interest rate is x% per annum, the daily rate of interest is therefore (x/365) %, including weekends and bank holidays.

Suppose for example that a business has an overdrawn balance on its account of $30,000 on Monday, and it pays interest on the overdraft at 10%. If there are no receipts or payments into the account during the week, the overdraft interest payable for the week would be approximately $(7/365) \times 10\% \times \$30,000 = \$57.53$.

5.1 Example: cash management and an overdraft

Ryan Coates owns a chain of seven clothes shops in the London area. Takings at each shop are remitted once a week on Thursday evening to the head office, and are then banked at the start of business on Friday morning. As business is expanding, Ryan Coates has hired an accountant to help him. The accountant gave him the following advice.

'Revenue at the seven shops totalled $1,950,000 last year, at a constant daily rate, but you were paying bank overdraft charges at a rate of 11%. You could have reduced your overdraft costs by banking the shop takings each day, except for Saturday's takings. Saturday takings could have been banked on Mondays.'

Comment on the significance of this statement, stating your assumptions. The shops are closed on Sundays.

Solution

(a)   A bank overdraft rate of 11% a year is approximately $11/365 = 0.03\%$ a day.

(b)   Annual takings of $1,950,000 would be an average of $\$1,950,000/312 = \$6,250$ a day for the seven shops in total, on the assumption that they opened for a 52 week year of six days a week (312 days).

(c)   Using the approximate overdraft cost of 0.03% a day, the cost of holding $6,250 for one day instead of banking it is $0.03\% \times \$6,250 = \$1.875$.

(d)   Banking all takings up to Thursday evening of each week on Friday morning involves an unnecessary delay in paying cash into the bank. The cost of this delay would be **either** the opportunity cost of investment capital for the business **or** the cost of avoidable bank overdraft charges.

It is assumed here that the overdraft cost is higher and is therefore more appropriate to use. It is also assumed that, for interest purposes, funds are credited when banked.

Takings on	Could be banked on	Number of days delay incurred by Friday banking
Monday	Tuesday	3
Tuesday	Wednesday	2
Wednesday	Thursday	1
Thursday	Friday	0
Friday	Saturday	6
Saturday	Monday	4
		16

In one week, the total number of days delay incurred by Friday banking is 16. At a cost of $1.875 a day, the weekly cost of Friday banking was $\$1.875 \times 16 = \$30.00$, and the annual cost of Friday banking was $\$30.00 \times 52 = \$1,560$.

(e)   *Conclusion.* The company could have saved about $1,560 in bank overdraft charges last year. If the overdraft rate remains at 11% and revenue continues to increase, the saving from daily banking would be even higher next year.

6 Investing surplus cash

A **temporary cash surplus** should be invested to earn income. When cash is invested, the choice of investment will depend on how quickly the cash might be needed, and the risks of a fall in the capital value of the investment (eg investments in shares of other companies).

Companies and other organisations sometimes have a surplus of cash and become 'cash rich'. The cash surplus might only be temporary, but while it exists the company should seek to obtain a good return by investing or depositing the cash, without the risk of a capital loss (or at least, without the risk of an excessive capital loss).

Three possible reasons for a cash surplus are:

- (a) Profitability from trading operations
- (b) Low capital expenditure, perhaps because of an absence of profitable new investment opportunities
- (c) Receipts from selling parts of the business

A company might keep surplus cash in liquid form to **benefit from high interest rates** that might be available from bank deposits, when returns on re-investment in the company appear to be lower. Another reason for holding on to cash is to have cash available should a **strategic opportunity** arise, perhaps for the takeover of another company for which a cash consideration might be needed.

If a company has no plans to grow or to invest, then surplus cash not required for transactions or precautionary purposes should normally be returned to shareholders. Many businesses will be able to cover their precautionary cash needs by means of their overdraft facility, and so a small cash surplus for transaction purposes may be all that is needed.

Surplus cash may be returned to shareholders by:

- (a) Increasing the usual level of the annual **dividends** which are paid
- (b) Making a one-off **special dividend payment**
- (c) Using the money to **buy back its own shares** from some of its shareholders. This will reduce the total number of shares in issue, and should therefore raise the level of **earnings per share**, assuming that the company can earn more on its ordinary activities than it would from investing its cash. Repurchase of a company's own shares is sometimes called a **share buy-back**.

7 The management of payables

A business should negotiate credit terms with its suppliers. **Trade credit** reduces the required investment in working capital, and it is 'free'. However, credit terms should be observed, so that a good trading relationship with suppliers can be maintained.

Businesses give credit to their customers in order to win sales. Businesses that purchase goods or services from other businesses expect to be given credit, because it is a 'fact of life' in business.

7.1 The advantages of trade credit

The advantages to a business of receiving trade credit are that:

- (a) It reduces the required investment in working capital
- (b) It is a short-term source of finance, but has **no cost**

Suppose for example that a company has average inventories of $50,000 and average receivables of $90,000. If it took no credit, it would need to finance its inventories and receivables with $140,000 of long-term credit. If it takes credit, however, and has average trade payables of, say, $40,000, the required investment in working capital would be lower, at $100,000 (average).

Unlike credit to individual holders of credit cards, where interest is charged on unpaid balances, businesses do not usually pay interest on outstanding trade debts. Trade credit is 'free', and businesses therefore save money by taking the trade credit available to them.

7.2 Risks of taking credit

There are risks in taking credit.

(a) The money owed to creditors might become so large that a business is unable to pay all its debts on time, as they fall due. Suppliers might withdraw credit facilities. In extreme cases, a business might be forced into liquidation by its unpaid creditors.

(b) High levels of trade credit might increase the perceived credit risk of a business, so that banks might be more reluctant to lend, or might raise the interest rate at which it is prepared to lend to the business.

(c) A supplier might be unwilling to give credit to a small business unless it has some form of **guarantee**. If the business is a subsidiary company in a group, a supplier might be prepared to accept a guarantee of payment from the parent company of the group. If the business is a small owner-managed company, a supplier might insist on a **personal guarantee** from the owner/director. Individuals are reluctant to give a personal guarantee for business credit, and will avoid having to do so if they possibly can.

7.3 Factors in the management of trade payables

The management of trade payables involves:

(a) Attempting to obtain satisfactory credit from suppliers
(b) Attempting to extend credit during periods of cash shortage
(c) Maintaining good relations with regular and important suppliers

7.4 Interest on late payments

Under legislation in some countries businesses can claim statutory interest if their invoices are not paid on time. A payment is 'late' when it is received after the end of the contractually agreed credit period; or after the credit period in accordance with trade custom and practice or in the course of dealing between the parties. If this date or period cannot be established a payment is late if it is made after 30 days from delivery of the invoice for payment or of the goods and service, whichever is the later.

A reference rate is used to determine the late payment interest rate, which is fixed for each six-month period. The late payment interest rate that applies in the UK is the reference rate (currently 4%) plus eight per cent (i.e. currently 12%). This is applied on a daily basis to the full (sales tax-inclusive) amount of the outstanding invoice.

In theory this means that delaying payment to creditors is no longer a 'free' source of finance. In practice it seems that very few businesses have taken advantage of the legislation so far, probably because they fear that it will damage relationships with customers.

8 Taking early settlement discounts

When an **early settlement discount** is available from a supplier, a business should consider the financial benefits of taking the discount and paying early.

If a supplier offers a discount for the early payment of debts, the evaluation of the decision whether or not to accept the discount is similar to the evaluation of the decision whether or not to *offer* a discount. One problem is the mirror image of the other.

When a discount is offered for early payment, we can calculate the **cost** to a business **of not taking the discount**.

The cost of lost cash discounts can be estimated by the formula:

$$\frac{d}{100-d} \times \frac{365}{t}$$

where d   is the size of the discount. For a 5% discount, d = 5.

   t   is the reduction in the payment period in days which would be necessary to obtain the early payment discount

8.1 Example: trade credit and settlement discount

X has been offered credit terms from its major supplier of 2/10, net 45. This means that a cash discount of 2% will be given if payment is made within ten days of the invoice date, and payments must be made anyway within 45 days of the invoice date.

The company has the choice of paying 98c per $1 on day 10 (to pay before day 10 would be unnecessary), or to invest the 98c for an additional 35 days and eventually pay the supplier $1 per $1. The decision as to whether the discount should be accepted depends on the opportunity cost of investing 98c for 35 days. What should the company do?

Solution

If the company refuses the cash discount, and pays in full after 45 days, the implied cost in interest per annum would be approximately:

$$\frac{2}{100-2} \times \frac{365}{35} = 21.3\%$$

Suppose that X can invest cash to obtain an annual return of 25%, and that there is an invoice from the supplier for $1,000. The two alternatives are as follows.

	Refuse discount $	Accept discount $
Payment to supplier	1,000.0	980.0
Return from investing $980 between day 10 and day 45:		
$980 \times \dfrac{35}{365} \times 25\%$	23.5	
Net cost	976.5	980.0

It is cheaper in this case to refuse the discount because the investment rate of return on cash retained, in this example, exceeds the saving from the discount.

Note that the above method of estimating the cost of lost cash discounts is not quite accurate, as it ignores the compound nature of interest. A more exact formula would be given by:

$$(1 + \frac{d}{100 - d})^{365/t} - 1$$

However, this rarely makes a lot of difference to the answer. Returning to the example above, the more accurate answer would have been:

$$(1 + \frac{2}{100 - 2})^{365/35} - 1 = 0.235, \text{ i.e. } 23.5\%$$

In the exam, use this formula if you can remember it; otherwise the approximation given above will be acceptable.

Although a company may delay payment beyond the final due date, thereby obtaining even longer credit from its suppliers, such a policy would be inadvisable (except where an unexpected short-term cash shortage has arisen). Unacceptable delays in payment will worsen the company's credit rating, and additional credit may become difficult to obtain. As mentioned above, suppliers may also choose to claim statutory interest.

9 Working capital problems of small businesses

FAST FORWARD

Small businesses often have serious difficulties managing working capital, and consequently face severe cash flow problems. The main causes of the problems are weak negotiating power with suppliers, customers and banks, a lack of financial expertise and a lack of adequate information systems for monitoring and control of cash, inventories and receivables.

For small businesses, cash flow is often a major concern, and the need to control working capital is particularly important. The problems of small businesses are attributable largely to:

(a) Their small size, and weak negotiating position with banks, large customers and important suppliers

(b) A lack of financial skills

(c) Inadequate financial information systems

Small businesses lack **negotiating power**.

(a) A supplier might be unwilling to give as much trade credit to a small business as the business would like, because the business is not considered sufficiently creditworthy. Without trade credit, a small business has to find cash to pay its suppliers sooner. Occasionally, suppliers might even insist on cash with order. The small business cannot threaten to withdraw its custom unless the supplier gives more credit, because it is not a sufficiently important customer. If it switches to another supplier, the supplier's financial loss will not be large, and other suppliers are equally unlikely to offer better credit terms.

(b) Small businesses can have great difficulty in obtaining prompt payment from customers, particularly important customers and large organisations. The small business has to offer generous credit terms to its customers, who might otherwise go to a different supplier. In practice, many customers of small businesses then take longer credit than allowed by their terms of sale.

(c) Small businesses often rely on a bank overdraft facility. A bank, however, might not offer an overdraft facility sufficiently large to meet the requirements of the business. An overdraft facility might also be uncommitted, which means that the bank is able to withdraw it without notice. For a bank, the income from providing an overdraft facility to a small business (fees plus interest) does not justify a large amount of effort investigating the business, assessing its creditworthiness and then monitoring its overdraft closely.

(d) A small business might wish to arrange a bank loan. If so, a bank might insist on a personal guarantee from the business owner. The requirement to give a personal guarantee can act as a deterrent to borrowing.

Small businesses, by their nature, do not employ large numbers of employees. They usually lack individuals with the financial expertise to manage working capital efficiently.

(a) The management of receivables calls for the application of credit policies, and applying procedures for debt collection, which many small businesses do not have.

(b) Inventory management calls for an understanding of inventory holding costs, and the need to keep inventory levels under control.

(c) The link between working capital management and cash flow is not always properly understood.

(d) Management of small businesses are often unaware of the importance of banking receipts promptly.

Efficient management of working capital calls for information about the cash position of the business, outstanding receivables and late payers, inventory levels and revenue. Many small businesses do not have information systems in place that give their management sufficient information, either because the information is too costly to provide, or because management lacks the financial expertise to understand what information they actually need.

Chapter roundup

- **Cash flow management** calls for the efficient management of inventories, receivables and trade payables. Cash management is concerned with using cash received, and having access to another source of finance (eg an overdraft facility), in the event that cash flows from operations are insufficient to meet payment obligations.

- Cash is needed to pay creditors. Any surplus cash can then be used to purchase business assets, invest in financial assets or make payments to the business owners (shareholders).

- Cash flow problems can arise for loss-making businesses, businesses that are growing and investing more in working capital and non-current assets, businesses with a seasonal trading pattern and businesses facing large one-off expenditures.

- Cash management procedures should include procedures for banking receipts (cheques and cash) promptly, encouraging regular business customers to pay by BACS, and possibly arranging for regular payments from customers to be made by direct debit or standing order.

- An **overdraft** should be closely monitored and controlled, to minimise the interest cost and ensure that the borrowing limit is not exceeded.

- A **temporary cash surplus** should be invested to earn income. When cash is invested, the choice of investment will depend on how quickly the cash might be needed, and the risks of a fall in the capital value of the investment (eg investments in shares of other companies).

- A business should negotiate credit terms with its suppliers. **Trade credit** reduces the required investment in working capital, and it is 'free'. However, credit terms should be observed, so that a good trading relationship with suppliers can be maintained.

- When an **early settlement discount** is available from a supplier, a business should consider the financial benefits of taking the discount and paying early.

- **Small businesses** often have serious difficulties managing working capital, and consequently face severe cash flow problems. The main causes of the problems are weak negotiating power with suppliers, customers and banks, a lack of financial expertise and a lack of adequate information systems for monitoring and control of cash, inventories and receivables.

Quick quiz

1   How do cash flow problems arise?

2   What is BACS?

3   A business estimates that in the first three months of the year (90 days) its average overdraft requirement will be $40,000. It is charged 12% per annum on its overdraft balance. What is the expected cost of overdraft interest for the three-month period?

4   What might be the consequences for its working capital management of the weak 'market power' of a small business?

Answers to quick quiz

1   (a) Inadequate control of inventories, receivables and payables (b) inadequate cash management (c) making losses (d) seasonal trading patterns and the build-up to a busy trading season (e) growing the business and investing more in working capital and non-current assets (f) large one-off expenditure items.

2   Bankers' Automated Clearing Services. A banking system that allows users to make payments 'electronically'. Many businesses use BACS to make payments to employees and regular suppliers. Avoids the need to produce cheques, and speeds up the payments process.

3    $(90/365) \times 12\% \times \$40,000 = \$1,184$.

4   Suppliers unwilling to grant sufficient credit. Customers taking longer to pay than agreed. Banks unwilling to grant a sufficient overdraft facility, or to lend without a personal guarantee from the business owner.

Part F

Business combinations

15

Business combinations

Introduction

A business combination is the bringing together of separate entities or businesses into one reporting entity. Examples are where two businesses of similar size decide to merge their operations into a single new company, or where one business acquires another business.

This chapter considers how such mergers or acquisitions are carried out and regulated.

1 Definitions of merger and acquisition

Business combinations take place for various reasons. Strategic reasons might be to gain market strength, to grow a **business** more quickly than would be possible by internal growth alone, to diversify into other business areas, and possibly for defensive reasons.

A **business combination** is the bringing together of separate entities or businesses into one reporting entity. Traditionally, two sorts of combination have been recognised, a merger and a takeover (or acquisition).

A merger and an acquisition are both arrangements in which two businesses come together to form an entity with a single management.

Key term

> In a **merger**, two companies of roughly equal size join together. All the shareholders of each company become shareholders in the new entity. Typically, the merged entity is established as a new company.

Suppose for example that Rotherham Bank and the Bank of Wales agree to merge. A new company, RBOW, might be established. RBOW will issue shares to the shareholders of Rotherham Bank and Bank of Wales, in exchange for their shares in their respective companies. The former shareholders in Rotherham Bank and Bank of Wales will therefore become the shareholders of RBOW.

There will be a single management for RBOW, probably appointed from the management teams of both Rotherham Bank and Bank of Wales.

A merger usually begins with talks between the management of the two companies. If they agree on merger terms, these are then put to their respective shareholders, who then vote whether to approve the arrangement.

Key term

> In a **takeover** or **acquisition**, one company acquires ownership of another.

For example, ABC might make a bid to acquire XYZ. The bid takes the form of an offer to buy all the shares in the target company, for a stated price or consideration. The bid is made initially to the directors of the target company (XYZ), who must then pass on the details to their shareholders.

A takeover is successful if the bidding company acquires a controlling interest (more than 50% of the ordinary shares) in the target company. After a successful takeover, it is usual for the acquired company to retain its independent identity, but it will now be a subsidiary company. The successful bidding company is the parent company or holding company. Its assets will include: 'Investment in acquired company, at cost'.

It is usual for **purchased goodwill** to arise when a takeover takes place.

Key term

> **Purchased goodwill** is the difference between the price paid to acquire the shares in the target company, and the fair value of the underlying assets acquired.

For example, if ABC acquires 100% of the shares of XYZ for an agreed price of $5 million, and the fair value of the assets of XYZ is just $2 million, there will be purchased goodwill of $3 million. Purchased goodwill is reported as a non-current asset in the consolidated balance sheet of the group. The $3 million of purchased goodwill would therefore be reported in the consolidated balance sheet of the ABC group, and it will be subject to an annual impairment review. Any impairment loss that is recognised will therefore become an annual charge against the profits of the group.

Not all shareholders in the target company might agree to sell their shares, and after a takeover, there could still be a **minority interest** in the subsidiary. A minority interest is simply an interest in shares of a subsidiary company that is owned by shareholders other than the parent company of the group.

The distinction between mergers and takeovers is not always clear, for example when a large company 'merges' with another smaller company. The methods used for mergers can be the same as the methods used to make takeovers. In practice, the number of genuine mergers is small relative to the number of takeovers.

2 Reasons for a merger or an acquisition

The reasons for a merger or takeover should be strategic. When a merger or takeover is announced by a public company, it will explain the strategic reasons and expected benefits to the investing public.

The strategic purpose might be to achieve a target position in the market.

(a) **Growth**. A company may achieve growth through merger or acquisition more cheaply or more quickly than through internal expansion.

(b) **Diversification**. The long-term interest of shareholders might be best served by spreading risk through diversification into different business areas. This can normally be achieved more easily through merger or acquisition of an established business, rather than by setting up a completely new business.

(c) **Expansion into other parts of the value chain**. The value chain is made up of all the stages in delivering a finished product or service to the end consumer. It starts with the production of raw materials and components, goes through one or more manufacturing stages, then through distribution and retailing to the end consumer. A manufacturing company might seek to expand by acquiring the business of a supplier or the business of a distributor of its products.

(d) **Defensive merger**. Companies may merge in order to prevent competitors from obtaining an advantage in some way.

Though a merger or acquisition must satisfy some strategic business objectives, the company will expect to realise some further benefits such as

- operating synergies
- financial synergies
- Other

> **FAST FORWARD**
>
> Mergers and acquisitions should also have a financial objective, and should be expected to increase the wealth of shareholders. This can be monitored through changes in the share price.

Key term

> **Synergy** is often described as the 2 + 2 = 5 effect, whereby the sum of the combined entity is greater than the sum of its individual parts.

If company A, which makes annual profits of $200,000 merges with company B, which also makes annual profits of $200,000, the combined annual profits of the merged companies should be more than $400,000.

There are two main types of synergy:

(a) Operating synergy, and
(b) Financial synergy.

> **FAST FORWARD**
>
> Mergers and acquisitions often result in **operating synergy**, ie in higher profits from cost savings (economies of scale), or in higher sales and profit margins due to greater market strength.

Operating synergy arises from the benefits of either economies of scale in the larger entity, or the benefits of greater market power (eg higher sales volumes and profit margins). Economies of scale result in lower operating costs and higher profits. The effect of operating synergy is that the combined operating profits of the business after the merger or acquisition should be higher than the sum of the profits of the individual companies before the merger or acquisition.

The most common form of operating synergy is savings in labour costs. A merger or acquisition often results in job losses, because fewer people are needed to do the work in a combined enterprise than were needed before in the two separate companies. However, other duplicated resources might be eliminated (eg investment in equipment might be reduced). The enlarged enterprise might also be able to use its enhanced market power to negotiate better prices from its suppliers.

Financial synergies arise from benefits to the enlarged enterprise from:

(a) Better use of idle cash. A company with surplus cash earning low interest might earn a better financial return by investing the money in the acquisition of another business.

(b) A higher borrowing capacity, so that the business is able to raise more debt capital. The ability to borrow more improves access to sources of new capital and should also enable a company to reduce its weighted average cost of capital.

(c) Potential tax benefits, for example if the acquiring company is able to utilise accumulated losses in an acquired company, to reduce the total tax liabilities of the group.

Other benefits arising from a merger or takeover might be as follows.

(a) **Management acquisition**. If a company lacks a management team of sufficient quality to ensure continued growth, it may be best to seek an amalgamation with another company with aggressive and competent management.

(b) **Asset backing**. A company in a risky industry with a high level of earnings relative to the net assets may try to reduce its overall risk by acquiring a company with substantial assets.

(c) **The quality of earnings**. A company may reduce its perceived business risk by acquiring another company with less risky earnings. For example a company in an industry where profits tend to fluctuate sharply with changes in market conditions might take over another company in an industry with more stable and predictable profits.

The aim of a merger or acquisition should be to improve profits in the long term as well as in the short term.

(a) Acquisitions may provide a **means of entering a market** at a lower cost than would be incurred if the company tried to develop its own resources, or a **means of acquiring the business of a competitor**. Acquisitions or mergers in the UK which might reduce or eliminate competition in a market may be prohibited by the Competition Commission. Acquisitions or mergers affecting wider European markets might be subject to approval by the competition authorities of the EU.

(b) Mergers, especially in Britain, have tended to be more common in industries with a history of little growth and low returns. Highly profitable companies tend to seek acquisitions rather than mergers.

2.1 Factors to consider when investigating a takeover target

What a business is looking for when considering a takeover is to benefit from satisfying the strategic objectives of the takeover and realising the operating and financial synergies along with gaining any other benefits. It must, however, be careful to guard against the prospect of any adverse factors that may arise. Therefore, when considering any takeover it will be important to examine the potential positives and negatives. Important factors to consider in this respect would therefore be:

- **The business/markets/customers**

  - The operations of the target need to be a good strategic fit with those of the acquirer and offer the potential synergistic benefits.

  - The target business market should ideally be growing, and the trends and conditions of the market should be carefully considered.

  - The customer base should ideally be large rather than trade being concentrated on a few key clients.

  - Where only a few key clients do exist, the target is exposed to a significant, possibly unacceptable, business risk. In this situation, care needs to be taken with respect to any significant exposure the target may have to any customer and to any significant contracts the target has with customers to ensure they do not impose onerous conditions.

  - What is the businesses relationship with its customers, are they satisfied repeat customers.

  - What is the businesses relationship with its suppliers, are they reliable or have there been any disputes.

- **The business assets**

  - Consideration needs to be given to the age, quality and suitability of any assets in use along with whether they are owned or leased.

  - In respect of leased assets, the lease terms need to be considered to ensure any commitments are not overly onerous.

- **The technology/products/services**

  - Does the target have proper rights to any technology it uses, and to any products and services it provides, or is it dependent on joint ventures, franchise or licence arrangements in which case the terms need to be investigated.

- **The intellectual property**

  - Does the target have true ownership of any key patents, trade marks and intellectual property, or is it dependent on third party intellectual property and on licensing deals in which case the terms need to be investigated.

- **The people**

  - Is the target business dependent on a few key individuals, and if it is then how can their services be assured at least for the short term.

  - How good is the targets industrial relations, what is its relationship with its employees and how are they liable to react to a takeover.

- **The competition**

  - Who are the major competitors to the target and what is their position in the market.
  - Is market share expending or is it coming under pressure.

When initially considering a takeover target, these issues will be considered but many of them will be unanswerable. Eventually, as takeover negotiations get underway, the checking of these items becomes part of what is known as the **due diligence** process in which the acquirer will seek to confirm these points, so far as it is practicable.

2.2 Advantages and problems with mergers

When two companies merge, they are often in the same line of business, and the purpose of the merger is to create a larger combined company to compete in the market place. Occasionally, however, two completely different companies might merge. Indeed, a company might undertake one or more major acquisitions so that it can diversify into other markets and industries.

Companies should consider very closely the strategic reasons for the merger, to assess whether there are benefits to be obtained. There are differing views as to whether a strategy of diversification through mergers or acquisitions can be successful.

One argument is that by diversifying, a **company reduces its overall business risk**. If one of its operations performs badly, other operations in different industries might perform well. In contrast, a company that operates in just one industry is vulnerable to the economic cycle and conditions in that particular industry. In 2001, for example, there was a slump in the telecommunications industry, and all companies in the industry suffered a sharp fall in share price. Some fell into severe financial difficulties. An argument in favour of diversification is that if a company operates in more than one industry, it will be better able to survive a downturn in one of those industries.

A second argument in favour of diversification is that **top-quality management** is able to **run any type of business better than run-of-the-mill management**. If a company believes it has able managers, it could identify poorly-run companies, buy them, and turn them round. When an acquisition has been turned round, it can be sold off at a huge profit. Companies that specialise in this type of strategy are likely to own diversified businesses.

An argument **against** diversification is that it is **unlikely to add shareholder value**. By bringing together two or more companies in different industries, the benefits from cost savings or additional sales are negligible. Since future profits are unlikely to be affected by such a merger, investor expectations of future returns will not change. Since share prices reflect expectations of future returns, the overall value of a merged company will be unchanged. However, although the total value of the merged businesses might be unaffected, one set of shareholders might make a capital gain from the merger and the other set of shareholders might make a loss.

2.3 Example

For example, suppose that AB and CD are planning a merger. The companies operate in different markets, and no synergies are expected. AB currently makes annual profits of $20 million, and its shares have a market value of $250 million. CD currently makes annual profits of $15 million, and its shares have a market value of $190 million. The planned merger will be effected by creating a new holding company, ABCD, and half the shares in the new company will be given to shareholders in AB (in exchange for their AB shares). The other half will go to the shareholders in CD, in exchange for their shares. As a result of the merger, the former shareholders in each of the individual companies will own 50% of the shares in the new holding company.

If there is no synergy from the merger, there is no reason to suppose that the merger will create additional shareholder value. The value of ABCD shares should therefore be $440 million ($250 million + $190 million). However, the former shareholders in CD will have exchanged their shares worth $190 million for new shares worth $220 million, making a gain of $30 million. The former shareholders in AB, however, will suffer a corresponding $30 million fall in the value of their investment, from $250 million to $220 million. In these circumstances, the shareholders of AB would be well-advised to vote against the merger.

There are other potential disadvantages of mergers.

    (a)   The two merging companies will have different cultures and ways of doing things. If they merge their business operations, there will be a **culture clash**. Quite possibly, employees who are unable to adjust to the culture of the merged entity will leave to pursue their careers somewhere else.

For example, some opponents of the merger between computer hardware companies Hewlett-Packard and Compaq (2002) cited the difficulty there would be in combining the informal management style of Hewlett-Packard with the more formal management style of Compaq.

(b)   When the purpose of a merger is to increase market share by bringing together two competing companies, the deal might be investigated by the competition authorities. Mergers that are considered anti-competitive will be either prohibited, or allowed only subject to certain conditions (e.g. that certain parts of the merged business are sold off to a third party buyer).

A further argument against mergers that are made by a company as a way of diversifying their business operations is that there is no benefit for shareholders. Investors can achieve their own diversification by building up a portfolio of shares in different companies. Investors would probably argue that they can make better decisions about diversifying their investments than a company's management would on their behalf. Companies should therefore focus on industries in which they have particular competence.

2.4 Example

For example, suppose that a company manufacturing motor cars decides to diversify into boat building. A shareholder formerly owning shares in a car producer would now hold shares in a car producer and boat builder. If he had wanted to diversify his investment into boat-building, he could have bought shares in a specialist boat building company. If he wants to invest in a car manufacturing company but not in boat building, the diversification decision by the car manufacturer would affect him adversely. To avoid an exposure to investing in boat building, the investor would have to sell his shares in the car manufacturer and buy shares in another car producer that has not diversified.

3 The bid consideration

FAST FORWARD

In an acquisition, the **purchase consideration** might be shares in the bidding company, cash or loan capital. A cash purchase must be financed, and the cash will be obtained by issuing new shares, raising debt finance, or using existing surplus cash resources.

Key term

The **bid consideration** or **purchase consideration** is the amount that shareholders in a company are offered in exchange for their existing shares.

In a merger, the consideration is the number of shares in the new merged entity that shareholders are offered for their existing shares. For example, suppose that P agrees a merger with Q, to form a new company PQ. Shareholders in P might be offered, say, 2 shares in PQ for every share they hold in P. Shareholders in Q might be offered a different amount of consideration, say 3 new shares in PQ for every two shares they hold in Q.

In a takeover, the shareholders in the target company are invited to sell their shares. The bid is unlikely to succeed unless the target company shareholders believe they are being offered a price that is too good to turn down. If the target company is a public company with shares traded on a stock market, the offer price should be in excess of the current market price; otherwise, there is no reason for the target company shareholders to accept the bid.

3.1 The form of bid consideration

In a takeover, the consideration can take any of the following forms (or a combination of any of the following forms):

  (a)   Cash
  (b)   Share exchange (share-for-share offer or **paper offer**)
  (c)   Loan notes or loan stock

3.2 Share exchange

In a **share exchange**, the shares in the target company are purchased with shares of the predator company. For example, suppose that Large wishes to acquire Small. Large might have 100 million shares in issue, each currently priced at $5. Small might have 5 million shares in issue, each currently priced at $2. Large might make an offer to acquire Small, by offering, say, one new share in Large for every 2 shares in Small.

If the bid is successful, and if all shareholders in Small accept the offer, Large will issue 2.5 million new shares to purchase the shares in Small from their holders. Shareholders in Small will receive one new share in Large, valued at $5 (assuming no change in the market price) in exchange for every two shares they hold in Small, currently valued at just $4.

After the takeover, Large will have a share capital of 102.5 million shares. The value of these shares will depend on how the market price has reacted to the takeover.

3.3 Cash purchase

If the purchase consideration is in **cash**, the shareholders of the target company will simply be bought out. For example, suppose that the following information applies to two companies.

	Big	Minnow
Net assets (book value)	$1,500,000	$200,000
Number of shares	100,000	10,000
Earnings	$2,000,000	$40,000

Big negotiates a takeover of Minnow for $400,000 in cash.

As a result, Big will end up with:

  (a)   Net assets (book value) of:

         $1,500,000 + $200,000 − $400,000 cash = $1,300,000

  (b)   100,000 shares (no change)

  (c)   Expected earnings of $2,040,000, minus the loss of interest (net of tax) which would have been obtained from the investment of the $400,000 in cash which was given up to acquire Minnow.

When a takeover is paid for in cash, the bidding company has to obtain the cash from somewhere in order to buy out the shareholders in the target company. A cash purchase might be financed:

  (a)   From existing surplus cash resources of the bidding company
  (b)   By issuing new shares in the stock market to raise cash
  (c)   By raising debt finance, either by issuing bonds or by obtaining bank finance

When a company finances a takeover by issuing shares in the stock market to raise cash, the bid is a cash bid. The target company shareholders receive cash in exchange for their shares, even though the consequence for the bidding company is an increase in its issued share capital.

Sometimes, a company might acquire another in a share exchange, but the shares are then sold immediately on a stock market to raise cash for the seller. For example, A might acquire B by issuing shares which it gives to B's shareholders; however A's stockbrokers arrange to 'place' these shares with other buyers, and so sell the newly issued shares for cash on behalf of the ex-shareholders of B. This sort of arrangement, which is a mixture of (a) and (b), is called a **vendor placing**.

3.4 Loan notes as consideration

An acquisition might be partly financed by issuing loan notes or loan stock to the shareholders in the target company. Loan notes are loan stock with a maturity of up to about five years, at the end of which they are redeemed by the issuing company, usually at their face value. Until maturity, the issuing company pays interest on the notes.

Issuing loan notes or loan stock to finance a takeover has several advantages:

(a) The bidding company does not have to find the cash to pay the target company shareholders until the loan notes mature. However, it must pay interest.

(b) The target company shareholders are not liable for capital gains tax on the disposal of their shares until the loan notes are redeemed. Until then, their only tax liability is for income tax on the interest received. Loan notes might therefore make up some of the purchase consideration where the target shareholders are individuals, for example when a small private company is taken over by a public company.

3.5 The choice between a cash offer and a paper offer

Many takeover bids are financed by a share exchange, by a cash offer, or by a combination of share exchange and cash consideration. With a share exchange offer, there may be a cash alternative.

The choice between **cash** and **paper offers** (or a combination of both) will depend on how the different methods are viewed by the company and its existing shareholders, and on the attitudes of the shareholders of the target company.

FAST FORWARD

The effect on **earnings per share** and the share price after a takeover will depend to some extent on the form of purchase consideration chosen.

The factors that the directors of the bidding company must consider include the following.

(a) **The company and its existing shareholders**

(i) **Dilution of earnings per share**. Unless there is synergy from the acquisition, there could be a fall in the earnings per share (EPS) of the bidding company. The risk of a fall or dilution in earnings is greater when the acquisition is paid for by issuing new shares, because there are now more shares in issue.

(ii) The **cost to the company**. The use of loan stock (or of cash borrowed elsewhere) will be cheaper to the acquiring company than equity, because the interest payments on debt will be allowable for tax purposes. A direct consequence of using debt finance to pay for a takeover is that dilution of earnings might be avoided, even when there are no synergies.

(iii) **Gearing**. A highly geared company may find that the issue of additional loan stock either as consideration or to raise cash for the consideration may be unacceptable to its existing debt providers or shareholders.

(iv) **Control**. In takeovers involving a relatively large issue of new ordinary shares, the effective control of the company can change considerably. This could be unpopular with the existing shareholders.

(v) An **increase in authorised share capital**. If the consideration is in the form of shares, it may be necessary to increase the company's authorised capital. This would involve calling a general meeting to pass the necessary resolution.

(vi) **Increases in borrowing limits**. A similar problem arises if a proposed issue of loan stock will require a change in the company's borrowing limit as specified in its Articles of Association.

(b) **The shareholders in the target company**

(i) **Taxation**. If the consideration is in cash, many investors may find that they face an immediate liability to tax on a realised capital gain, whereas the liability would be postponed if the consideration consisted of shares (or loan notes).

(ii) **Income**. Where the consideration is other than cash, it is normally necessary to ensure that existing income is at least maintained. A drop may, however, be accepted if it is compensated for by a suitable capital gain or by reasonable expectations of future growth.

(iii) **Future investments**. Shareholders in the target company might want to retain a stake in the business after the takeover, and so would prefer the offer of shares in the bidding company, rather than a cash offer.

(iv) **Share price**. If shareholders in the target company are to receive shares in the bidding company, they will want to consider whether the shares of the bidding company are likely to retain their value.

The main advantages and disadvantages of shares or cash as purchase consideration can be summarised briefly as follows.

	Advantages	Disadvantages
Share exchange	No cash is needed to pay for the acquisition. No finance has to be raised.	There might be a dilution in earnings per share, and the share price might fall.
	The gearing of the company will be lower. This could therefore increase the ability of the company to raise further debt capital in future.	Existing shareholders will own a smaller proportion of their company after the takeover.
	For shareholders in the target company, there is an opportunity to hold equity in the post-takeover group.	Existing shareholders have to share profits with new shareholders.
		For shareholders in the target company, there is uncertainty about the value of the shares they receive (post-takeover), and so uncertainty about the value of the offer.
Cash, financed by share issue	See the first two advantages above, for share exchange.	See the first three disadvantages above, for share exchange.

	Advantages	Disadvantages
Cash, financed by debt capital	Low cost of finance, therefore possible increase in earnings per share after the takeover, even without synergy No new shares are issued. Existing shareholders retain their proportionate stake in the company.	Higher gearing will increase the perceived financial risk. The cost of equity is likely to rise. Company must be sure of having sufficient cash flows to meet the interest payment obligations.
Cash, using surplus cash	Surplus cash is probably earning a low return. Investing in a takeover should improve returns and earnings per share. No new shares are issued. Existing shareholders retain their proportionate stake in the company.	The cash could be put to other uses, such as paying a dividend to shareholders.

4 Impact of a merger or takeover on financial performance

FAST FORWARD

The **financial position of a company** after a takeover will depend partly on how the takeover has been financed, and partly on the effects of **synergy** (ie increases in operating profits).

A merger or takeover will have an effect on the financial performance of the enlarged enterprise. The effect can be measured in terms of:

(a)   Profits
(b)   Earnings per share
(c)   Return on capital employed

The effect on profits, earnings per share and return on capital will depend to a large extent on whether the merger or takeover results in **synergy** and an increase in the combined profits of the enterprise.

Purchased goodwill arising on an acquisition must be subjected to an annual impairment review. Any impairment loss that is recognised must be charged against consolidated profits and will depress earnings and earnings per share. The annual impairment review of goodwill is a fairly recent feature of company financial reporting, and it is not yet clear what effect, if any, it might have on takeover activity and share prices after a takeover. In the analysis that follows in the rest of this chapter, the possible impairment of purchased goodwill is ignored.

4.1 Example

Dance acquires all the share capital of Stage for $4 million. The purchase is in cash, but is financed by new borrowing at an interest rate of 8%. The annual pre-tax profits of Stage are currently $250,000.

Dance has 50 million shares in issue, and its annual pre-tax profits are $8 million. The tax rate is 30%.

What will be the effect on profits and earnings per share if there is no synergy from the takeover?

Solution

The current EPS of Dance is:

	$
Profits before tax	8,000,000
Taxation (30%)	(2,400,000)
Earnings	5,600,000
Number of shares	50 million
Earnings per share	11.2 cents

After the takeover, the profits and earnings per share will be as follows

	$
Pre-acquisition profits of Dance	8,000,000
Pre-acquisition profits of Stage	250,000
Synergy: effect on profits	0
Total profits before interest	8,250,000
Interest (8% of $4,000,000)	320,000
	7,930,000
Taxation (30%)	(2,379,000)
Earnings	5,551,000
Number of shares	50 million
Earnings per share	11.1 cents

In this example, the takeover results in a dilution in earnings per share, because the profits from Stage are insufficient to cover the interest cost of the debt finance.

The situation would be different, however, if some synergy is obtained. For example, suppose that in the example above, the takeover is expected to result in an increase of $100,000 in the combined profits. Profits and EPS would then be as follows.

	$
Pre-acquisition profits of Dance	8,000,000
Pre-acquisition profits of Stage	250,000
Synergy: effect on profits	100,000
Total profits before interest	8,350,000
Interest (8% of $4,000,000)	320,000
	8,030,000
Taxation (30%)	(2,409,000)
Earnings	5,621,000
Number of shares	50 million
Earnings per share	11.24 cents

Although the acquired company is fairly small, there would still be some improvement in profits and earnings per share as a result of the takeover.

Question 15.1   Synergy

Heap has acquired all the share capital of Soft for $6 million. The offer was in cash, and Heap obtained the finance by borrowing at 9% per annum. The current annual pre-tax profits of Heap are $4 million, and the annual pre-tax profits of Soft are $450,000. What is the minimum amount of synergy that should be obtained from the takeover to avoid a dilution in earnings per share? The rate of tax is 30%.

(For the answer to this question, see the Answer section at the end of this book.)

5 The position of shareholders

The **financial position of shareholders** after a takeover will depend partly on expected earnings per share (eg whether these are higher or whether there is dilution in earnings) and partly on changes in the P/E ratio. **Market perception** of a takeover is very important.

The main financial objective of a company is normally to improve the wealth of its shareholders. Wealth is largely measured by the value of the shares.

(a) In a merger, the shareholders of the merged company will expect the value of their new shares to exceed the value of their former shareholding in the pre-merged company.

(b) In a takeover, the shareholders of the target company will expect to receive a fair price for their shares. If the shares are traded on a stock exchange and have a market value, the price they receive should be higher than their current market value.

(c) In a takeover, the shareholders in the bidding company will also expect to benefit from the takeover, in the form of a higher value from their shares. The actual value of their shares after the takeover will depend, however, on what happens to the share price. The share price will depend to a large extent on the market's expectations of profits and earnings per share in the enlarged group.

5.1 Example

Vowel is considering making a takeover bid for Comma. The current annual earnings of Vowel are $12 million and the annual earnings of Comma are $4 million. It is expected that the takeover will result in cost savings of $2 million. The tax rate is 30%.

Vowel has 100 million ordinary shares of $1 in issue, and Comma has 20 million shares.

The price/earnings ratio for Vowel shares is 20.0 and for Comma is 15.0.

The bid would take the form of a share offer, with Vowel offering three of its shares for every two shares in Comma.

Required

On the assumption that the P/E ratio of Vowel remains unchanged after the takeover, and that the share price changes to reflect the expected change in earnings:

(a) How many new shares would Vowel issue?
(b) What will be the share price after the takeover?
(c) By how much will a holder of 1,000 shares in Comma benefit from the takeover?
(d) By how much will a holder of 1,000 shares in Vowel benefit from the takeover?

Solution

(a) Vowel will issue 30 million new shares to purchase the 20 million shares in Comma. There will be 130 million Vowel shares in issue after the takeover.

(b) Earnings and earnings per share after the takeover will be as follows:

	$	$
Pre-acquisition earnings of Vowel		12,000,000
Pre-acquisition earnings of Comma		4,000,000
Synergy: savings	2,000,000	
Less tax	(600,000)	
Increase in earnings		1,400,000
Total earnings post acquisition		17,400,000

Number of shares	130 million
Earnings per share	13.4 cents
P/E ratio	20.0
Share price post acquisition	268c

(c)   The EPS of Comma is currently ($4 million/20 million shares) 20c. The current share price of Comma is EPS × P/E ratio = 20c × 15.0 = $3.

A holder of 1,000 shares in Comma will exchange the shares, currently worth $3,000, for 1,500 shares in Vowel, which are expected to be worth 268c each, ie $4,020 in total. The gain on the sale will be $1,020.

(d)   The EPS of Vowel is currently ($12 million/100 million shares) 12c. The current share price is 12c × 20.0 = 240c. The takeover should result in an increase in the share price from 240c to 268c, an increase of 28c per share. A holder of 1,000 shares in Vowel would expect to gain $280.

5.2 The market values of the companies' shares during a takeover bid

Market share prices can be very important during a takeover bid.

5.3 Example

Suppose that Velvet decides to make a takeover bid for the shares of Noggin. Noggin shares are currently quoted on the market at $2 each. Velvet shares are quoted at $4.50 and Velvet offers one of its shares for every two shares in Noggin, thus making an offer at current market values worth $2.25 per share in Noggin. This is only the value of the bid so long as Velvet's shares remain valued at $4.50. If their value falls, the bid will become less attractive.

This is why companies that make takeover bids with a share exchange offer are always concerned that the market value of their shares should not fall during the takeover negotiations, before the target company's shareholders have decided whether to accept the bid.

If the market price of the target company's shares rises above the offer price during the course of a takeover bid, the bid price will seem too low, and the takeover is then likely to fail, with shareholders in the target company refusing to sell their shares to the bidder.

5.4 EPS before and after a takeover

FAST FORWARD

When a takeover is financed by a share exchange, and there is no synergy, there will be a **dilution in earnings per share** if the target company is bought on a higher P/E ratio multiple than the P/E ratio of the purchasing company. There will be an increase in earnings per share if the target company is purchased on a lower P/E multiple.

If one company acquires another **by issuing shares**, its EPS will go up or down according to the P/E ratio at which the target company has been bought.

(a)   If the target company's shares are bought at a **higher P/E ratio** than the predator company's shares, there is likely to be a fall in the earnings per share after the acquisition, assuming no synergy.

(b)   If the target company's shares are valued at a **lower P/E ratio**, there will be a rise in the EPS, even without synergy.

5.5 Example: buying at a lower P/E ratio

Giant takes over Tiddler by offering two shares in Giant for one share in Tiddler. Details about each company are as follows.

	Giant	Tiddler
Number of shares	2,800,000	100,000
Market value per share	$4	-
Annual earnings	$560,000	$50,000
EPS	20c	50c
P/E ratio	20	

By offering two shares in Giant worth $4 each for one share in Tiddler, the valuation placed on each Tiddler share is $8, and with Tiddler's EPS of 50c, this implies that Tiddler would be acquired on a P/E ratio of 16. This is lower than the P/E ratio of Giant, which is 20.

If the acquisition produces no synergy, and there is no growth in the earnings of either Giant or its new subsidiary Tiddler, then the EPS of Giant would still be higher than before, because Tiddler was bought on a lower P/E ratio. The combined group's results would be as follows.

	Giant group
Number of shares (2,800,000 + 200,000)	3,000,000
Annual earnings (560,000 + 50,000)	$610,000
EPS	20.33c

If the P/E ratio is still 20, the market value per share would be $4.07, which is 7c more than the pre-takeover price.

5.6 Example: buying at a higher P/E ratio

Redwood agrees to acquire the shares of Green in a share exchange arrangement. The agreed P/E ratio for Green's shares is 15.

	Redwood	Green
Number of shares	3,000,000	100,000
Market price per share	$2	-
Earnings	$600,000	$120,000
P/E ratio	10	

The EPS of Green is $1.20, and so the agreed price per share will be $1.20 × 15 = $18. In a share exchange agreement, Redwood would have to issue nine new shares (valued at $2 each) to acquire each share in Green, and so a total of 900,000 new shares must be issued to complete the takeover.

After the takeover, the enlarged company would have 3,900,000 shares in issue and, assuming no earnings growth, total earnings of $720,000. This would give an EPS of:

$$\frac{\$720,000}{3,900,000} = 18.5c$$

The pre-takeover EPS of Redwood was 20c, and so the EPS would fall. This is because Green has been bought on a higher P/E ratio (15 compared with Redwood's 10).

5.7 Buying companies by share exchange on a higher P/E ratio, but with profit growth or synergy

Buying companies on a higher P/E ratio will result in a fall in EPS unless there is profit growth to offset this fall. Growth in profits might come from the effects of synergy (cost savings etc). For example, suppose that Starving acquires Bigmeal, by offering two shares in Starving for three shares in Bigmeal. Details of each company are as follows.

	Starving	Bigmeal
Number of shares	5,000,000	3,000,000
Value per share	$6	$4
Annual earnings		
Current	$2,000,000	$600,000
Next year	$2,200,000	$950,000
EPS	40c	20c
P/E ratio	15	20

Starving is acquiring Bigmeal on a higher P/E ratio, and it is only the profit growth in the acquired subsidiary that gives the enlarged Starving group its growth in EPS.

	Starving group
Number of shares (5,000,000 + 2,000,000)	7,000,000
Earnings	
If no profit growth (2,000,000 + 600,000) $2,600,000	EPS would have been 37.14c
With profit growth (2,200,000 + 950,000) $3,150,000	EPS will be 45c

If an acquisition strategy involves buying companies on a higher P/E ratio, it is therefore essential for continuing EPS growth that the acquired companies offer prospects of strong profit growth.

Question 15.2
Total earnings and EPS

ABC has 40 million shares in issue. The annual earnings per share is 50c, and the current share price is $10. XYZ has 20 million shares in issue, annual earnings of 20c per share, and a share price of $6.

ABC is considering whether to make a takeover bid for XYZ. The bid would be worth $150 million. Two forms of consideration are under review:

(a)   A share exchange, involving the exchange of 3 shares in ABC for every 4 shares in XYZ
(b)   A cash offer of $150 million, financed by debt at an interest rate of 7% per annum.

It is estimated that the takeover would result in annual savings of $6 million. The tax rate is 30%.

It is expected that the P/E ratio of ABC after the takeover will be the same as now, but that the share price will change to reflect the expected change in annual earnings.

Required

What will be the effect on total earnings and EPS if the takeover goes ahead, all the shares in XYZ are acquired, and the acquisition is financed by: (a) a share exchange and (b) debt capital to pay for a cash offer?

(For the answer to this question, see the Answer section at the end of this book.)

Exam focus point

> The impact of a takeover on the share price of the acquiring company undertaking a share-for-share swap was examined in June 2006 for 12 marks.

6 Areas to investigate when considering an acquisition

FAST FORWARD

> Other factors in deciding whether to make a takeover bid, and if so at what price, include (a) the **quality of earnings** of the target company, (b) the **quality of the assets** of the target company, (c) the existence of **key personnel** and whether these can be retained after the takeover, (d) the possible effect of the takeover on **dividend policy**.

6.1 Factors in a takeover decision

Several factors will influence a decision to try to take over a target business. These include the following.

6.1.1 Price factors

(a) What would the cost of acquisition be?

(b) Would the acquisition be worth the price?

(c) Alternatively, factors (a) and (b) above could be expressed in terms of the highest price that it would be worth paying to acquire the business.

The value of a business could be assessed in terms of its earnings, its assets, its prospects for sales and earnings growth, or how it would contribute to the short-term and long-term strategy of the 'predator' company.

Different methods for the **valuation** of companies are covered in the next chapter.

6.1.2 Other factors

(a) Would the takeover be regarded as desirable by the bidding company's shareholders and (in the case of quoted companies) the stock market in general?

(b) Are the owners of the target company amenable to a takeover bid? Or would they be likely to adopt defensive tactics to resist a bid?

(c) What form would the purchase consideration take? An acquisition is accomplished by buying the shares of a target company. The purchase consideration might be cash, but the purchasing company might issue new shares (or loan stock) and exchange them for shares in the company taken over. If purchase is by means of a share exchange, the former shareholders in the company taken over will acquire an interest in the new, enlarged company.

(d) How would the takeover be reflected in the **published accounts** of the purchasing company? How might the reported profits of the enlarged group be affected, bearing in mind that purchased goodwill might have to be written down for impairment?

(e) Would there be any other potential problems arising from the proposed takeover, such as future **dividend policy** or service contracts for **key personnel?**

(f) Is the proposed takeover likely to be investigated by the Competition Commission, on the grounds that it might be **harmful to competition** in the industry? If so, what might be the outcome of the investigation? The Competition Commission can recommend that a takeover should not be permitted, or that a takeover should only be permitted on certain conditions.

6.2 A strategic approach to takeovers

A strategic approach to takeovers would imply that acquisitions are only made after a full analysis of the underlying strengths of the purchasing company, and identification of the target company's **strategic fit** with its existing activities. Possible strategic reasons for a takeover are matched in the table below with suggested ways of achieving the aim.

Strategic opportunities	
Where you are	**How to get to where you want to be**
Growing steadily but in a mature market with limited growth prospects	Acquire a company in a younger market with a higher growth rate
Marketing an incomplete product range, or having the potential to sell other products or services to your existing customers	Acquire a company with a complementary product range
Operating at maximum productive capacity	Acquire a company making similar products operating substantially below capacity
Under-utilising management resources	Acquire a company into which your talents can extend
Needing more control of suppliers or customers	Acquire a company which is, or gives access to, a significant customer or supplier
Where you are	**How to get to where you want to be**
Lacking key clients in a targeted sector	Acquire a company with the right customer profile
Preparing for flotation but needing to improve your balance sheet	Acquire a suitable company which will enhance earnings per share
Needing to increase market share	Acquire an important competitor
Needing to widen your capability	Acquire a company with the key talents and/or technology

6.3 Net assets per share and the quality of earnings

It might be supposed that when making a takeover bid, the bidding company will try to avoid a dilution of earnings (ie a reduction in the earnings per share). However, there are situations where a dilution of earnings might be accepted if there were other advantages to be gained from the acquisition.

(a)   A company might be willing to accept earnings dilution if the quality of the earnings of the acquired company is superior to the quality of its own earnings. Earnings have a high 'quality' when they are reliable, where customers are all 'blue chip' organisations and where prospects for growth are good.

(b)   A trading company with high earnings but with few assets might want to increase its assets base by acquiring a company which is strong in assets but weak in earnings. In this case, dilution in earnings is compensated for by an increase in net asset backing.

6.4 Example

Intangible has an issued capital of 2,000,000 $1 ordinary shares. Net assets (excluding goodwill) are $2,500,000 and annual earnings average $1,500,000. The company is valued by the stock market on a P/E ratio of 8.

Tangible has an issued capital of 1,000,000 ordinary shares. Net assets (excluding goodwill) are $3,500,000 and annual earnings average $400,000.

The shareholders of Tangible accept an all-equity offer from Intangible valuing each share in Tangible at $4.

Required

Calculate Intangible's earnings and assets per share before and after the acquisition of Tangible.

Solution

(a)   Before the acquisition of Tangible, the position is as follows.

Earnings per share (EPS) $= \dfrac{\$1,500,000}{2,000,000} = 75c$

Assets per share (APS) $= \dfrac{\$2,500,000}{2,000,000} = \$1.25$

(b)   Tangible's EPS is 40c ($400,000 ÷ 1,000,000), and the company is being bought on a multiple of 10 at $4 per share. As the takeover consideration is being satisfied by shares, Intangible's earnings will be diluted because Intangible is valuing Tangible on a higher multiple of earnings than itself, and there is no expected synergy. Intangible will have to issue 666,667 shares valued at $6 each (earnings of 75c per share at a multiple of 8) to satisfy the $4,000,000 consideration. The results for Intangible will be as follows.

EPS $= \dfrac{\$1,900,000}{2,666,667} = 71.25c$ (3.75c lower than the previous 75c)

APS $= \dfrac{\$6,000,000}{2,666,667} = \$2.25$ ($1 higher than the previous $1.25)

If Intangible is still valued on the stock market on a P/E ratio of 8, the share price should fall by approximately 30c (8 × 3.75c, the fall in EPS) but because the asset backing has been increased substantially the company will probably now be valued on a higher P/E ratio than 8.

The shareholders in Tangible would receive 666,667 shares in Intangible in exchange for their current 1,000,000 shares, that is, two shares in Intangible for every three shares currently held.

(a)	Earnings	$
	Three shares in Tangible earn (3 × 40c)	1.200
	Two shares in Intangible will earn (2 × 71.25c)	1.425
	Increase in earnings, per three shares held in Tangible	0.225
(b)	Assets	$
	Three shares in Tangible have an asset backing of (3 × $3.5)	10.50
	Two shares in Intangible will have an asset backing of (2 × $2.25)	4.50
	Loss in asset backing, per three shares held in Tangible	6.00

The shareholders in Tangible would be trading asset backing for an increase in earnings.

6.5 Dividends and dividend cover

A further issue which may create some difficulties before a merger or takeover can be agreed is the level of **dividends** and **dividend cover** expected by shareholders in each of the companies concerned. Once the companies merge, a single dividend policy will be applied.

6.6 Service contracts for key personnel

When the target company employs certain **key personnel**, on whom the success of the company has been based, the predator company might want to ensure that these key people do not leave as soon as the takeover occurs. To do this, it might be necessary to insist as a condition of the offer that the key people should agree to sign service contracts, tying them to the company for a certain time (perhaps three years). Service contracts would have to be attractive to the employees concerned, perhaps through offering a high salary or other benefits such as share options in the predator company. Where key personnel are shareholders, they might be bound not to sell shares for a period.

7 Conduct of a takeover bid

7.1 Takeover tactics

When a company wishes to acquire another public company, it is common practice to build up a holding of the shares of the takeover target, by purchasing shares in the stock market. Such buying may be done within a very short space of time, in an effort to avoid an upward move in share prices which might occur if the buying company's tactics were to become known in the market. Buying a quantity of shares quickly and unexpectedly is known as a 'dawn raid'.

In the UK, once a shareholding of 3% is reached, the purchasing company is obliged to notify the company whose shares it has bought. When a holding of 30% or more is reached, the purchasing company becomes obliged under the **City Code** (or **Takeover Code**) to make an offer to the remaining shareholders for all of their shares.

The offer price decided at this point is normally set below the maximum amount the bidder might be willing to pay for the takeover target, but above the current market price of the shares. An offer addressed to the board of the target company, which may be communicated either through a merchant bank or directly, will establish the board's reaction as hostile or not.

Although secrecy should be sought for this stage in negotiations, it may in fact be in the target company's interests to 'leak' information to the market in the hope of either raising the market perception of an acceptable price or inducing the purchasing company to abandon its bid. Secrecy ceases to be an issue when a formal offer document is sent to all the shareholders in the target company.

7.2 Will the bidding company's shareholders approve of a takeover?

When a company is planning a takeover bid for another company, its board of directors should give thought to how its own shareholders might react to the bid. A company does not have to ask its shareholders for their approval of every takeover. However, it is important to consider shareholder opinion.

(a)   When a large takeover is planned by a listed company, and the takeover involves the purchasing company in the issue of a substantial number of new shares (to pay for the takeover), Stock Exchange rules may require the company to obtain the formal approval of its shareholders. This approval would have to be obtained formally, at a general meeting of the company.

(b)   If shareholders, and the stock market in general, think the takeover is not a good one, then the market value of the company's shares is likely to fall. The company's directors have a responsibility to protect their shareholders' interests, and adverse market reaction to an offer might persuade the directors to think again.

A takeover bid might seem unattractive to shareholders of the bidding company for the following reasons.

(a)   It might reduce the EPS of their company (ie it might **dilute earnings**).

(b)   The target company might be in a high-risk industry, or might be in danger of going into liquidation.

(c)   The purchase price might seem excessively high, especially when the target company has very few tangible assets of value.

7.3 Will a takeover bid be resisted by the target company?

Quite often, a takeover bid will be resisted. **Resistance** may come from the target company's board of directors, who might adopt defensive tactics. Resistance might also come from the target company's shareholders, but they can refuse to sell their shares to the bidding company. → Glazer utd.

A bid is said to be **hostile** when it is resisted by the board of directors of the target company. In a hostile bid, the target company directors take what measures they can (ie the measures they are allowed to take under the takeover rules) to persuade their shareholders to refuse the offer.

Resistance might be overcome by offering a higher price. The board of the target company are required to act in the interests of their shareholders. Their main objection to a bid is often that the bid is too low. Raising the offer might therefore overcome this objection, and persuade the target company's board to recommend the new offer.

In cases where the target company is a **quoted** company, there will often be a large number of target shareholders, whose attitudes to the bid will often vary considerably. Because there are likely to be major differences of opinion about whether to accept a takeover bid or not, the London Stock Exchange has issued formal rules for the conduct of takeover bids, in the **City Code on Takeovers and Mergers**.

8 Contesting an offer: defensive tactics

The directors of a target company must act in the interests of their shareholders, employees and creditors. They may decide to **contest an offer** on several grounds.

    (a)   The offer may be unacceptable because the terms are poor, in particular the price is too low. Rejection of the offer may lead to an improved bid.

    (b)   The merger or takeover may have no obvious advantage.

    (c)   Employees may be strongly opposed to the bid.

    (d)   The founder members of the business may oppose the bid, and may appeal to the loyalty of other shareholders.

When a company receives a takeover bid which the board of directors considers **unwelcome**, the directors must act quickly to fight off the bid. The steps that might be taken to thwart a bid or make it seem less attractive include:

    (a)   Issuing a forecast of attractive future profits and dividends to persuade shareholders that to sell their shares would be unwise and that the offer price is too low. It would be better for them to retain their shares to benefit from future profits, dividends and capital growth. (Such profit and dividend forecasts can be included in **defence documents** circulated to shareholders, and in press releases.)

    (b)   Lobbying to have the offer referred to the Competition Commission.

    (c)   Launching an advertising campaign against the takeover bid.

    (d)   Finding a '**white knight**'. A white knight is a company that will come to the rescue, by making a takeover bid of its own, that the board of the target company finds preferable. The offer from a white knight might be higher, but there are also likely to be strategic reasons why the bid is preferred.

    (e)   Making a counter-bid for the bidding company. (This is rare, and can only be done if the companies are of reasonably similar size. It is called a Pacman defence.)

    (f)   Arranging a management buyout. The management team might wish to continue to run the business themselves, and face the loss of their jobs if the takeover is successful. They might therefore offer to buy the company, if they can find venture capital support. Their bid would need to match the offer from the bidding company.

(g) In some countries, the directors of companies are permitted to introduce a **'poison-pill'** to deter takeover bids. A poison pill is any arrangement that makes it more difficult or more expensive to make a hostile takeover bid. An example of a poison pill is a provision in the company's constitution giving existing shareholders the right, in the event of an investor gaining a shareholding of more than, say, 15% in the company, to subscribe for new shares at a large discount to the current share price. The issue of new equity at a discount to the market price would make a takeover more difficult and more expensive. Poison pills are not permitted in the UK.

Exam focus point

Defensive tactics were examined for 8 marks in the June 2006 exam. – *See exam q⁵*

8.1 Costs of contested takeover bids

Takeover bids, when contested, can be very expensive, involving:

(a) Costs of professional services, such as an investment bank (for advice)
(b) Advertising costs and public relations costs
(c) The cost of producing and distributing defence documents

8.2 Gaining the consent of the target company shareholders

A takeover bid will only succeed if the predator company can persuade enough shareholders in the target company to sell their shares. Shareholders will only do this if they are dissatisfied with the performance of their company and its shares, or they are attracted by a high offer and the chance to make a good capital gain.

9 Regulation of mergers and takeovers

FAST FORWARD

Takeovers and mergers are regulated. They might be forbidden if they are likely to restrict competition. The conduct of takeovers by public companies and some private companies is regulated in the UK by the City Code.

9.1 The Competition Commission

A company may have to consider whether its proposed takeover would be drawn to the attention of the **Competition Commission**. In the UK the **Office of Fair Trading** (the OFT) is entitled to scrutinise all mergers and takeovers above a certain size. If the OFT thinks that a merger or takeover might be against the public interest, it can refer it to the Competition Commission. Proposed mergers can be notified to the OFT in advance. If no referral is made to the Competition Commission within (normally) 20 days, the merger can proceed without fear of a referral.

The function of the Competition Commission is to advise the government. The Commission can make recommendations to the Department of Trade and Industry (or to any other body, including the companies involved in the bid).

The result of an investigation by the Competition Commission might be:

(a) A withdrawal of the proposal for the merger or takeover, in anticipation of its rejection by the Commission

(b) Acceptance or rejection of the proposal by the Commission

(c)   Acceptance of the proposal by the Commission subject to the new company agreeing to certain conditions laid down by the Commission, for example on prices, employment or arrangements for the sale of the group's products

9.2 European Union regulations on mergers

The European Commission has the power to intervene and to either block or authorise mergers above a certain threshold size. If the Commission finds that the merger raises some serious doubts as to its compatibility with the European common market, it will initiate proceedings to block the merger.

9.3 The Takeover Panel and the City Code on Takeovers and Mergers

The **City Code** is a code of behaviour which UK companies are expected to follow during a takeover or merger, as a measure of self-discipline. The Code has no statutory backing, although it is administered and enforced by the **Takeover Panel**. Once adopted, the 13th Company Law Directive of the EU will have statutory power in EU member states, bringing an end to the non-statutory approach to the regulation of bids and takeover deals currently used in the UK.

The nature and purpose of the City Code is described within the Code itself as follows.

'The Code represents the collective opinion of those professionally involved in the field of takeovers on a range of business standards. It is not concerned with the financial or commercial advantages or disadvantages of a takeover, which are matters for the company and its shareholders, or with those wider questions which are the responsibility of the government, advised by the Competition Commission.

The Code has not, and does not seek to have, the force of law, but those who wish to take advantage of the facilities of the securities markets in the United Kingdom should conduct themselves in matters relating to takeovers according to the Code. Those who do not so conduct themselves cannot expect to enjoy those facilities and may find that they are withheld.'

Companies subject to the Code include all UK public companies (listed or unlisted) and also some classes of private company.

The details of the City Code are outside the examination syllabus, but it might be useful to note some of the general principles that are applied.

(a)   All shareholders of a target company must be treated in the same way by a bidder. Some shareholders must not be given preferential treatment, or a better offer, than the others.

(b)   Any information provided during a takeover by the bidder or by the board of the target company must be made available to all the shareholders.

(c)   Shareholders must be given sufficient information and advice to enable them to reach a properly informed decision and must have sufficient time to do so. No relevant information should be withheld from them.

(d)   The directors of a target company are not permitted to frustrate a takeover bid, nor to prevent the shareholders from having a chance to decide for themselves.

(e)   Where control of a company is acquired by the bidder, a general offer must normally be made to all the other shareholders who have so far not accepted the offer. Control is defined as a holding of shares carrying 30% of the voting rights of a company, irrespective of whether that holding or holdings gives *de facto* control.

Chapter roundup

- **Business combinations** take place for various reasons. Strategic reasons might be to gain market strength, to grow a business more quickly than would be possible by internal growth alone, to diversify into other business areas, and possibly for defensive reasons.

- Mergers and acquisitions should also have a financial objective, and should be expected to increase the wealth of shareholders. This can be monitored through changes in the share price.

- Mergers and acquisitions often result in **operating synergy**, ie in higher profits from cost savings (economies of scale), or in higher sales and profit margins due to greater market strength.

- In an acquisition, the **purchase consideration** might be shares in the bidding company, cash or loan capital. A cash purchase must be financed, and the cash will be obtained by issuing new shares, raising debt finance, or using existing surplus cash resources.

- The effect on **earnings per share** and the share price after a takeover will depend to some extent on the form of purchase consideration chosen.

- The **financial position of a company** after a takeover will depend partly on how the takeover has been financed, and partly on the effects of **synergy** (ie increases in operating profits).

- The **financial position of shareholders** after a takeover will depend partly on expected earnings per share (eg whether these are higher or whether there is dilution in earnings) and partly on changes in the P/E ratio. **Market perception** of a takeover is very important.

- When a takeover is financed by a share exchange, and there is no synergy, there will be a **dilution in earnings per share** if the target company is bought on a higher P/E ratio multiple than the P/E ratio of the purchasing company. There will be an increase in earnings per share if the target company is purchased on a lower P/E multiple.

- Other factors in deciding whether to make a takeover bid, and if so at what price, include (a) the **quality of earnings** of the target company, (b) the **quality of the assets** of the target company, (c) the existence of **key personnel** and whether these can be retained after the takeover, (d) the possible effect of the takeover on **dividend policy**.

- **Takeovers and mergers are regulated**. They might be forbidden if they are likely to restrict competition. The conduct of takeovers by public companies and some private companies is regulated in the UK by the City Code.

Quick quiz

1   Name three features of a takeover that makes it different from a merger.

2   Why might the shareholders of the bidding company disapprove of a bid for a target company by their board of directors?

3   What factors might affect the choice between a cash offer and a paper offer in a takeover bid?

4   What is the name of the '2 + 2 = 5' effect on operating profits arising from a takeover or merger?

5   If a bidding company issues shares to buy a target company on a *lower* P/E ratio than the bidding company shares are valued at, what will happen to the bidding company's own EPS after the takeover?

Answers to quick quiz

1   (a) Management control. The bidding company takes over and controls the target company. There is no pooling of management teams. (b) Target company becomes a subsidiary company of the bidding company. (c) Purchased goodwill, to be shown in the group balance sheet and reviewed annually for possible impairment. (d) Possible minority interests in the share capital of the acquired company.

2   The takeover might dilute earnings and depress the share price.

3   (a) Dilution in earnings per share (b) cost to the company (c) effect on financial gearing (d) effect on control of the purchasing company (e) whether the target company shareholders are likely to accept a paper offer.

4   Synergy (operating synergy)

5   EPS will rise, even if there is no synergy.

16

Business valuations

Introduction

If an acquisition company is planning to launch a bid for a company it wishes to take over, it must decide on a bid price to offer to the target company shareholders.

The purpose of this chapter is to examine the possible methods that can be used to value a company, so that a bidding company's offered price is realistic and likely to be welcomed by the target company shareholders.

1 Reasons for business valuations

The main concern of this chapter is with methods of valuing the entire equity share capital of a company. It is not particularly concerned with how to value small blocks of shares that an investor might choose to buy or sell on the stock market.

Company shares are traded at their current market price on a stock exchange, and so it is important to understand why it might be necessary to value an entire business. A business valuation will be necessary:

(a) For **quoted companies**, when there is a takeover bid for the company. The offer price will exceed the current market price of the shares. If it does not, shareholders in the target company have no reason to accept the offer, when they can obtain the same price on the stock market. The offer price in a takeover bid is said to reflect a 'premium for control'.

(b) For **unquoted companies**, when:

  (i) The company wishes to 'go public' and must fix an issue price for its shares
  (ii) There is a proposed merger with another company
  (iii) Shares are sold privately by one shareholder to another
  (iv) Shares need to be valued for the purposes of taxation
  (v) Shares are pledged as collateral for a loan

(c) For **subsidiary companies**, when the group's holding company is negotiating the sale of the subsidiary to a management buyout team or to an external buyer.

2 Principles of valuation

When a business is valued, several basic principles should be applied.

(a) There should be a logical basis for the valuation.

(b) The valuation should be fair. In a takeover bid, the valuation by the bidder will reflect what the bidder considers financially justifiable, but should also have regard to what the target company shareholders are likely to accept.

(c) There is no single valuation that is correct. Different valuations can be made, using different valuation methods and different assumptions with each method. At the end of the day, the 'correct' valuation is the one that is agreed between the parties.

(d) In a takeover bid, there is likely to be a maximum price that the bidder is prepared to offer. The initial bid might be less than this maximum.

2.1 Relevance of accounting information to business valuations

The valuation of a business should be based on the available financial information. In many cases, particularly with private companies, the most significant information might be the financial accounts of the company.

However, accounting information might be unreliable.

(a) Financial statements provide **historical information** about past profits and earnings. They are not a guide to current earnings or future earnings.

(b) Asset values in the balance sheet of a company are not necessarily representative of the current value of the assets.

Even so, accounting information about earnings, dividends and asset values might be used – with caution – in a business valuation.

3 Methods of valuation

There are a number of different ways of putting a **value** on a **business**, or on **shares** in an **unquoted company**. It makes sense to use several methods of valuation, and to compare the values they produce.

Common methods of valuing shares are:

- (a) The earnings method (P/E ratio method)
- (b) The net assets method
- (c) Dividend based approaches
- (d) DCF-based valuation
- (e) A cash flow-based valuation

It is unlikely that one method would be used in isolation. Several valuations might be made, each using a different technique or different assumptions. The valuations could then be compared, and a final price reached as a compromise between the different valuations reached.

What matters ultimately is the final **price** that the buyer and the seller agree. The purchase price for a company will usually be discussed mainly in terms of:

- P/E ratios, when a large block of shares, or a whole business is being valued
- Alternatively, a DCF valuation or discounted free cash flow valuation
- To a lesser extent, the net assets per share.

Exam focus point

In December 2002 there was a question that presented a scenario in which a company was considering the sale of one of its subsidiaries. You were required first to calculate the value per share of the subsidiary using the net assets, dividend yield and P/E ratio bases. The remaining 11 marks of this 20 mark question were for discussion of the strengths and weaknesses of the methods used, and for comment on a bid received for the subsidiary. Provided you were familiar with the basics of these methods, it would have been reasonably straightforward to gain good marks on this question.

4 The price-earnings ratio method

This is a common method of valuing a controlling interest in a company. The **P/E ratio** relates earnings per share to a share's value. The P/E ratio is often called an **earnings multiple**.

Since P/E ratio $= \dfrac{\text{Market value}}{\text{EPS}}$

It follows that the market value per share $= \text{EPS} \times \text{P/E ratio}$.

A business can be valued by applying an appropriate P/E multiple to the company's total earnings.

- (a) The **total earnings** might be historical earnings in the previous financial year. Where annual earnings have fluctuated up and down in the past, the figure chosen for annual earnings might be an average annual earnings figure for the most recent few years. Where there are reasonably reliable estimates of future earnings, and these differ from historical earnings, a figure for estimated future annual earnings might be used.

- (b) The **P/E ratio** chosen for the valuation should be one that is appropriate for the type of company, the industry it is in, its business risk characteristics, and its financial risk characteristics (gearing level). A 'typical' P/E ratio for companies in the same industry or market sector might be selected.

Choosing a high P/E ratio will produce a higher valuation than if a lower P/E multiple is selected. A high P/E ratio may indicate:

(a) **Expectations** that the EPS will grow rapidly in the years to come, so that a high price is being paid for future earnings prospects. Many small but successful and fast-growing companies are valued on the stock market on a high P/E ratio.

(b) **Security of earnings.** A well-established low-risk company would be valued on a higher P/E ratio than a similar company whose earnings are subject to greater uncertainty.

(c) **Status**. If a quoted company made a share-for-share takeover bid for an unquoted company, it would normally expect its own shares to be valued on a higher P/E ratio than the target company's shares. This is because a quoted company ought to be a lower-risk company; but in addition, there is an advantage in having shares which are quoted on a stock market: the shares can be readily sold. The P/E ratio of an unquoted company's shares might be around 50% to 60% of the P/E ratio of a similar public company with a full Stock Exchange listing (and perhaps 70% of that of a company whose shares are traded on a junior stock market).

4.1 Example: earnings method of valuation

Spider is considering the takeover of an unquoted company, Fly. Spider's shares are quoted on the Stock Exchange at a price of $3.20 and with a recent EPS of the company of 20c, the company's P/E ratio is 16. Fly is a company with 100,000 shares and current earnings of $50,000, 50c per share. How might Spider decide on an offer price?

Solution

The decision about the offer price is likely to be based on deciding first of all what a reasonable P/E ratio would be:

(a) If Fly is in the same industry as Spider, its P/E ratio ought to be lower, because of its lower status as an unquoted company.

(b) If Fly is in a different industry, a suitable P/E ratio might be based on the P/E ratio that is typical for quoted companies in that industry.

(c) If Fly is thought to be growing fast, so that its EPS will rise rapidly in the years to come, the P/E ratio that should be used for the share valuation will be higher than if only small EPS growth is expected.

(d) If the acquisition of Fly would contribute substantially to Spider's own profitability and growth, or to any other strategic objective that Spider has, then Spider should be willing to offer a higher P/E ratio valuation, in order to secure acceptance of the offer by Fly's shareholders.

The P/E ratio on which Spider bases its offer will probably be lower than the P/E ratio that Fly's shareholders think their shares ought to be valued on. Some haggling over the price might be necessary.

(a) Spider might decide that Fly's shares ought to be valued on a P/E ratio of 60% × 16 = 9.6, that is, at 9.6 × 50c = $4.80 each.

(b) Fly's shareholders might reject this offer, and suggest a valuation based on a P/E ratio of, say, 12.5, that is, 12.5 × 50c = $6.25.

(c) Spider's management might then come back with a revised offer, say valuation on a P/E ratio of 10.5, that is, 10.5 × 50c = $5.25.

4.2 General guidelines for a P/E ratio-based valuation

When a company is thinking of acquiring an **unquoted company** in a takeover, the final offer price will be agreed by negotiation, but a list of some of the factors affecting the valuer's choice of P/E ratio is given below.

(a) General **economic and financial conditions**, and how share prices in general might be expected to move in the future.

(b) The type of **industry** and the prospects of that industry.

(c) The **size** of the undertaking and its **status** within its industry. If an unquoted company's earnings are growing annually and are currently around US$400,000 or so, then it could probably get a quote in its own right on the junior stock market and a higher P/E ratio should therefore be used when valuing its shares.

(d) **Marketability**. The market in shares which do not have a stock market quotation is always a restricted one and a higher yield is therefore required.

(e) The **diversity of shareholdings** and the financial status of any principal shareholders. When a controlling interest in the shares of a target company is owned by an individual, it will probably be necessary to offer a higher price for the shares.

(f) The reliability of profit estimates and the past profit record.

(g) The liquidity of the target company. Liquidity in this sense refers to the cash flows from the business operations of the company. Companies with strong operational cash flows should attract higher valuations.

(h) Asset backing. A P/E ratio-based valuation might be affected by the quality of the assets of the target company.

(i) The **nature of the assets**, for example whether some of the non-current assets are of a highly specialised nature, and so have only a small break-up value.

(j) **Gearing**. A relatively high gearing ratio will generally mean greater financial risk for ordinary shareholders and call for a higher rate of return on equity.

(k) The extent to which the business is **dependent** on the technical skills of one or more individuals.

4.3 Forecast earnings growth

When one company is thinking about taking over another, it should look at the target company's **forecast earnings**, not just its historical results. Often the management of the predator company will make an initial approach to the directors of the target company, to sound them out about a possible takeover bid. If the target company's directors are amenable to a bid, they might agree to produce forecasts of their company's future earnings and growth. These forecasts (for the next year and possibly even further ahead) might then be used by the predator company in choosing an offer price.

Forecasts of earnings growth should only be used if a reasonable and reliable estimate of growth is available.

5 The net assets method

The net assets method values the equity shares of a business at the value of the assets that are attributable to the shareholders. The net assets attributable to shareholders are:

	$	$
Value of tangible non-current assets		X
Value of intangible non-current assets, but only if these have a recognisable market value		X
Value of current assets		X
		X
Less		
Current liabilities	Y	
Long-term liabilities (eg long-term debt capital)	Y	
Nominal value of preference shares, if any	Y	
		Y
Value of net assets attributable to equity		X - Y

Intangible assets (including goodwill) should be excluded from the valuation, unless they have a market value at which they could be sold (for example patents and copyrights).

(a)   **Goodwill**, if shown in the accounts, is unlikely to be shown at a true figure for purposes of valuation, and the value of goodwill should be reflected in another method of valuation (for example the earnings basis, the dividend yield basis or the super-profits method).

(b)   **Development expenditure**, if shown in the accounts, would also have a balance sheet value unrelated to the worth of the company's physical assets.

5.1 Example: net assets method

The summary balance sheet of Cactus is as follows.

	$	$
Non-current assets		
Land and buildings	160,000	
Plant and machinery	80,000	
Motor vehicles	20,000	
	260,000	
Goodwill	20,000	
		280,000
Current assets		
Inventories	80,000	
Receivables	60,000	
Short-term investments	15,000	
Cash	5,000	
		160,000
		440,000
Ordinary shares of $1		80,000
Reserves		140,000
		220,000
5% preference shares of $1		50,000
		270,000
Non-current liabilities		
12% debentures	60,000	
Deferred tax	10,000	
		70,000
Current liabilities		
Trade payables	60,000	
Taxation	20,000	
Proposed ordinary dividend	20,000	
		100,000
		440,000

What is the value of an ordinary share using the net assets basis of valuation?

Solution

If the figures given for asset values are not questioned, the valuation would be as follows.

	$	$
Total value of non-current assets plus net current assets		340,000
Less intangible asset (goodwill)		20,000
		320,000
Less: Preference shares	50,000	
Debentures	60,000	
Deferred tax	10,000	
		120,000
Net asset value of equity		200,000
Number of ordinary shares		80,000
Net asset value per share		$2.50

The difficulty in an asset valuation method is establishing realistic asset values. The figure attached to an individual asset might vary considerably depending on whether it is valued on a going concern basis or on a break-up basis. The following list should give you some idea of the factors to be considered.

(a) Do the assets need professional valuation? If so, how much will this cost?

(b) Have the liabilities been accurately quantified, for example deferred taxation?

(c) How have the current assets been valued? Are all receivables collectable? Is all inventory realisable? Can all the assets be physically located and brought into a saleable condition?

(d) Can any unrecognised liabilities be accurately assessed? Would there be redundancy payments and closure costs?

(e) Is there an available market in which the assets can be realised (on a break-up basis)? If so, do the balance sheet values truly reflect these break-up values?

5.2 When is the net assets basis of valuation used?

The greatest drawback to a net asset valuation is that the business is valued on the historical cost or current value of its assets, without regard to the future earnings potential of those assets. A company with very few assets might have high earnings potential, particularly where they rely on the skills and know-how of employees, whose worth is excluded from a net assets valuation. For example, a software firm might operate with just a few items of IT equipment and software, and yet have very high profitability.

Despite the serious limitations of net assets valuations, it is always useful to calculate the net assets per share. The net assets basis of valuation should be used on the following basis.

(a) **As a measure of the 'security' in a share value**. A share might be valued using the earnings basis, and this valuation might be:

(i) **Higher than the net asset value per share.** If the company went into liquidation, the investor could not expect to receive the full value of his shares when the underlying assets were realised.

(ii) **Lower than the net asset value per share.** If the company went into liquidation, the investor might expect to receive the full value of his shares (perhaps more).

It is often thought to be a good thing to acquire a company with valuable tangible assets, especially **freehold property**, which might be expected to increase in value over time.

(b)   **As a measure of comparison in a scheme of merger**. If company A, with a low asset backing, is planning a merger with company B, with a high asset backing, the shareholders of B might consider that their shares' value ought to reflect this difference. It might therefore be agreed that something should be added to the value of the company B shares to allow for this difference in asset backing.

5.3 Current value methods of net asset valuation

A business might be valued on the basis of the current value of its net assets, either at net realisable value (NRV) or replacement cost.

The minimum valuation of a company should be the amount that its assets would fetch in a sale, after paying off creditors, if the business were to be broken up and the assets sold off piecemeal. This would be an NRV valuation. If a business is worth less as a going concern than it would be worth from selling off the assets separately, the economic argument would be to break up the business.

The seller of a business should therefore establish the NRV of its assets, and should not consider accepting any offer from the purchaser below this valuation. In normal circumstances, however, a going concern valuation should be much higher than an NRV valuation. An exception to this general rule might occur where the business owns an asset that is not being properly exploited, and could be put to better use by another business. Examples of such assets might be land and buildings or an item of intellectual property. If the business as a whole is not particularly profitable, the net realisable value of its assets might exceed a going concern valuation.

A **net replacement cost** valuation of the net assets of a business might be of interest to a would-be purchaser of a business. Net replacement cost is the investment that would be needed to establish a comparable business from scratch. Arguably, this is the maximum purchase price that a bidder might consider for a target business.

5.4 Example

Rust wishes to dispose of a subsidiary company, Russett, and has entered into discussions with a company interested in making a purchase offer for its shares. Russett would be sold as a going concern. The finance director of Rust has made the following assessment of the asset values and liabilities of Russett.

	Net book value (NBV) $	Net realisable value (NRV) $	Net replacement cost (NRC) $
Land and buildings	3,000,000	5,000,000	5,200,000
Motor vehicles	800,000	600,000	850,000
Other non-current assets	2,000,000	800,000	2,300,000
Inventory	50,000	10,000	52,000
Receivables	70,000	60,000	70,000
Trade payables	(20,000)	(20,000)	(20,000)
Long-term debt	(500,000)	(500,000)	(500,000)
	5,400,000	5,950,000	7,952,000

These valuations suggest that:

(a)   Rust should not be prepared to consider an offer for the shares of Russett at a price below $5,950,000.

(b)   The buyer might be reluctant to offer more than $7,952,000 to buy the shares, if its management felt a similar company could be set up for about that amount of money.

6 A dividend-based approach to business valuation

A dividend-based method is more appropriate for **small shareholdings**, because ownership of the shares does not give any control over decision-making, such as dividend decisions and retained earnings decisions (ie reinvestment of profits).

A dividend-based approach to share valuation measures the value of shares as the present value of the expected future dividends. It is more appropriate as a method of **valuation for small shareholdings in unquoted companies**. This is because small shareholders are mainly interested in dividends, since they cannot control decisions affecting the company's profits and earnings. (In contrast, a valuation of a controlling interest in a company should be based on earnings or cash flows rather than dividends).

A suitable offer price for a minority shareholding in an unquoted company is a price that compensates the shareholder for the loss of the future dividends by selling the shares. (The valuation method is unnecessary for small shareholdings in quoted companies, because any valuation will be based on the current market price for the shares.)

6.1 Dividend valuation model: no dividend growth

The simplest dividend capitalisation technique is based on the assumption that the level of dividends in the future will be **constant**. A dividend yield valuation would be:

$$\text{Share value} = \frac{\text{Dividend in cents}}{\text{Expected dividend yield}\%}$$

This valuation model was explained in the earlier chapter on the cost of capital. The share value is the present value of a constant annual dividend in perpetuity, discounted at the shareholders' cost of capital. Since the present value of $1 every year in perpetuity is $1/r$, the present value of an annual dividend of d cents in perpetuity is d/r.

In an examination question, look carefully to see whether the dividend yield given is net or gross – this will dictate whether you use the net or gross dividend to obtain the share value.

6.2 Dividend growth valuation model (Gordon's growth model)

It may be possible to use expected **future** dividends for a share valuation and to predict dividend growth. For this purpose, it is necessary to predict future earnings growth and then to decide how earnings growth will be reflected in the company's dividend policy.

The dividend growth model for share valuation, you may recall from the chapter on the cost of capital, is as follows.

$$P_0 = \frac{d_0(1+g)}{(r-g)}$$

where P_0 is the current market value ex dividend
       d_0 is the current dividend
       g is the expected annual growth in dividend, so $d_0(1+g)$ is the expected dividend next year
       r is the return required.

Question 16.1   Value of shares

Company A expects to pay no dividends in Years 1, 2 or 3, but a dividend of 7.8c per share each year from Year 4 in perpetuity.

Company B has just paid an annual dividend of 14.4c per share. Dividend growth is expected to be 3% per annum into the foreseeable future.

Value the shares of Company A and Company B on a dividend yield basis, assuming a required yield of 12%.

Year	Discount factor at 12%
3	0.712
4	0.636

(For the answer to this question, see the Answer section at the end of this book.)

6.3 The CAPM and dividend-based valuations

The **capital asset pricing model (CAPM)** might be used to value shares, particularly when pricing shares for a stock market listing. The CAPM would be used to establish a required equity yield.

6.4 Example: CAPM and share price valuations

Suppose that Mackerel is planning to obtain a listing and admission to trading on the Stock Exchange by offering 40% of its existing shares to the public. No new shares will be issued. Its most recent summarised results are as follows.

	$
Revenue	120,000,000
Earnings	1,500,000
Number of shares ($1 shares)	3,000,000

The company has low gearing.

It regularly pays 50% of earnings as dividends, and with reinvested earnings is expected to achieve 5% dividend growth each year. Summarised details of two listed companies in the same industry as Mackerel are as follows.

	Salmon	Trout
Gearing (total debt/total equity)	45%	10%
Equity beta	1.50	1.05

The current Treasury bill yield is 7% a year. The average market return is estimated to be 12%. The new shares will be issued at a discount of 15% to the estimated post-issue market price, in order to increase the prospects of success for the share issue. What will the issue price be?

Solution

Using the CAPM, we begin by deciding on a suitable β value for Mackerel's equity. We shall assume that since Mackerel's gearing is close to Trout's, a β of 1.05 is appropriate.

The cost of Mackerel equity is $7\% + [(12 - 7)\% \times 1.05] = 12.25\%$

This can now be used in the dividend growth model. The dividend this year is 50% of $1,500,000 = $750,000.

The total value of Mackerel's equity is $\dfrac{\$750,000(1.05)}{(0.1225 - 0.05)} = \$10,862,069$

There are 3,000,000 shares, giving a market value per share of $3.62. Since the shares that are offered to the public will be offered at a discount of about 15% to this value, the share price for the market launch should be about 85% of $3.62 = $3.08.

7 The discounted future profits method of valuation

The **discounted future profits** method of share valuation may be appropriate when one company intends to buy another company and to make further investments in order to improve profits in the future. The maximum price the purchasing company should pay is the present value of the future cash flows resulting from the acquisition.

The future cash flows from the acquisition are:

(a)   As cash outflows, the cost of any additional investment in non-current assets and working capital

(b)   As cash inflows, the cash operating profits from the business. Cash operating profits can be estimated as the operating profit before interest and tax, plus depreciation charges (since depreciation is not a cash expense).

The valuation might be based on expected future cash flows for a limited number of future years. This is because:

(a)   Estimates of profits into the longer-term future will be unreliable

(b)   Setting a maximum time horizon for the valuation in effect imposes a discounted payback period on the investment

This method of valuation is sometimes called a **free cash flow valuation**. The value of a business is said to be the present value of the estimated future free cash flows of the business, where **free cash flow** is defined as follows.

Annual free cash flow = Revenues – operating costs + depreciation – investment expenditure

7.1 Example: discounted future profits method

Diversification wishes to make a bid for Tadpole. Tadpole makes after-tax profits of $400,000 a year. Diversification believes that if further investments are made, the after-tax cash flows (ignoring the purchase consideration) could be as follows.

Year	Cash flow (net of tax)
	$
0	(1,000,000)
1	(800,000)
2	600,000
3	1,000,000
4	1,500,000
5	1,500,000

The after-tax cost of capital of Diversification is 15% and the company expects all its investments to pay back, in discounted terms, within five years. What is the maximum price that the company should be willing to pay for the shares of Tadpole?

Solution

The maximum price is one which would make the return from the total investment exactly 15% over five years, so that the NPV at 15% would be 0.

Year	Cash flows ignoring purchase consideration $	Discount factor 15%	Present value $
0	(1,000,000)	1.000	(1,000,000)
1	(800,000)	0.870	(696,000)
2	600,000	0.756	453,600
3	1,000,000	0.658	658,000
4	1,500,000	0.572	858,000
5	1,500,000	0.497	745,500
	Maximum purchase price		1,019,100

This approach, however, presents the following practical problems.

(a)   Estimates of future profits will be subject to uncertainty, and it would be prudent to use cautious estimates. Over-estimating future profits will result in an over-valuation of the business.

(b)   The definition of free cash flow given above does not allow for any changes in working capital investment from year to year. Due to increases or decreases in inventories, receivables and payables, 'sales revenue minus operating costs plus depreciation' may fail to reflect cash flows accurately. Working capital changes should therefore be included in the cash flow estimates where they are likely to be significant in amount.

(c)   Taxation on profits should also be included in the cash flow estimates, and the cash flows should be discounted at the after-tax cost of capital.

These problems mean that estimating free cash flow involves not just forecasting sales, costs and profits, but also working capital movements and taxation.

Question 16.2
Offer price

Fang would like to acquire the business of Tooth. Tooth has been earning profits of about $75,000 a year for the past six or seven years. The finance director of Fang has estimated that future annual profits are likely to be $85,000 if the takeover occurs and if a further $30,000 is invested in working capital.

It is also estimated that the annual depreciation charge of Tooth will be $20,000, and that annual capital expenditure to replace ageing equipment will be $25,000.

Fang applies a cost of capital of 11% to its business valuations, and a discounted payback period of six years for its investments.

What is the maximum price that Fang should be prepared to offer to acquire Tooth?

Note. Assume that capital expenditure takes place annually at the end of each year, but that the additional working capital investment would be required immediately.

Year	Discount factor at 11%
1	0.901
2	0.812
3	0.731
4	0.659
5	0.593
6	0.535

(For the answer to this question, see the Answer section at the end of this book.)

8 Problems with P/E ratio valuations and DCF valuations

All valuations are based on assumptions. Changing the assumptions (eg changing the estimate of annual earnings or profits, or changing the cost of capital or P/E multiple) produces a different valuation. Valuations are particularly difficult in situations where there are problems with estimates of annual earnings or the assessment of risk.

The most commonly-used methods for the valuation of a business are the P/E ratio multiple method and the DCF or discounted free cash flow method. However, there are several practical problems with each of these methods.

The main problem is to estimate a reliable figure for annual earnings or cash profits. Basing estimates of earnings or profits on current annual profits will be unreliable in the following situations.

(a) When the company being valued is **in financial difficulty**. Earnings-based valuations or DCF valuations are based on the expectation that the future profits will continue into the future. However, a company in financial difficulties might go into liquidation. If the risk of insolvency is high, a valuation based on the break-up value of net assets might be more appropriate.

(b) Earnings-based valuations and DCF valuations are difficult to apply to companies whose **business follows economic cycles**, with high profits in years when the economy is growing and falling profits in times of recession. It is usual in these cases to apply an average annual figure for earnings or profits over the economic cycle, but it is difficult to make a reliable estimate.

(c) Earnings-based valuations and DCF valuations might not be entirely appropriate in cases where the company has **valuable assets**, such as patent rights, that could be sold to another buyer. Earnings or profits estimates might not fully reflect the value of such assets. In these cases, the valuation should make an allowance for the market value of key assets.

(d) The company might have **under-utilised assets**, and its future earnings potential could be much greater than its current earnings, if the assets can be more fully utilised. A valuation that ignores the earnings potential of under-used assets will be too low.

(e) When a company is in the **process of restructuring**, it will be difficult to make a suitable estimate of annual earnings or profits. Restructuring might involve selling off parts of the business, closing down some product lines and cutting back on operating costs. Until the restructuring process is complete, it will not be clear just what future annual earnings might be.

Making a valuation of a private company is also difficult.

(a) A private company is not worth as much as a comparable public company. There is a greater risk element in an investment in a private company, and the cost of capital applied to a DCF valuation should reflect this higher risk. A higher cost of capital will result in a lower valuation. The practical difficulty is to decide how much allowance to put into the cost of capital to allow for the risk.

(b) Similarly, a P/E ratio valuation of a private company should adjust the P/E multiple downwards to allow for the higher risk element. Again, the problem is to decide by how much the multiple should be adjusted.

Whenever a P/E multiple valuation is used, it should be remembered that any 'error' in the choice of multiple can have a large effect on the valuation, and the resulting valuation could be much higher or much lower than it should be. For example, during the so-called 'dot com boom' in 1999 and early 2000, dot com companies were being valued on P/E multiples of 40 or more. When the boom came to an end and share prices collapsed, valuations were re-adjusted, and much lower P/E multiples were used.

Chapter roundup

- There are a number of different ways of putting a **value** on a **business**, or on **shares** in an **unquoted company**. It makes sense to use several methods of valuation, and to compare the values they produce.

- What matters ultimately is the final **price** that the buyer and the seller agree. The purchase price for a company will usually be discussed mainly in terms of:

  - P/E ratios, when a large block of shares, or a whole business is being valued
  - Alternatively, a DCF valuation or discounted free cash flow valuation
  - To a lesser extent, the net assets per share.

- A dividend-based method is more appropriate for **small shareholdings**, because ownership of the shares does not give any control over decision-making, such as dividend decisions and retained earnings decisions (ie reinvestment of profits).

- All valuations are based on assumptions. Changing the assumptions (eg changing the estimate of annual earnings or profits, or changing the cost of capital or P/E multiple) produces a different valuation. Valuations are particularly difficult in situations where there are problems with estimates of annual earnings or the assessment of risk.

Quick quiz

1 What guidelines should help to determine the P/E ratio on which to base an offer price for shares in an unquoted target company?

2 A company's profits before interest and tax are $18 million, interest is $4 million, tax is $3 million and dividends are $6 million. There are no preference shares. The company's shares are valued on a P/E multiple of 16. What is the value of the shares?

3 How should the net assets of a company be valued, for a net assets method valuation?

4 What is 'free cash flow'?

5 Give four situations in which an earnings-based valuation or DCF valuation are problematic, due to difficulties in estimating annual earnings or profits.

Answers to quick quiz

1   Look at the P/E ratio for other companies in the same industry or business sector.

Allow for gearing: the equity shares of a company with high gearing should be valued on a lower P/E multiple than shares of a company with low gearing, to allow for the higher financial risk. Select the P/E ratio of a company with similar gearing to the business being valued.

When a private company is being valued, reduce the P/E multiple to allow for the higher risk. As a rough guideline, use a P/E multiple that is about 60% of the P/E for a comparable public company.

2   Earnings = profits after interest and tax = $11 million. Valuation = $11 million × 16 = $176 million.

3   Tangible non-current assets + current assets minus all liabilities and minus preference share capital (nominal value). Non-current assets should be at a current value if possible, particularly valuable assets such as land and buildings. Intangible asset values should be included if these have a reliable market value or sale value (eg patents, copyrights). Any long-term investments should also be included where these have a measurable value.

4   Profits before interest and tax + depreciation – replacement capital expenditures. However, cash flow valuations should also allow for taxation on profits and changes in working capital investment.

5   (a)   Companies in financial difficulties and facing insolvency/loss-making companies
     (b)   Companies with annual earnings that rise and fall with the economic cycle
     (c)   Companies with valuable assets
     (d)   Companies with under-utilised assets
     (e)   Companies in the process of restructuring their business

Company restructuring

17

Topic list	Syllabus reference
1 Divestments and spin offs	6f
2 Management buyouts	6f
3 The appraisal of proposed buyouts	6f
4 Management buy-ins	6f
5 Going private	6f
6 Private equity and institutional buyouts	6f

Introduction

The management of a group of companies may decide to restructure the group, eg to sell off a loss-making company or a company that no longer fits into the management's strategic plans for the future.

This chapter considers various methods of restructuring companies and groups.

1 Divestments and spin offs

A company might occasionally undergo a restructuring. Methods of restructuring are **divestment** (selling off part of the business to an outside buyer), **demerger** or **spin-off** (creating two or more separate and independent companies in place of just one), or **liquidation**.

Although a company might pursue financial strategies for growth in earnings and shareholder value, there might be occasions when a decision is taken to restructure the business.

Key term

A **divestment** is the sale of part of a business for cash. The cash from the sale might be paid to shareholders as a special dividend.

In a **spin off**, a part of the business is established as a new and separate company, and the shares in the new company are distributed to existing shareholders in proportion to their ownership in the company. Spin-offs are also called **demergers**.

1.1 Example

ICI is one well known example of an enterprise which has undergone a spin off or demerger, splitting itself into two separate companies some years ago (as ICI and the pharmaceuticals company, Zeneca).

A spin-off or demerger is the opposite of a merger. It is the splitting up of a corporate body into two or more separate and independent bodies. For example, the ABC Group might spin off its 100% shareholding in a subsidiary, C, by distributing the shares in C to its shareholders in proportion to their shareholding. C would then be run as an independent company. Shareholders would now own shares in both ABC Group and C, and can treat them as separate investments. An investor might decide, for example, to keep his shares in C but sell his shares in ABC Group.

1.2 Reasons for divestment

The reasons for a divestment could be any of the following.

(a)   A company might wish to sell an unprofitable subsidiary, or a subsidiary that is making only small profits. The buyer, who would expect to make a better return by taking over the subsidiary, might perhaps be a group of the subsidiary's managers, with the management buyout team being backed by venture capital finance.

(b)   Subsidiaries that are not 'core businesses' and do not fit in with the group's strategic plans might be sold. Restructuring through divestment is often the result of a decision to focus on core businesses (the opposite of diversification).

(c)   Another company might offer a price for a part of the business that is too good to refuse. The sale would earn a substantial profit.

(d)   Some finance companies have specialised in taking over large groups of companies, and then selling off parts of the newly-acquired groups, so that the proceeds of sales more than pay for the original takeovers.

(e)   A company in financial difficulties might be forced to sell off some subsidiaries in order to raise capital to pay off debts.

(f)   A subsidiary with high risk in its operating cash flows could be sold, so as to reduce the business risk of the group as a whole.

Reasons for a demerger

FAST FORWARD

In a demerger or spin-off, shareholders receive shares in the newly-established companies. They can choose to hold on to their shares in both companies, or can choose to invest in just one of them (or neither of them) and sell their shares accordingly.

The reasons for a spin-off or demerger might be any of the following.

(a)   The business has two distinct parts, and each has different strategic objectives and needs its own dedicated management.

(b)   Splitting the company and putting each part under a different management might result in better decision-making and greater organisational efficiency.

(c)   When a business has two distinct parts, its shareholders have to invest in both businesses, when they might prefer to invest in one of the businesses but not the other. A demerger gives them the opportunity to sell their investment in one of the businesses and hold on to their shares in the other. Investors wanting to invest in both businesses can hold on to their shares in both demerged companies.

(d)   A company might consider that its shares are undervalued. In particular, they might consider that investors do not recognise the value of one particular part of the business. A decision to spin off this business as a separate public company would be intended to add to shareholder value.

1.3 Examples

Royal Doulton, the china producer, was demerged from its parent company Pearson, which also owns the Financial Times, in 1993. Pearson said at the time that the demerger was part of its decision to focus on the media.

In 2001, measures taken by British Telecom to overcome its financial difficulties included selling off parts of its business (eg operations in Spain and Japan, and its Yellow Pages business) and a demerger of its mobile phone division, BT Wireless.

The potential disadvantages of demergers are as follows.

(a)   Economies of scale may be lost, where the demerged parts of the business had operations in common to which economies of scale applied.

(b)   The smaller companies which result from the demerger will have lower revenues, profits and status than the group before the demerger.

(c)   The ability to raise extra finance, especially debt finance, to support new investments and expansion may be reduced.

(d)   Vulnerability to takeover may be increased.

1.4 Example

Daytime currently achieves annual earnings of $50 million. It has 100 million shares in issue and the shares are currently valued at $5 each. The directors of the company believe that the shares are undervalued. In particular, they think that the market does not appreciate the true value of its media division, Morning. They therefore decide to spin off Morning as a separate company, turn it into a public company, and apply for a listing for its shares.

Morning is established as a public company with 25 million shares and demerged. Shareholders in Daytime are given 1 share in Morning for every 4 shares they hold in Daytime. The shares are admitted to trading on a stock exchange.

As a result of the demerger, the earnings of Daytime fall by $15 million, and the P/E ratio of the company remains unchanged. The earnings of Morning are $15 million, and its P/E ratio is 20.

Required

How does the demerger affect the wealth of an investor holding 1,000 shares in Daytime at the time of the demerger?

Solution

Before the demerger

EPS of Daytime	($50m/100m)	50c
Share price		$5
P/E ratio	($5/50c)	10

After the demerger

EPS of Daytime	($35m/100m)	35c
P/E ratio		10
Share price		$3.50
EPS of Morning	($15m/25m)	60c
P/E ratio		20
Share price		$12

Investor with 1,000 Daytime shares	$	$
Value of:		
1,000 Daytime shares before the demerger		5,000
1,000 Daytime shares after the demerger (× $3.50)	3,500	
250 Morning shares after the demerger (× $12)	3,000	
Value of combined investment		6,500
Gain from the demerger		1,500

1.5 Liquidations

An extreme form of sell-off is where an entire business is liquidated. In a **liquidation**, the business is not sold as a going concern. Instead, the assets are sold off individually at their 'break-up value'. The income from a liquidation is unlikely to be high, unless there are valuable assets with a market value (eg land and buildings).

Liquidation will only be a sensible option when a company wants to sell part of its business, perhaps because it is making losses, and:

(a)   No one is prepared to buy it as a going concern, or
(b)   The business has individual assets with a high sell-off value.

Exam focus point

> Divestment and share valuation were examined together in June 2005. The question asked for possible reasons for divestment and then a valuation of the shares of the company being disposed of on a variety of bases.

2 Management buyouts

FAST FORWARD

> A divestment might take the form of an MBO or MBI. An **MBO** is a buyout of a part of the company's business by an existing management team, backed by venture capital providers. An **MBI** is similar, except that the management team making the purchase comes from outside the company.

Key term

> A **management buyout (MBO)** is the purchase of all or part of a business from its owners by a team of its managers.

For example, the directors of a subsidiary company in a group might buy the company from the holding company, with the intention of running it as proprietors of a separate business entity.

To the managers, the buyout would be a method of setting up in business for themselves. To the group, the buyout would be a method of **disinvestment** - selling off the subsidiary as a going concern. Management buyouts might easily be thought of as attempts by a company to sell loss-making subsidiaries. In fact, management buyouts more commonly involve the sale of **profitable** subsidiaries, which are being sold off simply because they do not fit in well with the group's strategic plans.

2.1 The parties to a buyout

There are usually **three parties** to a management buyout.

(a) There is a **management team** wanting to make a buyout. This team ought to have the skills and ability to convince financial backers that it is worth supporting.

(b) There are the **directors** of a group of companies, who make the disinvestment decision.

(c) There are **financial backers** of the buyout team, who will usually want an equity stake in the bought-out business, because of the **venture capital** risk they are taking. Often, several financial backers provide the venture capital for a single buyout.

2.2 Reasons why a company might agree to an MBO

The board of directors of a company might agree to a management buyout of a subsidiary for the same reasons that they might decide to divest a subsidiary by selling it to an outside buyer.

(a) The subsidiary may be peripheral to the group's mainstream activities, and may no longer fit in with the group's overall strategy.

(b) The group may wish to sell off a loss-making subsidiary, and a management team may think that it can restore the subsidiary's fortunes.

(c) The parent company may need to raise cash quickly.

(d) The subsidiary may be part of a group that has just been taken over and the new parent company may wish to sell off parts of the group it has just acquired.

The reasons for agreeing to an MBO rather than selling to an outside buyer might be that:

(a) The best offer price has come from a small management group wanting to arrange a buyout.

(b) If the business that is being sold off is quite small, or is making losses, there might not be an outside buyer interested in making an offer to buy it.

(c) When a group has taken the decision to sell a subsidiary, it will probably get better co-operation from the management and employees of the subsidiary if the sale is a management buyout.

(d) If employees in the subsidiary will be made redundant if the business is sold externally, sale to an MBO team would avoid the cost of the redundancies.

A private company's shareholders might agree to sell out to a management team because they need cash, or they want to retire, or the business is not profitable enough for them.

2.3 Disadvantages of an MBO

There are potential drawbacks to agreeing to an MBO.

(a)   The management team might have more difficulty than expected in raising the venture capital to finance the buyout.

(b)   The management team might lack the skills to make a success of the business, particularly if it is currently making losses.

(c)   The management team might try to give a gloomy picture of the state of the business, and hide important information from the parent company directors, in order to negotiate a lower price for the buyout.

(d)   A successful MBO might unsettle other managers in the group, and encourage some to attempt an MBO for their own part of the business.

The buyout team will have to find willing **financial backers**, and so it must convince them that it can run the business successfully. To help with the task of convincing the bank or other institution, the management team should prepare a **business plan** and **estimates of sales, costs, profits and cash flows**, in reasonable detail. If the parent company's existing shareholders have already indicated their willingness to sell, the management team should have reasonably free access to the sort of figures they need about revenues, costs, areas for improved efficiency and cost savings, and so on.

3 The appraisal of proposed buyouts

3.1 How likely is a management buyout to succeed?

Management-owned companies often seem to get better performance out of their company, probably because of:

(a)   A favourable buyout price having been achieved

(b)   Personal motivation and determination

(c)   Quicker decision making and so more flexibility

(d)   Greater attention to matters such as pricing, inventory control and debt collection

(e)   Savings in overheads: owner-managers will be more reluctant to spend unnecessarily than employee-managers, and will avoid unnecessary spending, for example on expensive property or company cars.

However, many management buyouts, once they occur, begin with some redundancies to cut running costs.

The prospects of success for a management buyout ought to be evaluated:

(a)   By the managers who are thinking of making the buyout

(b)   By the institutional investors who are being asked to put in venture capital to finance the buyout

(c)   By the vendor, where the vendor continues to have a trading interest

3.2 How should an institutional investor evaluate a buyout?

An institutional investor should evaluate a buyout before deciding whether or not to finance. Aspects of any buyout that ought to be checked are as follows.

(a) Does the management team have the full range of management skills that are needed (for example a technical expert and a finance director)? Does it have the right blend of experience? Does it have the commitment?

(b) Why is the company for sale? The possible reasons for buyouts have already been listed. If the reason is that the parent company wants to get rid of a loss-making subsidiary, what evidence is there to suggest that the company can be made profitable after a buyout?

(c) What are the projected profits and cash flows of the business? The prospective returns must justify the risks involved.

(d) What is being bought? The buyout team might be buying the shares of the company, or only selected assets of the company. Are the assets that are being acquired sufficient for the task? Will more assets have to be bought? When will the existing assets need replacing? How much extra finance would be needed for these asset purchases? Can the company be operated profitably?

(e) What is the price? Is the price right or is it too high?

(f) What financial contribution can be made by members of the management team themselves?

3.3 The financial arrangements in a typical buyout

Typically, the buyout team will have a minority of the equity in the bought-out company, with the financial backers holding a majority of the shares between them. A buyout might have several financial backers, each providing finance in exchange for some equity.

The financial institutions will probably regard their investment as either a short-term or a medium-term one. They might hope that if the company is successful, it will eventually be floated on a stock market, perhaps the second tier junior market, thus giving a market value to their equity, and the option to sell their shares if they wish to realise their investment. Alternatively, they might hope for a **trade sale** to another company in the industry.

Investors of venture capital usually want the managers to be financially committed. Individual managers could borrow personally from a bank, say US$20,000 to US$50,000. This should be enough to commit them without hurting them too much.

The suppliers of equity finance might insist on investing part of their capital in the form of **redeemable convertible preference shares**. These often have voting rights should the preference dividend fall in arrears, giving increased influence over the company's affairs. They are issued in a redeemable form to give some hope of taking out part of the investment if it does not develop satisfactorily, and in convertible form for the opposite reason: to allow an increased stake in the equity of a successful company.

3.4 Financial benefits to the management team

Venture capital providers hope to make large returns from their investments. At the same time, they recognise that success depends on having a motivated and hard-working management team. The financing agreement will therefore usually provide for:

(a) Basic salaries for the management. These will be reasonable but by no means excessive

(b) An initial equity investment, that the individual managers pay for themselves

(c) A bonus scheme or incentive scheme that rewards the management team for success. The incentive might take the form of cash bonuses if profits exceed a given target figure, and/or an equity incentive, perhaps in the form of low-cost shares or share options when certain strategic targets are reached.

The most effective form of incentive scheme is one that rewards the beneficiaries in proportion to the amount of success they achieve.

3.5 Possible problems with buyouts

A common problem with management buyouts is that the managers may lack sufficient experience in financial management or financial accounting.

Other problems are:

(a)   Tax and legal complications

(b)   Difficulties in deciding on a fair price to be paid

(c)   Convincing employees of the need to change working practices

(d)   Inadequate cash flow to finance the maintenance and replacement of tangible non-current assets

(e)   The maintenance of previous employees' pension rights

(f)   Accepting the board representation requirement that many sources of funds will insist upon

(g)   The loss of key employees if the company moves geographically, or wage rates are decreased too far, or employment conditions are unacceptable in other ways

(h)   Maintaining continuity of relationships with suppliers and customers

---

Question 17.1   Cash flow

Why do you think that cash flow might be a crucial problem for many management buyouts?

(For the answer to this question, see the Answer section at the end of this book.)

---

4 Management buy-ins

A '**management buy-in' (MBI)** is a term used when a team of outside managers, as opposed to managers who are already running the business, mount a takeover bid and then run the business themselves. A management buy-in might occur when a business venture is running into trouble, and a group of outside managers see an opportunity to take over the business and restore its profitability.

Key term

> **Management buy-in**: the purchase of all or part of a business from its owners by new managers from outside the business.

To the company making the sale, an MBI is simply a form of divestment. Unlike a trade sale to another company, however, the divested business is taken over by the external management team, and the team will be backed by venture capital finance.

The issues to be considered in an MBI are similar to those in an MBO. In addition:

(a)   An important issue for the venture capitalist is whether the external management team has the necessary skills to make a success of the investment, not having been previously involved in the business.

(b)   The attitude of the employees of the divested business should also be considered. They will need to be reassured about their future employment prospects, and their pension rights will have to be protected.

5 Going private

Occasionally, a shareholder or group of shareholders in a public company whose shares are traded on a stock market might **take the company private**. They offer to buy the shares of the other shareholders, de-list the company's shares and re-establish the company as a private company.

Public company status is often beneficial, because:

(a)   Its shares are more marketable, and can be traded on a stock exchange

(b)   It has better access to new sources of finance than a private company, and so should be in a better position to grow its business

(c)   It can finance takeovers by issuing new shares, and develop the business through acquisitions rather than having to grow internally.

The expected benefits of going public do not always happen. Occasionally, a company that has gone public in the past might revert to private status.

A public company 'goes private' when a small group of individuals, possibly including existing shareholders and/or managers and with or without support from a financial institution, buys all of the company's shares. The company de-lists its shares, and the shares are no longer traded on a stock exchange. The company then changes its status from public limited company to private company.

When a public company goes private there may be a shareholder or small group of shareholders (eg members of a family) who still own a substantial proportion of the equity capital.

The reasons for going private might be any or several of the following.

(a)   The shareholders believe that the stock market is undervaluing the shares. They therefore buy back the shares from other investors (at what they consider to be a bargain price) and take the company private in order to obtain the benefit of all the profits of the company.

(b)   The purpose of going public might have been to gain access to sources of capital. If the company finds that it is unable to raise capital, its major shareholders might decide to offer to buy out the other shareholders and take the company private again.

(c)   The major shareholders might want to avoid the threat of a takeover by another company.

(d)   The major shareholders might wish to avoid conflicts between the long-term needs of the business and the short-term expectations of institutional shareholders. They might believe that the long-term interests of the company are being damaged by excessive attention to current profits and dividends. Going private will remove the need to produce annual profits and dividends to satisfy the market.

Other advantages in **going private** could include the following.

(a)   The annual costs of meeting listing requirements (complying with the Listing Rules of the relevant Listing Authority) can be saved. Similarly, stock exchange fees can be saved.

(b)   The company is protected from volatility in share prices which financial problems may create.

(c)   Shareholders are likely to be closer to management in a private company.

6 Private equity and institutional buyouts

Private equity funds are commonly misunderstood as investing in assets which were not available in the public market, this is not the case. The expression 'private equity' refers to the fact that the fund raises its money from private individuals rather than from public markets. The money raised by private equity firms may, however, be invested in either private or public assets.

There are many categories of private equity ranging from finance providers (venture capital, growth capital, angel investing, mezzanine finance ect.) to buyouts funds (leveraged buyouts, institutional buyouts).

An institutional buyout is where an investment institution/fund buys out a target and takes it private. An private equity buyout is where an private equity fund buys out a target and takes it private. The objective of this activity is obviously to make money for the institution or private equity firm. This will be achieved through efficiency improvements in the acquired business which will then ultimately be sold on or refloated.

In order to achieve these benefits, the buyout fund will often bring in new management teams to focus on value enhancement, perhaps to the detriment of employee relations. Such funds are often depicted as unscrupulous asset strippers, though others would argue that they are champions of business efficiency that maximise the value of a business and the use of its resources. The latter view has some credence since there would be little benefit to be gained from buying out an already highly efficient business.

Question 17.2   Reasons for change

Over the next week, get hold of the *Financial Times*, the *Wall Street Journal* or other good business newspaper section in your country and look through it for current examples of companies restructuring by divestment, demerger, MBO, MBI, going private or private equity/institutional buyout. Try to establish the basic reasons behind the change.

(For the answer to this question, see the Answer section at the end of this book.)

Chapter roundup

- A company might occasionally undergo a restructuring. Methods of restructuring are **divestment** (selling off part of the business to an outside buyer), **demerger** or **spin-off** (creating two or more separate and independent companies in place of just one), or **liquidation**.

- In a demerger or spin-off, shareholders receive shares in the newly-established companies. They can choose to hold on to their shares in both companies, or can choose to invest in just one of them (or neither of them) and sell their shares accordingly.

- A divestment might take the form of an MBO or MBI. An **MBO** is a buyout of a part of the company's business by an existing management team, backed by venture capital providers. An **MBI** is similar, except that the management team making the purchase comes from outside the company.

- Occasionally, a shareholder or group of shareholders in a public company whose shares are traded on a stock market might **take the company private**. They offer to buy the shares of the other shareholders, de-list the company's shares and re-establish the company as a private company.

Quick quiz

1 What is the main difference between a divestment and a demerger?

2 What might be the reasons for divestment?

3 What might be the reasons for a demerger?

4 Why might a company agree to an MBO rather than selling the business to an external buyer?

5 Why might a company go private?

Answers to quick quiz

1   In a divestment, a part of the business is sold to an external buyer. In a demerger, a part of the business is set up as an independent company, and shares in this company are distributed to existing shareholders.

2   (a)   To sell off an unprofitable subsidiary or a subsidiary that makes low profits

(b)   The company wishes to focus on its core businesses, and has decided to sell off non-core operations.

(c)   To make a large profit when another company makes an offer that is too high to refuse.

(d)   The company is in financial difficulties and must sell some businesses to raise cash.

(e)   To reduce the overall business risk of the company by selling off a high-risk operation.

3   (a)   The company consists of two distinct businesses with different characteristics.

(b)   The unified company is undervalued. Demerger is expected to unlock value and so increase shareholder wealth.

(c)   Shareholders are given the choice of continuing to invest in both separate businesses, or to invest in only one of the businesses and sell their shares in the other.

(d)   Decision-making and efficiency will be improved by having two independent management teams.

4   (a)   The MBO team offers the best price.

(b)   Another buyer cannot be found.

(c)   The convenience of selling to buyers who know the business.

(d)   Management and employees are more likely to co-operate in the sale arrangements.

(e)   The owner of a private company might want to retire, and wishes to pass ownership to a management team.

5   Going private needs an individual shareholder or group of shareholders with sufficient finance (or financial backing) to afford the cost of buying out the other shareholders. The shareholders organising the restructuring might consider that:

(a)   The stock market undervalues the company

(b)   Public company status has not given the company access to new sources of finance as originally hoped

(c)   The company is vulnerable to an unwanted takeover bid if it remains public

(d)   The company's management are making decisions that damage the long-term interests of the company, in order to satisfy the short-term concerns of investors about profits and dividends.

Answer to chapter questions

Chapter 1

Answer 1.1

No formal answer is provided to this activity, as it will depend on your own research.

Answer 1.2

Critics of the PFI argue that the government is allowing private sector firms to pay for the building of hospitals and schools in return for payments over a long period into the future, typically up to 30 years. The private sector companies will earn a high return, to be paid for by taxpayers in future years. The financial policy of 'get now, pay later' shifts the financial burden from current taxpayers to future years, hence the accusation of 'mortgaging' the future.

Chapter 2

Answer 2.1

	X $	Y $
Total cash flows	14,000	15,000
Total depreciation (Cost minus expected residual value)	8,000	7,000
Total profits after depreciation	6,000	8,000
Average profits (4 years)	$1,500	$2,000
Value of investment initially	10,000	10,000
Eventual residual value	2,000	3,000
	12,000	13,000
∴ Average value of investment (÷ 2)	6,000	6,500

The accounting rates of return are:

$$X = \frac{\$1,500}{\$6,000} = 25\%$$

$$Y = \frac{\$2,000}{\$6,500} = 31\%$$

Both machines would provide an ARR in excess of the minimum required, but Machine Y would be chosen because it has the higher ARR.

Answer 2.2

Annual depreciation = $150,000/5 years = $30,000 per annum

Year	Capital expenditure $	Working capital investment $	Net operating profit after depreciation $
0	(150,000)	(15,000)	
1			(20,000)
2			10,000
3			50,000
4			40,000
5		15,000	20,000
Total			100,000
Average			20,000

The average investment = $75,000 in non-current assets + $15,000 in working capital = $90,000.

(a) ARR = ($20,000/$90,000) × 100% = 22.2%.

(b)

Year	Capital expenditure $	Working capital investment $	Cash flow (profits) $	Net cash flow pa $	Cumulative net cash flow $
0	(150,000)	(15,000)		(165,000)	(165,000)
1			10,000	10,000	(155,000)
2			40,000	40,000	(115,000)
3			80,000	80,000	(35,000)
4			70,000	70,000	35,000
5		15,000	50,000	65,000	100,000

The payback time is 3 years + $\dfrac{35}{35 + 35}$ x 12m = 3½ years

(c) The project exceeds the target ARR of 15%, but fails to pay back within the maximum permitted period of three years. The project would not be undertaken.

Chapter 3

Answer 3.1

It is assumed that all variable costs are relevant costs.

		Net cash flow $
Increase in sales	10,000 × $20	200,000
Increase in variable costs	10,000 × $8	(80,000)
Increase in annual contribution		120,000
Increase in fixed cost spending		(80,000)
Increase in annual cash profits		40,000

Answer 3.2

Year	Cash flow	Discount factor at 12%	Present value
	$		$
2	40,000	0.797	31,880
3	30,000	0.712	21,360
			53,240

The present value of the future returns, discounted at 12%, is $53,240. This means that if Spender can invest now to earn a return of 12% on its investments, it would have to invest $53,240 now to earn $40,000 after 2 years plus $30,000 after 3 years.

Answer 3.3

Savings are 75,000 × ($3 – $2.50) = $37,500 per annum.

Additional costs are $7,500 per annum.

Net cash savings are therefore $30,000 per annum. (Remember, depreciation is not a cash flow and must be ignored as a 'cost'.)

The first step in calculating an NPV is to establish the relevant costs year by year. All future cash flows arising as a direct consequence of the decision should be taken into account. It is assumed that the machine will be sold for $10,000 at the end of Year 4.

Year	Cash flow	Discount factor	PV of cash flow
	$	12%	$
0	(90,000)	1.000	(90,000)
1	30,000	0.893	26,790
2	30,000	0.797	23,910
3	30,000	0.712	21,360
4	40,000	0.636	25,440
		NPV =	+7,500

The NPV is positive and so the project is expected to earn more than 12% per annum and is therefore acceptable.

Answer 3.4

Time	Cash flow	Try 14% Discount factor	PV	Try 16% Discount factor	PV
	$		$		$
0	(4,000)	1.000	(4,000)	1.000	(4,000)
1	1,200	0.877	1,052	0.862	1,034
2	1,410	0.769	1,084	0.743	1,048
3	1,875	0.675	1,266	0.641	1,202
4	1,150	0.592	681	0.552	635
		NPV	83	NPV	(81)

The IRR must be less than 16%, but higher than 14%. The NPVs at these two costs of capital will be used to estimate the IRR.

Using the interpolation formula:

$$IRR = 14\% + \left[\frac{83}{83+81} \times (16\% - 14\%) \right] = 15.01\%$$

The project should be accepted as the IRR is more or less exactly the minimum return demanded. It is therefore just acceptable, ignoring risk and uncertainty in the cash flow estimates.

Answer 3.5

Cash flows

Year		$	Replace every year $
0	Buy		(30,000)
1	Running cost	(14,000)	
1	Residual value	18,000	
1	Net cash flow		4,000

			Replace every 2 years
0	Buy		(30,000)
1	Running cost		(14,000)
2	Running cost	(18,000)	
2	Residual value	10,000	
2	Net cash flow		(8,000)

			Replace every 3 years
0	Buy		(30,000)
1	Running cost		(14,000)
2	Running cost		(18,000)
3	Running cost	(27,000)	
3	Residual value	0	
3	Net cash flow		(27,000)

Year	Discount factor at 12%	Replacement every year		Replacement every two years		Replacement every three years	
		Cash flow	PV of cash flow	Cash flow	PV of cash flow	Cash flow	PV of cash flow
		$	$	$	$	$	$
0	1.000	(30,000)	(30,000)	(30,000)	(30,000)	(30,000)	(30,000)
1	0.893	4,000	3,572	(14,000)	(12,502)	(14,000)	(12,502)
2	0.797			(8,000)	(6,376)	(18,000)	(14,346)
3	0.712					(27,000)	(19,224)
			(26,428)		(48,878)		(76,072)
	Annuity factor		0.893		1.690		2.402
	Equiv. annual cost		$29,595		$28,922		$31,670

The optimum replacement cycle is every two years.

Chapter 4

Answer 4.1

The NPV will increase – the lower the cost of capital the higher the present value – but the IRR will stay the same. The IRR is calculated by reference to the level and timing of cash flows. It may be compared with the cost of capital but it is not dependent on it.

Answer 4.2

The PV of the cash flow items, and the NPV of the project, are as follows

Year	Discount factor at 9% $	PV of equipment cost $	PV of running costs $	PV of savings $	PV of net cash flow $
0	1.000	(8,500)			(8,500)
1	0.917		(1,834)	4,585	2,751
2	0.842		(2,105)	5,894	3,789
3	0.772		(3,088)	6,176	3,088
Total		(8,500)	(7,027)	16,655	1,128

The project has a positive NPV and would appear to be worthwhile. The changes in cash flows which would need to occur for the project to break even (NPV = 0) are as follows.

(a) Plant costs would need to increase by a PV of $1,128, that is by $\frac{1,128}{8,500} \times 100\% = 13.3\%$

(b) Running costs would need to increase by a PV of $1,128, that is by $\frac{1,128}{7,027} \times 100\% = 16.1\%$

(c) Savings would need to fall by a PV of $1,128, that is by $\frac{1,128}{16,655} \times 100\% = 6.8\%$

Answer 4.3

(a) The most optimistic assumptions are that the project will last 5 years, the product will sell at its expected price and the residual value of the equipment will be 30% of its cost.

Year	Equipment $'000	Working capital $'000	Cash profit $'000	Net cash flow $'000	Discount factor	Present value $'000
0	(500)	(100)		(600)	1.00	(600.0)
1			180	180	0.89	160.2
2			180	180	0.80	144.0
3			180	180	0.71	127.8
4			180	180	0.64	115.2
5	150	100	180	430	0.57	245.1
					NPV	192.3

(b) The most pessimistic assumptions are that the project will only last for three years and that the selling price will be 10% less than expected, reducing the annual cash profit by $30,000. The resale value of the equipment at the end of year 3 will be about 45% less than its original purchase price. A resale value of $275,000 might therefore be chosen. Alternatively, a slightly more pessimistic resale price of about 50% of cost ($250,000) might be used. It would probably be too pessimistic to assume a resale value of just 20% or 30% of cost at the end of year 3. A resale value of $275,000 is assumed in this solution.

Year	Equipment $'000	Working capital $'000	Cash profit $'000	Net cash flow $'000	Discount factor	Present value $'000
0	(500)	(100)		(600)	1.00	(600.0)
1			150	150	0.89	133.5
2			150	150	0.80	120.0
3	275	100	150	525	0.71	372.8
					NPV	26.3

With pessimistic assumptions, the project should still have a positive NPV, although only of about $26,000.

Answer 4.4

NPV calculations are not shown here.

The ratio of NPV at 10% to outlay in year 0 (the year of capital rationing) is as follows.

Project	Outlay in Year 0	PV of cash flow	NPV	Ratio	Ranking
	$	$	$		
A	50,000	55,700	5,700	1.114	3
B	28,000	31,290	3,290	1.118	2
C	30,000	34,380	4,380	1.146	1

The optimal investment policy is as follows.

Ranking	Project	Year 0 outlay	NPV
		$	$
1	C	30,000	4,380
2	B	28,000	3,290
3	A (balance)	2,000 (4% of 5,700)	228
NPV from total investment			7,898

Chapter 5

Answer 5.1

The cash flows at inflated values are as follows.

Year	Fixed income	Other savings	Running costs	Net cash flow
	$	$	$	$
1	2,500	500	(1,000)	2,000
2	2,500	525	(1,100)	1,925
3	2,500	551	(1,210)	1,841
4	2,500	579	(1,331)	1,748

The NPV of the project is as follows.

Year	Cash flow	Discount factor	PV
	$	16%	$
0	(5,000)	1.000	(5,000)
1	2,000	0.862	1,724
2	1,925	0.743	1,430
3	1,841	0.641	1,180
4	1,748	0.552	965
			+ 299

The NPV is positive and the project would seem therefore to be worthwhile.

Answer 5.2

(a)

	Annual
	$
Profit before tax	25,000
Add back depreciation	20,000
Taxable profits	45,000
Tax at 30%	13,500

(b) The cost of the equipment is $120,000 (6 x annual depreciation or 4 × annual capital allowance).

Year	Net cash flow $	Discount factor 8%	Present value of cash flow $
0	(120,000)	1.000	(120,000)
1	31,500	0.926	29,169
2	31,500	0.857	26,996
3	31,500	0.794	25,011
4	31,500	0.735	23,153
5	31,500	0.681	21,452
6	31,500	0.630	19,845
		NPV	25,626

Chapter 6

Answer 6.1

Share price	Cumulative no. of shares tendered at this price (000)	Total receipts at this price ($'000)
$1.70	800	1,360.00
$1.25	2,150	2,687.50
$0.85	3,950	3,357.50
$0.50	6,350	3,175.00

The strike price should thus be $0.85 to maximise receipts.

Answer 6.2

	$
Three shares 'cum rights' are worth (× $4)	12.00
One new share will raise	3.20
Four new shares will have a theoretical value of	15.20

The theoretical ex rights price is $\dfrac{\$15.20}{4}$ = $3.80 per share

	$
Theoretical ex rights price	3.80
Price per new share	3.20
Value of rights per new share	0.60

The value of the rights attached to each existing share is $\dfrac{\$0.60}{3}$ = $0.20.

We will assume that a shareholder is able to sell his rights for $0.20 per existing share held.

(a) **If the shareholder sells all his rights:**

	$
Sale value of rights (900 × $0.20)	180
Market value of his 900 shares, ex rights (× $3.80)	3,420
Total wealth	3,600

The shareholder would neither gain nor lose wealth. He would not be required to provide any additional funds to the company, but his shareholding as a proportion of the total equity of the company will be lower.

(b) **If the shareholder exercises half of the rights (buys 450/3 = 150 shares at $3.20) and sells the other half:**

	$
Sale value of rights (450 × $0.20)	90
Market value of his 1,050 shares, ex rights (× $3.80)	3,990
Total wealth	4,080

	$
Total value of 900 shares cum rights (× $4)	3,600
Additional investment (150 × $3.20)	480
	4,080

The shareholder would neither gain nor lose wealth, although he will have increased his investment in the company by $480.

(c) **If the shareholder does nothing, but all other shareholders either exercise their rights or sell them, he would lose wealth as follows.**

	$
Market value of 900 shares cum rights (× $4)	3,600
Market value of 900 shares ex rights (× $3.80)	3,420
Loss in wealth	180

It follows that the shareholder, to protect his existing investment, should either exercise his rights or sell them to another investor. In practice, if he does not exercise his rights, the new securities he was entitled to subscribe for might be sold for his benefit by the company, and this would protect him from losing wealth.

Answer 6.3

(ii) and (iii) are true.

(i) is incorrect – a bonus issue increases the number of shares in issue with no corresponding increase in capital, thus share price is likely to fall.

(iv) is incorrect – a placing does not involve a public offer.

Chapter 7

Answer 7.1

Year	Cash return	Discount factor at 6%	PV of return
	$	$	$
1	8	0.943	7.54
2	8	0.890	7.12
3	8	0.840	6.72
4	108	0.792	85.54
Value of bond			106.92

The bonds will be valued at $106.92. They are valued above par, because the interest payable on the bonds (8%) exceeds the current yield required by bond investors in this type of bond.

Answer 7.2

(a)

	cents
Cost of warrant	68
Exercise price	780
	848
Current share price	762
Premium	86

(b) The warrants do not have an intrinsic value yet, because the exercise price is higher than the current share price. The warrants will not be worth exercising unless the market price rises above the exercise price.

(c) The warrant will probably rise in value by 10c. The gain for investor A will be (10/762) 1.3%. The gain for investor B will be (10/68) 14.7%. However, investor A will be entitled to dividend payments on the shares, whereas there are no dividends payable on warrants. Warrants are delayed equity.

Chapter 8

Answer 8.1

(a)

	Current $	Year 1 $	Year 2 $	Year 3 $
Non-current assets	100,000	120,000	140,000	160,000
Working capital	20,000	30,000	40,000	50,000
Total assets minus current liabilities	120,000	150,000	180,000	210,000
Debt capital	(30,000)	(30,000)	(30,000)	(30,000)
Total net assets	90,000	120,000	150,000	180,000
Equity at start of year		90,000	110,000	135,000
Retained profits (one-third of profits)		20,000	25,000	25,000
Equity at end of year	90,000	110,000	135,000	160,000
Shortfall in funds	0	10,000	15,000	20,000

(b) This shortfall could be eliminated by:

    (a) reducing the required amount of non-current asset investment
    (b) reducing the required amount of working capital
    (c) improving profitability
    (d) reducing dividend payments
    (e) raising new capital, either debt or equity.

Answer 8.2

	$'000
Prior charge capital	
Preference shares	500
Debentures	4,700
Long-term bank loans	500
Prior charge capital, ignoring short-term debt	5,700
Short-term loans	120
Overdraft	260
Prior charge capital, including short-term interest bearing debt	6,080

Either figure, $6,080,000 or $5,700,000, could be used. If gearing is calculated with capital employed in the denominator, and capital employed is net non-current assets plus **net** current assets, it would seem more reasonable to exclude short-term interest bearing debt from prior charge capital. This is because short-term debt is set off against current assets in arriving at the figure for net current assets.

$Equity = 1,500 + 760 + 1,200 + 2,810 = \$6,270,000$

The gearing ratio can be calculated in any of the following ways.

(a) $\dfrac{\text{Prior charge capital}}{\text{Equity}} \times 100\% = \dfrac{6,080}{6,270} \times 100\% = 97\%$

(b) $\dfrac{\text{Prior charge capital}}{\text{Equity plus prior charge capital}} \times 100\% = \dfrac{6,080}{(6,080+6,270)} \times 100\% = 49.2\%$

(c) $\dfrac{\text{Prior charge capital}}{\text{Total capital employed}} \times 100\% = \dfrac{5,700}{12,520} \times 100\% = 45.5\%$

Chapter 9

Answer 9.1

Cost of capital $= \dfrac{12(1+0.04)}{96} + 0.04 = 0.13 + 0.04 = 0.17 = 17\%$

Answer 9.2

(a) *Equity*. Given a 5% annual increase in dividend in perpetuity, the cost of equity capital may be estimated as:

$\dfrac{60,000(1+0.05)}{585,000-60,000^*} + 0.05 = 0.17 = 17\%$

* Market value of equity **ex div**, not cum div. The current dividend must be subtracted from the cum div price.

(b) *Preference shares*. The cost of capital is $\dfrac{6c}{40c} \times 100\% = 15\%$

(c) *Debentures*. The cost of capital is the IRR of the following cash flows.

Year	Cost $	Interest $	Tax relief $	Net cash flows $
0	(95.30)			(95.30)
1		10	(3.00)	7.00
2	100.00	10	(3.00)	107.00

		Try 10%		Try 8%
Net cash flow $	Discount factor	PV $	Discount factor	PV $
(95.30)	1.000	(95.30)	1.000	(95.30)
7.00	0.909	6.36	0.926	6.48
107.00	0.826	88.38	0.857	91.70
		(0.56)		2.88

The IRR is approx $8\% + \dfrac{2.88}{(2.88 - -0.56)} \times (10 - 8)\%$

$= 9.67\%$

(d)   *Weighted average cost of capital*

Item	Market value $	Cost of capital	Product $
Ordinary shares*	525,000	0.170	89,250
Preference shares	40,000	0.150	6,000
Debentures*	190,600	0.0967	18,431
	755,600		113,681

* ex div and ex interest

$$WACC = \frac{113,681}{755,600} = 0.150 = 15.0\%$$

Answer 9.3

(a) $7\% + (11\% - 7\%) \times 0.9 = 10.6\%$

(b) $\dfrac{5.3c}{0.106} = 50$ cents

Chapter 10

Answer 10.1

	$
Profits before tax	9,320,000
Less tax	2,800,000
Profits after tax	6,520,000
Less preference dividend (8% of $2,000,000)	160,000
Earnings	6,360,000
Number of ordinary shares	10,000,000
EPS	63.6c

Answer 10.2

EPS = 30c

Dividend cover = 1.5 times

Dividend per share is therefore (30/1.5) 20 cents.

Dividend yield = 4% = Dividend per share/Share price

Share price = Dividend per share/Dividend yield = 20c/0.04 = 500 cents.

Chapter 11

Answer 11.1

If a market is at least semi-strong efficient, for the vast majority of investors public information cannot be used to earn abnormal returns (i.e. returns above the expected level for the amount of systematic risk involved). The implication is that fundamental analysis, such as that performed by fund managers, is a waste of time and money, and the average investor should simply select a suitably diversified portfolio. Thus it will be easier and cheaper to invest in a tracker fund than an actively managed fund, most of which have been shown to generally under perform the share index, particularly once high management costs have been deducted from returns.

Answer 11.2

The effect of each event on the share price will depend on the efficiency of the market.

(a) If the market has strong form efficiency, it is likely that the profit warning will be anticipated by the market. The share price will fall ahead of the announcement The value of the company will fall by at least $10 million, and more, if future profits are also expected to be lower than originally anticipated. If the market displays semi-strong form efficiency, the share price will fall on the announcement of the profits warning.

(b) If the market has strong-form efficiency, and the profitability forecast of the company management is believed, the value of the company should rise by $45 million - $25 million = $20 million, in expectation of higher future profits. The share price should rise ahead of any public announcement of the project by the company. If the market has only semi-strong form efficiency, and if investors believe the company's profitability forecast, the share price should rise when details of the project are announced to the market. (If the market has only weak-form efficiency, the share price will not be affected at all by the investment and the future profits it will generate.)

Chapter 12

Answer 12.1

The clue to the approach is in the name! You need to reconstruct the balance sheet from the ratios provided. As current liabilities is the 'base' for two ratios, we will put that at a nominal value of 1:

Non-current assets	2.5
Current assets:	
Inventory (*balancing fig.*)	0.6
Other (quick)	1.9
	2.5
Total assets (non-current + current)	5.0
Current liabilities	(1.0)
Net assets	4.0

Now, sales: total assets = 2.2:1 ∴ total assets = $44m/2.2 = $20m. Using the above structure, inventory must be $20m x 0.6/5.0 = **$2.4m**

Answer 12.2

(a) The cash cycle is (70 + 50 – 25) = 95 days.

(b)

					$m
Receivables	$\frac{70}{365}$	×	2,065.0	=	396.0
Inventory	$\frac{50}{365}$	×	1,478.6	=	202.5
Payables	$\frac{25}{365}$	×	1,478.6	=	(101.3)
Working capital					497.2

(c) In the original exercise, the comparable investment in working capital, defined narrowly as inventories plus trade receivables minus trade payables, was (119.0 + 329.8 – 236.2) = $212.6 million.

The investment in working capital is much higher in (b) because the cash cycle is much longer. **A longer cash cycle means a higher working capital investment.**

Chapter 13

Answer 13.1

It is assumed that inventories and trade payables will increase in proportion to the increase in sales, ie by 20%.

Increase in sales (20% × $60 million)	$12,000,000
	$
Increase in contribution (20% × $12 million)	2,400,000
Increase in bad debts (2% × $72 million)	1,440,000
Increase in net profit	960,000
	$
New average receivables (1.5/12) × $72 million	9,000,000
Old average receivables (1/12) × $60 million	5,000,000
Increase in receivables	4,000,000
Increase in inventories (20% of $11 million)	2,200,000
	6,200,000
Increase in trade payables (20% of $4.5 million)	(900,000)
Increase in working capital investment	5,300,000
Return on investment from change in credit policy = ($960,000/$5,300,000) =	18.1%

The return is above the target of 17%, and the new credit policy is financially justified.

Answer 13.2

Current annual sales ($36,500 × 12)	$438,000
Sales if discount is introduced (× 125%)	$547,500
Increase in sales	$109,500
Contribution/sales ratio	10%
	$
Increase in contribution	10,950
Cost of settlement discounts (1/3 × $547,500 × 3%)	5,475
Increase in net profit	5,475
	$
New average receivables (10/365 × $547,500)	15,000
Current average receivables (30/365 × $438,000)	36,000
Reduction in receivables	(21,000)
Increase in inventories	25,000
Increase in trade payables	(15,000)
Net reduction in working capital investment	(11,000)

The discount policy, on the basis of the figures given, would increase annual profits by $5,475 and reduce the working capital investment by $11,000. The policy is therefore financially justified, whatever the company's target return on capital.

Answer 13.3

(a)   Re-order level = 15 days lead time x 16 units per day = 240 units.

(b)   Average consumption during the supply lead time = 8 days x 10 units = 80 units. This means that the average buffer inventory will be (240 – 80) units = 160 units. At a cost of $12 per unit per annum, the cost to the company will be $1,920.

(c)   The maximum inventory level will occur when a new delivery of the item (500 units) is received, the supply lead time has been at its shortest (4 days) and daily consumption during the supply lead time has been at a minimum (6 units each day). Only 24 units will be consumed during the supply lead time. When the new supply is received, the number of items in inventory would then be 240 – 24 = 216 units. With the new delivery of 500 units, the inventory level would rise to 716 units. This is the maximum inventory level.

Answer 13.4

The total annual cost at the economic order quantity of 500 units is as follows.

	$
Purchases 4,000 × $96	384,000
Ordering costs $300 × (4,000/500)	2,400
Holding costs $96 × 10% × (500/2)	2,400
	388,800

The total annual cost at an order quantity of 1,000 units would be as follows.

	$
Purchases $384,000 × 92%	353,280
Ordering costs $300 × (4,000/1,000)	1,200
Holding costs $96 × 92% × 10% × (1,000/2)	4,416
	358,896

The company should order the item 1,000 units at a time, saving $(388,800 – 358,896) = $29,904 a year.

Chapter 14

Answer 14.1

A fall in the company's cash balance or an increase in the bank overdraft. Also, probably, a fall in inventory levels as the company cuts back on purchases, and a reduction in receivables as the company chases late payers more aggressively. Possibly also an increase in trade payables as the company takes the maximum available credit from suppliers. Eventually, unless the situation improves, the company will become insolvent.

Answer 14.2

The benefits are similar to those provided by other on-line cash management systems of banks, but with the difference that access is via the internet. The benefits are the ability to check the current cash position at any time in order to monitor and manage cash flows closely. Possibly also some reduction in bank charges, depending on the fees charged by the bank for internet transactions. Possibly some speeding up of cash receipts, if customers can be persuaded to make direct payments into the internet bank account.

Chapter 15

Answer 15.1

There is no increase in the share capital of Heap, which means that dilution in earnings per share will not occur if the total pre-tax profits (and earnings) of Heap remain at least the same as before.

	$
Profits of Heap	4,000,000
Profits of Soft	450,000
Combined profits before interest, assuming no synergy	4,450,000
Interest (9% × $6,000,000)	540,000
Combined pre-tax profits, assuming no synergy	3,910,000
Pre-tax profits of Heap	4,000,000
Synergy required to prevent reduction in pre-tax profits and earnings	90,000

Pre-tax profits would need to increase by $90,000 per annum. This is the difference between the profits obtained from the business of Soft ($450,000) and the interest cost of the debt raised to finance the acquisition ($540,000).

Answer 15.2

(a)   If the acquisition is financed by a share exchange

	$	$
Earnings of ABC (40 million × 50c)		20,000,000
Earnings of XYZ (20 million × 20c)		4,000,000
Savings	6,000,000	
Less tax (30%)	(1,800,000)	
		4,200,000
Total earnings		28,200,000
Number of shares post-acquisition		55 million
(40 million + (3/4 × 20 million))		
EPS		51.3c
Expected P/E ratio ($10/50c)		20.0
Expected share price		$10.26

(b)   If the acquisition is for cash, financed by debt

	$	$
Earnings of ABC (40 million × 50c)		20,000,000
Earnings of XYZ (20 million × 20c)		4,000,000
Savings	6,000,000	
Interest on debt (7% × $150 m)	(10,500,000)	
Net fall in pre-tax profits	(4,500,000)	
Less tax (30%)	1,350,000	
Net fall in pre-tax earnings		(3,150,000)
Total earnings		20,850,000
Number of shares post-acquisition (no change)		40 million
EPS		52.1 c
Expected P/E ratio ($10/50c)		20.0
Expected share price		$10.42

Chapter 16

Answer 16.1

Company A

The value of a constant annual dividend of 7.8 cents in perpetuity at a cost of capital of 12% is

7.8c/0.12 = 65c.

However, the dividends will only begin in Year 4, which means that the value of 65c per share is a present value in Year 3. To convert a Year 3 value to a present value (Year 0), we need to apply a Year 3 discount factor to the Year 3 valuation.

Share price = 65c × 0.712 = 46.28c, say 46c.

Company B

$$P = \frac{14.4c\,(1.03)}{(0.12 - 0.03)} = \frac{14.832c}{0.09}$$

= 164.8c, say 165c per share.

Answer 16.2

It is assumed that the working capital investment is recovered at the end of Year 6, ie the inventories and receivables are converted into cash.

Annual cash operating profits are expected to be ($85,000 profit + $20,000 depreciation) $105,000.

Year	Working capital $	Capital investment $	Cash operating profits $	Net cash flow $	Discount factor at 11%	Present value $
0	(30,000)			(30,000)	1.000	(30,000)
1	-	(25,000)	105,000	80,000	0.901	72,080
2		(25,000)	105,000	80,000	0.812	64,960
3		(25,000)	105,000	80,000	0.731	58,480
4		(25,000)	105,000	80,000	0.659	52,720
5		(25,000)	105,000	80,000	0.593	47,440
6	30,000	(25,000)	105,000	110,000	0.535	58,850
						324,530

The maximum price Fang should offer is around $325,000.

Chapter 17

Answer 17.1

The financial structure for an MBO often involves a high level of debt capital. The company therefore needs to earn sufficient cash flows from operating activities to cover high interest costs, before any cash is available for capital spending or dividends. Unless an MBO is immediately successful, cash flow problems are likely to arise, with inadequate cash to meet essential commitments, and the MBO team might have to go back to the venture capital backers for additional funding.

Answer 17.2

This will depend upon your particular research.

Mathematical tables

MATHEMATICAL TABLES

Present value table

Present value of 1, ie $(1+r)^{-n}$

where r = discount rate
       n = number of periods until payment

Periods (n)	Discount rates (r)									
	1%	2%	3%	4%	5%	6%	7%	8%	9%	10%
1	0.990	0.980	0.971	0.962	0.952	0.943	0.935	0.926	0.917	0.909
2	0.980	0.961	0.943	0.925	0.907	0.890	0.873	0.857	0.842	0.826
3	0.971	0.942	0.915	0.889	0.864	0.840	0.816	0.794	0.772	0.751
4	0.961	0.924	0.888	0.855	0.823	0.792	0.763	0.735	0.708	0.683
5	0.951	0.906	0.863	0.822	0.784	0.747	0.713	0.681	0.650	0.621
6	0.942	0.888	0.837	0.790	0.746	0.705	0.666	0.630	0.596	0.564
7	0.933	0.871	0.813	0.760	0.711	0.665	0.623	0.583	0.547	0.513
8	0.923	0.853	0.789	0.731	0.677	0.627	0.582	0.540	0.502	0.467
9	0.914	0.837	0.766	0.703	0.645	0.592	0.544	0.500	0.460	0.424
10	0.905	0.820	0.744	0.676	0.614	0.558	0.508	0.463	0.422	0.386
11	0.896	0.804	0.722	0.650	0.585	0.527	0.475	0.429	0.388	0.350
12	0.887	0.788	0.701	0.625	0.557	0.497	0.444	0.397	0.356	0.319
13	0.879	0.773	0.681	0.601	0.530	0.469	0.415	0.368	0.326	0.290
14	0.870	0.758	0.661	0.577	0.505	0.442	0.388	0.340	0.299	0.263
15	0.861	0.743	0.642	0.555	0.481	0.417	0.362	0.315	0.275	0.239

	11%	12%	13%	14%	15%	16%	17%	18%	19%	20%
1	0.901	0.893	0.885	0.877	0.870	0.862	0.855	0.847	0.840	0.833
2	0.812	0.797	0.783	0.769	0.756	0.743	0.731	0.718	0.706	0.694
3	0.731	0.712	0.693	0.675	0.658	0.641	0.624	0.609	0.593	0.579
4	0.659	0.636	0.613	0.592	0.572	0.552	0.534	0.516	0.499	0.482
5	0.593	0.567	0.543	0.519	0.497	0.476	0.456	0.437	0.419	0.402
6	0.535	0.507	0.480	0.456	0.432	0.410	0.390	0.370	0.352	0.335
7	0.482	0.452	0.425	0.400	0.376	0.354	0.333	0.314	0.296	0.279
8	0.434	0.404	0.376	0.351	0.327	0.305	0.285	0.266	0.249	0.233
9	0.391	0.361	0.333	0.308	0.284	0.263	0.243	0.225	0.209	0.194
10	0.352	0.322	0.295	0.270	0.247	0.227	0.208	0.191	0.176	0.162
11	0.317	0.287	0.261	0.237	0.215	0.195	0.178	0.162	0.148	0.135
12	0.286	0.257	0.231	0.208	0.187	0.168	0.152	0.137	0.124	0.112
13	0.258	0.229	0.204	0.182	0.163	0.145	0.130	0.116	0.104	0.093
14	0.232	0.205	0.181	0.160	0.141	0.125	0.111	0.099	0.088	0.078
15	0.209	0.183	0.160	0.140	0.123	0.108	0.095	0.084	0.074	0.065

Annuity table

Present value of an annuity of 1, ie $\dfrac{1-(1+r)^{-n}}{r}$

where r = discount rate
       n = number of periods

Periods   **Discount rates (r)**

(n)	1%	2%	3%	4%	5%	6%	7%	8%	9%	10%
1	0.990	0.980	0.971	0.962	0.952	0.943	0.935	0.926	0.917	0.909
2	1.970	1.942	1.913	1.886	1.859	1.833	1.808	1.783	1.759	1.736
3	2.941	2.884	2.829	2.775	2.723	2.673	2.624	2.577	2.531	2.487
4	3.902	3.808	3.717	3.630	3.546	3.465	3.387	3.312	3.240	3.170
5	4.853	4.713	4.580	4.452	4.329	4.212	4.100	3.993	3.890	3.791
6	5.795	5.601	5.417	5.242	5.076	4.917	4.767	4.623	4.486	4.355
7	6.728	6.472	6.230	6.002	5.786	5.582	5.389	5.206	5.033	4.868
8	7.652	7.325	7.020	6.733	6.463	6.210	5.971	5.747	5.535	5.335
9	8.566	8.162	7.786	7.435	7.108	6.802	6.515	6.247	5.995	5.759
10	9.471	8.983	8.530	8.111	7.722	7.360	7.024	6.710	6.418	6.145
11	10.37	9.787	9.253	8.760	8.306	7.887	7.499	7.139	6.805	6.495
12	11.26	10.58	9.954	9.385	8.863	8.384	7.943	7.536	7.161	6.814
13	12.13	11.35	10.63	9.986	9.394	8.853	8.358	7.904	7.487	7.103
14	13.00	12.11	11.30	10.56	9.899	9.295	8.745	8.244	7.786	7.367
15	13.87	12.85	11.94	11.12	10.38	9.712	9.108	8.559	8.061	7.606

(n)	11%	12%	13%	14%	15%	16%	17%	18%	19%	20%
1	0.901	0.893	0.885	0.877	0.870	0.862	0.855	0.847	0.840	0.833
2	1.713	1.690	1.668	1.647	1.626	1.605	1.585	1.566	1.547	1.528
3	2.444	2.402	2.361	2.322	2.283	2.246	2.210	2.174	2.140	2.106
4	3.102	3.037	2.974	2.914	2.855	2.798	2.743	2.690	2.639	2.589
5	3.696	3.605	3.517	3.433	3.352	3.274	3.199	3.127	3.058	2.991
6	4.231	4.111	3.998	3.889	3.784	3.685	3.589	3.498	3.410	3.326
7	4.712	4.564	4.423	4.288	4.160	4.039	3.922	3.812	3.706	3.605
8	5.146	4.968	4.799	4.639	4.487	4.344	4.207	4.078	3.954	3.837
9	5.537	5.328	5.132	4.946	4.772	4.607	4.451	4.303	4.163	4.031
10	5.889	5.650	5.426	5.216	5.019	4.833	4.659	4.494	4.339	4.192
11	6.207	5.938	5.687	5.453	5.234	5.029	4.836	4.656	4.486	4.327
12	6.492	6.194	5.918	5.660	5.421	5.197	4.988	4.793	4.611	4.439
13	6.750	6.424	6.122	5.842	5.583	5.342	5.118	4.910	4.715	4.533
14	6.982	6.628	6.302	6.002	5.724	5.468	5.229	5.008	4.802	4.611
15	7.191	6.811	6.462	6.142	5.847	5.575	5.324	5.092	4.876	4.675

List of key terms and index

These are the terms which we have identified throughout the text as being KEY TERMS. You should make sure that you can define what these terms mean; go back to the page highlighted here if you need to check.

REVIEW FORM

BPP Learning Media always appreciates feedback from the students who use our books. We would be very grateful if you would take the time to complete this feedback form, and return it to the address below.

Name: _____   Address: _____

_____

How have you used this Text?
(Tick one box only)

☐ Home study (book only)

☐ On a course: college _____

☐ With 'correspondence' package

☐ Other _____

Why did you decide to purchase this Text?
(Tick one box only)

☐ Have used complementary Study Text

☐ Have used BPP Texts in the past

☐ Recommendation by friend/colleague

☐ Recommendation by a lecturer at college

☐ Saw advertising

☐ Other _____

During the past six months do you recall seeing/receiving any of the following?
(Tick as many boxes as are relevant)

☐ Our advertisement in *ACCA Finance Matters*

☐ Our brochure with a letter through the post

Which (if any) aspects of our advertising do you find useful?
(Tick as many boxes as are relevant)

☐ Prices and publication dates of new editions

☐ Information on Text content

☐ Facility to order books off-the-page

☐ None of the above

What BPP products have you used? *(Tick one box only)*

☑ Text   ☐ Kit   ☐ Passcards

☐ i-Pass   ☐ Home Study package

Your ratings, comments and suggestions would be appreciated on the following areas

	Very useful	Useful	Not useful
Introductory section	☐	☐	☐
Chapter introductions	☐	☐	☐
Key terms	☐	☐	☐
Quality of explanations	☐	☐	☐
Case examples and other examples	☐	☐	☐
Questions and answers in each chapter	☐	☐	☐
Key learning points	☐	☐	☐
Quick quizzes	☐	☐	☐
List of key terms and index	☐	☐	☐

	Excellent	Good	Adequate	Poor
Overall opinion of this Study Text	☐	☐	☐	☐

Do you intend to continue using BPP Products?   ☐ Yes   ☐ No

Please note any further comments and suggestions/errors on the reverse of this page

Please return to: Pippa Riley, BPP Learning Media Ltd, FREEPOST, London, W12 8BR or e-mail pippariley@bpp.com

Review Form (continued)

TELL US WHAT YOU THINK

Please note any further comments and suggestions/errors below.